UNITY MITFORD: A QUEST

UNITY MITFORD: A QUEST

David Pryce-Jones

WEIDENFELD AND NICOLSON LONDON

ISBN 0 297 77156 6

Printed in Great Britain by
Cox & Wyman Ltd
London, Fakenham and Reading

For my father — and in memory of my mother

Ich kenne Knaben, die zur Mandoline
Dir von Verbrechen reden, dass dir graut.
Ich kenne Mädchen, die mit süsser Miene
Ins Dunkel gehen . . .

Hans Bethge

Vorbei sind die Kinderspiele,
Und alles rollt vorbei —
Das Geld und die Welt und die Zeiten,
Und Glauben und Lieb' und Treu'.

Heine

CONTENTS

ILLUSTRATIONS

The author and publishers are grateful to the above owners for permission to reproduce their pictures; the remaining photographs are from private collections.

INTRODUCTION

My quest for Unity Mitford was started in Berkeley in the summer of 1968, when I was teaching creative writing at the University of California. By a fluke it had suited Jessica Mitford to exchange her house there with mine, so she was in London while I sat and worked in the room built out over her back garden, its walls shelved, the shelves book-distended. The most striking Mitford possessions in the house were the pencil drawings of some of the sisters by William Acton, younger brother of Harold, done in about 1934. There were Coronation chairs with blue velvet seats and royal monograms, and Lady Redesdale's set of Lunéville china. Also a copy of The Protocols of the Elders of Zion whose pages were often underlined or scored in the margin with exclamations like 'Too true!' and 'I always said so' in a hand which I took to be Lady Redesdale's. One afternoon, my wife handed me the book which she had hit on, Lion Feuchtwanger's Jew Süss, open at the fly-leaf to show a signature and a date, 'Unity Mitford June 1930'. Her handwriting was both bold and childish, its well-rounded letters suggesting that she was not much in the habit of forming them, but could do so with schoolroom decorum, had she a mind to it. Among her idiosyncrasies were a Greek 'e', and a diagonal line through a capital 's' so that it had the air of a dollar sign. Her ink was usually clear blue, as on this fly-leaf.

Jew Süss is an unlikely novel for an English schoolgirl aged fifteen to be claiming and dating for her own. Translated into English by Edwin and Willa Muir in 1925, it is one of those fife-and-drum parades like The Robe or Ben Hur, which are apparent invitations to rub along with the celebrities of the past. Here were dukes, courtiers, the grandeurs and miseries of a principality in eighteenth-century Germany, but above all, the Jew, Süss, constructed upon a historical model, to be sure, but highlighted to represent his kind, the amasser of a fortune far beyond avarice, lover of jewels and Christian women, puppet-master of the state but doomed from the start. Into the character of Süss, Feuchtwanger poured the ambivalence that an emancipated communist sympathizer like himself felt, unable to forgive or forget his own residual Jewishness, proud even of the anachronism he despised. Feuchtwanger played into the hands of anti-semites through the trashy way in which he exploited ancient symbols as sensation, as creepiness, for instance writing of Rabbi Gabriel having on his forehead 'the furrow made by the sacred letter Shin, the first letter of God's name, Shaddai' or else depicting a young peasant planting flowers in a forest clearing to read 'Josef Süss, Pig-Jew and Sathanes'. For the sake of romantic fiction, the novelist was providing those very images of irrational excitation, that shuddering sense of at last being led by authority into the presence of darkness revealed, which inspired Nazi anti-semitism. The novel adapted into a notorious film of the period, but Feuchtwanger could hardly pretend that the basis for mystification was not his. People were right to be afraid of his Süss, but they were also right to be afraid of their fear, like any pagans in a world whose gods have given them only fire.

Through possession of this very copy of Jew Süss, Unity leaped into a living dimension. Previously she had been a myth, no more flesh and blood than Süss was, a caricature in a penny-dreadful shocker; a storm-troop English maiden, one who had got away, a silhouette blacked with gossip. She had been a fascist among fascists. More, she had been the intimate friend of Hitler. In the hour of his triumph, he had permitted this English girl to prostrate herself in obeisance to him. That was her claim to fame. In the surveys of the time, such as The Long Weekend by Robert Graves and Alan Hodge, or Malcolm Muggeridge's The Thirties, Unity rated a mention as a phenomenon, like a comet blazing a trail too erratic to be charted. She had escaped her own poster-publicity, an advertising campaign come to nothing. Yet she must have offered motives and justifications for herself and her beliefs. Had Feuchtwanger's novel been a stepping-stone?

My father had known her. At about the time when Jew Süss would have been in her hands he had often been enough with the Mitfords to qualify as a 'Swinbrook sewer', one of the Oxford aesthetes to whom Lord Redesdale made such a point of being contrary. As a matter of fact it can have been no great surprise for them to venture upon this particular Farve, as he was generally called, for most of them had fathers cut of the same cloth. It was not Lord Redesdale who was exceptional, but his children. My father had been an Eton contemporary of Tom's, the brother sandwiched between two older and four younger sisters – above the line, so to speak, being Nancy and Pam, my father's friends too. Unity, born five years after Tom and four after Diana, headed the 'little ones' with Jessica and Deborah (more usually Bobo, Decca and Debo in the family) and according to my father, they used to play a game of sticking a fork into the back of a hand, or an arm, to see who could stand pain best. (Jessica has described how 'Hure, Hare, Hure, Commence-ment' was a game involving the pinching of arms.) Then again, Jessica had been invited from her finishing school in Paris, in 1934, to lunch at Royaumont, my grandmother's house near Chantilly. A story about this has survived. Asked what her father did, Jessica had replied, 'He skates.' Then what does he do in the summer? 'He puts his chin in his hand and thinks about skating.' Whereupon she had clenched her fist in a communist salute. The following year, an aunt of mine was at Ischl, which had never lost its appeal since the Emperor Franz Josef had spent his summers there. People had taken to sporting their allegiances in their button-holes, and my aunt had in her hat the badge of Prince Starhemberg's Stahlhelm, the right-wing rivals to the Austrian Nazis, but meeting Pam in the street handed this badge to her as requested, on the grounds that it would annoy Unity so much. If vignettes of the kind were to be picked up within reach, what more might there be in the world in which Unity had moved by inclination?

Home-base in the quest for Unity is Hons and Rebels, Jessica's account of her childhood and upbringing. It has that special nostalgia of things affectionately remembered. An obviously loving, if harried, mother and father, seven healthy and beautiful children, in the Cotswold village of Swinbrook, in a house built by its owner on an inherited estate of several thousand acres – these are the circumstances for that rooted existence which is in the English genius, and it is not only the privileged few who have felt the pulse of the ideal. The Mitfords were fortunate. Swinbrook was a way of life, indeed to Jessica it was nothing else, like an enclosed citadel. In isolation, protected, but also indulged, the household imagination thrived. As children must, they invented pastimes, and if some of them, 'Hure, Hare, Hure', for example, were unkind, at least it was all a binding against the grown-ups.

Nancy Mitford's novels are also commemorations of the endless games upon which this family life was constructed. Only lightly fictionalized, what is more, for their distinction between reality and invention was impossibly thin. It was as if everyone were engaged on a permanent acting-out of the challenge 'Truth or Dare' which bold children like to play. There is in this a hankering after perpetual adolescence, a conspiracy never to grow up. The colder and harder the world, the warmer and more intimate the nursery remains, a secret to all except those who shared it too. The Mitfords are held together far more by their myths, common and extraordinary, than they are divided by later vagaries.

Jessica was three years younger than Unity but three years older than Debo, betwixt and between. She has described how the three of them particularized their mutual feelings. 'Unity and I made up a complete language called Boudledidge, unintelligible to any but ourselves, into which we translated various dirty songs (for safe singing in front of the grown-ups) and large chunks of the Oxford Book of English Verse. Debo and I organized the Society of

Hons, of which she and I were the officers and only members. Proceedings were conducted in Honnish, the official language of the society ... Occasionally Unity and I joined in the forbidden sport of "teasing Debo".'

Boud, pronounced Bowed, the first syllable of Boudledidge, was the nickname exchanged between Unity and Jessica, a reassurance that they were ganging up together. Out of this childhood, and these ceremonies and safeties, the one evolved as a fascist and the other as a communist: one experience but two outcomes, opposed in externals, though in fact complementary. Sequestered, sheltered Swinbrook became a famous battleground of the nations. Tacitly, the children may have avoided the grown-ups but they fought out in miniature the political crisis of their society. The world had not been allowed into the nursery: very well, the nursery would have to make do for the world.

Simple wishes come true simply. Jessica saw the parting of the ways like this: 'It was the year of Hitler's accession to power. Boud's announced intention was to go to Germany, learn German and meet the Führer ... Boud wouldn't be teased about her devotion to the Nazis. She was completely and utterly sold on them. The Nazi salute – "Heil Hitler!" with hand upraised – became her standard greeting to everyone, family, friends, the astonished postmistress in Swinbrook village ... Family relationships took a sudden turn, and Boud and Diana, formerly far from friendly, became thick as thieves. Diana accompanied Boud to Germany and was also admitted to the Nazi inner circles. Their activities soon reached the newspapers and a columnist reported that Hitler had declared them to be "perfect specimens of Aryan womanhood" ... I still loved Boud for her huge, glittering personality, for her rare brand of eccentricity, for a kind of loyalty to me which she preserved in spite of our now very real differences of outlook ... Sometimes we even talked of what would happen in a revolutionary situation. We both agreed we'd simply have to be prepared to fight on opposite sides, and even tried to picture what it would be like if one day one of us had to give the order for the other's execution.'

This fantasy descends piping hot from the age of dictatorships, it was not private like Boudledidge, but widespread among whole layers of supposedly thoughtful and literate people, intellectuals even, who were affirming that mere or 'necessary' murder would never stand in the way of their principles. Whatever their cause, they would be all the purer for sacrificing to it their nearest and dearest. Put to the test, some of these people might even have been true to their theories, so deep a hold did their moral corruption acquire. In the California where I absorbed Hons and Rebels, it was a commonplace to come across up-against-the-wall threats to execute whole categories of imagined enemies, of course pretending that in some circumstances hate is not itself hateful. How to have one's cake and eat it has become a finer art since the thirties, and those who plot violence tend to be living and behaving indistinguishably from those their violence is directed against. Unity's example is extreme and sensational, but tens of thousands of radicals – that blanket expression now properly covering the Right as well as the Left – have pictured the ordering of executions, and found it a sleight-of-mind, a sentimental contrivance, great fun to live with.

Eighteen months after I had left Berkeley, I was invited to write a profile of Nancy Mitford, and therefore went out to see her at Versailles. In spite of her insistence on things French, her set manner of being an expatriate and contented, she was implacably English, a confident Mitford with the exaggeration and vocabulary which means membership of a restricted upper-class club. She may have laughed at Muv and Farve, and worked them and the sisters and the uncles and aunts up into caricatures, but the romp was based on the securest of foundations. She had travelled a short distance, and the values of Swinbrook had come along too.

In her house the furniture was discriminating. Some of the most beautiful pieces had belonged to her grandfather, the first Lord Redesdale, who had returned from his diplomatic mission in Japan in the 1860s with examples of his good taste in his baggage. There were also luxuriant portraits by Helleu. It amused Nancy to talk about herself and her parents, and that entity 'the sisters', and we settled straight into the embroidery of day-to-day life which is the stuff of her novels. 'We roared' is a Mitford expression, to mean that a story has come to its proper ending. Unity used it. Nancy used it. To see the world as a joke, a complete joke, and nothing but a joke, is hardly a philosophy, but has its stoicism. She was already in great pain from the cancer which would kill her. As well as 'Hideous', she had nicknamed Unity 'Head of Bone and Heart of Stone' and over the years had levelled out her affections for her. In a *Sunday Express* interview in November 1968 she had said, 'with her the whole Nazi thing seemed to be a joke. She was great fun. She used to drive round Central Europe in a uniform with a gun. Unity was absolutely unpolitical. No one knew less about politics than she did.' That was what she repeated to me too, but she went further, saying that Unity had reached the point of discussing marriage with Hitler. This had so appalled his staff that they had insisted on having her followed, to check her out. The subsequent report had cleared Unity as a security risk, but created other obstacles. According to this anecdote, Hitler is supposed to have told Unity that he could not think of marrying someone who had been behind the hedge with half his army – the words were Nancy's. When Unity had shot herself, this report was apparently among the papers which the Germans, being methodical, had packed up and sent home to England with her, though I do not think Nancy claimed to have seen it. (Now the quest is over, by the way, I am confident that there was no such report; nor, if there had been, would Hitler have handed it to her; nor did her papers come back with her to England, where the authorities would have confiscated them, and the family saw them only after the war; nor, finally, does it seem likely that she had been behind the hedge with half Hitler's army, a typically Mitford shaft of drama.) I said that I ought to try describing Unity's life because it was representative in the way that usually only fiction can be. The sisters would not care for that, Nancy thought, though it ought to be done while there were still people alive to remember.

My imagination was unleashed by two further stories, which afterwards I discovered were set-pieces of Nancy's. At the beginning of the war, she told me, she had been with her mother on Inchkenneth, the island which the Redesdales had bought in 1938. Their London house in Rutland Gate was to be turned into a centre for East End evacuees, and Nancy had to leave Inchkenneth to organize it. Lady Redesdale had rowed across with her to the next-door island of Mull, and was driving her on to Salen, from where the ferry left for Oban on the mainland. It was a calm, hot day and if Hitler had not started the war, Nancy had remarked, she could have stayed to enjoy perfect weather. Lady Redesdale had stopped the car, and told her to apologize for such a slander against Hitler, or else lift her suitcase out of the car and walk. Finally Unity, at the end of her life, used to improvise religious services with her mother as congregation in the ruins of the ancient chapel on Inchkenneth. One day a stranger had intruded on their worship. Lady Redesdale whispered to Unity to look over her shoulder, and there stood a man in a belted overcoat, with a lock of hair plastered down on his fore-head, a bristle of a moustache ... At the end of the service the man had vanished into thin air. They tried to trace him, they wondered whether a malicious journalist might have been impersonating Hitler, but the boatman swore that nobody had crossed the water.

The apparition lingers. The ghost of Hitler hovers behind Europeans as they go through the motions of civilization in the ruins of his continent. Unity had been more than a by-stander, she had engaged the man's affection, the girlfriend of the greatest national enemy; they might have talked of marriage; the Hon. Mrs Adolf Hitler; the Führer as Swinbrook sewer startling the village postmistress; dreams of childish revenges, teasings, exorcised upon whole masses of people suddenly brought to submission. What was to be made of this fantastic relationship? Doing my work on the profile of Nancy, I began to read the newspaper cuttings on Unity. I found that I was pursuing a figure recognizable enough, the society creature who takes advantage of her position to smash it up, whose seasons were marked by brawls instead of balls, and proud of it too. Hundreds had simultaneously stampeded along the highway to Moscow and Madrid; she had taken the turning to Germany, their mirror-image. Their country, their upbringing, their good fortune, had given such people the freedom to criticize everything as by right, but they had surrendered it as frivolously as old clothing, because values were of less concern, less style, than the act of rejection. Marxism and Nazism were contexts in which they seemed to be doing more than saying boo and sticking their tongues out. Here was a perfect case of the true believer, the person who swallowed dogma whole, including the racialism and anti-semitism which have cast a pall over humanity. Without such guilts and passions as hers, the breakdown of decency and tolerance is not to be understood.

Of the remaining sisters, Lady Mosley was kind enough to receive me, in her flat in Paris. To grasp Unity in all her contradictions, Lady Mosley felt, it would be necessary to have been her close friend, open to the idea that fanatical as she was, she was also eccentric, lovable, and by the end of the thirties, maturing. Her friends had been fond of her, loyal, and among those she mentioned to me was a special confidante, Mary, an English girl who had been constantly with her in Munich, but had not been in touch since the war.

Lady Mosley herself would be the person to write about Unity with inside knowledge, deploying such papers as have survived. But anyone coming to those papers, say in ten years' time, will have nothing much else in support; so many of the principal people in this story are dead already. Others, for instance Baldur von Schirach or Ian Colvin, died at the moment when I was contacting them. Besides, Unity was nothing of a writer, her language was trite, quite without insight. Her behaviour was comment enough for her. The more I heard of it, the greater grew the determination to learn what exactly she had been up to in Germany. I could reconstruct what she had done, the externals, describing the impact she had made upon others, her social climate. As I talked to those who had known her, I came across more and more untapped material, in England or Germany, until in the end I had worked my way round Unity, obtaining a portrait which, as Lady Mosley had warned, had its contradictions. Her supporters and detractors did not line up automatically according to their politics, as might have been expected, for there were anti-Nazis who kept a soft spot for her, in spite of everything. I have let those whom I interviewed speak for themselves. I have sometimes rearranged the shape, but not the matter, of what they told me, their narrative inconsequences having arisen because my questions had been asked in the wrong order.

Unity does not yet belong to history proper, but is still a part of living memory. Eye-witnesses are often considered to be less reliable than documents, and that seemed another reason for reporting much direct speech. I spoke directly to well over two hundred people who had known her, and corresponded with half as many again. Only five of those whom I approached, three in England (where rumour of Unity has gone to ground) and two in Germany, refused to talk to me. The Germans in a way had cause, one of them being Frau Brandt, whose husband, a personal doctor of Hitler's, was hanged by the Allies for initiating medical experiments on concentration camp inmates; the other being Maria Goebbels, sister of Dr Goebbels, the aunt of the six little children murdered by their parents in the Berlin Bunker in the last days of Hitler, but children of whom Unity had been fond. More usually, after I had spoken to someone, I was forwarded on with an introduction to someone else, the enthusiasm and offers of help snowballing on the way, generating luck, as often happens. The method had selected itself. Like me, people wanted to know the truth about Unity, they were prepared to put themselves out, tracing long-lost acquaintances, rummaging in old trunks, checking diaries and letters. To everybody quoted in the book goes my gratitude for allowing themselves to be part of the quest. I want also particularly to thank the following:

Countess Almasy-Kuefstein; Dr E. Andraskay; Brigitte Arora, for keeping my German correspondence straight; Dr Andrew Barlow, present owner of Inchkenneth, where he received me and lent me books; Lutz Becker; Robert Benewick; Baroness Bentinck; Clarence Braun-Munk; Mrs Lucy Butler; Lady Cairns for permission to publish correspondence between Sir Hugh Cairns and Mr E. J. Crawford; Dr Eugen Dollmann; Dr Robert Forgan; Father Lorincz von Gyömörey and his sister Baroness Stoerck; Egon Hanfstaengl; Mr Anthony Hardcastle, who showed me Asthall; Mr and Mrs Christopher Harris; Sir William and Lady Hayter; Col. Roger Fleetwood Hesketh, and his brother Peter, and his sister Joan; Sir John Heygate Bt; Heywood Hill; Gertraud Junge; Judith, Countess of Listowel; Dr Brigitte Lohmeyer, cultural counsellor of the German Embassy in London; Mr and Mrs Angus Macintyre; Mrs Hamish Mackenzie who has been so hospitable to me in Munich; Mr and Mrs Duncan Mackinnon, for showing me round Swinbrook; Sir Donald Makgill Bt; Karl E. Meyer; Leonard Mosley; Adam Munthe, for information about Tidö Slott; Mr and Mrs Anthony Rhodes; Miss Scatchard, headmistress of St Margaret's, Bushey; Herr Roland Schaub for allowing me access to his father's papers; Her Excellency Frau von Scherpenburg; Josephine Sinclair; John Saumarez Smith; Christopher Sykes; A. J. P. Taylor; George Theiner, for obtaining and translating Czech references; Peter Uppard; Mrs Yolande Warner; Simon Wiesenthal.

My aunts, Hélène Propper de Callejon and Liliane de Rothschild, were something like private tracing services.

The librarians of the *Daily Express*, the *Daily Mail*, the *Daily Mirror*, the *Daily Telegraph* and *The Times*, made their clippings readily available. The Wiener Library and its assistants deserve special thanks for taking what amounted to a collective interest in this book. The London Library is always exemplary. I should also like to single out Herr Raillard of the Bundesarchiv in Coblence for his willingness to provide information and photostats for me; and the staff of the Bayerische Staatsbibliothek in Munich were also most helpful.

ELDERS AND PROTOCOLS

The *Water Beetle*, Nancy's collection of essays, opens with a tribute to the Mitford nanny, Blor, and in it Unity's naming is cleared up. To have been christened Unity Valkyrie, a combination which does sound far-fetched but very deliberate, seemed to her an augury, with prophetic overtones. When appropriate in later life, she did not scruple to play up an explanation. Credulous Germans believed it, when she told them that her parents had been so dismayed by the declaration of the First World War that they had put all their pro-German aspirations into her names. The whim was a sentimental convenience for the Nordic-Teutonic image of herself which Unity sought to cultivate, stressing the Valkyrie, and becoming comically pedantic about spelling it *Walküre*, as Germans do. Nancy refuted the whole correction. In the summer of 1914, she wrote, she had been in Grandfather Redesdale's house in Kensington High Street, with Pam, Tom and Diana, Blor and Ada, the nursery maid, 'because my mother was, as usual, increasing the number of the others, an occupation which I thought extremely unnecessary. On 8 August a girl was born; she was christened Unity, after an actress my mother admired called Unity Moore, and Valkyrie after the war maidens. This was Grandfather Redesdale's idea; he said these maidens were not German but Scandinavian. He was a great friend of Wagner's and must have known. Then we all went back to Victoria Road.'

Grandfather Redesdale appeared to be a worldly-wise diplomat of the old school, and perhaps had not expected his tribute to Scandinavian war maidens to be taken seriously when the troops were marching past his house, off to France. The following year, he published his *Memoirs*, and the two volumes were a runaway success, testimonies to a career lived to the full in the embassy at St Petersburg, then in Pekin and Japan. He had met the celebrities of the day, and relished them. In 1912 he had been invited by Siegfried Wagner, the composer's son, to the Bayreuth Festival. A drama there, he noted, was more like a religious ceremony. 'Wagner holds their mind in the thralldom of his genius ... the Early Christians in the Catacombs could hardly have been more reverent.' It was not possible to have foretold how the Nazi mind was to stay in thralldom to Wagner and his hell-fire anti-semitism.

At Bayreuth, indeed at Haus Wahnfried, the Wagner house, lived a friend for Lord Redesdale to see, Houston Stewart Chamberlain, a toiler in the shadow of Wagner, whose daughter Eva he eventually married in 1918. In 1911 the English translation of Chamberlain's book, The Foundations of the Nineteenth Century, had appeared with a lengthy introduction by Lord Redesdale, humble in his respect for its 'pages adorned with brilliant passages of the loftiest eloquence'. Born in 1855, Chamberlain was the son of an English admiral. He had been brought up in France and Germany, where, in Lord Redesdale's words, 'he plunged heart and soul into the mysterious depths of the Wagnerian music and philosophy'.

In practice, this meant adopting the theories of race which were then being conjured as purely self-serving political responses to the new-found purposes of Bismarck's Germany. The Foundations of the Nineteenth Century was an influential book because it vulgarized plain nationalism, the pan-German nationalism which owed its glory, and its obscurity hitherto, to professors and intellectuals. If Germany was to have so uplifting a historical role, then it was as well to minimize and denigrate those who would be having to make way for this role. The high legacy had come from Greece and Rome, and the Germans were the true heirs. The merest storm-trooper could read his respectability into a text like this. '"The entrance of the Jews" has exercised a large, and in many ways an undoubtedly fatal, influence upon the course of European history since the first century.' Since Christ was Jewish apparently, much exercise had to be spent surmounting that stumbling-block. Chamberlain goes into shapes of skulls, blood measurements, magical functions, blind will; he will generalize upon anything and everything to set Jews apart, as a race, as a religion. Jews have either too much history for him, or too little. The bogus apparatus of justified racial persecution was at hand, and the Nazis had only to pick it up from him. 'That the Teuton is one of the greatest, perhaps the very greatest power in the history of mankind, no one will wish to deny.' But the Teuton has been contaminated by mixture with non-Aryan half-breeds and Jews. 'No argument about "humanity" can alter the fact that this means a struggle.'

The association of Unity with Chamberlain through her grandfather won her a place by divine right in the Nazi scheme of things; it was a source of wonder to Hitler, and he referred to it often to her and to others as proof positive of the way breeding and blood are the masters of destiny. Chamberlain, foreshadowing Unity, had to choose between England and Germany. A renegade, he was naturalized German in 1916, and in his propaganda essays he became the Lord Haw-Haw of the First World War. His hope was for a future state organized on the lines of the German army. The Weimar Republic he went so far as to call the *Judenrepublik*. The influence on Hitler and *Mein Kampf* has been acknowledged. The two men met in Wahnfried in September 1923, and shortly before the November *putsch* that year Chamberlain was writing to Hitler a letter which was to be treated as revealed truth by Nazis: 'You are not really as you have been portrayed, a fanatic ... A fanatic influences heads. You warm hearts. The fanatic talks everyone down. You want to convince them, only to convince them – and this is why you have succeeded ... That Germany in the hour of her deepest need should have given birth to a Hitler bears witness to its living strength.'

Lord Redesdale had been marginally embarrassed to explain smoothly 'the extraordinary interest of Chamberlain's special chapter upon the Jews and their entry into the history of the West. I have already hinted that with some of his conclusions I do not agree: but I go all lengths with him in his appreciation of the stubborn singleness of purpose and dogged consistency which have made the Jew what he is.' The breeziness with which he formed up behind Chamberlain's pamphleteering and militaristic prejudices ought to be unusual in so experienced a man, but can only be reflecting his cast of mind.

In the years of his retirement Lord Redesdale acted the conscious dynast. In 1880 he pulled down the old Georgian house, Batsford, which had come to the family when a Freeman heiress had married a Mitford, and built himself its present version, a late-Victorian castle, a pile, domestic in its lack of actual fortification, but wholly heraldic, the great hall and tower and angularities designed to impress. The rhetoric of the man rises there for all to admire, an exclamation in red stone. Batsford today has an arboretum, some of it planted by Lord Redesdale, with his collection of bamboo species partly surviving, as well as some Japanese statuary. When he died in 1916, his eldest son Clement had already been killed in France, leaving two small daughters, Rosemary and Clementine, the latter born posthumously. The title therefore passed to the next son, David, Farve already to his growing children. Not that Unity knew much of Batsford, for by the time she was four, in 1918, it was sold and her parents moved some dozen miles away to Asthall.

As if one grandfather who thought fit to make public observations about the Jews was not enough, Unity had two. Thomas Gibson Bowles was Conservative Member of Parliament for King's Lynn, a true-blue Victorian card, a naval commander with a belief that the British navy ought to outnumber the rest of the world's fleets put together. Among other interests he owned the *Lady* (for which Nancy wrote in her early days, and which remains in the hands of the Bowles family). The commander's tang blows strong through his book *The Log of the 'Nereid'* (1889), a description of a journey he undertook with his four young children, George and Geoffrey, Weenie and Sydney – in other words Uncles George and Geoff, who later were scarcely on speaking terms, 'the vile Aunt Weenie' as Unity was habitually to call her, and Muv. On the title page Commander Bowles designated himself Master Mariner, and below that he trails a nursery epigraph: '"I waunt to go to sea, velly much" – Weenie.' Weenie's book it was, and an illustrated frontispiece showed her as a bold, half-sulky child, arms akimbo, one leg crossed before the other, with ropes and tackle around. From their earliest days she and her sister wore sailor suits and eccentric yachting caps and stockings. Where Weenie was concerned, love and licence were unchecked. Little Sydney hardly rated a mention in the log. Her mother had already died, and nobody and nothing appears to have come between Sydney and neglect, which may explain why when she in turn became a mother, she was remote, ineffectual, unphysical, not caring to hug her children nor to be hugged by them.

Foreign parts were not much to the commander's taste. For Egypt he reserved the language of the prophet Ezekiel, 'They shall be there a bare kingdom.' In Jerusalem, the Wailing Wall was a sight for jeering at: 'Certainly if any Jews come from the neighbourhood of Hatton Gardens, they would hardly fail, at the mention of these precious stones, to reflect that they cost a deal of money, or to mourn with the greater emphasis over them. But, in truth, I don't see what the Jews have got to wail about. If they have been expelled from Jerusalem, they are the rulers of London, Paris and Berlin. If they are no longer governors of Palestine, they are the tyrants of Europe, and I cannot believe that they really hold themselves to be worse off for the change. Nor shall I believe it till I see the great house of Rothschild abandon London in order to set up as bankers in Jerusalem; Baron de Hirsch leave Paris in order to make a railway from Jerusalem to Jericho, with a free refreshment bar at the place where the man fell among thieves; and all the Jewish controllers of the European Press, from Mr Levy Lawson downwards, cease printing startling intelligence in the West, and take to achieving the largest circulation in the world in Hebrew near the Gate of Damascus.' And much more besides. Old Lord Redesdale had expressed himself more fluently.

As for Uncle Geoff, though in her autobiography Jessica pokes fun at him and his crackpot writing of letters to the newspapers, his absurd fads about diet, the fertilization of soil and the pasteurization of milk (fads shared by his sister Sydney, whose inverted adherence to Mosaic diet laws, according to Jessica, 'was enforced as rigidly as in any orthodox Jewish household ... because my mother had a theory that Jews never got cancer') – he is to be found writing to a fascist paper, the *Weekly Review*, on 28 November 1946, when anti-semitism had already run its full course. 'It does not matter who wrote or forged or plagiarized (kidnapped) the 'Protocols of the Elders of Zion'. Somebody must have written them. The one thing that does matter is that the predictions in the Protocols have come true up to now. What can prevent the remaining predictions from also coming true? The whole programme and plan of the Protocols is aimed against the "Gentiles" they name so often, and the plan has largely succeeded already. Their prophetic value is plain. The Protocols ought accordingly to be widely published and easily obtainable so that all Gentiles can read the future foretold for them by such true foretellers in the past.'

A Hon (the 'h' was pronounced), then, Unity was from the age of two, but a rebel she was to become only by way of disobedience, for the deeper outlook of superiority and indifference to others which is at the base of every racial theory, anti-semitism included, was natural to her elders, as it was to be to her.

A coda is provided by Uncle Jack, fifth of Grandfather Redesdale's nine children, and the only one to have headed in an unlikely direction, and then not for long. Expelled from Eton, he had not been able to enter the diplomatic service for which his father had destined him. In October 1913, he announced his engagement to Marie-Anne Friedländer-Fuld, whose father, 'officially rated as the richest man in Berlin, made a large fortune in coke and its by-products', as James W. Gerard wrote in My Four Years in Germany, summing up the period 1913 to 1917, when he had been American ambassador to the Kaiser.

On 5 January 1914 the Daily Mail correspondent in Berlin turned to lyric prose. 'Amid scenes of splendour rivalled only by royal functions, the three days' festivities in connection with the marriage on Tuesday of Mr John Freeman-Mitford and Fräulein Marie-Anne von Friedländer-Fuld, only child of the German "Coal King", began tonight with the traditional "wedding eve" party in the marble mansion of the bride's parents in the Pariser Platz. The bride and bridegroom described themselves as "Baby" and "Jack" in the facsimile autographs on the gilt-embossed menu-programmes. Three hundred guests bearing names famous in war, politics, diplomacy, finance, and letters, and government, made the occasion one of the most notable events in the history of German society. One of the great banker guests said to me that the fortune of the bride's father could not be much under £10,000,000.' To forestall comment that one of the largest fortunes in Germany might eventually be transferred to England, Uncle Jack was promoted to be a partner in his father-in-law's business.

Among the three hundred guests, as it happened, was my grandfather.

Because she had been expecting my mother, my grandmother had stayed at home. Nearly ninety now, she writes to me that Baby Friedländer-Fuld had been good-looking and brilliant; that she had bought Van Gogh's *L'Arlésienne* and other French impressionists well before she was twenty. 'She was a great friend of Rathenau and of Max Reinhardt. Her second husband was Kuhlmann [who had been secretary in the German embassy in London at the outbreak of war]. Her third husband was Rudi Goldschmidt-Rothschild. How did the marriage come about in the first place? It was the idea of the Kaiser's brother, Prince Henry of Prussia, who had many friends in England. Why did it not last? Very simply because never consummated. Asked for details of the wedding, your grandfather assured me that he thought he was in Venice . . . one needed a gondola as the tears of the bridegroom came in waves. You can imagine that neither of the families did anything but try to hush up the whole affair.'

Ten weeks after the marriage, Baby started proceedings for an annulment, alleging 'masculine indolence and an unbearable selfishness'. During the twenties and thirties she continued to live in the marble mansion on the Pariser Platz, and after the Nuremberg Laws were passed, so it is said, the Star of David which she wore was of yellow diamonds. She spent the war in America and died in 1973. She and Unity could well have met in Berlin, though it would have been accidentally, for Unity did not enjoy any mention of the lady who had been, however briefly, her Jewish aunt.

2

SISTERS, COUSINS, SEWERS

The Redesdales, Muv and Farve, were a handsome couple, all that they ought to have been outwardly, conventionally. They imposed, they looked solid. Yet their firm front was actually cardboard, which spurred their spirited children to break through it and see what might happen next. Errant Edwardians that they were in a modern age which was stranding them, the Redesdales had only one tactic – they resisted all encroachments upon them until it was hopeless, and then they surrendered unconditionally. Lord Redesdale was a brave man, distinguished as a soldier, a simple patriot, with puzzled contempt for those not like himself, such as Catholics, Jews or foreigners, especially Germans, a church-goer, in short every inch a gentleman. Lady Redesdale matched him, full of the domestic virtues and good works, with enough dottiness to stop her being insipid. Knowing nothing of the world at large in all its complexity, they had neither the inclination nor the intellectual means to find out about it. They preferred their home, and its pursuits. They expected their children to be like themselves. Faced with originality, they were defenceless. The onslaught of Unity, for example, was to knock them down flat. Nothing is more curious in their lives than the way that this innocent-minded couple were converted by her from hating the Germans to admiring them, becoming enthusiastic Hitlerites themselves, to the point of disaster, their marriage eventually breaking upon these rocks.

'"From Batsford Mansion to Asthall Manor to Swinbrook House to Old Mill Cottage" was our slogan to describe the decline of the family fortunes from Grandfather's day.' This *Hons and Rebels* dig was close to the bone. A Marxist might interpret the scattering of the Mitford children over the social target as evidence of the decline and fall of the gentry. Lord Redesdale was as improvident as an aristocrat is supposed to be. His investments were not prudent. At the age of twenty-three, after he had been wounded and decorated in the South African war, he bought a gold mine, uncannily called the Swastika Mine, near Culver Park, in Canada. Sir Harry Oakes had the adjoining concession. In summer the Redesdales would go prospecting. They camped in a shack where Muv cooked and washed, and Farve conferred with Shee, the foreman. The adventure was debonair and carefree, an escape from obligations, but although a table-turning session at Asthall once promised that the gold was there, no rich lode was ever located.

The Swinbrook estate, as well as several hundred acres in Northumberland, had been inherited, and with this came the urge to build. Asthall had originally been a large farmhouse, one among several in Cotswold stone in a buried village. It sits right beside the Windrush, one of the prettiest of Oxfordshire streams. No sooner had Lord Redesdale moved in than he set about major improvements, adding panelling, ceilings, battlements, throwing out a schoolroom and a cloistered passageway to the tithe-barn, itself converted to a ballroom with separate rooms above it. The bell-board in the kitchen today shows the names of these rooms, whose walls the children had painted. Unity's room is decorated with a potent little horned demon. The nurseries, and Nanny Blor's room in the main house, are still painted the dark shiny blue which was known as Redesdale blue, a colour repeated in all their houses.

But in 1928 Asthall was sold to the father of the present owner, Mr Anthony Hardcastle. He explains that Lord Redesdale had been very anxious to sell. 'The Redesdales had suffered from a ghost here, they had the notion that a Grey Lady haunted the house. Lord Redesdale liked the shooting, going out with old Everett, the keeper, though once he told my mother that the best sport would be a manhunt. I remember Unity out on a horse.' There was also a less intangible, urgent reason for selling, in that the work at Asthall had hardly been finished before Lord Redesdale had another fit of building folly, and embarked upon Swinbrook, or South Lawn, to give that house its name, only a couple of miles away from Asthall but still on his estate. Asthall and the Grey Lady had lasted seven years. Afterwards Lady Redesdale used to say that none of their troubles would have happened if they had stayed there.

To console everyone for the upheaval, Lord Redesdale bought a house in London, 26 Rutland Gate, in a Kensington not so different from Thackeray's. On the ground floor were the dining room and Lord Redesdale's study, with drawing room and ballroom above according to the canons of Victorian entertaining. Overhead were five more floors of bedrooms, graduating from landing to landing, from parents to children, to governesses, to nannies and parlourmaids and kitchenmaids. Unity and Jessica shared a bedroom on the third floor. Honnish games could be devised – for instance dodging the parents by means of the two staircases or the lift – but Rutland Gate had about it something official, with the time-limits of an excursion or a holiday. Rutland Gate was property, a stake, and not a stamping-ground as their house

in the country was. Besides, in order to pay for itself, it was let for long
stretches. Much of the Swinbrook estate was tenanted, and even the shooting
rights there had to be let when Lord Redesdale was particularly feeling the
pinch.

While Swinbrook was being built, in the winter of 1925 to 1926, Lord
Redesdale moved his family to Paris, in order to be out of harm's way for
the duration. Swinbrook could have done with ageing, with a Grey Lady. As
a house, it was an imposition, a Mitford barracks with picket-line formality,
perhaps because everyone who might have softened its design was away in
Paris. The original conception had been cottagey, with elm doors and latches
and bobbins, but it was discovered that elm warped, and the woodwork had
to be scrapped. Cotswold fireplaces and oak beams became the order of the
day, then varnished floors, slippery and bare. Downstairs, the drawing room –
facing towards forsaken Asthall – ended white, tunnel-like, the prettiness
chilled. Next to it was the Closing Room, amusingly depicted in *Hons and
Rebels* as the place where Farve would at last close his eyes in peace. Eighteen
bedrooms upstairs, spartan whitewashed rooms, without wallpaper, but with
a stripe painted round as a cornice. Unity's stripe was yellow. The sewing-
maid, Gladys, had a room in which to sew the girls' dresses, but as fortunes
declined, she was dismissed – as was Turner, the chauffeur. Then the sewing
room became the DFD or Drawing Room from Drawing Room, divided
down the middle, with Unity and her Nazi trophies to one side, and Jessica
and Communism to the other – the barricade, in fact, was here. The schoolroom was on the second floor, demarcated from the adults by a green baize
door. And still the fires smoked, damp crinkled the new plaster, the bills
were ceaseless.

Financial speculation depleted Lord Redesdale's resources no less than his
building. 'Marquise fails in slander suit', the heading of a *Morning Post* article
of 29 January 1930, compressed a row which typified Lord Redesdale's punt-
ing of money upon his hunches, in this instance the wireless inventions of a
Spanish, or more improbably a Chilean, marquis. To have said that the marquis was not a nobleman proved no slander, but Lord Redesdale was no
better off for the satisfaction in the courts. That March, in the House of
Lords he demanded that British creditors should receive justice from the
southern states of America, which had defaulted on their loans in the Civil
War. His defence of the peerage and the hereditary system offered one of the
more obvious butts for his children, though the suggestion of his that the
abolition of the House of Lords would 'undermine the foundations of
Christianity' attracted the derision of the political scientist, Professor Harold

Laski, no less. To back Hitler through thick and thin was only to continue displaying his unerring eye for a dud cause. He was not taken seriously. His speeches had never alarmed.

With this poor lovable ogre of a father, and a blindly opinionated mother, Unity was bound to have a childhood out of the ordinary. It was not a matter of living comfortably. Arrogance and assumed superiority went with obedience to the social code, and out of this English blend has been generated a great deal of energy, but confusion as well. Insecurity as a source of aggression is a modern theory which would have baffled the Redesdales entirely, but the sale of Asthall, and the leap up the hill to Swinbrook, certainly did uproot her for a second time, and perhaps psychologists would explain that her passion for Hitler and for Nazism over-compensated for a father-figure and a tight-knit family framework.

Was Unity naughty, thoroughly against the grain, or was her behaviour naughty only because it attracted the grown-ups' attention and broke their daily tenor, which was the worst of naughtinesses in a traditional household of the time? Self-expression was allowed only within the bounds of discipline. Yet Unity was not thwarted or narrowed deliberately. She grew up to that rhythm of the nannied class, of alternate indulgence and punishment. Parents were like judges in a court of last appeal, and bad manners and spoilt behaviour came before them almost as a test of character. Show-off did lead to retribution more automatic than thoughtful, and that in turn provoked the couldn't-care-less outlook, which sparked real anger, and so the vicious spiral was enlarged. Children do not have to be from a well-off background to prepare for their self-destruction in this way, but then the majority know when to stop, which Unity did not.

Neighbours were not much to the Redesdales' liking, and the country-house round was done with a slight show of duty. There were the Herman-Hodges at Sarsden, where Unity at one time had dancing lessons; John Buchan and his children at Elsfield; the McCalmonts at Adlestrop; the Andrews at Bibury; the Watneys at Cornbury, the Goodenoughs, Mrs Goodenough unconsciously triggering one epic row when she mentioned to the Redesdales that she had seen Nancy and Mary Milnes-Gaskell at the station, off to lunch in Oxford with Brian Howard, arch-sewer.

Abbotswood, a house extended by Lutyens at Stow-on-the-Wold, belonged to Mark Fenwick, who had five daughters, the youngest of whom today is Mrs Constantia Arnold. On 2 June 1923 her sister Hilda married 'Boy' (later General Sir Bertram) Sergison-Brooke of the Grenadier Guards, and Unity was one of her bridesmaids. Photographs show her in a silk dress with a bow, a heavy wreath round her forehead, as cherubic a nine-year-old as any mother could hope for. Mrs Arnold's portrait of the Mitfords shows a family circle in the full sense. 'In the school holidays I used to stay with them for a week at a time, first at Batsford, then at Asthall, which was fifteen miles from Abbotswood. Nancy was my real friend. I used to adore going there, though frightened of Farve. He wore canvas gaiters, with knickerbockers and boots, and he had a thumb-stick, and always wore a hat out of doors. A thick-set man, good-looking with his clipped hair and moustache. He and Lady Redesdale had blue eyes. He was not quite as stupid as he'd like to make out, though I remember someone asking him what he read, and he answered, I don't read. His stock-in-trade was to make those outrageous remarks which children really can't take. He'd shout and rage and you never quite knew where you were. It was a very happy household, though, not suppressed, oppressed or depressed, whatever they may say. They never went to school, so were thrown upon each other. And there were masses of servants, a French governess, and Miss Price, another governess, Blor, and Mabel the parlour-maid. The little ones, including Bobo, lived a life of their own upstairs. We used to muck about, giggling, riding a good deal. At one of the Asthall fêtes, Farve brought a huge wireless with a horn. At one of their fancy-dress parties Unity went as Queen Victoria. Their cousin, Tim Bailey, was being Moses in the bulrushes, just lying in his crib.'

Over at Hatherop Castle, rebuilt in the 1870s, were the Bazleys. Lady Bazley, like Lady Redesdale, held no brief for boarding school, but had the PNEU system of education in the house, which involved posting exercises off to a central examiner in London. For a year Nancy lived at Hatherop, which had to do for her formal education. Frances Bazley is now married to the novelist Richard Hughes. Her half-brother, Christopher Cadogan (killed in the war), was one of the many young men in Munich whom Unity was to promise to introduce to Hitler. 'The Redesdales were terribly grand,' said Mrs Hughes, 'quite unapproachable. Nancy told endless stories about them, she also had a brother-worship of Tom. Dancing class was twice a week at Hatherop. All the little Mitford girls came on a Wednesday. They were all dressed up in white, with sashes and beautiful shoes. Nurses and under-nannies were there, it was a matter of prestige, we didn't have time to talk, we had to watch. I noticed Unity a lot, she was so beautiful, she was more silent than the others, quite an innocent face, with china-blue eyes. At Hatherop we usually had a dance in the summer in the garden, and the Mitfords did the same in their turn – it was the right thing to ask each other. Just about every year, around Christmas, we used to get up a play, with old clothes and so on, but one year we got ambitious and started to hire from Clarksons, the wig people, and we did the play in the drawing room.

The Mitfords had walk-on parts. We had a governess called Essex Cholmon-delay, a cousin of Stella Benson's, she produced it.'

When I wrote to Miss Cholmondelay about this play, she replied, 'I only saw Unity a few times when she and her sisters came over to Hatherop. *Quality Street* was being produced for a party of neighbours and Nancy persuaded her family to be the schoolchildren in one scene. Jessica was delightful, but Unity, then about twelve, remained very shy and aloof. She never unbent and I suppose she hated the whole thing.'

If neighbours had to be tolerated, cousins were a given fact of life. For com-pany, for entertainment and breaks from Swinbrook, the Mitfords depended upon an array of cousins. Favourites among them were the Baileys, the Farrers, and the Churchills – Lady Churchill's mother and Grandmother Redesdale having been sisters. Tim Bailey, the guest who came by crib to the fancy-dress party, was one of the four sons of Aunt Weenie and Colonel Bailey, and they lived at Maughersbury Manor, at Stow-on-the-Wold. For family occasions such as Christmas, or for what was known as 'spending the day', they were driven over to their cousins. Tim Bailey said, 'The Old Dave was how my father called Lord Redesdale, they were two of a kind. My mother and Aunt Sydney were also very alike, they had the same set of neck. Every summer in August we used to have Bailey Week, for the four brothers, and we did the traditional things of those days, playing tennis and cricket, and having a dance on the Saturday. Dick, my eldest brother, and Tom Mitford were at Eton together, and so was Jim Lees-Milne who came over from Broadway. Lees-Milne was the one who couldn't do anything. All of us were once made by my father to build a wall of Cotswold dry stone. Jim went off on his own, and as he returned, he came past the wall just as it was being finished, and it collapsed. Randolph Churchill used to be with us for the holidays, his mother had been my mother's bridesmaid. Bobo was a non-games player, she was the wrong shape. In age she was the exact contemporary of my brother Chris, and they were inseparable. The famous scene was once when we were staying at Asthall, and Bobo and Chris had picked every strawberry out of the greenhouse before breakfast. They were professionally naughty, nobody in the history of corporal punishment was more beaten than those two. For one of the fêtes at Asthall, Bobo stood on the main road and diverted all the traffic down to the village, the trucks crawling along those tiny lanes. When Bobo was in Munich later on, she'd send Chris a telegram about her plans for coming home. That little Morris of hers had an Oxford-shire numberplate, UD 9999. Chris went on seeing Bobo but not much after 1933, he did not want to know about Nazis. He became Lord Wavell's

ADC and was killed in the war. I took Aunt Sydney and Debo and Tom to one of Mosley's last big rallies in London. Tom wouldn't sit with us, I suspect he didn't want to be identified.'

Chartwell, where the Churchills lived, was within less easy range, but visits were nevertheless regularly exchanged in the holidays between the Mitfords and the Churchills. Winston Churchill, 'Cousin Winston', was not much seen by the children, for whom he had little time, though he did single out Diana Mitford, calling her Dynamite, and it was hard and ironical that he had to order her detention in Holloway Prison in the war, as though in an ultimate disposal of a squabble. The Redesdales never cared for Churchill's politics at any stage, and late in life Lady Redesdale took to referring to him as 'that wicked man'. Diana and Randolph Churchill, and Diana and Tom Mitford were all more or less growing up together, while Unity was expected to pair off with Sarah Churchill, exactly her own age, and who was to become the actress.

Here was a crowd of children, according to Sarah Churchill, among whom it was all too possible to feel lonely, not rough enough. 'Diana Churchill and Randolph and Tom left out Bobo and me. They used to have midnight feasts, Randolph would tie a string round Diana's toe, to jerk it when it was time, but Bobo and I were not in on this. We minded. They used to bully us. The older children had a special tease, that they would lock the younger ones into cupboards if they ate *pâté de foie gras* (on the grounds of protecting geese from cruelty). Randolph was the leader of this. The threat was always there, so we formed up, principally Bobo and I, and decided to go into the cupboard anyhow, and we were locked up in it. Sometimes we also used to sit in that linen cupboard. We had a game in which Randolph led the rest of us, he was a Major. I was Private Jones, a ranker. They used to march us over banks of high stinging nettles. Tom didn't do anything to me but he used to make Bobo be his slavey, and whip her fat little legs. At Swinbrook Bobo had the bedroom next to mine and used to rap on the wall the rhythm of "Slowly Crushed to Death in a Lift" which had been a headline from a paper. Its subtitle was "Man's Long Agony in a Lift-shaft". This jingle would so upset Debo that she would cry, and the penalty for that was to have pocket money docked. Therefore the horrid jingle had to be rapped or whistled. The story of the arm was invented to get the better of Bobo's tapping. This story was about a medical student and his girl. He had got a frozen arm and hung it up by the light, so when she got into bed she reached up to pull the light and held this frozen arm. The girl was known to be easily scared and everyone was waiting for her screams. Silence. After a bit they forced their way in and she was sitting up in bed, the moonlight on her face, eating the arm. Bobo was full of mischief. I wasn't physically frightened of her but all the same . . . Once we were all sent home by Lord Redesdale for throwing slates off the roof at Swinbrook, they went clattering down into the garden. There was a shindig. Bobo and I had not been part of it, and we came rushing in as fake goody-goodies saying that we hadn't done it, we were counterplotting against the older children. We came out together as debutantes in the end, spending time in the ladies' loo, gossiping, playing cards. I used to go to the library and fall asleep. We were all shattered by what happened to Bobo. Just as war was breaking out, Tom was having lunch with us and my father asked, What do you think Bobo will do? Tom said, I think she'll shoot herself.'

Brayfield belonged to Major Dennis Farrer and Aunt Joan, one of Lord Redesdale's four sisters. On the Buckingham–Bedford borders, that soft landscape of water and willows and huge churches, Brayfield is an architectural ramble, an extended Georgian house with a Victorian conservatory and an iron verandah on the garden facade. Major Farrer was a distant relation of Lord Redesdale's in his own right, and the two of them had travelled as young men to Ceylon. The shooting season brought them together, their families motoring across country. Brayfield was a rival gathering-point for cousins, for Rosemary and Clementine Mitford (now Mrs Bailey and Lady Beit) used to stay there too, and so did the Romillys, with their sons Giles and Esmond. Of the five Farrer children, Barbara was Pam's contemporary, while Ann and Joan (known as Robin) matched Unity and Jessica, the boys bringing up the rear. In Boudledidge, the girls' names were translated into Idden and Rudbin, though Jessica and they were, and are, prone to address each other as Sister, as in the American movies which impressed them. More properly, Rudbin is Mrs Paul Rodzianko, having married the late Colonel Paul Rodzianko, once of the Russian Imperial Guard, a noted horseman and author of a book about his experiences, *Under Tattered Banners*.

Mrs Rodzianko said, 'Asthall was very haunted. I remember hearing this odd tick-tock of water. Holy fear: I remember the feeling. We were anyhow frightened of staying there or at Swinbrook. Nancy thought we had rather a thin time, but she was very sharp, we had no real reason to fear her, but we did all the same. Her favourite story to us was about witches boiling little boys in cauldrons. Uncle David I didn't have any fear of, he was just like Bobo, he went bull-headed at things, he had loves and loathes, one of the latter being my eldest sister, and he was beastly to her. The Mitfords led us into terribly bad ways and daring escapades. The cardinal sin was getting on to the roof, at Swinbrook or Brayfield.

'Uncle David and Muv breakfasted with us in the dining room. We all had lunch together and once we were old enough, we were allowed down to dinner, changed. Bobo and I used to go to the village shop, which was also the post-office, to buy whipped cream walnuts, she adored that kind of thing. She ate quantities of cream and potatoes. She was big but not unduly fat. She rode but didn't hunt like the others. The question, What shall we do? nearly always got the answer, Let's go skating. Unity got a bronze medal for it. Frau Witter, a German woman and the wife of the pro, used to skate with Lord Redesdale, he was fond of her. Unity was a strong personality, if ruthless. I remember her and Decca reading Chrome Yellow when it was the "in" thing. Unity was the bright white hope, far and away the most loved, they caught from her all the excitement. Uncle David was frightfully pleased to have such brilliant and clever daughters, but he was mad about Unity. We used to stay with them in London too, and be taken to the National Gallery, to see the Blakes, to Westminster Cathedral, and go climbing the tower there. Miss Hussey, the governess, took us to St George's swimming baths, where we jumped off the high-diving-board, Unity too.

'In 1928, Unity and I were schoolgirls, and went with Muv by train on an educational trip, for about a week, to Bruges, in a little hotel there, and on to Ghent. We saw the Van Eycks, Unity enjoyed herself, she was keen on the eating. She spoke French but neglected it. Muv thought my mother was going to do nothing for us, so she lent us the mews cottage, always known as The Garage, at Rutland Gate, in 1932, the big house having been let. Muv took another house in Tite Street and she brought me out with Bobo, and had a dance there in January. Then we used to have girls' lunch parties. She was presented at Court in May, and soon afterwards Diana gave this ball for us. There was a lot of chat about dressing when she came out, she was always rather gorgeous with strange, gaudy things, and the pet rat too. There was a fancy-dress ball in the Albert Hall, and I also remember going with her to the Victoria Palace music-hall – at that stage she had plenty of admirers.

'Like all Mitfords, she had a one-track mind, she became completely caught up in fascism – there was a vacuum and that was what rushed in to fill it. Once she was off with Oswald Mosley and Diana, and away to Germany, she could think of nothing else, and neither could Diana. Oh Rudbin, they're Jews, she would say when I was in a fury at the way they were being treated. They're just Jews and must be got rid of. She talked a lot about the Führer, and said that he was very celibate. I married in 1936 and lived in Lenham Heath in Kent. Bobo stayed there in July 1939, on her way back to Munich for the last time. I asked her what would happen if there was a war. She said she would kill herself.'

Of Unity's society moment, Mrs Rodzianko has some souvenirs in her scrapbook: a photograph of a group in front of a fierce sports car, as at a point-to-point, with the explanation, 'Fitz Orchard, Bobo, Me, Rosemary Bailey, at the Stanmore Riding School 1932, The Cup Competition'. Also a double portrait clipped from a Sunday Pictorial in the same year, 'A new portrait of the Hon Unity Mitford, a 1932 debutante, and her cousin Miss Joan Farrer.' Then Easter weekend at Brayfield, in April 1935, has two pages of photographs of Unity and Jessica, their father and Uncle Jack, Major Farrer and his daughters and two young men, Neil Hodgkin and David Wilson (killed in the war). Some of these snapshots were taken by Unity. And another page has six watercolour sketches by her, like cigarette cards in size, somewhat linear but appealing, of people in costume at the fancy-dress ball given by Bryan and Diana Guinness at Biddesden, which was a highlight of her 1932 season – here are John Sutro, as a cupid with a bow and tiny wings and gold hair; Oliver Messel, the stage designer, in a Roman uniform of toga and high-heeled buskins and vast feathered helmet; someone else, un-identified, holding a trident; Nancy, as a Marie-Antoinette peasant, a floral wreath round her shoulders; Diana, chaste and lanky in white, but faceless, which must have been an intentional jab; and finally a self-portrait, in a blue-and-white eighteenth-century dress, 'Me' firmly written underneath, but crossed out in favour of 'Bobo'.

That Nazism filled a vacuum for Unity finds confirmation in Hons and Rebels. Unity appears there as huge and sullen, caught in claustrophobia, permanently about to ignite through spontaneous combustion in the rarefied atmosphere of Swinbrook. The objections were neither moral nor political, for abstract questions of the sort were not posed by Muv and Farve. Unity was bored. She was restless. Her place in the family shifted, in that she could not pass muster with the older sisters, and did not attract the apple-of-the-eye affection lavished on Decca and Debo. There was nothing for it except self-assertion. To tease, or to be teased. 'Her immense, baleful blue eyes, large, clumsy limbs, dead straight tow-coloured hair, sometimes in neat pig-tails but more often flowing loose, gave her the appearance of a shaggy Viking or Little John. She was the bane of governesses, few of whom could stand up for long to her relentless misbehaviour.'

If governesses were intimidated by scale and broodiness, so was Farve. 'She had perfected a method of making my father fly into a rage by the simple expedient of glowering at him in a certain way at meal-times. She would sit silently stowing away quantities of mashed potatoes, her eyes fixed on Farve with a sombre, brooding glare. He would glare back, trying to make Boud drop her gaze, but she invariably won out. Crashing his fists on the table, he would roar: "Stop looking at me, damn you!" I envied her this accomplishment, at the same time pointing out that she was taking unfair advantage of my father's sub-human aspects: "Poor Farve, he's like a lion, not able to stand being fixed by the Human Eye."'

Unity's experiences, of course, were most closely paralleled by Jessica's, and the insistence on details and mutual games seems only to point up the absence of purpose from which they suffered. Jessica said, 'Bobo derived from Baby, my mother used to call her Little Babe, which became Little Bobe. As a child she knew lots of poetry by heart, most of the Oxford Book of English Verse, and tons of Shakespeare, my parents made us recite it. We used to go often to Stratford. She adored Arthur Rackham's illustrations, and Doré. She read quite a lot, including Huxley and Waugh, she was a terrific Brontë fan, and was attached to mystic things like Blake, or the weird and off-beat, Edgar Allen Poe and Hieronymus Bosch. She had the two volumes of Bentham and Hooker, the naturalist's guide to English flowers, and she knew every specimen in it. She liked picking bunches of flowers and arranging them for flower paintings, she used to decorate furniture by painting flowers and ivy on it. Once she had a real oil paint-box as a present, I got at it and squeezed out all the tubes and she never got another. Our musical upbringing was pretty bad, but we were all made to practise the piano. We used to sing those songs from my mother's song-books from 1900 to 1930. That's when Mark Ogilvie-Grant came into his own, with "The Last Rose of Summer", "I Dreamed I Dwelt in Marble Halls", with our make-up innuendo words. [Mark Ogilvie-Grant, another Swinbrook sewer, illustrated Nancy's early books and was bizarrely rendered as the Songster of Kew in her Pigeon Pie.] Bobo was always whistling a lot, tunes of the day, hymns. She used to start whistling in the middle of things. It was the despair of my mother at dinner parties – "Oh God Our Help in Ages Past", that kind of thing. I used to call my parents the Revered Parents, which became the Revereds, then simply Male Revered and Female Revered, and so down to Fem and the Male. This they didn't like, so they docked our allowance. We also called them The Poor Old Male and The Poor Old Female, TPOM and TPOF for short. We must have been the only children of our generation who were never forced to eat anything. As a child Bobo loved mashed potatoes and milk and chocolate, the choc tuppenny bars. Her teeth were oddly brown and nicked, they looked like Stonehenge, it may have had something to do with the way we had to put forks directly into our mouth without the food touching our lips, my mother having discontinued napkins. Or, more likely, the mashed potato and chocolate diet.

'Boudledidge grew up in very primitive fashion. Pal was Bal, equals Baddle, equals Boudle. Ch would be je; picture would be bigjure or bigjer; chair would be jer. T was d, and it went from there of its own accord. We were starting it at about the age of seven, and went on perfecting it until about ten. The language had to go with the facial expression, which was one of great sorrow, and the noise was pressed out of the side of the mouth. "Uuge and objegzionable" I called her, and when we quarrelled I would urge her to "gommid id", meaning that she should go and commit suicide – when she did, my mother reminded me of that, as though I had second sight.

'As for Honnish, that was a language between Debo and me. Kenoy is Honnish for hen, so a phrase like "in a woy kenoy" in Bobo's letters is a borrowing, she would have been too old for Honnish, which was more an accent than anything else. There were really two Hons cupboards. The main one was at Old Mill Cottage which belonged to my mother, and where we used to be when London and Swinbrook were both let. In the dining room, the wall was terribly thick, and in one recess had a bread oven built into it, large enough to hold three children, Debo, her chum Margaret, and me. Bobo used to be allowed into the Hons Cupboard but she had little part in it. In Swinbrook it was the linen cupboard.

'There were the Nasty Ladies. She used to have a recurrent dream, and repeat it in the morning, of a giant steamroller, vast, coming down the road with immense yew hedges on either side, and the steamroller fitted exactly between them so there was no escape. Three Nasty Ladies operated this steamroller, one had the gears, another was steering. The Nasty Ladies dressed like nannies in black, with nanny boots and bonnets, or a straw boater, but black. I caught the same dream from her. As well as the Nasty Ladies, she had Madam, an imaginary person of baleful influence who was responsible for her naughtiness, instructing her to do things not allowed, like stealing strawberries. I had stuffed toys as constant companions, Bobo used to stick pins into them, Nimmy a cat and Shooshoo a rabbit, so I wrote *Danger* on them, but spelled it Dangu, as we were taught phonetically, and everybody laughed. Just as Tom made her his slavey, she took it out on me by making me her "faithy servy" or faithful servant. She had a special whistle – three notes with a fourth up a bit – and if I didn't arrive, she pretended to be a ghost, or waylaid me.'

Madam had a living model in Mrs Violet Hammersley, also known as Mrs Ham, The Widow, even The Wid. The Hammersleys had lived in Lowndes

Square close to the Bowles's, and the families had also met in yachting days in the north of France. Mrs Hammersley had spent her first seventeen years in France, where her father, though neither a diplomat nor a spy, was somewhat nebulously employed by the Foreign Office. Somerset Maugham had a similar background of the British Embassy in Paris, and was her lifelong friend, as indeed were many writers, Logan Pearsall Smith, Arnold Bennett, the Sitwells, Beerbohm, as well as the New English Art Club world of Tonks, Wilson Steer, Augustus John. After the death of her husband, Mrs Hammersley based herself in the Isle of Wight, a blue-stocking, a woman of letters in her own right, an enigmatic but persistent presence. At Asthall Mrs Hammersley had asked Unity right out what Madam looked like, to hear a portrayal exactly of her own pale white face, thin nose, black clothes and mauve shawl. Not someone to miss the point, especially with children, she had laughed, a clever successor to the Grey Lady. Rosamond Lehmann in *The Swan in the Evening* has described the imprint: 'In those days I believed Violet Hammersley to be a witch; I feared she might change me or bewitch my mother. My tastes too tuppence-coloured to admire that elegance of hers in the high Spanish style which made her one of nature's works of art and caused all painters to wish to set down a reflection of her, I thought her very ugly. Her low-toned intensity in conversation troubled me; so did that hooded sombre gaze which impaled her interlocutor, especially when politics and finance were in question, and seemed to me literally to put out tentacles.'

When the Redesdales went overboard for Nazism, she was too fascinated to keep her fingers out of the pie. Their perpetual family crises fuelled her manic-depressive side, she probed at what she called 'Jessica's ball-room communism', and she was to propose herself as a visitor to Unity in Munich, where she would have been an agitated familiar. The Lehmann children, like the little Mitfords, were each addressed as 'Child' by Mrs Hammersley, and she would tirelessly inform the one set of the doings of the other (writing to Nancy regularly until the end of her life). Only once, though, did she come over from Swinbrook with Unity to introduce her – as one 'child' protégée to another – to Rosamond Lehmann, then married to Wogan Philipps and living at Ibstone in Oxfordshire. Rosamond Lehmann said, 'Unity was in full flood about Hitler. Wogan at the time was in the International Brigade in Spain, I was deeply involved in anti-fascist activity. She was a horror figure. I thought her very queer and affected. Apparently she took a dislike to me, I heard afterwards. She talked defiantly about Germany, it was awkward as Violet had very much wanted me to make friends with Unity.'

.   .   .   .   .

Attempts to burst the bounds of Swinbrook were in vain because Unity refused to put herself out for others, she made no concessions. At no point in her life did she bother to be friendly or charming with run-of-the-mill contemporaries. People had to like her as she was or not at all. If they approved, well and good, and if not, then they had only to reject her, as she rejected them. This pose of defiance pressed her down into teenage gloom, and when later extended into adult relationships, was horribly damaging. For pose it certainly was, a kind of misguided precaution to forestall being disliked. Rather than find that she had been left behind, she preferred to remove herself from the running, and this had to be made to look deliberate, colourful, justified. She had plumped early for rudeness and eccentricity, twinned characteristics of those who fear that they may not be able to make a real human mark as they would wish. And even Mitford gaiety was part and parcel of the pose of defiance, as Jessica describes it.

'When I was about nine, a farmer gave me an unwanted lamb. That was Miranda. So Bobo, thinking it unfair, got herself a goat, therefore we had quarrels over the merits of sheep and goats. The Harrods Pet Shop was where we went constantly buying. Enid, Bobo's grass snake, came from there. She used to take it everywhere. You could throw Enid into the sea and she'd come back through the waves, we'd think she was faithful. She used to go to deb dances with Enid round her neck. Ratular, her pet rat, came from Harrods too, and so did Sally the salamander. She usually had a rat or two, but not a dog of her own, because when she was old enough to have one, she went off to St Margaret's.

'Other cousins we stayed with were the Stanleys, Lyulph and Victoria, at Penrhos – Muv somehow knew about us bathing there once with no clothes on, and was credited with second sight – and the Airlies at Cortachy. The Airlies were Christian Scientists, and Bobo tested their faith by placing up-ended drawing-pins on their chairs at Swinbrook, and mixing castor-oil in the salad.

'While Swinbrook was being built, we lived for a six-month stretch in Paris, in the Avenue Victor-Hugo. On the first night in the hotel Blor took a loathing to the food, which was breaded veal cutlets, with lemon. My mother loved Paris, we had lessons with French governesses, learning to sing French songs, bowling hoops in the Bois. Paulette Helleu, daughter of the artist, came round and told us how much she had cried at a funeral in the church opposite. A lot of time afterwards was spent funeral-watching out of the hotel windows. But the first real trip abroad was to Sweden, when I was eleven and Bobo fourteen. We saw the sights of Stockholm, and were invited to Tidö Slott by the von Schinkels, my mother was nervous about taking it up. [Tidö, at Västmanland, about an hour from Stockholm, had been built between 1625 and 1645 in the classical northern style by Oxernstierna, Charles ix's famous general, and is one of the most notable of Swedish houses. The von Schinkels, Carl-David and his wife Carola, had inherited it in 1913.] The von Schinkels were very hospitable, meeting us in Stockholm and driving us out. Dinner was at nine o'clock that night, and the two boys, about our ages, were up, the four children sitting apart from the grown-ups. We had no common language, so I started making signs, pretending to ride to see what their reaction was. Bobo never said a word.

'We had sumptuous rooms. In the morning a maid brought up two jugs, one of chocolate, one of cream. I drank most of that, and I was walking up to the ancestral hall when I threw it all up. Bobo at last came into her own, she and my mother got cloths and cleaned it up. The whole idea was concealment. After lunch, visitors came and we were taken with them on a tour of the castle, coming to the fresh stain. I said that it must be blood welling where one of the ancestors had been murdered. All the time Bobo was as sullen and rude as could be, she was in a totally black mood, continuously so – a prolonged fit of sulking that lasted till she was eighteen. The melancholy left her fit for anything, for any kind of illumination. At one end of the family she was daggers drawn with Diana, and at the other end with me. Nancy and Bobo had a very strange relationship. Nancy was prime tease only after we got old enough to take it. Tom was the one person everybody always liked. When Bobo was about sixteen, my father's feelings for her shifted from total loathing to adoration. He would have favourites, as well as Rat Week, and you never knew when your turn for that would crop up. For a bit she was his favourite, and then again after they went to Munich and got sold on Hitler. By 1931, when she was about to come out – by then she had a great flashy ring and a fake tiara and capes and velvets from a theatrical costumier, and used to wear it all to dances, to my mother's annoyance – we began to form our deep friendship, becoming each other's favourite sister.'

Pursuing his favourite pastime, Lord Redesdale would lead excursions to the skating rink at Oxford. Part of the attraction for the girls was Al, the instructor, into whose strong arms it was possible to contrive to collapse. Unity was a moderately good skater. On one occasion, when she had fallen flat on her face, she was asked why she had not put out her hands, and her answer entered the family repertoire, 'I was waiting to see if nature would prompt me.'

Once Swinbrook was completed, Lord Redesdale went farther afield for winter sports in Switzerland, to Pontresina. St Moritz was only a few stops farther along the local railway, but altogether more expensive and fashionable, the scene for Uncle Jack, who had emerged from his short-lived marriage to become a somewhat Ivor-Novello model of a bobbish man-about-town, the inspiration behind the International Sportsman's Club in Grosvenor House, and eventually secretary of the Marlborough Club. St Moritz, with the Cresta run, was Uncle Jack's element; his set included the skating champion Sonja Henie, and the young blonde who under the name of Sheilah Graham was making her way upwards from the East End of London where she had been born, towards friendship with Scott Fitzgerald and a position as a Hollywood columnist. In her book *Beloved Infidel*, she has a photograph of the St Moritz skating rink, and the touchingly rapturous caption, 'At twenty-one, Sheilah had mixed with England's most exclusive society' – in fact, the assembled Mitfords on a bench, not only Uncle Jack, but Unity on his left, sitting forward a little, long-suffering, her face apparently too large for the beret on top of it: 'true gentlefolk', Sheilah Graham considered them.

This St Moritz high-life was in the winter of 1930. The following year, Sheilah Graham found herself lunching at Quaglino's with Tom Mitford and Randolph Churchill. Tom, she reports, had been struck all of a heap in Munich. 'Unity, with fervent admiration, had introduced him to Hitler – all Germany would follow him, and very soon, she insisted. They had both been invited to Hitler's home. It had been a remarkable experience. Of course, some of Hitler's ideas were shocking, yet – Tom and Randolph began a long debate about the historical role of democracy and fascism.'

In 1931 Hitler was still some way from seizing power; and Unity's admiration of the man, her introduction of Tom to him, the debates with Randolph, all true enough, have been brought forward here a few years.

Mabel, the parlourmaid, has long retired to the Somerset where she was born, but the Mitfords remain the family which was hers over so many years. 'When I went there first Lady Redesdale was a very proud lady, and when I left she used to hold me in her arms. Not his Lordship, he was never proud like that. I went as a temporary, I was thirty. When I saw that round table at Asthall with all of them sitting at it my hair stood up on end. When Unity wanted seconds, she didn't ask, she sat there and opened her eyes wide, looking at me – oh what an appetite. I wore a blue uniform, the Redesdale colour. One Christmas Lady Redesdale said to me, I want to dress up as you, and so she did, sitting at table dressed as me. We used to have some big do's at Asthall, all that dressing up. Nancy always won the prize. She came to view round the house once, disguised as Mrs Hardcastle's sister. I showed her round the ground floor. You know how strict Annie was, well Annie did the bedrooms, and it had been arranged we would all stand up in the nursery for the visitor, just so. Nancy had a white wig on, and had padded her figure out. What a dear little girl, she said, giving Decca a hug. But Decca struggled, until Nancy's twinkle became a laugh. She was always full of that nonsense. You knew where to find her, lying back in a chair reading. [About Annie, the head housemaid, Unity had made up a jingle:

> Annie and Nanny are talking together,
> They talk of such things as *gurls* and the weather,
> When suddenly Nanny says, Oh lor,
> Just look at the lock on the lavatory door.

Gurls was emphasized in the pronunciation of Annie and Nanny.]

'Bobo was full of wickedness, and so was Chris Bailey. They took those strawberries. We had candy sugar to smash up for coffee, and I used to keep it on the top shelf in the pantry – that Chris would say to Bobo, I know it's there, and they'd stand up on a table and reach it. I caught them and gave their backsides a smack. They were aged eight. One day those two went into my dining room. There were cruets laid down, but they'd gone, so I went upstairs and said, Bobo's taken my cruets. They'd hidden them under the bushes in the cloisters. She was a handful, all her life. She'd jump out of the cloisters to frighten poor Annie. She was awful to Miss Hussey. Headstrong. When I went with Decca, Bobo said, I used to be your pet, Mabe, but now it's all Decca.

'She went to Germany and was full of Hitler. I said, Don't mention his name in front of me.

– Mabe, you don't know Hitler, you'd like him.

– Oh no I wouldn't, and I don't want to know him.

– You just wait and see, Mabe, you'll be fighting the Russians.

'She had pictures of Hitler, she used to boast about meeting him and all of them. She was dead against the Jews. I said goodbye to her outside Rutland Gate, she was just going away the summer the war started, and she went and put her arms round me, Goodbye, she said, and don't hate Hitler so much, you'll come in with Germany, you'll see. Then I prayed, kneeling upstairs in my little kitchen, Please God will you let Russia help us, and it came out that way.'

Miss Hussey, also called Whitey or Steegson, whom Mabel thought had had such an awful time, was singled out for a particular practical joke recorded in *Hons and Rebels*. 'Boud found out that she had a deadly fear of snakes, and left Enid, her pet grass snake, neatly wrapped around the w.c. chain one morning.

We breathlessly awaited the result, which was not long in coming. Miss Whitey locked herself in, there was shortly an ear-splitting shriek followed by a thud. The unconscious woman was ultimately released with the aid of crowbars, and Boud was duly scolded and told to keep Enid in her box thereafter.' In 1922 Miss Hussey, who had been trained at Ambleside, began a stretch of two and a half years at Asthall, after which she went to India, returning to the Mitfords at Swinbrook, in 1931, for another two years. 'So very interesting, India,' was a phrase of hers which percolated down from the schoolroom. A song of the period, 'Lover dressed in jade', was adapted to 'Steegson dressed in jade'. If awfulnesses there were, Miss Hussey has ceased to dwell on them. She too lives in the West Country. 'I had been there a short time when the girls lined up to tell me, You are the thirteenth governess we've had. But for those first two years, Unity was a very healthy, beautiful girl, with something a bit different about her – I got on well with her. At midday lunch she sat close to her mother, who would keep an eye on her. Unity had a wonderful skin, almost transparent, and she had a look of a little St Joan of Arc which I've never forgotten. I often reminded Lady Redesdale of that look. She was brilliant and charming. She had all sorts of hobbies. She stuck cloves into oranges for pomanders. Pam had been kept rather behind. Diana (aged twelve) had been pushed forward. It was difficult for somebody younger like Unity, they had all to do separate lessons. Lady Redesdale was wonderful, she had brought them all along and taught them their sums and tables. Unity could read quite well when I arrived. Starting at nine o'clock every morning, they did two hours with Lady Redesdale. We kept to the proper school year, so that in the holidays I went home and somebody French, a mademoiselle, came to teach them the language. In term time we used to go into Oxford, for shopping at Elliston and Cavells, for books at Blackwells, to skate in the rink behind the Regal Cinema. We went to plays, and once the whole family heard Kreisler give a concert. We used to canvass locally. When Nancy came out, they rented a house in Gloucester Square for three months, and in that winter of 1923–4 we went to the Wembley Exhibition with Diana and Unity – that was the year of the discovery of Tutankhamen. There was a model of Buckingham Palace in butter. Bobo went on the Big Dipper and boasted of it, Jessica had not been allowed to come. Unity had a strawberry roan and I went riding with her in the valley of the Shadow of Death, as we called it, between Asthall and Burford. In the holidays sometimes I took them to Brayfield to stay with the Farrers. And much later, 1932, I think, she and I went to *Pineapple Poll*, with Bryan and Diana Guinness and Evelyn Waugh too, though the parents had warned us off seeing Diana. Lord Redesdale knew that the girls ought to have a better education. Some of the governesses had let them down badly. I found their English better than mine. I used to give them subjects to paint, often taken from the Bible. Unity chose "Abraham and his seed for ever" with masses of dots for the seed. She did drawings and paintings rather like Blake. Such imagination. Generally I used to show her drawing book to Lady Redesdale. Anything she wanted to do she could do well.'

The Margaret who had been uniquely co-opted into the Society of Hons had no surname that I was aware of, and it took time and luck before I could identify her as Margaret Durman, who had married a man in the Royal Air Force. In fact she was living once more close to the scenes of her childhood, and was kind enough to offer me a guided tour of them. High Wycombe has swollen from an eighteenth-century county town into a dormitory for London, with light industry of its own too. Still, on its edge, is an almost untouched enclave, The Rye, though new housing laps up to it. Daws Hill rises steeply behind, once part of the estate which has belonged for so long to the Carrington family, and whose thickly wooded crest conceals the present large base for the American military. Across The Rye runs a lane, with a little stream alongside, and at its first bend stands the old workhouse, converted into Box Tree Cottage, where Margaret Durman was born. Opposite, a hundred yards on, is Old Mill Cottage, bought by Lady Redesdale in the early twenties from Lord Lincolnshire, a great-uncle of Lord Carrington's. The L-shaped house blocks two sides of an open yard, off the road, the square completed by the mill which stands apart, and used to be let to Mr Mason, the miller. It is picturesque, without the stiff-upper-lip of Swinbrook. At the back, Dean Garden Wood is a thicket. Wisteria drapes over the fence as it always did; the rose climbing over the door which led from Lady Redesdale's sitting room into the garden is tall and strong. That room was mauve and pink, its furniture upholstered in chintz with cabbage-roses on it, and in one corner was a plaster bust of Unity. The library, with a bow window on to the yard, is more of an enlarged entrance hall. In the nursery upstairs was a grandfather-clock case, the works removed, for displaying special treasures. The children's bedrooms were in the elongated part of the house, giving over the yard, with Unity's room in the middle, doors on either side, so that it was something of a distended corridor through which the others used to pass. Below, in the angle of the house, another door on the yard opens into the old dining room (a kitchen now, for the place was sold after Lady Redesdale's death in 1958 and divided in two), and there is the Hons Cupboard.

Margaret Durman said, 'When I was about six or seven, they must have come here, Debo being my age, Unity about thirteen. Nanny Dicks, Blor that is, was with them. The cook and the gardener, the Stobies, came with the family, it was plain cooking Lady Redesdale liked, her favourite being chocolate mousse, and it was the same with Unity. The Redesdales had two parlourmaids. The cottage was so small that they couldn't sleep the maids and the Stobies, so my grandmother gave the Stobies a room, and that was how I first met the girls, they were slipping across furtively to ask me out for a walk, escaping from Nanny Dicks. I seemed a suitable child, I did as I was told, where perhaps others would not have done. The girls had governesses, they were tearaways – my mother was thoroughly glad when they moved away and I went to commercial school. Lady Redesdale let them follow their bent right from the start, it was up to them how they'd behave and who they'd marry, they were always talking about that. I first saw Lord Redesdale when he had come back from gold-mining in Canada. He came into the yard, we had been sitting round a log fire in the library. Debo was pleading with Muv to let me stay – I called her Muv too, but I was too terrified of him to say Farve in his hearing. Debo told me that he had not found any gold but she held up something with a glitter in it, quartz probably, and said, You're only a village girl, if you've never seen it, this is gold in coal.

'Debo, Decca and I played enormous games in the mill. We used to stand in the corn and sink in, and to get us out the miller would start the mill so the corn would be pulled down for grinding. We'd play in the hay-loft – to get up through the trapdoor we'd have to climb a ladder, and once there, swing on a rope from one bale to another. I have a bad head for heights and I never could get down that ladder. I'd always been a quiet child until they descended on me. This wasn't a game for me at all. We also loved to sit on the chicken-house roof, above Muv's White Leghorns and white bantams, to discuss Counter-Hon measures for when Unity would come, horrible schemes or annoyances to bait her, or Tom, and sometimes even Nancy. Unity would be back for holidays, from St Margaret's, I suppose, she had been playing lacrosse, I remember. I was warned by Muv, You mustn't tease Unity – and Nanny Dicks used to say so too – they'd be furious with us for teasing Unity. She used to tease back, mind you, but because I wasn't one of the family she didn't tease me so hard. Unity had enormous hands and feet, and a loud voice, she was likable, very sweet to me really. Debo had said I had to be with her in the Hons Society, and Unity would answer, She's not a Hon, she's a Counter-Hon so she must come with me. Another game was to see if we could cross Mill Yard and go round the whole garden and into the house without anyone spotting us. Debo and I were one team,

Decca and Unity another. The Honnish language was a way of communicating without Muv and Farve knowing what was up.

'Meetings of the Hons took place in the baker's oven in the dining room. Lady Redesdale had rush-seated chairs there, and we had to stand on one of them, to get a lift up into the opening of the Cupboard. The oven just held three, you had to squash in crouched up with hands round your knees. Decca was usually the first in, to crawl along the whole length of it. On one famous occasion we managed to get the maids to push back the chairs, the oven door was shut and the table laid, and there we were hidden. We were supposed to have tea in the nursery. I used to run home for meals otherwise. Will they miss us, we wondered, and soon they were shouting for us. I felt so uncomfortable when we emerged, it wasn't my house in which I could get away with something like this, I hardly dared go again. We used to hold meetings of the Hons two or three times a week in that oven to hatch up schemes. Unity was much too large to have climbed in that oven but she did get on to the chicken-house roof. We kept things from her. On Sundays we couldn't play at all, they went to church, the Rev. Float was the vicar, and I had to go to Sunday school.

'Debo and I reared white guinea pigs, rough-haired ones. Unity's goat was tethered in the orchard where the Shetland ponies were. Debo loved to ride and we did that at Swinbrook where I was invited several times. Hooper the groom was another faithful old retainer who came here, with Mrs Hooper. Lady Redesdale bought them a small house, you'd see him in his polished leather gaiters, with old knickerbockers, just like Lord Redesdale himself. Pam had Irish wolfhounds, grey and woolly, Unity loved them. They'd take them out for walks and when the rain came on, they'd come over to Box Tree Cottage for me. Walking was a great occupation, especially in the rain, up Wendover Way, to Bassetsbury Lane, into Wycombe. They'd arrive dripping wet in the shops, at Tracy's the grocer, or W. H. Smith's, the employees would be terrified of them, you'd see them cower. They'd buy Country Life, or something, just going in for fun, they'd put it down on Lady Redesdale's account and later when she found out there'd be a row.

'For four or five years we saw them every holidays – they were probably letting Swinbrook – except after Christmas when they were off to St Moritz. One Christmas they were in London and I was allowed to stay there for two or three nights. They would go to London at odd times but otherwise were here pretty permanently. When the Chelsea Arts Ball came round, they had a great time, Nancy, Diana, Pam and Unity, they wore headdresses, and were very slinky, and extraordinary things would happen which they'd report. Muv used to say, You're not to tell the children what you've been doing, Unity!'

3
HARD KNOCKS
WITH LAUGHTER

Boarding school has its seasonal dreariness of trunks and trains, but what to other girls might have been unnecessary and perhaps heart-aching departures, looked like liberation at Swinbrook. Readers of Nancy's novels and *Hons and Rebels* may conclude that the Redesdales would have saved themselves much expense of spirit had they resorted to the safety valve of sending their children away to be educated. Boarding schools break inherited superiorities, for the lesson is learnt there that no rights exist without obligations, and those who will not learn it are put through miseries. Miss Hussey had been replaced by a fourteenth and a fifteenth governess, and still the Redesdales hesitated. Nancy thought that they dreaded the vulgarizing effect boarding school might have, and her own enrolment at the Slade Art School was a revolutionary break. While the family had been in Paris, Diana had been allowed to attend the smart Cour Fénélon; Unity went for a disastrous term to Queen's Gate, a London day school near Rutland Gate, only to be expelled in short order; Jessica was sent, also as a day-girl, to St Bernard's Convent across The Rye. By the time the Redesdales were in a frame of mind to experiment with boarding school, Unity was fifteen.

St Margaret's, Bushey, S.M.B. to its pupils, was chosen because the Farrers were there, and so were Rosemary and Clementine Mitford. Bushey, more-over, was conveniently in reach. Mrs Rodzianko said that Unity had longed to go there 'to gain more ample room for wickedness, fresh fields to conquer'. An altogether exceptional school might have hauled Unity out of herself, but it was late in the day to start excavating for her intellectual curiosity. St Margaret's had high standards which were not open to manoeuvring. Above the main entrance is a plaque with the date of its inauguration at Bushey, 1895, and the late Gothick-revival building, by Waterhouse, is considerable enough to imbue that date, as if for ever, through the yellow stock bricks and wine-red stone facings, the *fin-de-siècle* religious aestheticism of the chapel, the lattice-work, tower and wings, in the very idiom of Batsford. The Victorian institutionalism was calculated, for St Margaret's had been intended as a school for the orphaned daughters of the clergy. Only in 1902 were fee-payers allowed in, their numbers rising until by Unity's time they accounted for half the places, fashionable girls mostly. With Dickensian steadfastness, distinctions between the fee-payers and the free orphans were perpetuated, the former, for instance, wearing thick blue cloaks, while the latter had thinner serge which could be seen through if held up to the light; a popular means test. All wore blue gym tunics, or skirts and jerseys, though more variety was permitted in summer.

The school, as Unity will have entered it, has been described by another old girl, Lady Violet Powell (née Pakenham) in her autobiography *Five out of Six*. Breakfast at eight o'clock, chapel twice a day, a walk round the garden on Sundays, the school motto on hymn-books, studies of Shakespeare and trips to the Old Vic, the local riding school, dances, recitation in the school hall – it is churchy, pi, humdrum maybe, but neither humourless nor unbearably restrictive, merely chafing.

The tone had been set long since by Miss Boys, headmistress since 1908. Emancipated herself along the lines of the new ladies' colleges at Oxford and Cambridge, she was determined that others should have the benefit of well-adjusted progress. The school was organized to express her enthusiasm for a tight curriculum, Christianity and the Girl Guides. The school Games Song compresses the flavour of bonhomie into lines like these: 'We all shall learn hereafter/To take hard knocks with laughter./However hard those knocks may be,/we'll play right fairly still/ and honour yet the school we love,/The school upon the hill.' Miss Boys' brother was a clergyman, high church, and Miss Boys liked to suggest that any girl about to be confirmed should write a confession, which she would read and then burn in the fire. Her vice-regal presence was hardly mitigated by her mongrel elk-hound, Stracks, which was constantly scratching itself. On Sunday evenings, supper consisted of dry bread and potted meat which was known as Potted Stracks. In this headmistress, tall and powerfully built, with an autocratic intelligence, and a gold medallion round her neck, Unity had met her match, for once.

The aura of Miss Boys is not so easily dissipated. Her St Margaret's survives in the fixtures and fittings, and intangibly too. To the left of the entrance hall is the room where Miss Scatchard now sits as headmistress, but with the sofa of Miss Boys. Once parlourmaid to Miss Boys, Catherine Occleshaw has been at the school since 25 February 1925, and she said, 'Unity and her Mitford cousins were harum-scarum. Lady Airlie came to present the prizes, that was a good day for Unity, being related. We were very Victorian at that stage. Unity rebelled against the school rules, that was in her nature, she was expelled for it. Once she came back on a visit, and she was displaying this swastika in her lapel, very pleased with the effect of her friendship with

Hitler. They asked her to take it off, with the old S.M.B. badge which she had no right to be wearing anyway. It was defiance. They get so full of their own importance.'

Miss Scatchard was able to dig out of the files a card. 'Mitford, Unity Valkyrie. E [for entry] September 1929. Form IVa. L [for left] December 1930. July 1930, Junior Cambridge.' No words had been wasted there by Miss Boys. It was possible to work out that Unity had been in Nicholson's, one of the four houses, and that her wearing of the swastika had been in 1938 at the Christmas sale, which is held every year in the first week of December. Upstairs the dormitories are unchanged since she was there, with beds for sixteen girls in each, and curtained cubicles for privacy. The assistant matron supervising the dormitory has a staff room of her own, partitioned off. The Oak Room, where Miss Boys had taught and had received parents, including Lord Redesdale for a sticky final interview, has elaborate bookcases and furniture hand-carved for it, and a portrait of Miss Metcalfe, otherwise Metty, who had taught at the school as long and faithfully as Miss Boys.

Mrs Rodzianko had already tried to recall the exact wording of Lord Redesdale's supposed Parthian shot to Miss Boys, after Unity's expulsion. She had put me in touch with a contemporary, Mrs Evie Barnett, who proved word-perfect. 'Madam, your shape suggests a measure of self-indulgence totally unsuited to the religious position you pretend to hold.' Could such a gentleman really have said such a thing to such a lady, or is this an undying dormitory giggle? Mrs Barnett had been lower down the school than Unity, but thought that a clique had formed around her, self-entitled The Frabjous Five, '... through the mists of time I think three of them were Cynthia Charrington, someone called Jean McPherson Grant and Pamela Dillon who became Lady Onslow'.

The Frabjous Five was not a phrase familiar to Cynthia Charrington, now Mrs Carnegie. Unity, she says, drew well at school, mostly nudes, to be shocking. One day, in a discussion of what they would like to do as grown-ups, Unity had asserted that she would like to be a power behind the throne. Mrs Carnegie's sister, Mrs Rollo Hoare, could corroborate. 'At school we were all guides, but she was deliberately not. When I went to Munich, and was at a pensionat of the university, I met Unity and Diana at the opera. Unity was covered with swastikas, I told her that I had never thought that was what she was going to be, and she reminded me that she had wanted to be a power behind the throne. She had not met Hitler then. Diana had a flat in Munich, Unity was there a lot.' The date was the autumn of 1934, as will be shown.

Unity is said to have resented the religiosity of the school violently enough to have brought about a collision. That she did refuse to be confirmed is true, but that she staked out her ground by establishing an Atheist Society seems to be an exaggeration, for nobody can confirm it, and in all likelihood here was another dare which became a Mitford fact. As for her expulsion, *Hons and Rebels* has the authorized legend. She had been sent away from school, it seems, 'simply for saying one word, when she had been called on to recite before the assembled school, board of trustees, and parents. The word was "rot", which she had added to the line, "A garden is a lovesome thing, God wot".' Her contemporaries, Frabjous Five or not, would have been bound to attend any such recital, but none of them recall this happening, nor anything like it. Quite the contrary, it turns out that for several years already the improved line had been a chic throw-away between the girls, serving either as a greeting in the passages, an all-purpose cliché, or even as a complaint against some request from a mistress. Nevertheless, Boxing Day 1930, when she heard that she had to leave St Margaret's, remained one of the blackest days of her life, and she was always to harp on it. It was her first experience of being confronted by a reality which would not go away at her command; the external world, hitherto so obedient, had suddenly rounded, and she was the one shown to be out of step in her disobedience, her own Nasty Lady. Such a conclusion called for a measure of introspection which she never acquired, then or later. Instead, the whole shock had to be embellished into an amusing story until its meaning was lost.

Lady Onslow said: 'Through the Stanleys, the Mitfords are our cousins. Clementine was going to St Margaret's, so I went. My mother didn't believe in education either, I'd been to nine schools, but at St Margaret's I settled down, it was so funny. I adored it. I don't remember meeting Bobo originally but we were together in Form Va, and struck up friendship. I was a year younger than her. She wasn't very bright. She was impervious to everyone else's feelings. I never saw her cry. Form Va had Miss Metcalfe, Metty. What you all want, dears, is what I call uncommon sense, she was always giving us that advice. Bobo was no good at spelling. Once in a scripture lesson we had the passage about he who calls his brother a fool is in danger of hell fire. Bobo put her hand up and asked, Supposing your brother is a fool? Put your hand down, Unity Mitford, was the answer. I fell about, and so got rebuked too. They always called you by your first and last names. Girls at St Margaret's don't run down the corridors, Unity Mitford – she knocked into everything, she had a complete disregard, and was a great one for trying to be funny. But she earned a bit of respect, somehow, she got away with so much. Each dormitory had that loose-box off it where a mistress slept, and Metty used to make an ice-cream of jam and skimmed milk for her favourite girls, putting it out to freeze on her window-sill out there. Metty rather liked Unity, who sometimes got ice-cream.

'Miss Fisher taught botany, and was teased by Bobo. There was Miss Pyrton, for French. Miss Pendleton was called The Bun from the way she did her hair, she taught music and had written the accompaniment to the Games Song, which was properly called the Games Tea Song. Bobo was very keen on The Bun, she had a pash on her, but one had the impression that she was pretending because it was half-shocking. I remember her saying: Don't you think I'm terribly in love? and how we used to go into huddles about it. Excuses to join the loved one would be found – There's The Bun walking round the asphalt [the path round the school grounds]. In chapel we often sang the Clough poem, *Say not the struggle naught availeth*. [This line has been inscribed on Unity's tombstone. Miss E. F. Birney succeeded Miss Boys, and at Unity's death was asked by Lady Redesdale for the whole text 'of which Unity had been particularly fond'. It seems a strange stamp that St Margaret's should have put upon her at the very last.] Will you rise for the hymn, Miss Boys would say, taking the service. The chaplain was Mr Summers, he was always yawning. It's not you who should be yawning, Bobo said, but us. She was very atheistic.

'Her talent was for drawing. She drew naked figures in her rough note-book, an Adam and an Eve, and you can guess what they were doing. That was not at all the thing, she was told to stop, and that if she persisted she would have to get a new rough notebook at her own expense. Which made no impression. The wilful flaunting of the rules became too much for the school in the end. Sadly I had an autograph book with a drawing by her in it, but it was stolen. She was a good artist.

'Once or twice I stayed at Swinbrook, I had one more term at St Margaret's after Unity left, and afterwards I used to go over to the cottage at High Wycombe from a kennels where I was learning about dogs. Bobo always said she'd been listening through the walls there – she could hear her parents talking in bed. In the holidays she used to come to lunch with us in Wilfred Street, next to her sister Diana's house in Buckingham Street. Nancy was writing *Highland Fling*, Bobo told me with great pride and excitement, and had made ninety pounds out of it. One incident was evidence of her disregard for other people's feelings. I had an aunt, Hilda Dillon, known to be an active teetotaller, and she was also a British Israelite who believed that the English were the lost tribes of Israel. Unity spent the whole lunch mocking her, everybody was very uncomfortable. We were both still at St Margaret's, so it must have been in the spring of 1930.

'She was really a suicide, she was so self-destructive. The greatest disgrace we could have was to be made to stand outside Miss Boys' door. Bobo would contrive to be sent to stand outside the door. You never knew if she was doing the big act or not. The Mitfords seemed not to get the point, on purpose. In Va, I never heard of the Frabjous Five, and I cannot connect her with any girl except me. That she chose me for a friend might reveal the element of sadism in her. The "God wot rot" story certainly isn't quite true, we all went wandering about with it on our lips. There was no question of publicity about it. What she got the sack for was a fine disregard for the rules of the school.

'After I had left St Margaret's, my mother put me to work in the offices of the British Union of Fascists, in Lower Grosvenor Crescent. Lady Makgill, who ran the women's section in the office, was also a cousin of mine, she had been Esther Bromley before she married Sir Donald Makgill. Donald and Esther used to take me out. I was the office telephonist, Hon Pamela Dillon, christened Hallo Girl, as some paper put it. For thirty shillings a week, I was arranging meetings, and I stewarded some of them, but I was there only for three months, I was completely a-political, and got out at that stage. During that time Bobo and Mary Ormsby-Gore came in one day. I was in my black shirt, and we went out to lunch. I was terrified of them both. That was how I met her again, and I used to go to tea at Rutland Gate, but then she was going on alarmingly about the Führer. You thought she had to be fooling when she was being sincere.'

4

'I TOO COULD BE ARTY'

Rites and humours among the Mitfords had hardened in Unity's adolescence. The stigma of being one of the little ones was off-loaded by behaving as if there were no natural order of things. Independence had been longed for at any price; expulsion from St Margaret's apparently headed it off. By then the realignment within the family was under way, that *renversement des alliances* whereby Unity became Diana's favourite sister, in place of Jessica, as explained in *Hons and Rebels*. That Diana and Unity would draw together was likely in any case, as the four-year gap between them grew less and less significant with age. The decisive decade of Unity's life was spent under the influence, the shadow, of this one sister whose attainments and glamour she did her best to square up to, if not to rival.

As Mrs Bryan Guinness, after her marriage in the summer of 1929, Diana, party-goer and hostess, was receiving before she was twenty-one the most unpredictable of press consecrations, that of Society Beauty, a celebrity on account of her looks and position. Her name was a ready-reckoner on any list. The disapproval of the Redesdales, presumably representing caution as against cutting a dash, was out-distanced, they were the Dull Old beached by the Bright Young Things. Treasure-hunts, those most exclusive of outings, expressed exactly what fun it was to create minor nuisances in public, by bagging other people's dogs or lamp-posts. 'Masked parties, Savage parties, Victorian parties, Greek parties, Wild West parties, Russian parties, Circus parties, parties where one had to dress as somebody else, almost naked parties in St John's Wood, parties in flats and studios and houses and ships and hotels and night clubs, in windmills and swimming baths, parties at school where one ate muffins and meringues and tinned crab, parties at Oxford where one drank brown sherry and smoked Turkish cigarettes, dull dances in London and comic dances in Scotland and disgusting dances in Paris.' And was not *Vile Bodies* dedicated 'with love to Bryan and Diana Guinness', and Evelyn Waugh himself to be met in 'Buck Street', the Guinness house in Buckingham Street? The Swinbrook sewers had come into their own, their suavity and witticisms and affectations were in daily currency. Harold Acton, John Sutro, Brian Howard, Cecil Beaton ('Unity was not really a member of the Biddesden gang,' he says, 'she would not talk to people, only to herself'),

Robert Byron, Mark Ogilvie-Grant, Christopher Sykes, James Lees-Milne, the Heskeths, each and every clever friend of Diana's, and Nancy's too, were expected to be the groundswell of Unity's life, and so they were as a matter of fact, even after she had gone off at a tangent on the Nazi fancy-dress party, which she interrupted to bring the latest news home to the Aesthetes. Talented, artistic, rich or skilled at getting by, they were tougher than they looked, and formidable to a near-debutante just sacked from school, in the hiatus of her seventeenth year.

Biddesden, near Andover, in Wiltshire, was the country house of the Guinnesses, within range of Swinbrook, if Lady Redesdale wished to drive over with the little ones. A women's page article in the *Daily Telegraph* of 20 January 1932 gushed about the place, 'There is something more than a little uncanny about the perfection of this Queen Anne house, built in 1711, with its garden and 300 acres ... Mrs Guinness during the last six months has taken enormous trouble to bring out the exquisite grace of the rooms by the use of clear pastel colours used in a simple youthful way ... curtains of Madonna-blue glazed linen are being quilted by the miners' wives in South Wales ... in the dining room the George III panelling has been painted very pale duck-egg green ...' A swimming pool was added, its copper-domed gazebo decorated with mosaics of Bacchus by Boris Anrep (who was to include Diana among other select portraits on the mosaic floor of the National Gallery). Tchelitchew and Henry Lamb painted Diana's portrait; Stanley Spencer was a frequent visitor; Dora Carrington did a *trompe l'oeil* on the wall of Biddesden of a maid peeping out of a dummy window. Carrington's infatuated love for Lytton Strachey had propelled her into his house at Ham Spray, near Biddesden, but no further into his affections, his homo-sexuality being no secret. Writing to Lytton Strachey in a letter dated 14 September 1930, Carrington pointed up her expectations of the Guinnesses as new friends and patrons. 'The Guinnesses so far haven't bought any portraits and Henry [Lamb] has embarked on a life-size enormous family group with a dog the size of a grey cow, which if he doesn't sell, I should think would cost a fortune in paint, and canvas. I thought one of Bryan very pretty. But surely if it wasn't of a lovely young man, not a very good picture? And I completely agree about Diana's portrait. It gave one no impression of that Moon Goddess effect. I failed I fear to confide anything and I could see by their expressions that as I left they were saying I was cold and reserved.'

Over the next few months, Carrington grew into a Biddesden intimate, and by 28 July 1931 she was writing to Lytton Strachey, 'I went with Julia [Strachey] to lunch with Diana today. There we found 3 sisters and Mama

Redesdale. The little sisters were ravishingly beautiful, and another of sixteen very marvellous and grecian [Unity's seventeenth birthday was ten days off]. I thought the mother was rather remarkable, very sensible and no upper-class graces ... The little sister was a great botanist and completely won me by her high spirits and charm.' This is certainly a make-weight to the sulkiness usually reported of Unity at the time. Carrington's letters and diaries reveal the disturbing reliance she put upon Biddesden as Lytton Strachey's cancer stole over his life and hers. To be abandoned to an existence without him was to despair. She was nearly killed at Biddesden on a bolting horse in February 1932, and a month later she borrowed one of their guns to shoot herself, victim of a passion so far beyond reason that it could never have had any proper outlet – a figuration exactly like Unity's where Hitler was concerned.

The Bright Young Things who were Unity's exemplars used humour as a strategy. The stainless spites they directed at others were their own protection. The cruelty of the Waugh/Mitford novels has often been caught, but the weak child's need to jeer before being jeered at is there too. Their heroes are victims, Bolters, getting away with it by the skin of their teeth, integral part of the outrages they resent but survive. Treasure-hunts and fancy-dress parties vanished overnight in the real hard shock of the Depression and instability, and of all that will-of-the-wisp group only those with the grit and the gifts for individual achievements were heard of again. Bright Young Things is a figment like 'perpetual revolution' today, but extreme fashionable outlooks stick people in their formative moments, as pins do butterflies, and here was enough to take the place of the education Unity never had, but not enough to contain her. She never quite realized that the party was over before she joined in.

John Betjeman said: 'It was Miss Pam I was keen on. She had a council house on the estate which Bryan let to her, she kept the cows and looked after the milk round. I knew the Mitfords through Bryan marrying Diana. I never went to Swinbrook, but often to Biddesden and to Buckingham Street. There was a wonderful maid at Biddesden called May Amende. Their architect was George Kennedy, brother of Margaret Kennedy who wrote The Constant Nymph, he was a great friend of Henry Lamb, The Doctor, because he was a qualified doctor. When I knew Unity she was just out of school. I always used to call her Unity Valkyrie, by both names. She was a joyful version of Miss Pam, she spoke like them all, she used all those phrases of theirs. Diana was the leader of the sisters, lovely if you like that kind of Brunnhilde looks. Nancy was the warmest.

'Bryan had just published a book of poems, he used to do conjuring tricks, and we sang rounds, the old favourites like, Here I go sure and slow, Sang the Turtle down below. There was a piano in the room where we dined, as I remember. We also sang evangelical hymns, Unity Valkyrie was very fond of them. Like the Moody and Sankey one,

> There were ninety nine that safely lay
> in the shelter of the fold,
> but one was out on the hills away,
> far off from the gates of gold.

May Amende was terribly shocked by the way we sang hymns. We sang them in the car too, going to look at old churches, a whole group of us, and attending evensong too if we could find it. Terribly high church. Unity Valkyrie was funny, she had a lot of humour which doesn't come out in the accounts of her. We very much enjoyed communal games, Grandmother's Footsteps. Once we went to Lytton Strachey at Ham Spray and played statues there, with Unity Valkyrie, I do believe. It was a sort of Oxford set, we used to see things as an endless party.

'Unity Valkyrie was very keen on film stars and cinema. For a while I was press critic of films for the *Evening Standard*, I had to see films in the mornings. The man who looked after Metro-Goldwyn-Mayer publicity was Mervyn McPherson, he gave little entertainments for the critics before the showing of MGM films, and I brought Unity Valkyrie along to one of them. I had no idea of her being political and all that.'

John Betjeman took me to tea with May Amende, not far away from the Highgate house where he himself grew up, and the school where the American master who had once taught him was T. S. Eliot. May Amende had witnessed every stage of one of the more inspired of Buckingham Street hoaxes, when Brian Howard in the role of a German expatriate painter, 'Bruno Hat', confectioned some paintings to be exhibited in a gallery. The artist himself, who then appeared in a wheelchair, was Tom Mitford, much disguised.

May Amende said, 'Unity was a lot at Biddesden. She sang hymns, yes, the Alexander hymns, the mission hymns at the back of the English hymnal, they have a roaring chorus. Randolph Churchill practically lived with us, he came to Biddesden for his honeymoon. After the move from Buckingham Street, Unity used to come more to Cheyne Walk, it had been Whistler's house. Its drawing room ran front to back. There was a house-warming party – Diana was dancing with Sir Oswald Mosley, that was the first time I'd seen him. Next day he telephoned, I answered of course, and he was in such a hurry that he said to me, Darling when can I see you again. Lady Cynthia Mosley came to the Biddesden fancy-dress party as a shepherdess. They had a party too to hear Gypsy Smith at the Spurgeon Tabernacle in Newington Butts. Gypsy was a great revivalist and went to the Albert Hall. Oh my, we're going to be saved, they said as they set off, Unity with them.'

Through working for the architect George Kennedy, Lady Pansy Pakenham had met Henry Lamb, whom she married in 1928. She went to Swinbrook, once, she says, from her home at North Aston, to see Nancy – with a friend – Evelyn Gardner, or She-Evelyn when she later became Evelyn Waugh's first wife – 'thus catching sight of the gloomy father'. Lady Pansy said: 'The Guinnesses had Knockmaroon, just outside the gates of Phoenix Park in Dublin, and through August 1930 they had a continuous house-party, including Nancy and Hamish Erskine, more or less enagaged then – he was flattered, he was four years younger than she, and she was waiting on him hand and foot. Henry did the portrait of Diana with the dog at Knockmaroon, he did studies for it and painted her head, and then did the composition in his studio. Bryan said he'd like a separate picture of her. We lived at Coombe Bissett, and used to come over to Biddesden. Betjeman visited us from Biddesden – one of his fantasies was about Henry as a doctor in the First War, and he wrote a poem, which has since been lost:

> I too could be arty, I too could get on
> with the Guinnesses, Gertler, Sickert and John.

'The party at Biddesden must have been just before Unity's coming-out dance, which Henry went to. It was a fête champêtre. Mosley was there, and Diana was telling everyone how thrilling she found him, like having a crush on a film star. Henry was very austere and hated everything flashy. Mosley was throwing his weight about, Henry observed him, and Diana must have caught the expression on his face, for she said, You're thinking what a frightful bounder he is. Later in the year, Lady Castlerosse was at Biddesden, she was separated from her husband, she became a great friend of Diana's – she was getting into a different world. In the autumn Henry painted the second picture of Diana, sitting on a sofa, at the height of her beauty. Tom Mosley [he is Tom to his friends, Kit to Diana] had been hanging about when the picture was being painted. Henry went round shortly before Christmas, finding them tying up parcels and sobbing. The fascist boys were all devoted to Lady Cynthia. Henry became very stuffy about it all. Diana's attitude was love-me-love-my-dog. Bobo was shy, farouche, like a caricature of Diana, the features exaggerated by a bigger face, more chin.

'My sisters Violet [Powell] and Julia [the late Lady Julia Mount] were more her contemporaries at St Margaret's, and they and their governesses used to meet up at swimming baths. Julia and Bobo, I think, were quite fond of each other, they went together to an old girls' day at St Margaret's [the Christmas sale of 1938, as we saw]. In the train Bobo announced, I want to have a lot of sons for cannon-fodder. Outraged, Julia had replied, I expect you'll only have one and die in childbirth. The Mitfords cry if you say something tough, and Bobo began to cry now, saying, I don't think I shall, I've got very wide hips. Julia had the last word, That doesn't count, the outside measurements don't count.'

As a debutante Unity would be expected to participate in more of those polite rituals for which she had hitherto shown derision. Try as they might, even more enlightened mothers could not hide the dutiful aspects of bringing out a daughter. To be presented at Court, to have one's name on a list and duly to accept invitations to balls, was to admit to a station in life. Obligations were imposed, simple ones perhaps, of looking as pretty as possible, making conversation and greeting the host and hostess, but the submission was plain: the young men in white ties were potential husbands, the young girls were being set fair to become the kind of ladies their mothers were. Competition among the girls had its spur, in that some of the young men were indeed catches, owners or heirs of houses and fortunes. The press, however, was greatly responsible for the sweep-stake, tuft-hunting element of the London season. Between the wars, the space devoted to society news was out of all proportion to the events. Gossip columnists complicitly vied to appoint one or two Debutantes of the Year. Girls who were plain or dowdy, who for some reason failed to be noticed, had a thin time of it, and anyone of sensibility could be forgiven for disliking this particular showroom. Evasive action was always possible, either by sticking to cronies, or by becoming a licensed eccentric, 'doing one's thing' in the language of a later generation. Enid the grass-snake, or Ratular, could be brought in a handbag to dances and released to maximum effect; notepaper could be stolen from Buckingham Palace to write thank-you letters on. This was to repeat the good old carry-on of being naughty when there were no appropriate sanctions; to indulge pranks without nanny noticing; to be sent to stand outside the headmistress's door without threat of expulsion. Unity would not be invited again – very well, that just fitted the bill. She was not the first to realize that a debutante, above anyone else, was encouraged to have her cake and eat it. More insidiously, she wished to be seen brushing aside the attention she had attracted.

Elizabeth Powell (now Lady Glenconnor): 'I also came out in January 1932. I made friends with Unity at Queen Charlotte's Ball. We were both nearly six feet tall, bringing up the back of that procession with the cake, rebellious girls in white, it was ghastly. That was a great bond, we were both what was called at the time "very bolshie". I saw her quite a lot, I went to stay at Swinbrook that winter, the other guests were Mary Ormsby-Gore, Robin Campbell and Claud Phillimore. I was impressed by the way the Mitfords talked about their parents. Bobo seemed very sophisticated and free. One could float over everything in this frivolous way. In 1933 Unity used to stay in our house in Hyde Park Gate, she would change into her black shirt and was always rushing off to the East End to play ping-pong with the boys. It wasn't allowed by her parents, they tried to stop her, that's why she came to us, she was quite different from everyone else, more in her extraordinary behaviour than her character.'

In the middle of January, a suitably advanced date in the season, the Redesdales launched her with a dance at Swinbrook, and then they moved to London, the house they took in Tite Street possibly being Mrs Hammersley's. That February, the Sunday Graphic had a paragraph, 'A young writer who will shortly be back in London is Miss Nancy Mitford who in a week or two's time will have completed her new novel. She tells me that she finds it easier to write in the country, and probably more amusing, since her mother, Lady Redesdale, gave a ball last week for her youngest sister, who rejoices in the name of Unity Valkyrie. Lady Redesdale does not share her daughter's talents for writing, but she is an excellent baker. She claims that in the past she herself has made all the bread required by her family and that twenty minutes twice a week sufficed for the task.'

Such publicity created its own momentum. On 10 March, the Daily Express had a large photograph of Unity, to explain among other things that 'she will find it difficult to retain her obvious clear-eyed freshness throughout the season, which year by year seems to become for debutantes more of an endurance test than a period of social delights'. The William Hickey column which contained this glum reprimand was in fact written by Tom Driberg – his colleague on the Evening Standard's Londoner's Diary backed him up that very same day by printing another photograph of Unity. At the end of March, the Daily Mail picked this up in exactly the return-of-service style practised by the competing gossipmongers in Vile Bodies: 'Miss Unity Mitford who is one of this year's debutantes has the unusual second name of Valkyrie. She possesses the most lovely natural colouring and is very attractive. Doubtless her elder sister Nancy will be able to advise her throughout the season if necessary . . .'

'I thought that the prettiest girl at Epsom was Hon Unity Mitford.' Daily Express, 2 June. More attention in Ascot Week. The Tatler of 6 July reported on the Royal Air Force Display at Hendon, and printed a large photograph of

Lady Redesdale, scanning the skies as though in some apprehension, flanked, says the caption, by 'The Hon Pamela Mitford and Miss Joan Villiers', which can only have been a leg-pull for the two are in fact Unity and Joan Farrer, or Rudbin. (The following week the *Tatler* had a full-page portrait of Hitler as man-about-town, with the curious information that he had refused to look the camera in the eye.)

That night, 6 July, Unity went to Mrs Somerset Maugham's party, in her house in the King's Road. Syrie Maugham, in the words of the gossip-writer, 'as usual had done the whole place with white flowers. Her guests included Noel Coward and Gladys Cooper, Osbert and Sacheverell Sitwell, and Sir Oswald and Lady Cynthia Mosley' – though if Unity had a glimpse of her future brother-in-law and Leader, she did not speak to him.

A few hundred people at most circle on this merry-go-round, their acquaintance is as superficial as it is regular, and no changes are to be rung there. These dances are interred in dead gaiety, except for the one given on 29 June by the Rothschilds. Unity had become a friend of Nika Rothschild, for whom this ball was given. 'I have rarely seen such a dazzling display,' Eve in the *Tatler* was unable to refrain from finger-pointing prose, 'and our hostess Lady Rothschild was wearing what must be the largest pearl necklace in the world.' The scene apparently evoked pre-war functions in Vienna or Berlin or one of the other European capitals. To the vapours of *Jew Süss* Unity had been able to add next to no experience of Jews. The Oxfordshire country-side contained no Jewish neighbours, or if it did, none of them had impinged upon Swinbrook; obviously Jewish girls did not attend a school for clergy orphans like St Margaret's. In the Biddesden set, John Sutro was Jewish, though *sui generis* in his comic gifts, Brian Howard might have been trapped by the Nuremberg Laws, while a figure like Mark Gertler, though spoken about, was too peripheral for her to have met. Two years later, Unity would not have permitted herself to set foot in a Jewish house for a ball, unless to disrupt it. Two years later, Unity's attacks on Jews would be a central, missionary feature of her existence, but what she personally knew about them, first-hand, was characterized by nothing more than one or two Jewish wits or dandies, and Lady Rothschild's ball.

Diana's ball for Unity and Joan Farrer (Rudbin) was on 7 July. 'This popular hostess of 22 years of age,' so the *Evening Standard* previewed the occasion, 'only moved last April into a house which enables her to entertain on a large scale ... The 300 guests will dance in a white ballroom, and supper will be served at refectory tables in the two sparsely furnished dining rooms, with their austere white walls and picturesque arches. The note of austerity is continued throughout the house. The old walls and ceilings – they were built in 1760 – are perfectly plain, in the palest tones of blue, pink and gold. Mrs Guinness is also planning to make good use of her old-world garden for the dance. No dinner parties are being arranged, and guests will come straight on from their own homes to Cheyne Walk. In attendance there will be maids wearing the charming green and white floral dresses that the hostess has chosen in place of uniform.'

Osbert Lancaster was there: 'I dined with Jim Lees-Milne, we all went on. It was the time of the Mrs Barney case, she was the daughter of the government broker, Sir John Mullens – she'd been accused of shooting a young man but was then acquitted. It was also the slump, and there was a nasty feeling about the upper classes. The crowd outside the dance was not in a pleasant mood, their remarks were all about Mrs Barney. Also as I was going up the stairs two footmen pushed everybody away and two more came carrying Augustus John downstairs. He'd already passed out.'

One of the names cropping up most often as a new friend made in the season was Mary Ormsby-Gore's. She is also in the position of being able to compare Unity before and after the conversion to Nazism, because Robin Campbell, whom she married in 1935, was posted as a member of the Reuter's bureau to Berlin (but that has its chronological place). Mary Ormsby-Gore is now married to Sir Lees Mayall, of the Foreign Office. She was one of the few friends whom Unity treated as an equal; she usually called her 'Gore'. Mary has Unity's copy of The Arabian Nights. In her album are photographs taken at Wootton in Bedfordshire, where the Ormsby-Gores lived, of Unity, in the spring of 1934, rather preciously posing with an arum lily or standing with Mervyn Phipps, son of the then British ambassador in Berlin. Mary's father, William Ormsby-Gore, later Lord Harlech, was secretary of state for colonies until 1938; he was also a Zionist sympathizer and had long been in touch with Weizmann. He had a loathing for anti-semitism, and at the League of Nations condemned it in Germany, which was rare for a Conservative politician, and did not appeal to Chamberlain. David Ormsby-Gore, the present Lord Harlech, who has been ambassador in Washington, is younger than his sister Mary but remembers how Unity's swastikas in the visitors' book at Wootton infuriated his father. 'When Bobo turned up with her Nazi sympathies, he shut himself in his study. He was too tactful to let himself be quarrelled with, but he hated her opinions, and we knew it. Bobo saw herself in a very dramatic role, talking about how she was training her bladder to last for twelve hours at a stretch without going to the loo, because she might have to go on a long journey. There might be a great holocaust and she would find herself on the road. She seemed marginally mad, at least so exaggerated that rational conversation was impossible.'

Mary Ormsby-Gore: 'I met her at a ball in 1932 when I came out too, and we became great friends immediately. We neither of us enjoyed the season. I got engaged and married Robin. She wasn't an English rose, she didn't dance a great deal. The men she danced regularly with were David Rhys, Lord Archie Gordon, Ronnie Greville [now Lord]. She did have a fellow called Norman, an American, a dress designer. He asked, Will you trip down the red carpet with me? which amused her. He had a flat off Gloucester Place and wore an opera cloak with red lining. Wally Cruishan, who appeared in revue, was his friend, and they seemed dashing to us. Unity hated Robin, and said he had Chinese eyes. She said, 'You can see Robin's got Chinese blood. The Mitfords are pure bred Aryans. What about me, I asked her after that, to be told, You've got filthy blood. By then she had taken to race politics.

'Al, the skating instructor, had been embarrassed by her falling into his arms, for the sake of being picked up. "I adore Al with true devotion" she sang to an old tango tune. She was fun, she used to giggle and giggle, but in photos she looks severe because Diana had said that smiling wrinkled the skin, so she put on her photography face.

'I went to her coming-out party, which was very glamorous. She had a beautiful frock made for it, grey lace with white ruffles, by Norman Hartnell, on account of its colours known by her as "milk-and-water". She was very proud of it. She was strange. In an antique shop that year she bought a big mask and called it "my Pygmalion". Ratular used to be put in my bath at Swinbrook, although usually she wore it on her body. That was shock exhibitionism. And what do you think of our Female? Bobo asked me about Muv when I first went there. She always wore her hair differently, like Diana, a fringe being the favourite way. Her legs used to worry her, and her front teeth were bad. With two grey stoppings.

'She began to go to the East End, and I went to one meeting with her. Pamela Dillon came too. You're so cowardly, Bobo used to say to me, when she and Pamela had to decide on which beat to sell Blackshirt. I went to their office before they started off. I was forbidden to go to The Eatonry, 2 Eaton Square, or Diana's bolt-hole. Jonathan and Desmond, her two sons, were there, Jonathan was dressed as a girl and Bobo said, When I get married you're going to be my bridesmaid. She adored children and marrying.

'One day she took me to Selfridges saying, Let's make a record, and she spoke into it, The Yids, The Yids, We've gotta get rid of the Yids, and there's my voice protesting in the background. She had a Boudledidge pronunciation of "The Leader". I'd have seen her on her visits to England in 1935 and 1936, I went to Rutland Gate and she came to us, but no longer on such bosom terms.' (The ending of Graham Greene's Brighton Rock exploits the novelty of recording one's own voice. Unity's words were a standard chant of the Blackshirts as they marched through the East End.)

A fête champêtre the fancy-dress party at Biddesden may have been, but more than that, it was a turning point. For the guests could not fail to draw conclusions, as Henry Lamb had, from the presence of Sir Oswald Mosley and the attention he paid to Diana: the two were affiché, visibly so, to the gaze of the entire Biddesden set. It is enough to quote an item from the newspapers of 16 June 1933, reporting what had gone through the courts the previous day: 'In an undefended suit Mrs Diana Guinness of Eaton Square prayed for the dissolution of her marriage with Mr Bryan Walter Guinness on the grounds of his adultery with Isolde Field at an hotel at Brighton in March last.' The hotel in Brighton, of course, was one of those well-appointed inconveniences which arise when the law is an ass. Singing out of Tune, Bryan Guinness's first novel, published in May 1933, has a hero Arthur, who marries Agnes, a girl with more beauty than brains or experience. Agnes likes parties and flirting and such up-to-date japes as a port-hole in her front door, which of course the press glorify. Subdued as it is, the novel has observations about the drift apart of a couple incompatibly married, as Agnes 'seemed to be converted to some worldly heresy of lovelessness, heretical enough in itself, but which by the evacuation of her heart, would leave her dangerously exposed to more damnable heresies still.' On impulse, in pursuit of night-club fancies, Agnes runs away with another man. Arthur agrees to be the guilty party, Miss Simkins, a hotel chambermaid is produced, and the decree nisi follows – the donnée is not far to seek.

In the metaphor of the day, Diana had forsaken the Aesthetes: attached to Mosley she was to join forces with their enemies. It was a notable defection, a farewell to the twenties, a first line-up to a flag. Mosley at this stage was emerging from the collapse of his New Party, the chrysalis out of which the British Union of Fascists hatched. He had already zig-zagged from the Conservative party into, and out of, the Labour party. In the general election of 27 October 1931, the New Party had fared even more humiliatingly than the communists, Mosley himself not being returned for Stoke-on-Trent, Lady Cynthia's former constituency. In January 1932 Mosley had arranged to have an audience in Rome with Mussolini, which hardened his resolve to emulate the European fascists. Harold Nicolson, the go-between of this meeting in Rome, but then at the end of his New Party tether and about to break with Mosley, wrote in his diary for 18 January 1932 that Mosley 'does not want to do anything at present. What he would like would be to lie low till the autumn, write a book, then rope in Winston Churchill, Lloyd George, Rothermere and if possible Beaverbrook, into a League of Youth. Then launch an autumn campaign.' The autumn campaign was not as Mosley had hoped, but by the end of October his supporters were wearing the uniform of the black shirt, their first indoor meetings and parades had been held in London, not without disturbances of the peace, and English fascism was a political fact. Instead of Churchill and the others in the League of Youth, Diana was roped in, and then Unity.

5
THE BIG PUSH

Arthur, the fall-guy of *Singing out of Tune*, had been given a rendezvous to lunch with his Agnes 'at the Art School of the London County Council in Vincent Square which she frequented. He arrived in some trepidation at the great brick building.' In fact Unity had enrolled there early in 1933, and stayed until Easter, long enough for the label of art student to be tied round her neck, even years later when she was away in Munich. At the time, the Redesdales had taken another house, 2 Grosvenor Crescent, conveniently near enough to Vincent Square for Unity to walk to her classes. Otherwise she was at a loose end, alternately listless, or in a suppressed thrill about the Eatonry break-through into the high affairs of the country. Lady Redesdale spotted the obvious; she lectured more than usual about not lying round the house wasting time. Not that Unity was prepared for concessions, she worked neither hard nor regularly at her drawing. For two days a week she attended classes, and also went once or twice in the evenings when she was supposed to be making model theatres, although she did not progress far enough to start one. A convincing reason for choosing this art school as a pastime was that Mary Ormsby-Gore was a student there. Also Bryan Guinness had been to Switzerland after Christmas with Ruby Lindsay and her daughter Rosemary Peto, who was at the art school too. A friend whom Mary and Rosemary Peto had in common was Antonia Meade, nicknamed Coney, and then taking lessons as a cellist from Caspar Casado. Coney used to drop into Vincent Square (she was shortly to marry Sir Ralph Jarvis, and she died only a few years ago). For a while Unity appeared to be finding a niche for herself among contemporaries who were not exactly bohemian, but independent and congenial.

Rosemary Peto: 'It was Sickert's old school. Walter Bayes was principal, Gertler, Bernard Meninsky, Adrian Allinson were among the teachers. Next door was a school for cooking and waiters, so we could profit by having five or six friends to lunch for a subsidized meal costing one and threepence, cooked and served by trainees. Mark Ogilvie-Grant was at the school then. I'd been at school with Mary and through her I met Bobo. One rather tiresome teacher attacked Mary by calling her father First Commissioner of Shirks [he was then at the Office of Works]. We didn't do a proper course.

They all dazzled me. We'd lunch and go to the movies – one of them had a pistol and would shoot at the villain with it, just bang-bang as in Westerns. At deb balls Bobo amused herself with a yo-yo, she was expert at it, and played it with the hand which was supposed to be at the back of the young man. At art school Bobo once said to me that Diana had lent her the Eatonry, and they were going to have an orgy there, but I was scared stiff. I heard about it afterwards. Everybody had been sick, and there had been a lot of necking. Bobo was fun in the way she impressed and shocked but as an acquaintance I didn't like her much.

'Before I came out, I used to meet her again quite often at Sir Ian and Lady Hamilton's. They had a house in Hyde Park Gardens and gave enormous luncheon parties for twenty or thirty people, mixing politicians, publishers, painters, distinguished elderly men and some young. The young men when I had my row there with Bobo were Jim Lees-Milne and Lajos Lederer. We'd finished lunch and were coming down from the place where we'd had coffee. Bobo was wearing a swastika in her button-hole. The Nazis had just done something particularly horrible, and I said, It's shocking that you are wearing that. She answered, If you had any sense you'd be wearing it too. Once she boasted that it was such fun to have supper with Streicher, as he'd have the Jews in after the meal, they'd be brought up from the cellar and be made to eat grass to entertain the guests. She was like a blank wall, with this thick obtuse quality.' *The Diaries of Sir Robert Bruce-Lockhart* has this entry for 17 July 1936, 'Lunched at the Ian Hamiltons and sat between Lady Muir (Mademoiselle Stancioff – she was the wife of Sir Kay Muir Bt, and a daughter of a former Bulgarian Minister in London) and Unity Mitford. Latter is madly pro-Nazi and will not speak to her sister Nancy because she is anti-Nazi.' Far from abhorring Unity's swastika, the Hamiltons were to become leading enthusiasts for making a deal with Hitler, who received them personally to show his appreciation that an English general of the First World War championed him as a lover of peace. Bruce-Lockhart worked for the *Evening Standard* and items about Unity which appeared regularly in its Londoner's Diary during the thirties were written or prompted by him: as good an example as any of how detestation of a cause like Nazism will prevent a man from noticing that he is actually airing it, and in this case, spicing it too. Two years later, incidentally, on 30 June 1938, Harold Nicolson, whose ear was as close to the ground as Bruce-Lockhart's, had an entry in his diary indicating how comment on Unity's behaviour did the rounds: 'Dine with Rob Bernays and Miss Mitford, Unity's cousin. She says that Unity does not hope to marry Hitler. It is merely adoration. Hitler likes her because of her fanaticism. She wants the Jews to be made to eat grass. Miss Mitford herself is not in favour of the Jews eating grass.'

From the art school that February, Unity and Mary went together for an outing to Cambridge, to see Claud Phillimore, then in his last year as an undergraduate (today the distinguished architect). He and Lord Duncannon, now Lord Bessborough, shared an elegant Georgian house in Jesus Lane called Little Trinity, where they gave the two girls lunch. Afterwards several of their friends dropped in and stayed on to tea, including David Lloyd (now Lord Lloyd, whose wife is an Ogilvie cousin of Unity's), Victor Rothschild (Lord Rothschild, the brother of Nika) and Gerald Cuthbert. The star of the afternoon, though, was the actress Phyllis Neilson-Terry, hugely tall as even Unity could think, and still handsome in spite of her age. She had been invited by Lord Bessborough, already then a man of the theatre. Sitting apart from the others, Unity and Victor Rothschild had a long conversation about Diana and Bryan Guinness and their divorce, the repercussions of which were highly gossip-worthy at the time, and then they moved on to incest, a beloved Mitford topic (Tom, as the only brother of six sisters, had more than his share of this joke). Mary Ormsby-Gore joined in loudly enough to be overheard by Phyllis Neilson-Terry, who appeared shocked by the low tone of the general discussion on incest which had been sparked off – which, no doubt, was mainly for her benefit.

Friends in an undergraduate circle are assumed to be, to have been, or to be about to be, in love with one another, in a fast but light minuet of affections, and here was no exception. Unity had just been introduced to Gerald Cuthbert (killed in the war), a conspicuously good-looking man, intelligent, musical, and until her departure for the grand passions of Nazi Germany, she was to have a faible for him. She also took away from Cambridge a copy of William Beckford's Diary in Italy and Portugal given to her by Claud Phillimore, a volume which went with the Nonesuch edition of Vathek that had been his Christmas present to her.

Claud Phillimore: 'Muv and Farve were friends of my mother's family. When my mother used to tell Muv her best stories, she could not help noticing how Muv would simply observe, I know. I came into the family chiefly through Pam, with whom I went to Salzburg with a group of friends in 1930, when I had just gone up to Cambridge. From that summer I got gradually to see them all, though Diana and Nancy least. I used to go to Biddesden, and was at the famous fancy-dress party in June 1932. David Long (Lord Long, killed in the war) was dressed as an eighteenth-century blacksmith, and Cecil Beaton was commenting from the side-lines. A lot of people had costumes designed by Oliver Messel for the C. B. Cochrane production of Offenbach's La Belle Hélène [which helps to explain Unity's six water-colours, already described]. Diana was in white, Mosley in black, suitably. A huge bonfire was lit in front of the house and we danced in the long down-stairs drawing room. Bryan's mood of melancholy permeated the thing. I was staying at Swinbrook, and had driven over all dressed up, with about six or eight people including Brenda Pearson [sister of Lord Cowdray]. I stayed there many times, invited either by Pam or Unity or Muv, though less after Unity went to Germany. Heavens knows what we did. Skating at the Oxford rink. Farve was expert at that. He was no great communicator, wrapped up in his preoccupations. We spent an enormous amount of time at the piano with Muv playing hymns or songs like "After the ball was over".

'I was never in love with Unity, though I enjoyed her company and was fond of her, anxious about her. It always seemed to me that she was deter-mined to do something against convention. She had quite a strong masculine streak in her. She would go off to BUF meetings in Oxford, donning her black shirt which couldn't be taken seriously. She enjoyed doing it to pro-voke, because it was revolutionary. She was immensely influenced by Diana, and I suppose not well balanced. She also went to the East End, and one felt it was a pity to be mixed up with that. She wore the fascist emblem to flaunt her outrages, to bait her parents. After the Hesketh dance that year, Muv was rather disapproving of us. And Unity was becoming disapproving of Nika Rothschild, she was actively developing anti-Jewish feeling. She swallowed a lot of it whole from the Oxford fascists. She hadn't an inquiring mind. The Mitfords were thwarted but not in the way they thought they were.'

The Heskeths were only slightly less numerous than the Mitfords, and paired off in age accordingly. Their mother had more or less standing pre-texts for a dance in her house in Wyndham Place, but none of the Heskeths can exactly date this particular occasion (which may have marked the coming-out of Joan Fleetwood-Hesketh, youngest but one of the sisters), but it was before the Redesdales left 2 Grosvenor Crescent, probably in the first fort-night of March. Beforehand Mary Ormsby-Gore invited Unity to dine, with Claud Phillimore, and Norman who hoped to trip down the red carpet, the two men not having met previously, and not caring for each other when they did. Mary left the dance early but Unity stayed to the end, at a table in the supper room with Claud Phillimore and Norman, to be joined there by Gerald Cuthbert and his sister Vida. Norman became drunker and drunker on champagne, holding forth in his broad American about nothing at all. Finally he started trying to kiss Unity in front of everybody, so Claud Phillimore had to rescue her by asking her to dance. Then he and Nika

Rothschild, Gerald and Vida Cuthbert, all wanted to sit up talking in someone's house, so Unity suggested Grosvenor Crescent, as it was large and they would not be overheard, but when they arrived there, at four in the morning, Lady Redesdale met them in the hall. She had been at the dance earlier, had returned and stayed up reading in front of the fire. Everybody was embarrassed, but unexpectedly Lady Redesdale left them to talk the dawn in. As a consequence, Norman was cut out, he and his *outré* manners had become boring; he was also trying to persuade Unity to order a dress from him, which she had no intention of doing. In fact he returned to America.

During these weeks at Grosvenor Crescent Unity met Mosley. A taboo had to be broken, for he was *persona non grata* with the Redesdales, who were reviling him as 'that man'. Upset by the divorce and frightened that their other daughters might suffer the social consequences and be ostracized for one reason or another, the Redesdales had warned Unity off Diana, which must have served to increase her disposition to admire Mosley. But at another party of the Maughams, at Christmas, Unity had been introduced to Mosley, speaking to him, which she had not had the opportunity of doing at the Maughams' six months earlier. For the future, Somerset Maugham maintained a novelist's interest in Unity. His secretary, Alan Searle, has told me how he used to accompany Maugham every year to Munich for the carnival and the opera. They stayed at the Vierjahreszeiten Hotel and in 1936, he believes, Unity was invited to dine with them there. She spoke only of her family. Perhaps she was aware that Maugham's books had been burnt in 1933 and he was on the black list maintained by Goebbels' ministry.

Unity was not altogether precise in her re-telling of what was to her a larger-than-life encounter, but it seems to have been one fine morning, on a day when she was on her way home to lunch from the Vincent Square art school. She dropped in on Diana at the Eatonry, and the two of them stood in the sunshine on the balcony outside the drawing room, waiting for Mosley, who at last arrived. Unity had been excited, having an impression of a great and important man, charming as well, whom she found it easy to get on with, when she had expected him to be frightening, in the Redesdale image of a rather wicked, cruel-looking monster. What she noticed instead was someone with black hair, black eyes and moustache and clothes, but a very white face, altogether a black-and-white contrast, as stark as at the Biddesden fancy-dress party. ('Where Mosley is so like Hitler,' a thoughtful profile in the *Observer* had just noted, 21 January 1933, 'is in his sense of the dramatic. There is an extraordinary atmosphere of drama about a Mosley meeting, a sense that great things are about to happen.')

.   .   .   .   .

For Easter, Diana and Nancy went on a journey to Belgium with Roger and Peter Hesketh, Nigel Birch (Lord Rhyl now) and Lord Hinchingbroke (who married Rosemary Peto, and eventually relinquished his title to revert to his name of Victor Montagu), the last two being friends of Tom, representative of the 'Fat Fairs' whom Nancy liked to treat as if they were already characters in her fiction. The rest of the family, Unity included, left Grosvenor Crescent for good, to be at Swinbrook for the Easter holidays. Art-student days simultaneously stopped, but as though to make amends for her scrappiness, or for neglect of any talent she might have, Unity started the picture, more properly the collage, of 'Hannibal crossing the Alps'. The inventiveness was not hers, she was actually copying a model. Some time earlier, when the family had been at High Wycombe, Lord Redesdale had ordered a writing table from one of the town's furniture factories, and he took Unity with him on the day when he went to see about this. She had noticed hanging in a dusty corner a picture of Hannibal crossing the Alps, and she admired it enough to ask one of the workmen about it. He answered that Mr Skull, the proprietor of the furniture factory, had bought it for its Chippendale frame, and would probably throw the picture out. Unity made her father ask its cost, whereupon Mr Skull presented it to Lord Redesdale, and he in turn had it framed for Unity. Tom also admired it, and he now commissioned Unity to do one like it for him, for which he would pay £2. She bought a piece of cardboard, three feet by two, a little larger than the original, and hoped to complete the work in a fortnight. The original was in fact naif, not to say primitive, and as she found she was improving upon it, she became absorbed. The mountains in the background had been built out with paper, and the figures in the army were paper cut-outs, painted and glued on, small in the distance but growing bigger as they descended from the heights, until they were two and a half inches high in the foreground, with Hannibal himself to the front, on his horse. For her mountains Unity chose plasticine which gave a stronger relief. She painted the upper slopes white and sprinkled them with sham snow; shading the lower slopes grey, and then green at the tree-line. Over the details of the soldiers she took a great deal of trouble, amplifying the impressionistic columns of the original by painting or cutting out miniature silhouettes, and using coloured tinsel for armour and banners and spearheads. As her procession wound downwards, she orientalized it with elephants bearing castles on their back, and camels and chariots and cavalry – developing her inspiration, obsession rather, as a psychoanalyst might think, with pictorial images of a mass, as revealed already in her 'Abraham and his seed for ever'.

At the beginning of the year, Tom had moved into a flat of his own in

Swan Court in Chelsea (in which building Bryan Guinness was also to live after his divorce). The sitting room, done up by Diana, had white wallpaper with gold spots, and a place left for 'Hannibal' to be hung, as it was by the end of 1933, eight months after being commissioned. When Tom was sent abroad in the war, his possessions were put into storage, only to be destroyed by bombing, this picture too. This particular theme was so successful, though, that Unity repeated it at least four times, one of the *collages* being done as a labour of love for Hitler, though what he thought of this triumphal procession of a dictator from another age, and what he did with it, are equally unknown.

The season had again to be faced. A girl not yet quite nineteen, like Unity, was expected to follow up the initiation and serve a second year on the debutante circuit, unless provided with the excuse of an early engagement and marriage. Lady Redesdale might have suspected that Unity's acquiescence was too good to be true, and the 'milk-and-water' routine screened ulterior purposes. As a mother, she seems serenely to have accepted everything at face value; repressions may have come too easily to her. It is extraordinary that Unity was on the point of kicking over the traces once and for all, but nothing was done about it. Rutland Gate was again let for the summer to the Warren Pearls, who were bringing out their daughter Audrey (now Mrs Lawson-Johnston). Returning to London at the beginning of May, the Redesdales were able to settle into the mews cottage at the back of Rutland Gate, once its stables, and known by the family as The Garage. Tom had been occupying it for a *garçonnière* before moving into Swan Court. The Garage was far from comfortable, but at least it did not have to be rented and they were looked after there by Bob Lambert, who, like Hooper, was one of the servants keeping the family up to the mark, being over eighty, after a lifetime with succeeding Mitfords. Unity wanted nothing out of the arrangement except to be in London.

Outwardly, to the naked eye of the Redesdales, Unity was taking up where she had left off. On 15 May, Mary Ormsby-Gore had a dance given for her by her grandparents, Lord and Lady Salisbury, in their house in Arlington Street. At a ball of Nancy Astor's, Unity met up with Coney Meade, whom she had last seen at the Chelsea Arts Ball. With Coney was Sir Ralph Jarvis – Ralphie, to Unity – who had been in Palestine for several months, where he had been attached to the King and Queen of the Belgians during their visit to that country. Not only had he fallen for the Queen of the Belgians, he said, who was as musical as he was, but for the Jewish experiments of reclaiming the land, which was news to Unity. The Somerset Maughams had another of their frequent parties, which did not prove so enjoyable, and from which Mosley was absent.

At the Howard de Walden's ball, Unity stayed until the end, with Mary, and Hamish St Clair Erskine and Lord Archie Gordon. At about six in the morning, Unity, Mary and Hamish proposed a trip to Covent Garden, but Lady Mima Ormsby-Gore, Mary's mother, put her foot down on this typically Mayfair junketing. A scene ensued between Mary and her mother, as a result of which Unity and Hamish crept off by themselves, and in the first light of a beautiful morning wandered through the market, where they bought some gardenias. They were in evening clothes, and Unity was what she liked to call 'terrifically painted up for electric light', so that the workmen shouted 'Hallo Lizzie' and 'Lucky Gent' at them, in an Eliza Doolittle-ish scene. By the time Unity arrived home at The Garage, Lord Redesdale and Bob Lambert were already up and about, and amazed to see her. Since the Redesdales had decided to leave that Friday morning for Swinbrook, Unity, like any star-gazing girl, did not go to bed at all.

The Warren Pearls invited her to go to their dance, not in Rutland Gate as might have been expected, but at Hurlingham, where the whole club was taken over. Unity's party beforehand consisted of her cousin and old partner in naughtiness, Chris Bailey, and Vida and Gerald Cuthbert, the four of them getting into training first, by slipping away to the Ring at Blackfriars, for the all-in wrestling. This, and boxing, were sudden new fads of Unity's, both theoretically forbidden by Lord Redesdale, who was furious when he heard where the young people had been, but by then they were sitting safely in a Daimler hire car, with Muv and Uncle Geoff too, on the road to Hurlingham. The night was hot, and one of the two dance floors was out of doors, the grounds set out with little tables and lit by coloured fairy lights. After some drinks, Vida and Chris and Unity and Gerald divided into pairs and lay down under the trees by the lake. Though Unity may have hoped for such mild flirtation as was permissible in those illuminated and chaperoned circumstances, nothing of the sort happened; her hopes of love were in the mind alone.

Vida Cuthbert is now Mrs Derek Schreiber, and she said, 'I was a great friend of Nika Rothschild, and used to stay with her at Tring. Gerald too. I don't remember Bobo there. Nika liked Ambrose, the band leader at the Cumberland Hotel, and I had to sit there with her for dreary hours. Bobo probably came with us. She may have been jealous that Gerald preferred Nika to her, she found that out. The all-in wrestling was ghastly. Gouge his eyes out, give him a rabbit punch, and there we were in our long dresses. Unity did enjoy it, it had been her idea entirely. She admired strength and power.

She was very much for fine young men, she felt people should be tougher, and was then talking about Mosley as the Leader. She was the sort of person who'd make herself a sacrificial figure very easily.'

Scrapbooks of the period are so entertaining because the camera had just ceased to be a specialist's invention, becoming instead an everyday toy, to Unity an accessory like a handbag. She enthused over films and filming. The silent pictures of her childhood had evolved into talkies, always a brilliant objective for an outing with a governess to Oxford, or at the end of a High Wycombe walk in the rain. She had been spell-bound by The Petrified Forest, the silver heart-throbs of Dietrich and Garbo, whose simple moralities and happily-ever-after endings were ready-made for her. To shoot pistol caps at a Western is a gesture for the audience, which is not primed for it, and although such babyish behaviour was chic in the Bright Young Thing code, the excitement of the film had in some degree been admitted. Just so, in her Nazi fervour, Unity was to stand up in a West End cinema showing Disraeli and shout 'Heil Hitler', for which she was ejected. She was that member of the audience for whom an impresario prays, of immediate superficial involvement in the plot as presented. Boxing and all-in wrestling shared this spectator-sport theatricality, as the Nazi rallies were to in their turn, being mammoth politicized extensions of the call to gouge out eyes and to rabbit punch. But it was spurious. The question was: how to participate? To draw and paint is an individual act, impossible without the minimum of talent and self-knowledge. To make a film is a collective enterprise, and Unity is not the only person to have confused the mass impact of films with their dreary, expensive, prima donna production. She had the fancy of becoming a film director, and her main dream-offering was to be about Mosley and his movement, a strength-through-joy documentary. There is no evidence that she ever became practical about it.

Just as John Betjeman had invited her to a press-view, so John Sutro, hearing her express these film-making ambitions, responded. A Swinbrook sewer, once at his own fancy-dress party he had been the Emperor Nero, and Diana had been Poppeia. Mosley asked him to stand as a New Party candidate for St Marylebone, and Diana even took him to a meeting of fascist women, but then as now, he was interested in old loyalties, not new grudges. He was a director of London Film Productions, a company formed by his father, and at the time backing The Private Life of Henry VIII. Early in June he drove Unity to Elstree to spend the afternoon in the studio where this famous film was then in production. John Sutro introduced her to Alexander Korda, the director, and to Charles Laughton who, as Henry VIII, was engaged on a scene at Hampton Court. Tapestry walls had been faithfully reproduced on the set. To Unity's amazement, the work was slowness itself, and only four short sequences were rehearsed and shot, from every conceivable angle and distance, during the whole time she was there, between two o'clock and six. Korda's extravagance and folie de grandeur did not leave a mark on her alone. Since it was Derby Day, the afternoon was interrupted to listen to the broadcast of the race, after which Unity was ushered into a small projection room for a screening of Korda's previous film, The Girl from Maxim's, starring Frances Day.

At Whitsun, she met Diana Wynyard, who was more approachable than anyone at Elstree had been. Tom, at Swinbrook for the weekend, wanted to drive over on the Sunday to Biddesden, because friends of his, Prince Jean-Louis de Faucigny-Lucinge and his wife, were staying there, as were a number of others, Rosemary Peto and her mother Ruby Lindsay, Peregrine and Rosalie Willoughby, and an Egyptian, Georges Cattaoui, a man at home in every drawing room, like a character in the novels of Proust with whom he was indeed on intimate terms, and about whom he has written, and possibly over-written. Unity found him clever and charming – as he was: I met him in the last years of his life – and she overlooked his Jewishness. Like Unity, Diana Wynyard and a friend of hers, Harriet Cohen, the pianist, came to Biddesden for the day, which was boiling hot, with the party round the swimming pool all afternoon. (Harriet Cohen might have won a place in the Biddesden set on her own accomplishments but she was there through Marian Dorn and Ted McKnight Kauffer, the latter being one of the foremost graphic artists of the day, the designer of the wrapper of Singing out of Tune, as well as of Mosley's The Greater Britain.) Unity had thought Diana Wynyard very boring in Cavalcade (Noel Coward's play had brought the tears to his eyes, so Hitler told Sir Eric Phipps, the ambassador) but now found her much prettier in real life than on the stage or on the screen, and asked her about such favourite film stars as Clive Brett and John Barrymore. Diana Wynyard was then in Wild Strawberries, a play about the Brontës, starring opposite Ralph Richardson, another of Unity's pin-ups since she had first been taken on school outings to see him in Shakespeare at the Old Vic. Diana Wynyard said that Unity had only to come round to her dressing room one night after the play, and an introduction to Ralph Richardson would follow – as it did, about three weeks later, Unity being escorted by Christopher Bailey, her cousin.

Also that day Ruby Lindsay asked her to paint a picture for an exhibition at Sunderland House which was being organized for charity. For this, Unity made a collage out of 'Hannibal' materials, cutting up and sticking together pieces of coloured tinsel to depict a bowl of flowers. After the exhibition, the Brook Street Art Gallery offered to sell it, but without success. In November she fetched it from there, Tom spotted it in The Garage, and paid her three guineas for it, hanging it with his 'Hannibal'. This willingness on every hand to treat her fits and starts of artistic whim as adult expressions of personality, this eagerness to be her sponsor, her patron, even flatterer, may have been encouragement only normal for someone her age, but all these kind people could no longer ignore her parallel existence, Jekyll-like, encroaching daily, a secret that had burst its bounds, and perhaps they were manning the only defences in sight.

For The Garage was offset by the Eatonry, the regularized dullness of the former dispersed by the conspiratorial solidarity of the latter. The Eatonry must have appeared to Unity as the ideal kingdom whose citizenship she had been seeking, where the defiance of ordinary people with their ordinary rules was the norm. In April 1933 Mosley had paid his second visit to Mussolini and on his return he had written in the *Blackshirt* that 'fascism was the greatest creed that Western civilization has ever given to the world ... destined to become the universal movement of the Twentieth Century'. His own Defence Force of stewards had become fully operational, meetings could therefore be the dynamo of the party, to incite the faithful and intimidate the enemy, a tactic which was not to vary in spite of the obvious repugnance of the majority to a rhetorical and physical violence quite outside their civilized parliamentary traditions. Mosley's initial upsurge was deflected by private matters, surreptitiously whispered in Fleet Street – as early as the previous September the *Tatler* had observed Sir Oswald 'who has John Barrymore's good looks' and Lady Cynthia at the Venice Lido, where the young Bryan Guinnesses also were – and now by the sudden dramatic illness of Lady Cynthia. On 13 May she was operated upon for appendicitis. Mosley came straight from the nursing home to the Eatonry, to lunch. The dining room could seat only six, and the other guests were Unity and Teresa, or Baby, Jungmann (now Mrs Cuthbertson, who cannot recall who the other two men were). The conversation was cheerful, the two sisters rehearsing for Mosley the gamut of Mitford nicknames. Next day Lady Cynthia developed peritonitis and her condition worsened.

On 15 May, Unity called on Diana at tea-time. Lady Castlerosse arrived. The death of Lady Cynthia appeared only too probable, as unforeseen as its consequences were unforeseeable. Lady Cynthia had loyally tacked her husband's political course, from conservative to labour, to fascist, of whose women's section she was titular head. The fascists, 'the boys', were said to be devoted to her, and to resent strongly anything like innuendoes about their Leader in the press, or tattled behind the backs of hands. At the Salisburys' dance for Mary Ormsby-Gore later that evening, Unity ran into Hamish St Clair Erskine, who told her that Lady Cynthia had indeed died.

Next day Unity went round to her sister. Nancy was away at Swinbrook, the parents had hardened their hearts against the Eatonry, and Diana had nowhere to turn. The newspapers printed obituaries of Lady Cynthia, usually several columns long with accompanying photographs, fulsome in tone, emphasizing her prominence as a daughter of Lord Curzon, and wife of Mosley. Speculation about the probable course of the fascist movement had she not died so unexpectedly is without point, for nobody can guess whether her politics and her affections would have remained so biddable. Three years later, however, Sir Oswald was to marry Diana, a step which might otherwise never have been taken, or would have had to be preceded by a sensational divorce from Lady Cynthia.

A family truce being declared, Diana came on 6 June for the weekend at Swinbrook. The DFD barricades were up indoors, all the same, with some steady sniping across them, so Diana and Unity sat out in the garden and took stock. From now on, Unity was committed, though her thoughts were far from high-flown or ideological, the fascist movement simply sounding great fun to her. From now on, with the parade-ground spirit of a steady trooper, Unity referred to Mosley in letters and conversation as the Leader. In this conversion the personal touch was everything. On the Saturday, she went into Oxford and in the Cornmarket saw a uniformed fascist hawking the Blackshirt. Buying a copy out of curiosity, she told the seller that she knew the Leader, and observed that he was thrilled – in this encounter there are impulses to boost herself, somewhat snobbishly, and to patronize the rank-and-file. At any rate this copy was a gift for Diana, to ingratiate, and to be a starting-point for a further discussion about the fascist party and what it was trying to do. The Leader would have to be asked whether Unity could join, and if so, then a little emblem would be sent to her.

Ascot week followed. Unity was not in London, but at the races, anxious for news of her application to become a fascist by the back-stairs. The letter arrived at Swinbrook, so that through Diana she heard at last how pleased Mosley was. If she was clever, it appeared, she might be of great use to the party. And she would receive an emblem from Mosley himself when next they met. Her excitement was too tremendous to be contained, she showed the letter to Nanny Blor who said that of course she must not join. Here was a cat which had virtually released itself from the bag.

One more Swinbrook weekend and Unity was at the end of her novitiate, undergoing the secular equivalent of a laying-on of hands. Thursday 14 June was the eve of Diana's appearance in the witness-box in her divorce proceedings, and the sisters had rallied loyally, four of them, Nancy, Pam, Diana and Unity, meeting up at tea-time at the Eatonry. All except Pam had arranged to dine and go to a film. When Mosley arrived to see Diana at this point, he was shown into the drawing room, Nancy and Pam making themselves scarce during his call. Catching sight of Unity, Mosley threw out his customary straight-from-the-shoulder greeting of 'Hallo Fascist' and removed a party emblem from his coat, to give it to her. This emblem, the sisters were relieved to discover afterwards, was not the real gold one which 'the boys' had had specially made for him. Just as 'we roared' was appropriate for a joke, so 'I was very excited' ticketed Unity's political supremes. She was now very excited.

Leaving Eaton Square to kill time at The Garage before dinner, Unity was entrusted by Pam with a basket of very special strawberries for her parents. But on the way she dropped into a jeweller's shop to have a safety chain fitted on the emblem just donated to her by no less a personage than her Leader himself, and this was so much more special to her that she forgot the strawberries in the shop. Which was what she was blamed for in the whole day's work. The jeweller was found in the morning to have eaten the strawberries because they would not have kept.

Drama that evening was by no means over. Halfway through dinner at Eaton Square, the butler, William, announced to the reassembled sisters that Mr Erskine wished to speak to Mrs Guinness on the telephone. Reasonably enough, Nancy answered her fiancé instead, but Hamish Erskine had asked for Diana on purpose, to break the news that he was calling off the engagement with Nancy, after it had dragged for four years with more provisos and obstacles in its wake than happiness. Shortly Hamish himself then appeared, downcast, to be his own advocate with Nancy. Diana and Unity left them to it, walking by themselves to the Haymarket, where Edward G. Robinson's *The Little Giant* was being shown. On the way they passed fascist headquarters in 12 Lower Grosvenor Place. In their keenness, 'the boys' apparently had the BUF offices open at half past seven in the morning, and did not shut till two at night. 'A big push' was planned for September, a repeat of the previous autumn's League of Youth aspirations. For Unity, it was again awfully exciting. By 15 June, then, Diana had her divorce, though it was not absolute until December; Nancy was no longer engaged to the man of her choice; Unity was engaged to the cause which had chosen her.

· · · · ·

This emblem, farcical enough, and crass, as apparel is in the service of an allegiance, led without ado to more high jinks of the kind which dogged Unity – the banana skin was perilously close to that huge stride. For the emblem was not a membership badge into the party, but a personal favour, a guerdon, from the Leader, and he had taken the precaution of warning Unity not to wear it when she actually enrolled. 'The boys' would otherwise perceive that she had this signal mark of approval in advance, they would twig that she was Diana's sister, and might put two and two together. If any query arose, then Unity was to say that she had met Mosley two years before.

On the Friday after receiving her emblem, Unity was able to take the London air with it, so long as she remembered to unpin it, safety chain and all, on her return to The Garage. Care had to be exercised, for were Muv and Farve to find out that this was her passport to the fascist party, they would be furious. 'That man' was definitely out of bounds. No possibility occurred at the regular Swinbrook weekend of displaying her treasure. On the following Monday, however, the 19th, in London again, the emblem was restored to the lapel, and there it rested, the solemn warning notwithstanding, when Unity entered 12 Lower Grosvenor Place to join the party formally. She was taken upstairs to the women's offices, where one of Lady Makgill's secretaries (senior colleague, therefore, to Pamela Dillon) was sitting. Lady Makgill was out. Her stand-in was not as welcoming as Unity had anticipated, and asked why she wanted to join. Because she knew the Leader and had read his manifesto *The Greater Britain*; it was the blabbing to the Oxford fascist all over again. A monthly contribution was expected from the party member, from each according to his means, and Unity offered to pay five shillings, which she considered a lot, though Lady Makgill's stand-in did not appear over-impressed. Then the pledge had to be signed. Finally, in the party shop downstairs, she bought the back numbers of the *Blackshirt* (it had begun publication in February) and ordered it weekly.

At dinner that evening in Eaton Square, the experience, as recounted to Diana and Mosley, had its down-beat note about the lack of welcome to the new recruit. Unity said he had promised to give her a rubber truncheon; it would be delivered on the Leader's behalf at Eaton Square next day, for her to fetch there. But instead of dawning with this Excalibur of a truncheon, 20 June turned out to be the blackest day of her life so far, worse even than that Boxing Day when the doom of St Margaret's had been pronounced. For party headquarters, far from taking too little notice of the new recruit, had reported that fascist member Unity had strolled in there flaunting a high party emblem, and in the circumstances the humble process of enlisting was a rigmarole which had not been appreciated. Telephoning ensued, and strictures. If Unity was to be so tactless, so disregarding of the Leader's instructions, so damaging to his interests, then there could be no room for her in the party.

Complete misery, utter despair. Expulsion again, with punishment this time. The future of the fascist party, of the Leader himself, seemed in jeopardy. 'I was so excited,' that dream of the future, crumbled to ruins. The Leader whom she had hoped might promote her to a responsible position, must be despising her as a fool. She ate no lunch, she moped in The Garage, she thought seriously of putting an end to herself, and in this sad state Mary Ormsby-Gore found her. The desire to please was all the more frantic for being exploded on its first appearance.

Tea at Eaton Square was a twist of the knife. Nancy was there already, and so was Doris Castlerosse, though she took her cue and left the sisters to it. Diana was also fretful about the emblem, though Nancy could hardly be expected to treat the thing seriously, nor did she, her line being that Unity would always be making such blunders and had far better not be allowed to join. Where and how would the Leader's wrath fall? He was due at the Eatonry just before dinner, and it was arranged that as soon as possible Unity would have his verdict telephoned through to her. Baroness d'Erlanger's cocktail party had to be endured first, with Muv, who had stopped by to collect Unity. Dinner was at The Garage, with Muv and Farve and Tom, and in the middle of it the telephone rang. Unity rushed to answer – relief! – the Leader had been very sweet about it and it didn't matter very much and there was no need to have worried like that, and he was wonderful, though who he was could hardly be spelled out within earshot of Muv and Farve, in the dark as ever. With Tom she went off to see George Arliss in The King's Vacation, and confided in him about these upheavals, but he was no more sympathetic than Nancy had been. And so to the Astors' ball, at midnight, this blackest of days over, except for the shudder.

A way of squaring party headquarters had been devised. Should Lady Makgill persist in asking about the emblem, she was to be told that Unity had enrolled at Oxford, and acquired it there, which was believable enough. No time was to be lost. Lady Makgill had indeed telephoned The Garage in order to make an appointment with Unity, and it had been fixed for the following Monday.

For once the Swinbrook weekend was opportune. The house-party consisted of Pam, Mary Ormsby-Gore, Jean Follett (who married Lord Broughton and Vaux, and then Monsieur Guépin), James Lees-Milne, Claud Phillimore,

Gerald Cuthbert, Frank Oppenheimer (drowned before the war swimming at Madeira. He was the brother of Harry, chairman of the mining concern, Anglo-American), and Erwein Gečman-Waldek (an Austrian of Czech extraction – whose Léhar mode and spirits have enhanced many lives, including my parents'). They were to arrive on the Saturday, 24 June, and it had been planned that evening to attend the open-air performance of *A Midsummer Night's Dream* which Max Reinhardt had produced for the Oxford University Dramatic Society. It was noted that Reinhardt, world famous as he was, was working with undergraduates *faute de mieux*, having been one of the prime targets of the first onrush of official Nazi persecution which had just culminated with the book-burnings and the muzzling of prominent intellectuals and Jews – Einstein, Thomas Mann and Feuchtwanger were among many forbidden the practice of their profession, and whose immediate emigration was a siren of alarm.

On the ready-made excuse of picking up the theatre tickets early in the day, Unity therefore drove into Oxford, straight to the local branch of the BUF, at 6 King Edward Street. The main office was on the second floor of this old house, with the shop selling propaganda below, a standard arrangement designed to gain advantage in the event of an attack, the defenders rallying upstairs. The office door was kept shut. Knocking, Unity was told to enter, and was taken aback to find the room full of Blackshirts. Rightly guessing that the man at the desk was the branch head, Vincent Keens, she addressed him, saying that she had come to join the party. 'The boys' were sent away to the canteen upstairs while Keens cross-questioned her. He was actually Canadian, in his mid-thirties, fair though balding, with pale eyes, and one of the dozen organizers who toured the country full-time for the party, valued as a propagandist. Evidently Oxford received new members as sternly as London. Unity had to explain that she knew the Leader personally, and had read his book. Afterwards Keens was to confess to her that several undesirable girls had been pestering to join the party to have fun with 'the boys' and he had feared Unity was another, which became a firm joke between them. Imitating the Leader, he gave her his own badge, and escorted her to the canteen to be introduced all round. By which time he had realized that a most unusual new member was on the rolls, not a neighbourhood good-time girl at all, and he could hardly get over the genuine upper-class article wanting to join.

Back in Oxford in the evening with her friends for the play, Unity had first to collect a copy of *The Greater Britain* which typically she had left in King Edward Street, typically because she was scatter-brained, but also because she was contriving for another gust of high-life to sweep Mr Keens.

Claud Phillimore, James Lees-Milne and Gerald Cuthbert accompanied her to the BUF office. Keens introduced Mrs Parker, the organizer of the women's section locally, a lady with grey hair and what to Unity's ears sounded a terrible accent. She and Keens were equally hearty in their expressions, saying 'Blow in any time' and 'We're an awfully jolly lot.'

The contretemps with the emblem had been smoothed over, she was on a friendly footing with 'sweet Mr Keens', *A Midsummer Night's Dream* was lovely, everybody had dined at the Clarendon where Mary Ormsby-Gore had met up with them. Gerald Cuthbert might be no more in love with her than before, but the weekend was altogether an advance in other respects. On Monday she could face Lady Makgill at her new office in 233 Regent Street, with nothing to fear, and making the point, she bought herself her first black shirt on the strength of the interview. Unfortunately Lady Makgill had no fascist work for her.

Lady Makgill is now Mrs Esther Murray. She said: 'I created the women's section of the BUF in Lady Cynthia's day. They sent a subscription and their name was put on a list. Mosley was interested in farming matters and I organized agricultural meetings for him and travelled to them. I sometimes wore uniform but I was unlikely to have been doing so when Unity came in. After Lady Cynthia died, there was a short interim and I left, I was there only at the beginning. Then Mosley moved the whole thing to Whitelands (the former Whitelands Teachers' Training College, called Black House when it was the BUF headquarters, was in the King's Road, next to the Duke of York's barracks). I had a personal secretary and an assistant, it was quite big at one time. I now understand why Mosley played the Mitfords down. Unity Mitford didn't mean anything to me in those days. She was swept in by her sister. I didn't do much for her, though I would have done if only I'd known. Mosley wasn't pushing it. Honestly I don't think Unity had much involvement in the BUF, she may have been more active and prominent afterwards, but she left so early for Germany.'

The art classes of the beginning of the year were now replaced by gymnastic exercises and tap-dancing, an echo of Lady Redesdale's Good Body, also a conditioning for the 'big push' to come. Twice a week or so, Unity went with Diana to the Women's League of Health and Beauty in Great Portland Place. Returning home exhausted, they would dine at Eaton Square by themselves, or with Mosley. The Redesdales must either have resigned themselves to what they could not mend, or had their heads deep in sand. Mosley was hoping to proselytize personally among the rich and grand, trusting in the autumn rallies to cater to the masses. His belief in the power of the chosen individual was a naivety he himself personified, and the Carlylean glorification of the hero and heroism was an essential creed of his politics, which takes the glitter off the would-be Keynesian technocrat subsequently furbished up by apologists. A dead set was made at such eminent men as Lord Nuffield and Lord Rothermere. Small dinners and gatherings enfolded the professional attenders of London, hangers-on, *déclassé* aristocrats and younger sons, meddlesome dons, former public servants coasting on a knighthood and a pension, altogether an untrustworthy nucleus. One such meeting was held in the house – also in Eaton Square – of Lady Mosley, Sir Oswald's mother, on 6 July, by invitation only. Unity took along Mary Ormsby-Gore and Anthony Rumbold. Such a crowd had been assembled to hear Mosley that Unity had to stand by the door, though there she could catch the Leader's eye and was complimented by him afterwards for her beauty. At question time an elderly lady rambled on about an audience granted to her by Mussolini, and how the Duce was not to be bracketed with Hitler. When she shouted *Viva l'Italia*, Mosley had had enough of being lectured on his very own pitch, and snubbed her.

Sir Anthony Rumbold's father was ambassador in Berlin from 1928 to 1933, and his despatches had spelled out the Nazi menace more unambiguously than the Foreign Office liked. To suppose that Unity at this stage wished to get at the father's position by inviting the son to listen to Mosley would be to read too much into it. Sir Anthony Rumbold (an ambassador in his turn) said: 'Pam took me to Swinbrook. The first time, I was set upon by Bobo and Decca, who asked me, Are you a fascist or a communist? and I said, Neither, I'm a democrat. Whereupon they answered, How wet. After my finals at Oxford, in the summer of 1933, I came to London to amuse myself and I could well have seen Bobo once a week or so. The meeting in Lady Mosley's house was nothing but upper-class old ladies. He spoke much more of Italy than of his own movement. Also I went to an Albert Hall meeting with the Mitford girls. The Leader's going to make a speech, they said, Do come. From their house in Eaton Square we went to the Albert Hall [22 April 1934], to a box on the right-hand side looking towards the dais. We heard "England Awake" to the *Horst Wessel Lied*. Prearranged, straight up the aisle, marched the Leader, and made a long speech. Everybody in the box saluted, except me, I was embarrassed and slunk away. Diana and Bobo weren't in black shirts. I used to see her with Mary Ormsby-Gore, who will tell you how Unity once returned from Germany with a story of how she'd met an old woman, obviously Jewish, with a heavy bundle on her back, who had asked the way to the railway station. Bobo had said, I told her the wrong way because I saw how heavy the bundle was, wasn't that wonderful of me?

Mary couldn't stand her in the end. Nobody could. After that meeting in Lady Mosley's house, at the end of July, I went to Germany and was there till the following February, when Jacques de Beaumarchais, the present French ambassador in London, and I were attacked in the Café Benz in Schwabing by a Stormbannführer and his chauffeur, and I was kicked out of the country.' This incident was much publicized at the time, and Unity, though still at Swinbrook, can hardly have helped hearing about the beating-up of a friend.

Other summer weekends, other occasions to be off with 'the boys' selling the Blackshirt, an activist. On 8 July, for instance, she drove down from London with Farve, and on to Oxford by herself, spinning a yarn to him that she was spending the day with a friend called Schnozzle at Magdalen College. (Farve had been softened up since the days when Nancy was held to have been ruined for life by lunching at Christ Church.) Schnozzle was really John Bennett, a music scholar, of some means and elegance, and until an overnight conversion to fascism, a quiet man in the eyes of college contemporaries like Anthony Rumbold. His rooms were in New Buildings, the eighteenth-century part of Magdalen, and Unity found him there in a dressing gown, booked for an appendicitis operation in two days' time, so she went on to the King Edward Street headquarters, where she changed into her black shirt. At two o'clock an expedition set off to spread the fascist tidings in Abingdon. Mrs Parker's daughter Cavell, named with patriotic anti-German emotion after Nurse Cavell, took Unity in her car, along with a schoolmaster named Buswell, and a little Irishman, Jimmy O'Brien, who never stopped wise-cracking. Abingdon did not embrace them, as they went their separate ways. It was an impossible town to sell fascist propaganda in, the inhabitants said nothing but they stared. At last two young men bought several copies of the Blackshirt, and also of the Leader's Fascism in Britain, costing tuppence, but they had a reason, they were journalists, or so they claimed, from the Morning Post, and they were ready for a discussion about Mosley. One of them, whom Unity found the better-looking of the pair, asked, 'What about Mrs Bryan Guinness?' and as before, she blurted out that she was her sister, and had the same instant regrets. The elements of a good story for the Morning Post were here, but the young men seem to have passed it up; they offered to buy the stock of material if Unity would go on the river with them. Much as she would have preferred this, as the day was hot, she was there for fascism, and had to decline. The young men wandered away. Her reward was back at headquarters, when she was found to have sold more papers than anyone else. Vincent Keens took her to tea but could not press her to more than bread and butter and a little water. Then he saw her off on the local train home, surprised by her, so he confessed, into feeling quite romantic, and the two dubious young journalists in Abingdon could have given her no approval worth as much as that.

New-blooded for the party, she determined to participate in its first great recruiting march through London on 16 July, the Sunday of the weekend after her Abingdon adventures. A network of fibs had to be woven in order to be able to leave Swinbrook with Diana on a Sunday morning without Muv becoming suspicious. In the end the story was that the Film Society had a special afternoon showing of *Le Sang d'un Poète* which could not be missed. Had poor Muv but known, the Film Society met only in the winter. More than that, Unity had to pretend that her friend Elizabeth Powell had offered to put her up for the night, as it was forbidden to sleep at the Eatonry, or to stay alone at The Garage. The march started from Eaton Square, so it was convenient to spend the night with Diana, as she did.

Unity had her place in the column. Fascism for her was debutante life in reverse, literally in black instead of white. The recruiting march through London could be considered a Queen Charlotte's ball she really wanted to attend, suitably dressed to be sure, bringing up the rear for all to see. Fascism, like communism, like the season, had a calendar, had occasions, functions, meetings, stuffy rooms, acquaintances dedicated to an identical routine, so that preliminaries were unnecessary, common small-talk and above all a common purpose. Unity had known that she would never be a real success socially, nor would have wanted to be. Except for the instructors at the ice rink, she had found it impossible to make friends in an altogether different class from her own. With 'the boys' she was sure that she would get on better than with people of her own class – it is the pure lament of the thirties, this class guilt, like a national Last Post, sounding in one privileged life after another, to foreclose it. The values which had made Unity what she was also prevented her from being anything else. Boredom and the longing for a wider prospect certainly propelled her out of Swinbrook, but also an instinct for self-preservation, for if the class system was about to founder, there was no reason for her to go down with it. Thousands of well-educated young men and women of independent means, with connections and a stake in the land, looked at the future as she did but they rushed to save their skins and souls in communism. Communists and fascists both were impelled by fear, the anxiety of being in a scrap-heap instead of a social class, but the communists were able to offer with more plausibility the twin motor of hope, for the few brief, illusory years in which their propagandists were able to conceal the truth. And if these choices in class abandonment were less cerebral and articulate, well then, not everyone had a sister with a Leader to herself.

To trace Unity at fascist demonstrations, as at dances, is a needle-in-haystack task. BUF archives vanished either before the arrests of May 1940, which effectively put a stop to the party, or were then impounded by the Home Office, from whose maw nothing returns, but mention of her would be scant in them, probably no more than another record of membership. English fascism cannot be studied in detail until the histories of local branches are written. Survivors of the party may be interviewed, which looks like witch-hunting to many of them; they have put it out of mind, or out of sight, and turned over new leaves in plenty. Besides, the kind of dutiful paper-selling and demonstrating that has been seen was over a short period, less than a year. Once she was away in Germany, she did not drop the BUF so much as throw herself into National Socialism. Party activities in England came to look less glamorous to her, a trifle provincial perhaps, and she was sporadic about them, fitting them in at her convenience, should she happen to be home.

The 'big push' of the autumn, however, was the prelude to the gains of 1934, and the short span before the passing of the Public Order Act, when the BUF looked as if it might take hold, the mass meetings attracting conservative-minded people as well as the temperamentally discontented, while in the person of Lord Rothermere, the party had a press lord and his papers at their service for a while, which could well have been crucial. It is an irony that in order to keep up social appearances, Diana's divorce not becoming absolute until December, the Mitford element was subdued deliberately at the one point when Mosley made leeway.

Mrs Ann Beckett was married to John Beckett, once a Labour MP who in the House of Commons resorted to the Cromwellian device of seizing the Speaker's mace as a protest on behalf of Fenner (now Lord) Brockway, his colleague. A visit to Italy impressed Beckett as it had Mosley, whose party he joined, to be director of publicity. With William Joyce and John McNab, he broke from the BUF in 1937 to found the National Socialist League, but after a year he thought that Joyce's anti-semitism should be moderated, and with the old Duke of Bedford he then founded the erratic British Peace Party. Mrs Beckett said: 'Mosley was not damaged by the Mitford connection. The only person who damaged Mosley was Mosley. Very few people in the organization knew of Unity. I met her at gatherings, and was introduced to her, once was at a hall where Mosley gave an exhibition of fencing, the other fencer was Marjorie Aitken. I was secretary to Dr Robert Forgan in Black

House, with E. D. Randall who went to teach in Germany in 1935. When Black House was closed in 1935, we moved to George Street and then on to Tothill Street. Unity didn't come in much to Black House. She was hardly known to us. Mosley was on the ground floor, I was on the floor above, where Forgan was carrying on the organization itself, the membership rolls, and so on. We very seldom saw Mosley. The organization felt that Unity became obsessed with Hitler, the general feeling was that she was behaving in a rather foolish way. Lady Claire Annesley who worked for the Peace Pledge Movement was her friend. She had no circle of friends in the BUF. One heard about her. I always thought it was Joyce's influence after 1936 that gave the organization its reputation. He was the only violent anti-semite I knew then. He knew Unity, but the Joyces did not know her well.'

Unity, however, was selected as one of the BUF representatives on the delegation sent to Germany, to attend the Nuremberg Party Day, though it is possible that she was attached to the others as a favour, and paid her own fare, freelance style. The first *Parteitag*, or Party Day, had been held in 1923, for the purpose of assembling in one place disparate nationalist and anti-semitic groups, to parade, to absorb ideology, and create a focus for public attention. A second Party Day, in 1926, was held in Weimar as a provocation. No Party Days had been staged from 1930 until 1932 because the energies of the Nazis were concentrated on political assaults against the government. In 1933 the Party Day of Victory (so named by Hess) was a celebration, to be repeated every year in that prefabrication of tradition which was a Nazi speciality. What had amounted to glorified street-tactics in revolutionary days were to be transformed into colossal, calculatedly brutal, expressions of power. Germans and foreigners alike were to look at the might of the new state, either in ecstatic fulfilment of their new destiny, or in despair. As soon as he was in a position to do so, Hitler decided to remodel Nuremberg into the city for these monster annual rallies, planning stadiums, a Congress Hall, and an open-air assembly area in open ground around the Luitpoldhain and the Zeppelinwiese, the hitherto untouched outskirts of the city.

The 1933 rally began on 31 August. Four hundred thousand party members had been collected by special trains, the SA, the SS, the Hitler Youth being represented. One thousand chosen guests filled the main grandstand. Later these guests would be more discriminatingly picked, as potential supporters, heads of states to be wooed, tycoons, Germanizers of every stripe, even significant tourists or busy-bodies, but on this first Nazi festival they were plain fascists. The official Nazi brochure published within weeks to mark the occasion records, 'Even the foreign guests are swept off their feet by the spirit and determination of the Hitler Youth.' In this brochure is a photograph of the English delegation, with Unity the only woman, in a tweed suit with her black shirt, her hand up saluting, gloves on (see photograph no. 6). Two away from her is William Joyce (who in his *Dämmerung über England*, published in Berlin in 1940, his first year as Lord Haw-Haw, wrote, 'In 1933 I joined Sir Oswald Mosley's new movement, the BUF. I became one of the leading political speakers and writers of that movement; for three years I was Mosley's propaganda chief. These were marvellous times and I shall never forget them. I used all my influence in the movement to give the party a strongly anti-semitic direction – and I may say that I succeeded in that direction.'). Two farther away from Joyce is Alexander Raven Thomson, the Rosenberg of the BUF, author of a book on Spengler; 'this exceptional thinker', as Mosley calls him in *My Life*, 'one of the finest fighters for our cause we ever knew'. The officer with the Highlander cap and medals is a Captain Vincent. The two men in peaked caps are French fascists. A series of photographs was taken that day, some of them without Unity, and one is printed in the German edition of James Drennan's book, *Oswald Mosley, B.U.F. and British Fascism* (1933). (James Drennan was the pseudonym of W. E. D. Allen, an Ulster Unionist MP who had joined the New Party and supported Mosley until 1936.) Because Hitler addressed the League of German Culture on 1 September, and some of the foreign guests and delegations were present, his first meeting with Unity is sometimes dated then, and this is true in the sense that she must have set eyes on him and heard the sound of his voice. 'The first moment I saw him I knew there was no one I would rather meet,' she was to say soon after to the *Evening Standard*. The five days of the rally over, the English delegation came home from Nuremberg, though again Unity may have separated from the others and gone to Munich to discuss plans with Baroness Laroche for a return to finishing school.

By October, the pattern of spending the week at The Garage and the weekend at Swinbrook had been re-established. She was at Swinbrook on 27 October and again on 6 November, therefore bridging a meeting organized by Vincent Keens in the Oxford Town Hall at the beginning of November. Mosley spoke. The poisoned fruit borne back by the BUF delegation from Nuremberg was served to the public a week later, on 11 November, when Mosley said in a speech at Ealing, 'Whatever happened in Germany is Germany's affair, and we are not going to lose British lives in a Jewish quarrel.' There is no evidence that Unity was present at either meeting, but the supposition is likely. Her Christmas was spent at Swinbrook, and she stayed there well into the New Year.

.   .   .   .   .

Three days after Unity had marched from Eaton Square on the big recruiting drive, Nancy announced her engagement. The *Evening Standard* of 19 July wrote, 'She is twenty-nine and Mr Rodd is twenty-six. Peter Rodd was educated at Wellington and Balliol. He left Wellington at the age of sixteen, having reached the top of the school. On leaving Oxford he went to South America as a steward in a cargo boat. He had only £2 in his pocket when he arrived in Buenos Aires. After a number of adventures he went on a forest exploration trip with two companions. The British Consul is said to have wired to Sir Rennell [his father, later Lord Rennell] for instructions to stop him. The reply reported to have been sent was, "No. Why? Rodd." In 1931 Rodd stood as an MP in Camborne in Cornwall as a Conservative.'

Peter Rodd was a close enough friend of Evelyn Waugh's to be the proto- type of Basil Seal, freebooter-in-chief of his fiction. A man after Unity's heart, it might be thought. She went to Nancy's wedding on 5 December, at St John's, Smith Square, and three days later Nancy was writing to her from Rome, 'Why do people say they don't enjoy honeymoons? I am adoring mine.' (Quoted in Harold Acton's *Memoir* of Nancy.) Nancy, not Diana, might have been the elder sister for Unity to steer a course by, but the dragged-out affair with Hamish Erskine had been pallid, and lowered the emotional temperature. Peter Rodd, snatched on the rebound, was a *mauvais sujet* all right, to suit the Mitford taste, but he was no saturnine matinée star like Mosley. Nancy and Peter Rodd offered Unity too little, too late.

His sister-in-law, Lady Rennell, painted a portrait of him in 1929, his straw-coloured hair a shock, his stance arrogant, stocky. She has this picture at their family house, The Rodd, in Herefordshire. She said: 'He was a wild young man. A beautiful person. In 1930 or 1931 he was a correspondent for *The Times* in Germany and used to go reporting until he was sacked. At Oxford he'd been a communist, but after he married Nancy, he and she both wore a black shirt, for a very brief time. He took me to the Albert Hall meeting of Mosley's [22 April 1934]. Peter was interested in people and what they were up to. Unity and the Mitfords diverted him.'

Any fascist leanings shown by Nancy were a masquerade, one more of the impersonations she sprang on the unwary. Too sceptical of everything to raise indignation, she was merciless in the writer's pursuit of copy, and in 1934 she was at work on her third novel, *Wigs on the Green*, whose publication was held up, according to Jessica, by threats from Diana and Unity that they would never speak to her again, if it appeared. The novel is a bit of a spoof but it perfectly crystallizes Unity in her first year as a fascist. 'Her straight hair, cut in a fringe, large, pale-blue eyes, dark skin, well-proportioned limbs and classical features, combined with a certain fanaticism to give her the aspect of a modern Joan of Arc.' Eugenia Malmains is the physical spit-image of Unity, though Nancy could not resist grimacing in the very next paragraph, 'She was dressed in an ill-fitting grey woollen shirt, no stockings, a pair of threadbare plimsolls, and a jumper made apparently out of a Union Jack. Round her waist was a leather belt to which there was attached a large bright dagger.' Anything for a laugh.

Nor can the Redesdales have had much pleasure in their characterization as Lord and Lady Chalford, Eugenia's grandparents. The family jokes of TPOF for The Poor Old Female, and TPOM, The Poor Old Male, were hung on them in public. 'The twopenny bar shop' and 'the tubercular content of a pint of milk' were the contours of Swinbrook. For Eugenia, the BUF, here parodied as Social Unionists or the Union Jackshirts, is a village craze. How in the fastness of Chalford Eugenia came to hear of the Jackshirts, let alone be enrolled as one, remains an obscurity which nags, and Nancy's silence on this question was probably a peace-keeping compromise. Eugenia's only outside link with the party is to write articles for the *Union Jack* which are continually rejected. Was Nancy cutting Unity down to size, or was she sticking to the observation that Unity's fascism was Oxford-based? Captain Jack, the Leader, is in London, and his sole appearance in the novel is wonderfully sarcastic reportage of a scene at which Nancy had been present, as we have seen. Eugenia has found her way to Union Jack House 'where she spent a blissful morning with Comrades of the London branch. Her eyes still sparkled with excitement at the memory of her reception. The Captain had himself granted her an interview, warmly thanked her for all the work she had done on behalf of the Movement and had finally, as a token of gratitude, plucked, like the pelican, his own little emblem from his own bosom and pinned it, still warm, upon hers.'

As a Jackshirt at Chalford, Eugenia is still trammelled by Nanny, and Nancy rightly makes something of this. '"Get out you filthy Pacifist, get out I say, and take your yellow razor gang with you . . . The time is not ripe for a blood bath in Chalford."' Unity had not actually come to such a pass with Blor, but the Nanny in the novel is one of many reasons why Eugenia's fascism will not wash in Chalford. Fresh fields will have to be opened up, and Nancy has pointers to the future. Eugenia is drawing swastikas on her letters, she thinks Hitler is a wonderful man and choruses 'Heil Hitler', and about her grandmother, the filthy old female pacifist who has shut her up in her bedroom, she writes, 'She misuses me and tramples upon me as for many years France has misused and trampled upon Germany. It does not signify. Germany has now arisen and I shall soon arise and my day shall dawn blood red.' Reichshund as the name of Eugenia's dog is spot on target.

Eugenia's several racial thrusts are also taken straight out of Unity's mouth. "'Under our regime," she said, "women will not have lovers. They will have husbands and great quantities of healthy Aryan children.'"

None of this packed enough punch to stop the runaway short. Like a restoration comedy, it was tempered with grace, it was playful, too snug. Nancy thought of Unity with asperity, though she was loyal when she had to be. *Wigs on the Green* leaves Eugenia in full cry, as, in reality, Unity was far beyond any influence Nancy might have. Germany was her release from TPOF and TPOM and Nanny, and Nazism was to provide her with a bigger and better leader.

6

PICK-UP IN
THE OSTERIA BAVARIA

Some time in the spring of 1934 Unity crossed the divide, to live more in Germany than in England, in a version she herself fashioned and cherished of the fable of Beauty and the Beast. Nancy had in her possession Unity's specially bound *Nazi Song Book*, duly signed and embellished with the ortho- dox 'Heil Hitler!' and 'April 1934, Munich'. As we shall see, Unity arrived at Baroness Laroche's only after the summer term had begun, in May. Had she been somewhere else in Germany, was she in Munich briefly in April, idling before the term, or do the inscriptions in the songbook not commit her firmly to a time and place?

Jessica says that Unity went to live in Germany with full parental approval. Initially the Redesdales were pleased to see her taking an interest in anything, even Germany – hence the return to the old finishing school where at least she would have to master the language. Seventeen in the autumn, Jessica herself was ready for the traditional 'year abroad', and Lady Redesdale weighted already opposing poles by accompanying her to Paris, to help her settle in. This was in April, and it is most likely that Unity came out with them, dawdled a little and went on by herself to Munich. 'Bobo,' says Jessica, 'was in Paris with us,' but she is now uncertain quite at which point this would have been, whether on the way out to Munich in the spring, or during the summer break. Certainly Lady Redesdale, Unity and Jessica, were all together in Munich later in the year, in September/October. At any rate, one old Swinbrook-style rag had its run in Paris. Dorothy Wilde, Dolly to her friends, reincarnated, as she thought, her uncle Oscar Wilde's gifts and disasters, with a few more of her own too. Nancy had introduced her to Lady Redesdale. 'When I was in Paris,' says Jessica, 'we were all madly in love with Dolly Wilde. We sat on either side of her in a taxi, to see which of us could get our hand farther up her fur cape. My mother was driven mad by Bobo and I doing this. Bobo made up a parody of a hit-tune of the time,

Goodbye Dolly, I must leave you
though it breaks my heart to go.

Goodbye Dolly, I must leave you
for the front to face the foe.
All the soldier boys are marching . . .'

Although Unity is not identified by name, this zany conjunction of women
and the singing of the song has also been recorded by Bettina Bergery in a
privately printed volume 'Oscaria', In Memory of Dorothy Ierne Wilde.

When Jessica was at Royaumont that June for the lunch already mentioned,
she had been brought by Paulette Helleu, daughter of the famous artist, lifelong friend of my family's. Her apartment in Paris has hardly altered since her
father lived in it, with his work all around. Paulette Helleu* said: 'It was
a pension de famille they had lived in in 1925, the Villa St Honoré d'Eylau, opposite the church. Next door was an Institut de Bègues, for stutterers. The
Redesdales had asked my father to find them something not far from us.
Lord Redesdale was always turning up from England with a brace of pheasants.
Helleu made an etching of Diana in 1927 – she had come back to a flat in
the Avenue Victor Hugo as part of being "finished" – it was the last etching
he did before his death.

'My parents were friends of Mr Bowles. My father had a yacht at Deauville
and was on it for the season there. Mr Bowles used to bring his yacht alongside, with Sydney and Weenie on board. Uncle Geoff had asked to marry my
much older sister in about 1910. They invited me several times to Swinbrook
but I never went. I was one year younger than Nancy but got on better with
the little ones. They used to come to this house.

'Unity was very expressionless. My father used to call her La République
because she looked like the classic statue of the French Republic. She was
altogether rather plain and had very ugly hands, terribly heavy, the fingers
like sausages. They were strictly brought up and plainly dressed. I spoke
English to them, I don't think Unity spoke much French. I saw her next
when she came to Paris from Germany in 1934, she had her holidays and
Lady Redesdale did not want to, or did not dare to, take her back to London,
so they stopped in Paris. Lady Redesdale took a flat near the Champs de Mars,
and Unity was there with her. She wanted me to go to Germany. In 1935 she
sent me three postcards with Hitler's head on each in a different pose, to
invite me to Munich. She always called me up on her way through Paris, I
don't think she knew many French people, nor would they have wanted to
see her. Unity and I went out in Paris – she used to play an accordion – she
had tea in this very room. I looked on her as a rarity, un animal curieux. By
then she could speak of nothing but Hitler, boasting about her friendship

* Who, incidentally, has never been to Germany, and never saw Unity after 1935.

with the man. Actually she couldn't understand a joke, she had no sense of humour. She was obstinate as a mule. And wasn't there another English girl with her? Once I asked Diana, What does Unity do when she doesn't see Hitler? She thinks of him, Diana answered. And did Hitler give her the revolver? I think I had it from Unity that she had a gun given to her by Hitler?'

Luck was with me that paths to Unity led through people I or my family had always known. Questions about work in progress, which a writer usually ducks in this case often had open-ended consequences, with a ricochet of coincidences. Unity had apparently stuck in the minds of those who crossed her in her heyday. Baroness Bentinck is the daughter of Fritz Thyssen, the great steelmaster, and author of I Paid Hitler, a title which tells all, though no good came of it. Becoming Hungarian, and adopting the additional name of Bornemisza, the Thyssens had been obliged by law to buy a property in Hungary, and they picked on Rechnitz, once a Batthyány house, near the Austrian frontier. From Baroness Bentinck I first heard of Janos Almasy, their neighbour in Bernstein, another castle of the Counts Batthyány. Janos Almasy, she said, had been an astrologer and necromancer in the Wallenstein tradition, rather sinister-looking but invited everywhere, dashingly Nazi and Unity's bosom friend. Just as the invasion of Poland was concluded, Baroness Bentinck and her husband, a Dutch diplomat, drove over from Rechnitz to Bernstein for the day. When Janos eventually put in an appearance, he was in a dressing gown, having secluded himself away to cast Hitler's horoscope, which, he warned, portended catastrophes, collapse and death by his own hand – a memorable prediction after the first blitzkrieg of the war. If they were still alive, Janos and his brother Ladislaus, Laczy for short, and also called Teddy, would be invaluable on this quest for Unity.

More than that, Baroness Bentinck invited me to her daughter's wedding. At the reception I met Anthony Rhodes, the writer, who in earlier days as a schoolmaster had taught me Italian. Now his first novel, The Uniform, is a trim miniature of Munich as it was for the smart young English set there before the war, and Unity herself is echoed in 'That splendid girl, Deborah Sykes-Maclean, Ribblestock's daughter,' who was in the habit of attending Hitler's informal parties and finding the Führer 'really rather sweet ... terribly bashful, you know, and quite, quite retiring'. Anthony Rhodes' wife, Rosie, had been in Munich and from her I had a first description of what had in fact been Unity's incessant go-betweening. She said, 'I'd met her at the Laroche tea-parties. One had an inspection, likely people were picked out. Unity was good with younger girls, and I was told I could come to tea if I liked. It was understood what was intended. One came with the thought that it might be tea at the Carlton. She took one girl at a time. Hitler sat at one corner of his sofa, in the same place. One or two of the people with him were not in uniform and had their wives. We were about ten people in a ring, balancing one's tea-cup, we talked about weather and the opera. That must have been in November or December 1936, when Hitler was at the height of his respectability after the Olympic Games.'

And, added Anthony Rhodes, I had to meet his old friend Mary who had been inseparable from Unity. Mary, it may be remembered, had cropped up in my conversation with Lady Mosley as someone lost to sight, and she was the other English girl whom Paulette Helleu had referred to. To cut short the story, by a fluke here she was. She has never had political interests or instincts, but was caught up in a situation. Living in Munich, she had married a German whom Diana and Unity used to call Das Kind, like Mrs Hammersley's 'Child', and she was made to suffer for it during the war, as may be imagined, which is why she asked me to omit her surname. She did me the immense service of allowing me to make use of those extracts from her diaries or notebooks which refer to Unity.

'Wednesday, 7th November 1934,' is the first such entry, 'Dinner Diana Guinness. 7 – Rosenberg speech.' Rosenberg was a speaker as poor as he was long-winded, and they would have needed that dinner at seven o'clock beforehand. 'Wednesday 14th November. Lunch Diana, Unity, Rosemary and Armida Macindoe at Alte Pinakothek [lunch in the cafeteria of the Munich picture gallery, in other words].'

For Armida Macindoe I had only to ask my father, who could help because he had been staying with her mother in Portugal. Armida Macindoe is now Mrs Reid, married to a colonel of the Irish Guards. She said: 'I had been sent to the Gräfin Harrach at first, where Liz Paget [Lady Elizabeth von Hofmannsthal] and Pip Scott-Ellis [Marchesa de Vilallongay] were. The older girls could do as they liked but I was about sixteen and strictly supervised. I complained and said I'd like to go to Laroche's. Mary Gerard Leigh was there already. The address was 121 Königinstrasse, right down the far end of the street on the left-hand side. We had bicycles and used to bicycle to the opera house on Sunday mornings to queue for our tickets for the week. Mary Gerard Leigh and I went to the opera four or five times a week. The Baroness was easy-going. Her favourites among her English girls had been Penelope Dudley Ward [Lady Reed, wife of Sir Carol Reed and a close friend of Tom Mitford's but who had left Laroche's in 1931], and she used to say, Pempy would never have done that. The Baroness didn't appear at breakfast. Then Fräulein Baum would come, the governess who lived out, and we went with her to town. The Baroness taught nothing. Fräulein Baum taught German, we had piano, singing, painting, in afternoon classes to which we also bicycled. Lunch and tea were with the Baroness, supper in the schoolroom. The Baroness was asleep by nine o'clock and knew nothing if we went out. Annie the maid made the beds, cooked, and waited at table. Frau Hacha, the cook, was already old then.

'I'd been there for six months when Unity arrived. She was that much older than me. I was suspicious of anyone new, I looked on her with awe, but not because I knew anything of her ideas. She turned up at Laroche's for the summer term, a bit late for the start in May, the term ending in July. She was there again for the autumn term, September to Christmas. I don't remember her having lessons like we did, she wasn't in the schoolroom. She was freelance, she floated around. If she wanted something out of the schoolroom she'd just come in and fetch it. She had her black shirt and it was taken in its stride. One was too polite to pass remarks. She was fully-fledged pro-Hitler, that's why she'd bothered to come out. The Roehm *putsch* had her up in arms, saying that Hitler might have been killed. One heard that Hitler had gone into Roehm's room and said, *Schuft, du bist verhaftet* [Wretch, you are under lock and key] which became a catchword amongst us. Unity was terribly put out, and kept speculating about what might have happened. Fräulein Baum, Bäumchen to everybody, was more pro-Hitler than anyone. She and Unity had an admiration society together. Jews were being baited. One was told by the Baroness that if one saw anything like a scrimmage, one was to hurry by and not stand and stare. Unity was very anti-Jewish anyway, being a Mosleyite. About Jews being beaten up, she used to say, Jolly good, serves them right, we should go and cheer.

'During the autumn term Diana came out and took a flat off the Ludwigstrasse, she came again early in November. I also met Putzi Hanfstaengl with Unity, he was more of a means than an end, he introduced her to Nazis. I think I got on well with her. She used to go to the Osteria Bavaria restaurant and sit waiting for Hitler. She'd sit there all day long with her book and read. She'd say, I don't want to make a fool of myself being alone there, and so she'd ask me to go along to keep her company, to have lunch or a coffee. Often Hitler was there. People came and went. She would place herself so that he invariably had to walk by her, she was drawing attention to herself, not obnoxiously but enough to make one slightly embarrassed. But the whole point was to attract his attention. She'd talk more loudly or drop a book. And it paid off.

'That summer and autumn term we sat there in the Osteria Bavaria. At last one of the henchmen was sent over, it was what she had been waiting for and praying for. It was after lunch, we'd had a cup of coffee. I must go, I said, and hurried off. She was thrilled when she came home that the object of the exercise had been achieved, and she'd been noticed.

'At Christmas I came home, though I saw Unity a little in England, she could be nice though irritating if you couldn't get her away from Nazi talk.'

Rosemary Macindoe, Armida's younger sister, said, 'In October 1934 I went to Baroness Laroche's because Armida was there. So were Yvonne O'Neill and Rachel Irby. I loathed Fräulein Baum, she looked like a witch. I never went to school and couldn't concentrate. Unity had not yet met Hitler; every Friday he lunched at the Osteria Bavaria, and she used to go in blind adoration. He came in with a raincoat, an Alsatian, and a whip in his hand, and Unity said, Don't you think his eyes are marvellous? She had a phobia about Jews, she used to make us write on letters Juden sind hier nicht erwünscht [a Stürmer slogan, 'Jews are not welcomed here', to be found posted up by some Nazi mayors of villages, shopkeepers etc.]. Unity could say quite funny things but if she'd had any sense of humour she'd have laughed at herself. I liked Diana best at that time. She and I went to a singing class in which there was a Peruvian and we laughed about him – Unity and Armida went to another class as they spoke better German. I was very young and swept off my feet by Diana's bated-breath admiration of the Leader. Unity may have been in love with Mosley too, she was always talking of the Leader. They were glad to have supporters. Diana and Unity had just been to the Nuremberg Rally. The Germans had torchlight processions all the time, Unity was at one of them in her black shirt when we'd just met. For 9 November Diana and Unity got a press card, saying they were working for the English press, so we had tickets in the crowd opposite the Denkmal. [This memorial had been erected at the Feldherrnhalle, by the Residenz, near the spot where several Nazis had been shot down by the police during the abortive putsch engineered by Hitler on 9 November 1923, which was then commemorated as a red-letter day in the Nazi calendar, preceded for old times' sake by a speech from Hitler on the evening before, in the Burgerbräukeller where he had launched this enterprise.]

'Diana used to have dinner parties in her flat and I went there quite a lot. One of the SS men who used to come said he was a doctor in a children's hospital. I was frightfully innocent, and when he took us round it proved to be a hospital for venereal diseases. His name was Dr Bartel. There were three SS men in particular, Max was the first name of another of them, a curly-blond SS man whom we saw in the Brown House. [In her photograph album are snapshots: Diana in a tweed skirt and blouse, reading, with an old military print on the wall behind; Diana and Unity at the dining room table, with flowers on it, the lamp above draped with a beaded fringe; Diana at the upright piano, Unity standing over her. Also a sequence from the November 9th parade, of Goebbels with the sinister *Blutfahne*, the flag dipped in the blood of the dead, and of Hitler arriving with Hess.]

'They had records of the *Horst Wessel Lied*, Unity was always singing that, as well as the *Wacht am Rhein* and *Unsere Fahne*. She was always on about the Hanfstaengls too. The only other thing we did, Diana, Unity and I, was when we went out to Schleissheim [where the famous *Schloss* was at Hitler's disposal] to see army manoeuvres, or perhaps a flying show, and found we were somewhere near Dachau. There were endless jokes about it. If somebody does anything bad, they said, We'll send them to Dachau. I came home for Christmas but was out again in January 1935, with Lord Redesdale. He felt, I think, She's my daughter, what would *you* do?' And Mary's diary reads: 'Thursday January 18, 1935. Lunch Osteria, Unity, the Baroness, Rosemary, Lord Redesdale. All to Brown House to see Max. Carlton for tea with Rosemary. Lord Redesdale funny about Bobo's hair – thought she had dyed it.'

Mary Gerard Leigh is now Countess Kapnist. She was also only fifteen when she arrived at Laroche's in September 1932, staying until the autumn of 1934. She said: 'Unity wasn't a friend of Hitler's when I was there. She was always nagging Baum about how to meet him, and Baum also used to go with her to the Osteria Bavaria. Unity was alarming to be with, it was a small house and she made herself felt in it. When Lady Redesdale came round with Diana, and with Jessica who was out there in September, they could hardly cram into the Baroness's little *salon*. I have a firm memory of the *Oktoberfest*, with the daughters all losing their mothers in the public gardens on purpose. Unity slept next door to me, and I could hear her talking in her sleep. She'd suddenly scream out, and I complained to the Baroness about it, as well as about the portraits of Hitler all over her room, which she'd salute. She used to bring SA or SS men back and ask them to spend the night, but probably there was no sex in it. The maid was shocked, and the Baroness would speak with horror of it. Unity wore these scarves round herself. I remember thinking she was a bit mad.'

Two further vignettes of Unity on the eve of her break-through to Hitler are from contemporaries who were studying in Munich to more purpose. Tim Martin was learning German in order to qualify for the Foreign Office, and he says, 'Late in 1934 my mother came out to visit me, and shared a sleeper with Diana. Early in 1935 we were invited to lunch with her, on a hideous day of pouring rain. At the top of the lift stood these two great blondes, obviously stunning, who took our mackintoshes. One of them said,

I've met the most marvellous storm. Really, what was that? My dear, a storm-trooper. That was Unity. Then at lunch when my mother was explaining I'd just left Winchester, Diana asked, Did you know Ozzie Mozzie? He's years older than me, I said, and he was the biggest worm who ever went through the school. The blood rushed into Diana's face, Unity tittered, and I was speechless.'

Derek Hill, subsequently well known as a painter, was a seventeen-year-old student of stage design at the Munich Lehrwerkstätte, from the autumn of 1933 for some twelve months before going on to Vienna, and then China and Japan. He says: 'Chris Bailey used to take me from school at Marlborough to lunch with Pam at Biddesden. Going to Munich I had a letter from Pam with Unity's address. She was older than me but hardly seemed it, we were children really. We telephoned in the mornings, I must have seen her every week or so. I best remember picnics in the hills, going with her to Wies for the baroque church, and to Rohr and Weltenburg on the Danube. We went together to see the Valhalla, an enormous monument to the spirit of Germany somewhere in the direction of Weltenburg. Just like university students, we would chug about by train, or bus. Sometimes there was a car for these trips. Bobo and all of us once went for a weekend on the Starn-bergersee, there was some family we stayed with, not the famous Haus Hirt where people like Benjamin Britten and Peter Pears used to be. When Muv and Decca came out to Munich, there were evenings in their *pension*. The Café Heck played a great part in our lives because of its marvellous chocolate cakes with *Schlagobers* [whipped cream], she used to love them and sigh *Noch ein Pfund* [another pound, in pidgin German] as she ate them. She wasn't sexy and I should be surprised if she got up to anything. References to Max or others in her letters are probably a tease. Although she talked a lot about it, I never went to any meetings with her. She thought exactly what she was supposed to think, she scribbled *Schwein* over photographs of Roehm in her album. She used to try to steer me through the city so that we could pass the Dankmal on the Feldherrnhalle, for us to salute it. I refused. I was a con-scientious objector. Lady Redesdale also refused to salute it, so as punish-ment Unity used to lose her and leave her to find her own way back to the *pension*.'

The Brown House, fronting the Briennerstrasse, was the headquarters of the Nazi movement, a showcase example of pseudo-classical pomposity, ornate with bronze eagles, flags and such-like heraldry. Access to it, to Dr Bartel and Max and others, was through Dr Ernst Hanfstaengl, Putzi for short, whose name cannot be thrown into the narrative without more ado, though he will be found speaking for himself in due course. His memoirs, *Zwischen*

Weissen und Braunen Haus, which is more thorough and accurate than its earlier English version *The Missing Years*, describe his efforts to make Hitler more socially presentable, *salonfähig* as Germans say; also how after the abortive *putsch* of 1923 Hitler had sheltered in the Hanfstaengl house at Uffing, where Erna, a year older than her brother Putzi, had caught his eye. Harvard-educated, proud of his place in the world and of his talents, well off thanks to the family firm of art publishers, Putzi looked a gentleman, and was a firecracker, unstable, larger than life, of another stamp to the dulled gangsters in Hitler's immediate entourage. His office was upstairs in the Brown House, after its completion in 1931. He was entrusted with foreign press relations. For one thing, he had travelled abroad. He had met Diana and Unity in London; he had indeed met everybody worth meeting in London. At the Nuremberg Party Rally of 1934, the Year of Power, as it was christened, alternatively the Year of Unity (a coincidence which was made much of), Unity and Diana had a letter of recommendation to Putzi from Prince Otto von Bismarck, secretary in the German Embassy in London. Unity just squeezed the rally in before the autumn term at Laroche's. 'They were very attractive,' Hanfstaengl goes on in *The Missing Years*, 'but made-up to the eyebrows in a manner which conflicted directly with the newly pro- claimed Nazi ideal of German womanhood. Their set purpose was to meet Hitler, and on the way to the Deutscher Hof Hotel, where he was staying, there were so many frank comments from passers-by that I had to duck behind a building with them. I picked out my large, clean handkerchief and said, "My dears, it is no good, but to stand any hope of meeting him you will have to wipe some of that stuff off your faces," which they did ... Goering and Goebbels expressed mock horror at the idea of my trying to present such painted hussies to Hitler,' and the girls had to make do with the rally, and the mere vision of the loved one from afar. (Incidentally, photo- graphs of Diana at the 1934 Rally, with a black beret on the back of her head, and an unusual puddingy blankness of face, have been published several times, but mistakenly identified as Unity, notably in Nerin E. Gun's *Eva Braun* and Fritz Wiedemann's memoirs.) Pretty women were acceptable to Putzi, and there is pique in his remark that when the girls 'paid the proper respects to the Hess and Rosenberg cliques, they were, of course, welcomed as out- standing Nordic beauties. I am afraid they listened to my opponents in the party far more than they did to me, although I subsequently saw quite a lot of Unity in Munich, and even helped her to find the little villa near the English Garden where she rented an apartment.' In the German version, this reads more truthfully, for Streicher has been given the place of Hess, and the clause about the villa has been altogether omitted. Well before Unity had this flat, she had helped to bring about Putzi's precipitous flight from Germany.

English propagandists for Hitler consisted of those who for psychological reasons favoured authoritarianism, or of scared conservatives, anti-communists for the most part, who claimed Hitler as their crusader. A serviceable specimen of the latter was Colonel (later Sir Thomas) Moore, MP, whose self-bolstering line was accepted by more people than cared to admit it. In the Daily Mail on 25 April 1934, his first proposition was, 'surely there cannot be any fundamental differences of outlook between Blackshirts and their parents, the Conservatives.' By 15 August, in The Times, he had improved it: 'Rarely do we read ... anything of the social, educational or even moral achievements of the Hitler administration.' Housing, maternity clinics, the purging of dens of vice, were a generation ahead of the rest of the world. 'Hitler may have been guilty, either personally or through his followers, of what may seem to us, without lack of knowledge, crimes against his own people, but they are his own people, and he is responsible to them, not to us.' A lot could be slipped under that kind of a carpet, the Roehm purge, for instance. Dachau had been opened in 1933, and Buchenwald, and what price had to be paid for them in terms, say, of social welfare? Here was that argument of Mosley's, still maintained, that a German quarrel was nobody else's business. Not only was this morally repulsive, but politically ridiculous, for if the Germans were prepared to treat with total violence their so-called enemies of the state, whether Jews or not, then their foreign enemies could confidently expect worse, as proved the case.

Dietrich Aigner, the German historian, is of the opinion that 'when Mosley in 1934 turned to anti-semitism without a racial stamp, this happened more under the influence of the German example than under German propaganda'. That autumn, Mosley, to quote a BUF account, 'amid scenes of tumultuous enthusiasm took up the challenge flung at his movement by Jewry'. Unity was a German-inspired anti-semite of this Mosley stamp. When anti-semitism, among other Nazi flies, was cast over her, she swallowed it hook, line and sinker. The Blackshirt doctrine confirmed her parent conservatism, which included the anti-semitism of her background too. German mystique, German example, defiled her. She became the ne plus ultra case of the person who could excuse whatever Hitler did on the grounds that it was by definition the proper thing to do. Colonel Moore spoke for those in all classes, be it said, who had been shaken by the calamity and changes of the First World War, and who instinctively felt that the Germans at least were telling their people what to do, and that they had better submit and get on with it, as everybody would if they knew what was good for them. Unity differed from Colonel Moore only in that she acted out these simple convictions where she could be seen doing so. What the Nazis put into her mind came out in her behaviour with the undeviating logic of fanaticism.

Hitler was her one true purpose, and such an *idée fixe* may be thought to reveal the fearful void carried over from Swinbrook. Yet the English upper-class presumption of getting one's way by hook or crook did the trick. She was not to be put off, where others would have admitted their limitations. Women by the thousand abased themselves at Hitler's feet, they tried to kiss his boots, and some of them succeeded, even to the point of swallowing the gravel on which he had trod, according to Reck-Malleczewen, whose fastidious hatred of the vulgarian Hitler was genuinely conservative. As a figurehead, as a male in absolute power, Hitler's aphrodisiac effect was scarcely even sublimated in the more impressionable women who constituted his beloved mass audience. They moaned, they were hysterical, they fainted, for an intro-spective bachelor deficient in sexuality. They could obey, but not approach, and if that was the main sexual charge then Unity certainly shared it, unable to control herself. In Unity's knapsack was a lady's baton placed there by Nanny Blor, but to avoid being non-U was only manners; she had been able to profit by sitting day after obsessive day in the Osteria Bavaria, in a lady's version of a prostitute, waiting for the pick-up. In one respect Hitler was a final item in an intimate treasure-hunt, the object which could never be brought home, and in another respect he was a historical Big Daddy, patting the heads of blonde children. Restraint was impossible, in the frustration of apparently approaching the unapproachable; this was, so to speak, a mastur-bation of the spirit. She had herself to display.

Fräulein Baum, guiding-light, cheer-leader, was a Nazi Steegson, the only governess ever to have influenced Unity. To begin with, they were a fan club of two, Osteria squatters, co-conspirators to gain access to the Führer. Schoolroom stories proliferate about what went wrong, and these centre on the question whether Bäumchen was in fact Jewish, and covering up by pretending to be Nazi; and further, whether she was then denounced by Unity, or alternatively denounced her. In order to place Bäumchen in her setting (she died in the 1950s, having survived the war in Germany, as conclusive a piece of evidence as any against her supposed Jewishness), Munich must be understood as a rival Grand Tour resort to Paris, Salzburg or Florence, where the deficiencies of private English education were remedied, and country-house daughters could acquire the veneer of cosmopolitan culture. The exchange rate assisted, for those who cashed pounds into rentenmarks, then register-marks, were well off, while at the receiving end the *ci-devant* aristocracy, especially in Bavaria, had been squeezed to ruin by the post-1918 cycle of revolution, inflation, Depression and Nazism. One last-ditch defence was to open the family house to paying guests or boarders, especially sterling-funded girls whose parents were more often than not old acquaintances from better days, thus keeping up a house-party front. Countess Rex, Countess Mallortie, Countess Harrach, the Pappenheims, Anna Montgelas, Count Podevil, the Mirbachs, were staging-posts beside Baroness Laroche's. Their sons or relations, Ernst-Georg Mallortie, Guy and Karl-Erdmann Donnersmarck, Pipo Thurn and Taxis, Ruli Jank, were suitable escorts to the opera, to the Starnbergersee in summer, or skiing at Garmisch in winter. Young men came out from London, like Anthony Rhodes and Tim Martin as we have seen, but also Ulick Browne, Rory Cameron the writer, Tony Pawson, Michael Pitt-Rivers, Lord Dudley, all of them being prepared to make their mark no less than the girls. Many of them were independently rich, on allowances, owners of cars, carefree and heart-free, which obliged the countesses to rein in their charges, and the tennis parties, the expeditions, the picnics with the girls in local costume and the men in *lederhosen* were innocently decorous. The old Munich ladies, with exceptions, were disdainful of Hitler, he was 'that man' to them, but dangerous of course, and within the bounds of prudence they carried on as if he were not there. The Nazis let well alone, but they did realize the potential asset of so many well-connected young English people in their midst. If first impressions of Germany were favourable, and stuck, then their return home was likely to filter youthful Nazism through the English upper classes. Suitably formal occasions, such as the laying of the foundation stone of the Haus der deutschen Kunst in 1937 by Hitler (who broke the silver hammer as he did so, his superstitions erupting at once) were attended by massed rows of chic English girls. Unity was present when the silver hammer snapped; she cast herself into whatever Nazi reception or ceremony there was, the captive slave perpetually bound to the wheel. Governesses like Fräulein Baum would come into their own on an outing of this sort, herding the girls by tram, the factotum who did what the countesses would hardly consider, and with good grace too.

Originally Eva Maria Baum had been found by Countess Harrach, to give lessons to Mary St Clair Erskine, Hamish's sister (who herself was taken by Unity and Diana to meet Hitler in the Brown House, only to find that he was too busy to talk to them that afternoon). Countess Harrach's daughter Mechtild, otherwise called Cucca, who was in touch with Fräulein Baum for forty years, including throughout the war in Munich, has told me that she came from Silesia and definitely was not Jewish. Only some of the English girls seemed to think she was, and they judged by the standards of the time, on the poor woman's appearance. One of her favourite pupils was Mrs John Weaver, then Ursula Horlick, and she says: 'She was always talking about Hitler but on other subjects she was an inspired teacher. At weekends she'd take us to Nuremberg or to baroque churches. She was receptive to any willingness to learn. Her English was fluent but with archaic idioms. Her young man had been English, and he was assumed to have been killed in the war. She looked like a dachshund and referred to herself as "the *dachl*", with bright blue eyes very unexpected in that face. A high forehead, pale skin, thin nose, a small mouth which went sideways. She had dark hair cut short and in constant need of washing. She was thin on slightly bandy legs, with a large behind. Her hands were well kept, the cuticles cut, and she had a way of holding them up as a dog might with its paws. Returning to Munich in 1938, I was aghast at her, I would make her pass the Denkmal to do one salute after another, and while I was laughing a man fell off his bicycle heiling, which I thought funny, but she didn't. She was obsessed by Jews, fanatically Jew-conscious. My sister and I had been skiing and she said to us that because we were thirsty afterwards we must be Jews.'

Even the most self-hating of Jews would not have gone to such preposterous lengths as that remark. Nor at that stage did Jewishness have to be so despairingly concealed, and emigration was possible still. In any case, if Unity did denounce her in 1934 or 1935, Bäumchen was soon back at the old work. Mary's diary gives Bäumchen's address as Kaulbachstrasse 87, Flat 3 (Unity's telephone number, 32375, is there too), and under Wednesday 16 January 1935, is this entry: 'Lunch Osteria Unity and Lord Redesdale. A girl from Kenilworth (?) Arranged German lessons with Fräulein Baum – 3 marks – begin Monday. Unity was going to some SS thing.' 22 January carries on, 'Started lessons with Bäumchen – every day.' 29 January: 'We (Unity and I) helped Bäumchen teach English to a class of unemployed people.' 11 February: 'Bäumchen gone to Berlin to chaperone Penelope Dudley Ward.' Monday, 18 February: 'Bäumchen outburst.'

From that February on, Bäumchen fades out of Unity's life. A row certainly had split them. Unity is supposed to have denounced Bäumchen's Jewish secret, and to have spilled it to the Brown House (an act of which she would have been capable). Bäumchen was also doing the rounds of certain streets collecting for *Winterhilfe*, the Nazi charity, which Unity claimed was a pretext for some Jewish work or spying. In the reverse of this, Bäumchen is said to have denounced Unity as an English spy to the Brown House, which may be dismissed straightaway, for Putzi Hanfstaengl would without doubt have been brought in on the act, and he was not. More probably, gossip was blown up into the contemporary drama of denunciation, a very real threat to be feared. To pin a denunciation on to Unity is a plausible way of registering disgust at her behaviour, but not necessarily true for all that. (Another current charge against her, much repeated, is that she denounced Hamish St Clair Erskine's German governess for writing a letter complaining of the Nazis. Unity is alleged to have passed the woman's address to the Gestapo, who arrested her and put her in a camp. Hamish's sister Mary, however, disposes of this, because she says that they never had a German governess in the family.)

Jealousy of Unity is the probable reason for Bäumchen's outburst on 18 February. For Bäumchen was nurturing an ambition never to be fulfilled, while Unity, an intruder, had cut in on her, so to speak, on the inside track. On Monday 28 January, Mary notes, 'Hitler lunching Osteria – came and spoke to a woman at our table. He was also in Carlton at tea-time.' How tantalizing it must have been for Unity that another woman at her very table was singled out, especially as by then, according to Armida Macindoe, Hitler had bothered to inquire who she was.

She had not much longer to wait for her quarry. 9 February was a Saturday and Mary spent that weekend in the mountains, returning to hear the news. 'Hitler sent for Unity on Saturday and she had lunch at his table – thrilled to death, of course.' Then 18 February: 'Having tea Carlton – Hitler came and sent Brückner over to ask us to join them – Werlin, Mercedes man, and pressman Dietrich – nobody else.' Brückner, a Nazi from the very first, was more of a bodyguard than an adjutant. Werlin, director-general of Mercedes-Benz, had a spirited Hungarian wife, and a flat in Munich, and as a tycoon who depended on Nazi patronage, took the precaution of being friendly to everybody, Unity included. Dr Otto Dietrich, controller of press and publicity, and after Hanfstaengl's downfall in charge of foreign correspondents too, wrote *The Hitler I Knew*, one of the more thoughtful and informative of post-war Nazi autobiographies. In it he had this passage, 'At the same table in the Osteria Bavaria Hitler made the acquaintance of the Englishwoman Unity Mitford ... an enthusiastic follower of the British fascist leader Sir Oswald Mosley and a fervent admirer of Hitler. She had many private conversations about Anglo-German relations with Hitler, whose secret itineraries she usually guessed with great acuteness. Over the years Hitler frequently included her among the guests who accompanied him on his travels. She introduced Hitler to her father and her brother, when the two were passing through Munich ...'

·   ·   ·   ·   ·

Of all the Osteria Bavaria circle of Hitler's intimates, only Albert Speer survives. Then he was the young architect chosen to petrify Hitler's fantasies into thousand-year stone, but in the war he was promoted to be Minister of Armaments, for which he was sentenced at the Nuremberg trials to twenty years' imprisonment. When I went to see him, it was raining, and water lapped on a sodden drive and dripped off overgrown thickets. The house was shadowy, heavily furnished. Speer is a handsome man, and in his face is a residual toughness as of a tree which has been struck by lightning but survives the scar. 'I met her in the Osteria Bavaria. She was very romantic,' were his opening words about Unity. 'The Osteria was a small inn, it is still there, and hasn't changed much. Small tables. There was a wooden partition, and behind it a table to seat eight. An adjutant would phone the owner to warn that Hitler might be coming and to have the table clear. There was also a courtyard, with one table under a pergola and this was Hitler's favourite seat when the weather was not cold. Unity was quite often there, I was invited only every second or third time. Like me, Mitford [as he calls her] would be invited by the adjutant Schaub. She was highly in love with Hitler, we could see it easily, her face brightened up, her eyes gleaming, staring at Hitler. Hero-worship. Absolutely phenomenal. And possibly Hitler liked to be admired by a young woman, she was quite attractive – even if nothing happened he was excited by the possibility of a love affair with her. Towards an attractive woman he behaved as a seventeen-year-old would. She was influential with Hitler in that she was of the group in the Osteria.

'For those close to Hitler it was a nuisance. Schaub was angry that she was coming again. It was amazing that someone not German was around Hitler and could listen to details of party politics and far-ranging policy. Hitler made no secret of his thoughts, and astonishingly a Britisher was sitting there and listening. I heard only afterwards that she was a follower of Mosley. Hitler thought nothing of Mosley. I had the impression that she was British, you know, in this circle. The others round Hitler were cautious and did not want to say anything, but she was straight and said things Hitler didn't like. She had cheek. Hitler's line was to get along with the British. She pressed the point. He was sympathetic. They would argue and he appreciated frankness in her – he said, That's the British way. Though I wouldn't say his interest in her was from the political point of view; simply part of his admiration for the British was confirmed by her. If somebody made a remark, and then Hitler replied, No, well, that person did not counter, but she did, back and forth. I was astonished that Hitler did not say that he had no wish to see her again. Of course it was dangerous to have somebody talking to Hitler like that about problems, he was easily influenced by small episodes, so if Mitford brought something to his attention, he could get furious about it and a huge effort would be required to settle things.

'She saw in Germany only what she wanted to see, but she spoke to him about that, Bavaria and the Bavarians, opera and singers, the usual gossip. He wanted light relief. Her German was good enough to make herself understood. She was never bored and never boring. Her features were those of a woman with some intelligence, thinking in her own way, not the type of Eva Braun who had no serious interests.

'I never heard she was a spy. Somebody so close to Hitler must have been checked. Hitler's outspokenness was calculated, talking secrets knowing that rumours would spread. For instance the treaty with the Russians, I was with him often just beforehand, and knew nothing until it was signed and sealed. The Osteria circle was Hoffmann [the photographer], Wagner [Gauleiter of Munich], Bormann, Schaub, Dietrich, Morell [the doctor], Dr Brandt [another physician], Brückner. Streicher did not come there, even to us he was a shock, he exaggerated his bad side, he was fond of women and maybe there was an attraction there. Wagner was crude too, but had a higher intellectual level. Mitford never spoke about Jews that I can recall, it would have been quite normal if she had.

'I was often at the Berghof – at Berchtesgaden – but she was not there much as a guest, if at all. I would have known if she had been regularly. I could go without a phone call from the adjutant. She had to be invited. In the Berghof there was the snag of Eva Braun, who would have been angry, in a bad mood. She was at Bayreuth though. I remember driving along the autobahn from Berlin to Munich. She was sitting there on a steep embankment, looking very romantic over the Franconian landscape. I stopped and chatted. She was very sentimental. This must have been 1937 or 1938, she came that year to Bayreuth, but not with Hitler. She had strolled out from the festival and could go no farther because of the autobahn, so had sat down. She must have recognized my car, a racing Mercedes with a long hood, for she waved at me, which is how I recognized her.

'It was a shock to Hitler when she shot herself. He felt responsible for her committing suicide, I remember that was his reaction. About a year or so later she had been forgotten. People who were no longer in his view were quickly forgotten. That happened when I was sick, for instance. She got a bouquet with handwriting in hospital. I got one with a printed card.'

Speer concluded, 'I'm not surprised that her comments on Hitler were so limited, that she could say only how wonderful he was. I often saw people go in for an appointment in a sceptical frame of mind, only to emerge saying how wonderful he was. That was his fascination which nobody can explain. She would have slept with him, of course, she was more than willing but he would not have gone to bed with her. I doubt if he ever did more than take her hand in his. And think too, that he was in a difficult position, even if he had ever found himself alone with her.'

7

STORM-TROOP MAIDEN

After Christmas holidays at Swinbrook, Lord Redesdale had accompanied Unity back to Munich to discuss her plans, which was why he had invited Baroness Laroche out to lunch on 18 January, as we saw. Unity had outgrown Laroche's, impervious to even its minimal supervision. A full-time Hitlerite, as she had grown into being, would normally have been catered for by the party. In her foot-loose way, Unity had pulled down about herself a totalitarian system in which she had no place, an absurd contradiction she was never able to resolve, and therefore she was always to remain marginal, an exhibitionist and nothing else. The Brown House, or the Nazi press and publishing concerns reserved the usual niches for the usual fellow-travellers (whose opposite numbers in Moscow were similarly garnered in) but Unity seems never to have considered the humdrum course of working for the cause. She remained independently in Germany because she put her foot down to her parents, and they gave in, as ever. Before doing so, however, they turned to the Embassy. Sir Eric Phipps had taken up his post in Berlin in September 1933, and lost no time sizing up the Nazis. His caustic despatches shine. Lady Phipps was paid the compliment of being nicknamed 'die heilige Betschwester', or 'sob-sister', by Hitler.

Lady Phipps said, 'The Redesdales were distraught parents who came out in the winter of 1934–5. They'd been in Munich, they couldn't bear the idea of Unity having bolted. They stayed at the Adlon, which was next to the embassy in the Wilhelmstrasse. I don't remember whether we'd already had Unity to lunch or not – these sloppy English girls were always having affairs with dreadful SS types, and Eric had the trouble of clearing it up. If you were at all snobbish you asked the ambassador for help. Anyhow Unity came as a Deutsches Mädchen battleship of a woman, walking upstairs into the drawing room, and gave a Nazi salute. Eric was a small man, he stood on tiptoe and reached up to shake her hand which made it a bit ridiculous. Eric refused to let it influence the lunch party. She wanted urgently to talk about it all, she made it sound incredible, her story of sitting next to his table, determined to meet him. It was unlikely to work, Hitler was prudish, afraid of girls. I remember her telling me that her favourite among Nazis was Streicher. She brushed aside my protests, and said Jews were traitors. Her own wish was to think like that. It was all invention, she knew no Jews, it was her heart that ruled. The Redesdales were very concerned, they were nice but quite outside anything that was actually happening. With Hitler I got on rather easily. I sat next to him at a New Year banquet with the whole diplomatic corps. He was affably trying a few words of English saying Young lady, young English lady, Freeman, honourable lady, charming lady. Then I realized it was Unity Freeman-Mitford he was talking about.'

On leaving Laroche's, Unity's precise movements are problematical. Erna Hanfstaengl remembers her coming to stay with her for the first time in February, and this would not have been before the introduction to her brother Putzi from Prince Bismarck in the summer of 1934. A clue lies in Mary's diary: 'Thursday February 7th, 1935. Tea Regina [Hotel] Unity and Erna Hanfstaengl.'

Solln, where Erna Hanfstaengl then lived in a comfortable wooden house built at the turn of the century, was a fashionable outlying district of Munich, spacious but inconveniently far from the centre for someone like Unity. Nevertheless Erna was to offer her a home-base there, and Unity was to take advantage of it on and off until June 1939, when Hitler put a stop to their friendship once and for all. Erna Hanfstaengl was always watchful and circumstantial, aware that Hitler and the regime had to be handled with utmost tact, and though Unity liked to shock and alarm her, mobbing up a *grande dame* once more, she seems to have been reassured by the goodwill of someone much older. Erna was already fifty, with experience of administration in the family business, and inviolate personally through her fortuitous help to Hitler in a bad hour. Hers was one of the names journalists concocted into Hitler's romances. Unity may have envied the association, or admired it, or perhaps have been seeking a substitute for Lady Redesdale (which is what Erna thinks herself). In the event she was a guest welcomed at Solln whenever she wanted from early 1935 onwards, and living free off the fat of the land, always a consideration of hers.

On 1 October 1934, Mary had moved into the Munich university hostel for girls, the Studentinnenheim, or Marie Antonie Haus, on the Kaulbachstrasse, and for most of the year Unity lodged there too. From that date, what is more, run a series of photographs in Mary's album. Diana's stay in the Studentinnenheim is recorded as 'Summer 1935' and her great beauty is oddly in contrast to the simple cupboard, wash-basin and bed of the hostel room. The following page in the album has an elderly woman with a placard 'Jesus is Our King', unmolested at first, then being bundled away by SA men, to the caption 'One Form of Opposition'. The 1935 Party Rally photographs are of Tom Mitford, languid, pipe in mouth, of Putzi Hanfstaengl and Diana together, of Leni Riefenstahl, and a group of Unity, Diana, German friends including two helmeted airmen, and Michael Burn.

As for Unity, she is to be seen herself, coyly standing on the hostel's spacious terrace (in the diary: 'May 4th. Sunbathed all day with Unity on terrace'.) or in a series of poses with Diana. Another sequence is of her in a blue and white dress with Brian Howard, party-going at Fasching, the Lent carnival of 1935, his collar undone with an air of night-club distraction, lugubriously clownish. On 6 May 1935, the Silver Jubilee of George v was celebrated by the English colony of Munich in the Hotel Bayerischet Hof. To the printed programme bound in patriotic colours, with royal portraits, Mary had attached photographs of herself and Unity at the dinner, escorted by three young men in evening clothes, chinless wonders in stick-up collars, none of them identifiable. And in the Studentinnenheim, the *Sunday Express* correspondent, Sefton Delmer probably, caught her for an interview published on 26 May, with a little-girl photograph of her in an open-neck dress with a frilly collar. '. . . she is probably the only foreign woman in Germany to enjoy Hitler's acquaintance. Twenty years old, pretty, with shining blue eyes and flaxen hair, she seemed when I met her in Munich to embody the Hitler ideal of a Nordic woman. Her eyes lit with enthusiasm as she spoke to me of Hitler. "The hours I have spent in his company," she said, "are some of the most impressive in my life. The entire German nation is lucky to have such a great personality at its head. I should like to remain in Germany, because I like the Germans very much, but my parents will not allow it." As I left her in the students' home in which she has lived for the past year, she raised her arm in the Nazi salute and cried "Heil Hitler!"'

The Studentinnenheim period closed on 21 October 1935, on which day Mary moved again, into a room at the Pension Doering in the Ludwigstrasse, which runs parallel to the Kaulbachstrasse. Unity came too. Like the Studentin-nenheim, this building survives, almost alongside the Siegestor, or Arc de Triomphe, one of the grandiloquent monuments which give Munich its peculiar graveyard pall. The owner of the Pension Doering was Herr Heil-bronn, and as a Jew his property was confiscated, the title deeds being deftly transferred to himself by the leading Nazi lawyer who had the job of plundering for the Reich. Herr Heilbronn spent the war in America, the building was then restituted, and has been converted into offices for the science faculties of the university.

Mary said: 'In Berlin in 1933 I was staying with a cousin of Schleicher's. I met Roehm at a cocktail party through Mason-Macfarlane, the military attaché, and I was in Berlin during the Roehm purge [during which General von Schleicher, former chancellor, was among the murdered]. After a summer in the Harz mountains I went to Munich, for the university autumn term. Unlike Unity, I was a genuine student, doing a doctorate in linguistics. The Studentinnenheim was cheap, 60 marks a month. There was a cafeteria with a plat du jour, with meat for one mark, without meat sixty pfennig. I had a bit of money from my parents. Unity received an allowance of £100 a year, which were changed into register marks at twenty to the pound. I can't imagine how we all met or how we were all in the Studentinnenheim. She was the first intelligent person I'd met, such fun. The whole idea was to annoy one's parents, épater la bourgeoisie. One was so completely ignorant coming from my background, it was deadly. My father had been an agricultural engineer who sold ploughs but I had a guardian as both my parents were dead.

'Bobo told me about being sacked from school, she was unhappy about it, the school had been her one effort to conform. She had this thing about being different from everybody else. She used to go two or three times a week to Frau Bermann, a marvellous teacher of German. Tony Rhodes was there, and Peter Scott. We loved her. She'd been married to quite a well-known sculptor, but had an illness which left her paralysed from the waist down. She had tremendous guts, became a teacher, and you never saw her except sitting at a table, her top beautifully dressed. Very dark, in a rather Slav way, with sallow skin, absolutely à la page about the latest books and plays. She had a thing about Egypt and about cats, she kept a strange and terrifying cat which was always crouching on a cupboard, glaring. Her room was always full of flowers and her balcony a garden. [Frau Bermann lived in the Bismarckstrasse, and unlike Bäumchen was Jewish, and died of her wasting disease, 'just in time,' as one of her friends put it to me. Unity took no more lessons from her after 1935, as by then her German was roadworthy.]

'In the Studentinnenheim an American girl, Thora, lived upstairs, and one evening there was a terrific banging which finally got on our nerves. She was in love with a Bulgarian, we called him Brüderlein, she'd come to Munich for a thesis on Rilke. She married an Italian consul in Los Angeles, it didn't work out, but she got her Bulgarian after the war. She was another Romantic, as we all were. Anyhow the noise was her tap-dancing, we couldn't get over that. Bobo's room was either right above or below mine, we used to throw Knallerbsen, like little stink-bombs, to wake one another up, they'd hit the stone wall as we leant out of the windows, exploding with a shattering noise on impact. We used to do this in the street behind all sorts of worthy people. Lunching in the Osteria with Bobo I once had a handbag full of Knallerbsen and dropped it, with sensational effect as they all went off together. Hitler was at his table, and the SS reached for their guns.

'We always went there for lunch, it was cheap. Herr Deutelmoser, the owner, we called Domodossola, a sweet gentle old bachelor. Bobo, like everybody, loved him. The two waitresses, Fräulein Rosa and Fräulein Ella, had been there for years and years. My husband's parents belonged to a club of painters and artists, the Klub des Lebenskunstlers, whose head-quarters were there, so they had their *Stammtisch* and came every day. One of the young waitresses in the Osteria got engaged, and Hitler gave a wedding reception for her in Berlin. You've served me for so long, he said, now I'll serve you. And at a wedding party there, Hitler invited the bride and bride-groom over, the bride was too moved to be able to speak, she wept floods.

'Bobo was the one friend I had in Munich. She didn't give a damn about anything. The Hitler girls would shout at us in the street, *Schöne rote Lippen* or *Schöne gemaltes Bild* [Fine red lips! What a picture you are!], I would go out of my way to avoid them, but she didn't. English people came and went. Brian Howard was there a lot. [Mary's diary records many meals in 1935 with him and his mother. *Portrait of a Failure*, Marie-Jacqueline Lancaster's book about him, has an amusing story of a dilettante quarrel between them over Nazism, with Unity rounding it off, 'Just for that, Brian, I won't introduce you to the Führer!' A legend also floats around that one of the getaways which punc-tuated his affairs was arranged by Unity dressing him up as a woman, and, who knows, this is true to the spirit of them both, so it may even be to the letter.] Someone had an old Morris full of holes and I remember driving in it to Vienna with Bobo and Brian in the middle of the Ethiopian campaign. A big car passed us and we all jumped up and shouted, Viva Ethiopia! Tom Mitford came to Munich, so did Nancy with Prod [P. Rodd was easily shortened], Ward Price was around. Iris Mountbatten, too, she was a great friend of Bobo's, she used to throw a shoe at the maid when she woke her up in the morning. Putzi was around, and Bobo kept popping off to Erna's. There were all kinds of SS men, she liked to joke about Max as "my adju-tant", he was a null, nothing. She went out with Fritz Stadelmann, one of Hitler's junior adjutants, who wore glasses. Such men were handy to her, she liked the reflected glory.

'She was totally indifferent to others. All failures, people who hadn't passed whatever test it might be, assorted wets, were known as Poors. I was always taking things along in case it rained or was hot or whatever, and they used to tease me, You never know, they would say, that was a joke never allowed to fail. Most of my girlfriends loathed her. She wasn't a happy person. Not at all. She needed company. She always sought you out, but never gave a clue to her feelings. I asked Farve to buy me tennis rackets in England, and he did, but although Bobo spoke about her parents a good deal, her relationship with them was an armed truce. She was very cold, she had never known any love. I was not a bit suprised she killed herself.

'Moving out of the Studentinnenheim, I went to Louise and Caroline, the Baronesses Geuder zu Rabenstein, in a flat in the Kaulbachstrasse. Sisters, they were in their forties, their family castle near Nuremberg had been painted by Dürer. They went to the Gentlewomen's Aid and received food parcels, they had some small pension to live off otherwise. Caroline did *schaffende Arbeit*, in other words she made lampshades to sell to her richer friends. Louise was rabidly anti-Nazi. Their old mother still went walking down the Ludwigstrasse with her maid five yards behind. The sisters each had one impeccable suit made free of charge by the family tailor so they could go out to lunch or a cocktail, though not dine out. Actually Caroline lived in the Pension Doering, she was coquettish, her room was filled with pink cushions and had a portrait of an ancestor, a *Hofdame* at Frederick the Great's court. Some *Hauptmann* was her lover, and she was having an affair with a vet, *Meine letzte Liebe*, she sighed. She had a Belgian bulldog, I had a setter called Borries, and Bobo had Rebell, a black Great Dane, as well as her white rats. I once took a couple of them back to England for her in my pocket. Bobo adored Caroline because she was so game, never complaining about being ruined.

'My room was next to Caroline's at the end of a long corridor. The *pension* was on two floors, and became like home to us. I can't remember Bobo's room at all, except that she used Floris Red Rose bath essence and stank the house out. There was only one bathroom, and I used to sing in the bath, the maid thought my voice was lovely – she was Käthl, the *putzfrau*, we called her Kettle. Tom Mitford said he was going to push her out of the window because she had such fat legs and wore woolly knickers. When Chamberlain was in Munich for the agreement, she said, *Das ist ein Gentleman*. Fräulein Becker managed the *pension*, a big handsome woman from a family of hotel-keepers in Wiesbaden. On Saturdays we used to have *Streuselkuchen*, a kind of marzipan cake. Bobo got so fat in 1935 and 1936, she minded her size, she ate too much. She loved truffles and was greedy. Of course nobody could compete with Diana, for charm and looks. Ribbentrop had a shine on Diana, and I remember her walking round the *pension* calling him up: she was terribly rich and rented a proper apartment. Diana was the one my husband, *Das Kind*, preferred.

'Bobo had said, If I appear often enough Hitler will get to know me by sight. I used to go to keep her company. She knew where he was going, either because it was public knowledge or because her SS "adjutants" told her. So in the Carlton Tea Rooms [18 February] Brückner had come over and said, The Fuhrer invites you to his table, and over we went. We'd seen Hitler almost every day. That was the first time I'd got my setter and he was being walked as Hitler was just arriving. He saw Borries and said, *Das ist ein schönes Hund.* I went over to their table too, and had tea with them, about six of us in all. Of course he had found out who she was shortly before, and perhaps he thought she had a certain influence. After that, a phone call would come to the *pension* from Brückner to say, Will you have tea with the Führer – and in case it rang, Bobo would sit by the telephone until about two o'clock, that became the pattern of her day, first the tension, then the anti-climax or the frenzy of getting ready. A car came for us. We went a lot to his flat in the Prinzregentenstrasse, it was round the corner. The curtains would be drawn, it was always dark. Lovely flowers everywhere. He ordered lots of cream cakes which he'd be disappointed if we left, but he'd eat a bit of *knackebrod*. He had a great big globe on a stand; and liked to show us any new pictures he had. He was extremely nice and kind to us, a pleasant host, I treated him as any friend one might meet. He'd talk for an hour. He wanted to discuss music, education, social services. Tell me about Lloyd George, he'd say. I can't think he was alone with Bobo, that wasn't the relationship. Some of his staff were always present. Maybe when I wasn't there, odd occasions cropped up for them to be by themselves, but I heard him say time and again, I have no time for marriage, you see how I live. Often I heard him talk about marriage in general, and he'd say, No woman could stand five minutes of this, my life I gave to Germany long ago. With Bobo he was neutral. I never detected a shadow of flirtation. We were not scared by the occasion, it was easy-going, something to boast about to friends and family. For Bobo it was the high-light of the week. Her eyes would brighten and shine.

'I never believed in the Eva Braun story at the time. Bobo and I had our film developed at Hoffmann's. I first noticed Eva Braun's shoes, beautiful Italian shoes which I knew she couldn't get in Munich. I pointed them out to Bobo. She was just a little blonde girl behind the counter, always there. Hoffmann built her a house in Bogenhausen.

'Bobo had her gold party badge from Hitler. I don't remember her saying a word of admiration for anybody except Hitler. She used the others. It was power. Her urge was to get on the posters. Decca made the posters over Spain, and Unity adored being singled out too – it was some kind of in-security. She liked Streicher because it was a sure-fire way of putting up the backs of all decent people She hated the families in Munich who took in English boarders, the *erste Gesellschaft* [upper crust] would not see her and she loved it.

'Now and then we went on trips. I was with her at the Hesselberg when she addressed the crowd. I don't remember much except being utterly exhausted, too many people, all that shouting. She was so exhilarated. We went to Berchtesgaden at weekends to stay in a hotel, and we peered through the wire gates wishing we could get in. [Diary entry: 'Sunday July 7th 1935. With Unity to Berchtesgaden to see Obersalzberg and salt mine.]

'Every year Unity went to the Bayreuth festival, and to the Parteitag. At Bayreuth, Diana and Unity and I dressed up for *Parsifal* in our best frocks, in crimson, only to find everybody else in black. We stayed in rooms in the town, and had tea with Hitler at Wahnfried, the Wagner house. Wieland and Wolfgang Wagner and their two sisters were there. 1936 was the summer when Hitler sent his Mercedes to the *pension* to drive us to Bayreuth. Speer and his wife were there, and Goebbels and his wife. In Bayreuth a message came that the Führer wanted us to return with him on his private train, so they came rushing along to pack for us, and get us on board. Thousands of people were shouting "Heil! Heil!" along the track and we didn't sleep a wink in the excitement. I remember also having dinner with Hitler during the Spanish civil war at some crisis, and Goering and Goebbels kept bursting in with urgent messages, so we sat up half the night waiting for our meal. *Das Kind* and I went to the Olympic Games but we did not see Unity.

'Another clothes disaster was at the 1936 Parteitag. We were in the middle of a craze for wearing those cotton aertex shirts which were all the rage then. We got to Nuremberg much later than we should have done, they had all gone to the opera, and there was an *Absperrung*, a road barricade, for ten miles. We were with Putzi and he got us through. In the opera the women were dressed up to the nines. We had no seats, what's more, but General Blomberg was in the front of the box and Putzi appealed to him and some other generals – we called Blomberg the Heavenly B. [Then Chief of Staff of the Wehrmacht, Blomberg was disgraced in 1938 for marrying a former prostitute.] They made way for Diana, Bobo, Tom and me. In the interval we went round to a small private room at the back to see Hitler and there we were still in our cotton shirts, and dirty old skirts as well. [A photograph in her album dates this to a performance of *Die Meistersinger*, 8 September 1936.] Janos Almasy was at that Parteitag, and Johnny Lucinge, he couldn't stand it.

'Towards the end of the thirties we saw her less. *Das Kind* had his medical finals. I was in Austria from November 1937 until April 1938. Every now and again we met. She was much more with Hitler. Hitler, I know, said to her, Where's your friend? why doesn't she come any more? So I felt guilty and sent him a token, the photograph of Borries, something like that. I was tired of it all. *Das Kind* had done a period of compulsory service in the SS which had taught him how things were. His officer had said to them, Gentlemen, it is incumbent on you to use your heads. In the very last summer before the war, the new vice-consul in Munich, Weld-Forester, gave a party, to which Bobo and I went, and we handed him our coats, mistaking him for a servant. That June, 1939, I said to her that everybody was leaving, and she answered, Well I'm not. She had asked Hitler, she said, if there was going to be a war and the answer was, It all depends on your Chamberlain. I returned to England and my mother-in-law wrote to me eventually, Your friend has shot herself in the English Garden.'

'Tuesday May 7th 1935. Lunch Osteria, Hitler, Brückner, Dietrich, Hoffmann. He gave us both his latest photograph – signed. Also a postcard each.' Mary has preserved this studio impersonation of the man of destiny, his face iron-moulded. The scrawly inscription reads, 'Zum freundlichen Erinnerungen, von Adolf Hitler' – 'with friendly recollections' – and the date below, sure enough, 7 May. Others have observed how eerie the Nazi insistence was on photographing their moods of power, perhaps to fake the record, or as if sensing in the bone their evanescence. At any rate the photographs of Unity and her group friends, in the albums of Mary or of Michael Burn, have about them something hectic, a factitious comradeship, all straight lines of faces, smiles, and arms linked for the statement to the camera. Here is the jollity on the steps of the Brown House, with Unity and Sister Pam and Mary, Coleridge Hills and his wife (J. C. Hills, whom I cannot trace) and Baroness Ella van Heemstra, who was a Mosleyite with her first husband Ruston, and has since become the mother of Audrey Hepburn, the film star, with whom she lives in Switzerland.

Sister Pam's arrival on 14 June was jotted down in Mary's diary. Pam was with the Heskeths and Billa Cresswell, now married to the economist Sir Roy Harrod. Lady Harrod said: 'We had driven along the Rhine, through Wiesbaden to Munich, in three cars, Roger Hesketh's, his sister Joan's, and Pam's. Cuthbert Hesketh and a footman called John were also with us. For two days we stayed at the Vierjahreszeiten. Pam rang Unity up and she came round to see us. We were all five sitting in the foyer of the hotel, and Unity was looking at her watch all the time as she was going to meet Hitler. She was on tenterhooks, she didn't seem too sure of him. It was the year of the Jubilee and I had on a check cotton dress, red and white with a round collar. I'd got buttons covered with Union Jacks from Woolworths. The conversation turned to patriotism and Bobo said to me, Would you think of joining the National Socialist Movement? I answered, I would if I could get the buttons. Next day she came round to the Carlton Tea Rooms, or perhaps we met there. Hitler walked in and we all stood up but he didn't acknowledge Bobo, he showed no sign of recognizing her. Bobo didn't come on with us to Bad Ischl.'

Still more snapshots of that summer; of Mary and Michael Burn; of Erich, another SS man somehow detached for ever from his surname, and Michael Burn in the streets of Gmunden; of Diana at the Zeppelinwiese during the 1935 Nuremberg Rally, with Sigismund FitzRandolph of the German Embassy in London. Photographs too, of Michael Burn in shorts, and Unity over-dressed, a tiny puppy in her arms, at a labour camp, or *Arbeitsdienstlager*. This can be dated by Mary's diary: 'August 8th. Unity came back with a darling puppy called Flopsy.' And again, 'August 18th. Lunch Unity and Micky Burn.'

Among other assignments for *The Times*, Michael Burn in 1949 was to cover the rigged trial in Budapest of Rajk, the communist foreign minister who was hanged to suit Stalin's policies. By then he had also been a prisoner of war in Colditz. He is distinguished as a writer and poet. In 1935 he was an apprentice journalist, researching an article on German prisons. He had known Unity at London parties, and still possesses an engraved invitation from Lady Redesdale and Unity, in whose hand the card has been written on, to a sherry party at 2 Grosvenor Crescent, on 3 April, which makes the year 1932. When his parents, Mr and Mrs Clive Burn, gave a ball for their daughter Renée in the 1937 season, Unity accepted and her name is in *The Times* social column among those attending. In Germany Michael Burn was prepared to give the Nazis the benefit of the doubt, and Unity was eager to follow up his researches, and recruit him to the cause whole-heartedly. At the end of September she went in his footsteps round the Ettstrasse prison, which was the central police headquarters of Munich, and a starting-point for investigation. An official conducted her round every single cell, even the empty ones, so that she felt she could be sure nothing was being hidden. Michael Burn had been on the track of a man who had been denounced by a young boy, and this boy was himself being detained in the Ettstrasse prison pending the trial in the process he had triggered. Unity saw the boy, but drew no conclusions, not even about denunciation as a basis for legal action. Several *Rassenschänder*, those who had broken the race laws new-minted at the latest Parteitag, German girls among them, were in prison, and Unity talked to one whom she found very beautiful. After a while this girl asked if Unity were not English and then said, 'Fancy even an English girl being imprisoned for *Rassenschändung*.' But Unity had not come to share her cell, only to go over the same ground as Michael Burn. Possibly his article might fail to please; he was to be sure to post it to Dr Hagen of the Polizeidirektion in the Ettstrasse, and also as promised, to Stadelheim prison, where only a year before Roehm and his SA men had been butchered in cold blood. Fussing about a postal order she had wanted to return to him as it was for too large a sum, and also sending him a head of the Führer cut out and enlarged from a photograph she herself had made and of which she was very proud, she was writing to Michael Burn from Kaulbachstrasse 49 on 5 October in what was the very last fortnight, therefore, of the Studentinnenheim.

Michael Burn said: 'Lady Redesdale used to give these parties to make debs out of Bobo and Decca. I'd met Bobo at dances, Queen Charlotte's especially, and we were equally bored by them. I'd then gone over to Swinbrook from Oxford, to which I failed to return when I wrote a book about motor-racing. I'd been staying with Syrie Maugham at Le Touquet. Then I wandered about Europe, including Germany. I'd been nauseated by unemployment and believed Hitler had solved it, though I didn't see how. In Munich there'd been Tony Rumbold and Donald Maclean – and Bobo, though she was considered disreputable and a bit unwise for a budding diplomat to know. But we arranged to meet in the Osteria Bavaria. There she was, sitting at a table facing the door. I began chatting about London gossip when I noticed she wasn't paying attention. I said, Am I boring you? and she replied, It would be better if you didn't say anything, the Führer is coming. Sure enough, the procession came in. Bobo began to shiver all over. The Führer passed, stopped at the table, and said something to her, and went on to the inner yard. Brückner then came back and said, The Führer would like you to join us. I was of no interest, and she hurried off without me. That time [18 August] when Mary dropped her handbag full of Knallerbsen and everyone around Hitler whipped guns out, I thought, What a fool – it was terrifying. Working for the Gloucester Citizen as I was, I had an official letter of introduction from the Brown House to the effect that I was a representative of the Rothermere Press, in Germany, to refute the accusations made by the Jew Lorant in his book, and therefore to be granted every assistance. It was a wonderful laisser-passer. I'd already got to Dachau through Victor Cazalet. In 1935 I went back to the Nuremberg Party Day for the column I was doing in the Gloucester Citizen. I was beginning to see through it by then, I had no card, but was determined to enter. I was with Bobo. In the stadium we saw Streicher, at the top of the stairs to the stand for the Ehrengäste, or guests of honour. I was dressed in lederhosen, suitably Aryan. I told Streicher what I wanted, and was admitted. I heard Hitler speak. Afterwards I remember Bobo saying, Wasn't it awful when he said that bit about how he might die? There had indeed been a hysterical gasp from the massed crowd at the notion. Unity and

Diana were at the Deutscher Hof with Leni Riefenstahl. I remember the glitter in Leni's eyes as we went up in the lift.'

Two other English Ehrengäste travelling together with facilities from the Ministry of Propaganda to this Parteitag were Henry Williamson, the nature writer, and Mosleyite, and John Heygate, who had married Evelyn Waugh's first wife and was then working at UFA Films in Berlin. Both published accounts, the former in Goodbye West Country (1937), the latter in These Germans (1940). The SA ranks struck Williamson as having 'the spirit of English gentlemen who had transcended class-consciousness', which brought him to the exclamation, 'Heil Hitler! God Save the King!' Unity could not have summed up her world-outlook more neatly. John Heygate did not empty out his mind. 'At last we are in our places! Right gangway, top tier on the right, rather high up, but with a clear view in front of us, and almost immediately behind the platform on which the Führer will appear and speak . . . guests arriving among whom I note the leader of another kind of party, a religious party, Dr Buchman. I note blonde Nordic prototype, Unity Mitford, admirer of the Führer, with her sister Diana, looking to my mind even more beautiful and Nordic . . . to see Hitler and his show as it might be the Lord Mayor's.' In a letter to me, Sir John Heygate, as he now is, adds, 'Unity, Diana and Dr Buchman were seated on a bench immediately in front of Williamson and myself. I put my hat on their bench when we stood up for Hitler, and Buchman sat down on it.' These seating arrangements were all quite un-planned.

Michael Burn continues: 'Hitler, according to Bobo, had the greatest diffi-culty hiding photos of herself which Lady Londonderry used to give him. She reported a conversation she had with Hitler when he asked, What is your father's name? Hearing the answer, and not being sufficiently up in the aristocracy to understand about titles and names, he had patted her hand and said, Mein armes Kind.

'Erich was her SS man. He and I were having coffee in the Luitpoldcafé in Munich and I lost my temper about Nazis, so I threw a tray at him and stalked out. His comment was, Bei Engländer ist alles möglich – You can expect anything from the English. He wore civilian clothes, I think. He seemed more an escort than a lover. He was a photographer, or said he was, rather a nonentity. The kindest thing I'd wish to say was that she had a lot in common with those disgusted with the world of their upbringing. But her direction was unfashionable. She was fulfilled by a monster.'

Service to the Führer had to be in word and thought and deed, a poor con-summation of love, to be sure, but at least with the hopes of being accepted and rewarded. Everything had happened because the Führer had noticed her; therefore he would have to notice her still more; she had no other *entrée*. The opportunity lay, publicly, in anti-semitism, upon which thousands of careers were prospering. Vice-consul C. J. Phillips was reporting from Munich on 30 January 1935, 'Recrudescence of the anti-semitic campaign has been evident in Munich during the past few days. The campaign appears to coincide with the presence of Herr Julius Streicher at Munich who is no doubt the spiritual organizer.' Streicher's own speeches were invariably on the same single note, but on 19 April, for instance, at an Easter meeting in Nuremberg of Nazi teachers, of which he had been one himself, he said, 'The number of Jew bastards in Germany is terribly large. We must not believe that we have yet obtained the victory. A hard path lies before us.' 'The anti-Jewish campaign,' wrote Seymour Gainer, the Munich consul-general on 3 May, 'is making rapid strides in Upper Bavaria, whereas previously it was in its intensest form confined to Bavaria.' On which, incidentally, the Foreign Office minute reads, 'The plate-glass industry must be having a boom.' Does the policy of appeasement need further explanation?

The following week, on 9 May, in another speech at Nuremberg, Streicher gave what must have sounded like encouragement from the home front to Unity. He had had occasion, he said, to congratulate the leader of the British fascists upon one of his speeches. The very next day the Nazi press published the text of the telegram in reply from Mosley to Streicher. 'BUF Headquarters. To Herr Streicher. The Stürmer. Nuremberg. Please accept my very best thanks for your kind telegram which greeted my speech in Leicester. It was received while I was away from London. I value your advice greatly in the midst of our hard struggle. The power of Jewish corruption must be destroyed in all countries before peace and justice can be successfully achieved in Europe. Our struggle to this end is hard, but our victory is certain.'

In *Oswald Mosley* (1975), Robert Skidelsky's long biography, this cable is nowhere mentioned, a most extraordinary omission, while the relation of Mosley and his movement to Streicher is not even hinted at, let alone weighed as it should have been. It is Skidelsky's contention, in brief, that the BUF legitimately exercising their rights in the East End of London ran into Jews and communists, often one and the same, who sought to deny those rights, and therefore received what was only their deserts. The anti-semitism of the BUF, in this view, was not a primary impulse or characteristic of the movement, but a by-product of the marches, a little local difficulty. The Jews, then, had only themselves to blame if they were attacked. 'A Jewish malaise of this time was to be obsessed with fascism. If some Jews found it intolerably provoking they certainly went out of their way to be provoked.' Malaise is not an adequate description for reactions to what was perceived, rightly and tragically, as the preliminaries of an unprecedented assault on Jews wherever they were. Mosley's telegram to Streicher has nothing to do with establishing the right to demonstrate in the East End, and it cannot be made to square with apologetics which dispose of the victims by calling them the aggressors. There is no possibility of interpreting 'The power of Jewish corruption must be destroyed in all countries before peace and justice can be successfully achieved in Europe' as anything but generalized anti-semitism. Streicher's valued advice was of the clearest. Such a cable from Mosley to him was a declaration that the English fascist contribution to persecuting Jews would not be restricted to local issues, but on the contrary was integrated into the international movement of anti-semites.

Streicher himself had long been unmistakable for what he was. His party card was Number 2, Hitler's being 7. Throughout the twenties, he had been a loyal agitator for Hitler, imprisoned in 1923, and again in 1926 when he falsely accused the socialist mayor of Nuremberg of stealing an overcoat from the city relief stores. Otto Strasser thought him a sexual pervert. In 1928, writes Gustav Regler in his autobiography, Das Ohr des Malchus, Streicher 'showed me photographs of naked girls who had affirmed to him that they had slept with Jews, but they had repented in good time and now were his mistresses'. The Stürmer had been a provincial sheet with a circulation of 28,000 when Streicher bought it for 40,000 reichsmarks from the previous owner's widow and transformed it into a blend of anti-Jewish raving and incitement to violence. The Stürmer had to be bought by some institutions and distributors under compulsion, so its circulation figures, and even its influence, are uncertain, but by the middle of 1935 about 100,000 copies were sold fortnightly. In the end the sale rose to four or five times that number. Streicher's declared income from it was 80,000 marks annually.

Although Streicher had been a Swabian originally, Hitler appointed him Gauleiter of Franconia. To reward him for the years of struggle, the Kampfzeit, and to acknowledge his anti-Jewish supremacy, on 29 March 1933, Hitler made him chief of the Central Committee of the Defence against Jewish Atrocity and Boycott Agitation. That July he had some Jews arrested and taken to a meadow to tear out grass with their teeth. He would boast of his cruelties, for example how after the Roehm purge he had whipped a Dr Steinrück in his cell in prison. Though the publicity was calculated terror, personal sadism was blatant. A small squat man, his head shaven, he had a predilection for swaggering in public. He carried a whip, and used it. At the end of 1934, Jews in the village of Gunzenhausen, in his Franconia, were murdered by SA men who were not brought to justice. On 12 February 1935, Hitler attended his old friend's fiftieth birthday. Nor, when Streicher was disgraced in 1940 for pocketing Jewish money and property so openly that even Nazis complained, could Hitler skimp his auld-lang-syne feelings for the man. 'This Streicher affair is a tragedy,' we read in Hitler's Table Talk, 'I can't help thinking that in comparison with so many services, the reasons for Streicher's dismissal are really slender. All that's said about his alleged disease is false. Streicher only had one disease and that was nympholepsy.'

This, then, was the man with whom Mosley had exchanged messages. As we have seen, first-hand experience of Nuremberg and Streicher's despotism had been gathered by BUF delegations there in 1933 and 1934, not to mention whatever Unity and Diana may have related. There was nothing secretive about Streicher. Nothing secretive, either, about Mosley's Leicester speech in April which had attracted Streicher, with its clamour, 'For the first time I openly and publicly challenge the Jewish interests of this country commanding the press, commanding the cinema, dominating the City of London, killing London with their sweat-shops. These great interests are not intimidating and will not intimidate the fascist movement of the modern age.' In the very first issue of Stürmer in 1934, the British fascists were laughably misrepresented. 'Mosley is the tool of the Jews. Mosley has admitted that he has Jewish blood in his veins.' The tenth issue continued as fancifully, 'The Party which in England strives in this anti-semitic spirit is led by a certain Mosley. This man acknowledges nothing of a Jewish or a race problem. He is therefore not opposed by the Jews, on the contrary they praise and support him.' By the forty-eighth issue, however, in 1935, 'Mosley is a great speaker, a fearless fighter but above all things a subtle diplomat. With his nationalist policies, he has for a considerable time been annoying and challenging the Jews.'

What part did Unity play in converting Streicher to champion Mosley, in bringing about the rapprochement of the telegrams? Karl Holz, administrative editor of Stürmer, in confessing to the paper's error about Mosley, mentioned that 'our representatives' had been given the opportunity of convincing themselves of the BUF's genuine anti-semitism. In an interview with Reuters Streicher confirmed that his information about the BUF came 'from a person I sent to the spot'. Whether this is a euphemism for Unity cannot be nailed down, but the presumption remains. The following interview with Unity is the only further light which can be thrown on the question, and it was published in the weekend Münchener Zeitung for Saturday/Sunday, 22 and 23

June 1935, under the title *Eine Britische Faschistin erzählt* – Confessions of an English fascist girl. The photograph by Delowi had Unity as she preferred, the right side of her face in half-profile. Peculiarly (out of guilt? or conspiracy?) her name nowhere appeared.

Lord Redesdale, hereditary member of the English House of Lords, belongs to the Conservative Party. As an Englishman of the old school and a relation of Winston Churchill's, his attitudes towards Germany are not exactly friendly, but nevertheless he is an elderly gentleman with an objective mind who has taken pains to do justice to the character of Nazi Germany and the new age. One problem, however, weighs heavily on this peer: his twenty-year-old daughter has become a member of the English fascist party. With all her heart and soul! She does not bother one bit about standing on her dignity as might be expected. She distributes broadsheets in the London streets, and carries on propaganda for the fascist party wherever she can. But we want to let her speak for herself, for right now she is living in Munich.

'The struggle of the British Union of Fascists for power in the state will be actively supported by the women who have found their way into the party, to a greater extent perhaps than was the case in the period of struggle of the national socialist movement in Germany. Women in England take care of many party jobs which in German eyes ought to be done by men. I have distributed broadsheets for our party in London, I have canvassed from house to house, in the Jewish districts of London as well as in working-class areas, and have done my utmost for the party of our Leader Mosley, and in an emergency I have also lent a hand to chucking out of the hall any women who have broken up our meetings.

'We British fascists have our struggle made terrifically hard by the well-known national tendency to do things traditionally. Our anti-semitism has called Jewry in England to account. In the press we are either completely ignored or laughed off. Caricatures, for instance of Mosley as an actor, or an Italian dancing-master, are supposed to lower us in public estimation, but they tend to demonstrate how fundamentally our Leader is feared.

'Oswald Mosley has a military disposition, he was educated at a military college, was a combat airman in the World War and is a fanatical patriot. Returning wounded from the War, he certainly did not find his homeland brought low and conquered, as Adolf Hitler did, but for all that the country was bitterly divided. Today our opponents try to find a way of blaming him for the fact that his shattering experience at the front took so strong a hold of his imagination that he collected round him a group of people who also wanted to develop the collective life of the country, the brand new spirit that came with experience of the front. Our enemies write it off as political irresponsibility that he crossed over from the Independents to the Labour Party, for a time was the youngest member of the government and in the end when the working-class party did not adapt his programme for unemployment, proceeded to found his New Party in 1931. To us that's the finest evidence of his honourable endeavours to win through to the collective spirit which one day will go down in history as the main intellectual current of the years after the war [*die geistige Strömung der Nachkriegszeit* – could she have expressed herself thus in German or English?]. Anyone who has ever heard Mosley speak knows that he is a man imbued with his sense of mission and an unshakeable belief in the victory of his cause.

'Oswald Mosley is our Leader, and we English fascists are behind him with the same enthusiasm as today the whole German people are behind their wonderful [*herrlich*] Führer. We British fascists have a lot to learn from Germany. On account of the way we are laughed off or dismissed, we know we shall be slandered, but even so will be taking another step forward, and the moment our Jewish enemies are ready to attack us – the time for this, we know, is likely to be soon – then our struggle at last will reach its final decisive stage. The British fascist party is a party of front-line soldiers and youth. Hitler had his SA and Mosley has his "Iron Front" [thus in the German] and he himself once told me, "I admire Hitler's national socialist movement: when at last we hold the helm of state in our hands, friendship between Germany and England will prevail."*

This long interview in a prominent paper was considered significant enough for official notice, though not because Unity's example was so bizarre in itself, but because through her the BUF was being championed openly by a Nazi personality as notorious as Streicher. The British Embassy forwarded to the Foreign Office its own full and faithful précis of the interview (F.O. 371/18859), with these introductory remarks, 'You may like to know that the *Münchener Zeitung* of the 22nd June contains an interview with the Hon Unity Mitford on the subject of Fascism in England. Miss Mitford, although only 20 years of age, appears to represent Sir Oswald Mosley at Munich, and has been living there since September.' The minutes, initialled by Ralph Wigram, for once are pointed: 'The Embassy do not seem to know about Miss Mitford's acquaintance with the Chancellor which is very curious indeed. She is a student in Munich – and it is true that her family are friends of Sir O. Mosley but I can't believe she "represents" him. I understand that she sees Herr Hitler very often in Munich.'

The *Münchener Zeitung* interview was published to coincide with the meeting on that Sunday at the Hesselberg, where Unity was so exhilarated but Mary, faithful companion, had found the people and the noise too much for her. Well she might have done, for the Hesselberg is not a large hill, but gently rounded, in beautiful rolling country outside Nuremberg, and by no means an ideal weekending site for a fervent throng, Bavarian peasants for the most part, whose Nazism had to be maintained at a level temperature. This particular bread-and-circuses on the Hesselberg was a contribution of the local

---

* The translation of this article, as of all the German, printed or spoken, is mine, though some Nazi expressions defy Mitfordese approximations.

emperor, Streicher, in honour of himself and his tribunes, but its hard political purposes were tricked out. Midsummer Night allegedly had been greeted in the historical past by huge fires here; Baldur, a mythical ancient, was associated with fire, and so was St John the Baptist; the Thing, or tribal moot of the Teutons, might also have been held in just such a place. Folklore, legend, Christianity, paganism and community amusements had been twisted together under the swastika to offer something for everybody. For forty-eight hours, columns of people swarmed towards the hill on foot or by car, through the surrounding villages of Dinkelsbühl and Wassertrüdingen and Gunzenhausen. Peasant costume was de rigueur, with Nazi armbands. Ritual offerings of bread and ham, and intermittent folk-dancing rehearsed to look impromptu, completed the would-be Breughel background.

On the 22nd Streicher had spoken at ten at night, exhorting the listeners in the dark to be revenged upon the Jews, 'who after the war had tried to make an end of the German race', and all in his own rhetoric, he warned them to be on the watch against Jews and to keep their bodies clean. Bonfires were lit to commemorate the war dead.

The early part of Sunday morning was devoted to gymnastics and a display of aerobatics, until at ten o'clock Streicher appeared again, with Goering and Frau Goering, whom he had fetched at Rothenburg station. With them was Unity. (The Nazi press, in particular the Fränkische Tageszeitung, one of the nine local newspapers controlled by Streicher, besides the Stürmer does not specify whether Unity had been staying with Streicher, or had arrived separately. That April she had been to the wedding of Goering and Emma Sonnemann, his second wife, the actress, and conceivably she could have come with them. But Goering was believed not to have cared for Unity, an impression confirmed to me by his daughter Edda, now living in Munich, who of course had only her mother's hearsay to go on.)

The Prominenten, in the useful German phrase for high-ups, Goering and his wife, General Karl Bodenschatz his adjutant, Obernitz, a local SA veteran, Streicher and his adjutant König, were ushered on to a specially erected platform, in a jostle of loudspeakers, standards and banners. Goering was to address the crowd, but on the spur of the moment, Streicher first introduced Unity to them. The Fränkische Tageszeitung reports how he did so, after yet another random burst of hectoring: '"But we have one thing to say to those witnesses among us from England. You have no idea as yet that it is the Jew who first split our people into political parties. You still do not realize that the Jew brought political parties and strife to you too. The English people are ready for an honourable peace, but it is the Jew who does not want peace. The day will come when it will be recognized by all peoples

1 Aged nine: a bridesmaid at a wedding at neighbouring Abbotswood.

2 Swinbrook was built to Lord Redesdale's plans, and the family
moved into the house in 1926.

3 Lady Redesdale (*centre*) took Unity and Joan Farrer to the RAF Display at Hendon at the height of their coming-out season, and this photograph appeared in the *Tatler*, 6 July 1932.

4 Three sisters. Unity (*left*), Diana (then Mrs Bryan Guinness, *centre*) and Nancy, at the wedding of their cousin Lord Stanley of Alderley to Lady Audrey Talbot, 3 March 1932.

5 Unity, at her finishing school, Baroness Laroche's, in the late summer of 1934, with her sister Diana. She had improvised this uniform.

6 ABOVE The Nuremberg Party Rally of 1933 was her first experience of Germany. With the B.U.F. delegation was William Joyce, later Lord Haw-Haw (flanked by French fascists in the front row), Alexander Raven Thomson (with moustache) and Captain Vincent (with Highland bonnet and medals).

7 BELOW Putzi Hanfstaengl, here with Diana, was in charge of foreign Press relations. He has described how at this 1934 Party Rally he had to use his handkerchief to wipe the extravagant make-up off the Mitford sisters, to bring them in line with Nordic womanhood.

8 Lunching with Lord Redesdale and Baroness Laroche at the Osteria Bavaria in Munich, on 18 January 1935, just a short month before making friends with Hitler there, in what was his favourite restaurant.

9 ABOVE 'She affirmed in some wonderful words her solidarity with the German people and the struggle of Julius Streicher' – who stood behind her on the platform at the Hesselberg midsummer meeting, 23 June 1935.

10 LEFT The mysterious Erich, nominally a photographer, who perhaps had a watching brief on Unity, waiting with Diana at Nuremberg airport.

11 In full fighting kit on the Hesselberg. Gauntlets were an important part of this; gloves were for civilian occasions.

of the world exactly what they can expect from the Jews, who told Christ that His father was the devil." Then the Frankenführer called to the microphone the English girl who had come as a guest to the Hesselberg. She affirmed in some wonderful words her solidarity with the German people and the struggle of Julius Streicher.'

Basil Newton of the British Embassy, shortly to be posted to Prague where he joined tremulously in the appeasement chorus, was in the crowd. His despatch to the Foreign Office somewhat took the sting out of the day (on which, in London, the Anglo-German Naval Treaty had been signed, a step on the war-path). Newton estimated a crowd of twenty thousand, which is a tenth of the figure in the Nazi press. He wrote, 'After the Deputy Gau Propaganda Chief Schöller had opened the proceedings and the Hon Unity Valkyrie Freeman-Mitford had made a brief speech testifying to the sympathy of the German people with the efforts of Herr Julius Streicher, General Goering addressed the assembly. He began by attacking those opponents of the regime who reproached National Socialism with having created a new heathenism. Midsummer Day celebrations, he declared, were also holy ... Goering then turned to the question of Anglo-German relations and expressed Germany's pleasure at the recent declaration of His Royal Highness the Prince of Wales. The German ex-servicemen and the German nation cheerfully grasped the hand which had been stretched out at them.' (F.O. 371/18858.)

This speech by the Prince of Wales to the British Legion, on the theme of old soldiers' comradeship between England and Germany, had not been vetted before delivery, and was most injudicious, the basis for the certainty of the Nazis, Hitler included, that here was a future King of England favourable to them, as indeed he was keyed up to be. (See Frances Donaldson's *Edward VIII*, especially for the pro-German sentiments behind this particular speech of his.) To extemporize a speech out of Unity was timely opportunism on Streicher's part. No doubt he realized how spotlighted she was by Hitler's recent attentions, and he could do himself a good turn by promoting her, but in the immediate moment when Germany was apparently winning English complicity in her political aims, if not approbation, what with royal speeches and the Naval Treaty, a member of the British ruling class could be stood up on a Nazi platform; the Prince of Wales's glittering coin could be repaid in kind.

Keeping up the pressure, maybe even astounded by such an ally from such a quarter, and wishing to spread curiosity, the *Fränkische Tageszeitung* on Monday 24 June, when the Hesselberg was being tidied up, published another interview under the title 'Miss Mitford Replies' – whatever else, another editorial orchestration of Streicher's. At the risk of tedious repetition, it is given here. The interviewer is identified only as H.D., a staff writer. One photograph showed Unity in profile, another of her at the microphone with Streicher.

Miss Unity Mitford, tall and blonde, is sitting opposite me. There's nothing cool and superior about her, though English girls are often considered to be just that. She is thrilled by the fabulous experience of the Frankentag [as the Hesselberg meeting was also known]. She is thrilled by the new Germany and its Führer Adolf Hitler. The mention of Adolf Hitler brings us straight to the problem why the majority of English people find it so difficult to fall in with the German national socialist movement. To my question, 'Can you understand how unconditionally grateful we Germans are to have a Führer embodied for us in the person of Adolf Hitler?' the answer comes loud and clear. 'If only England were inspired enough to have someone of your Führer's greatness, then everyone would fall into line and even the English would have to recognize that this system would not mean the denial of personal freedom. For years I have belonged to the Mosley movement and know how his struggle appeared to have no prospects. When Mosley introduced uniforms, it was generally agreed that no Englishmen would be found to wear uniforms of their own free will. But the course of the last few years has shown that plenty of Englishmen, and certainly those of better stock [Rasse] can be found to subordinate themselves to one man's leadership.

Question: Why do we hear so little of the Mosley movement these days?

Answer: At present the Mosley movement is ignored in the main papers, as once happened in Germany to the national socialists. The *Daily Mail* did once break through this boycott and regularly reported on our movement. [The next sentence was printed bold.] But big business is very often strongly influenced by Jews and it issued threats of completely withdrawing its support. Therefore the proprietor of this paper was compelled to limit what was published about us. So then we put together a paper for ourselves, which is still only small, but even the *Völkische Beobachter* was once a sheet of the kind.

Question: The Mosley movement originally was not anti-semitic. How did the change happen?

Answer: The Jews in England were not so visibly a danger as in Germany. But Mosley very soon recognized that the Jewish danger may well work its evil way from country to country, but fundamentally it poses a danger to all the peoples of the world.

Question: How strong is the Mosley movement today?

Answer: For the time being Mosley puts no figure to it, not being in a position to do so. But the movement grows steadily. At the coming elections we shall put up some candidates in the certain hopes of winning seats in the House of Commons. But that will be only one more spring-board and there can be no looking back until we have swept the whole nation with us.

Question: How did you come to the Mosley movement?

Answer: For years I have been a personal friend of Mosley, and so committed myself early to his political way of thinking.

Question: When did you first hear of Julius Streicher?

Answer: Many years ago now, and always only horrible and nasty things. But I also heard that many Germans applauded him. So I always had a firm wish to meet him one day. Now I am happy and grateful that I am acquainted with the national socialist fighter Julius Streicher. Above all I have long been reading the *Stürmer* with the greatest interest.

Miss Mitford is a student and for some months now has been studying in Munich university. She first came to Germany in 1933. She was fortunate enough to have been able to experience the first Reichsparteitag of the Third Reich, and since then has been an enthusiast for the Reich and its creator. She hopes to take part in this year's Parteitag. Then we may hope to be able to portray to our readers how Miss Mitford will have had further experiences of Nuremberg.

Official representative of Mosley in Munich or not, Unity could hardly have waved the BUF flag any harder or any better. While she was in the news, while the iron was hot, she had struck. Her own personal friendship with Mosley going back 'for years' was likely to be broadcast in print outside Germany, justifying that troublesome emblem without further family indiscretions. At this point, our readers may well wish to be spared yet another of these grisly contemporary documents, or prefer to seek relief in mockery as Nancy did in a letter to her, dated 29 June (quoted in Harold Acton's *Memoir*), 'Darling Stoneyheart, We were all very interested to see that you were the Queen of the May this year at Hesselberg. Call me early, Goering dear, For I'm to be Queen of the May! Good gracious, that interview you sent us, fantasia, fantasia.' But Unity herself was raising the stakes. Instead of having her Nazism relayed at second hand, she decided to trumpet it for herself. Her letter to the *Stürmer*, in its thirtieth issue, the last number of that July (the paper carried no exact dates), was her Hesselberg speech writ large, just as much a put-up job, in the sense that she was riding publicity for all that it was worth, and so of course was Streicher, with more tactical ability. Was the whole promotion his?

'The letter from an English girl' was disingenuously presented as arriving in the post-bag, though it occupied the centre of a page, its space doubled by a large photograph of her in her black shirt. Unity had written: 'Dear Stürmer! As an English fascist I should like to express my admiration for you. For a year I have been living in Munich and each week have read the *Stürmer*. If only we had such papers in England. Ordinary people in England have no idea of the Jewish danger. English Jews are always presented as "decent".

Perhaps in England Jews are cleverer with their propaganda than in other countries. I cannot otherwise explain the undoubted fact that our struggle is as hard as could be. Our worst Jews work only behind the scenes. They do not come out in the open and therefore we are unable to show them in their true horror [Entsetzlichkeit] to the English people. We urgently need a publication like Stürmer to tell people the truth. They will soon see, it is to be hoped, that in England too we shall be victorious over the world-enemy, in spite of his cunning. We look forward to the day on which we shall declare with full power and might "England for the English!" Jews out! With German greetings! Heil Hitler! Unity Mitford. P.S. If you should happen to find room in your paper for this letter, please print my name in full. I do not want my letter initialled U.M. for everyone should know that I am a Jew-hater [Judenhasserin].'

This worked the trick, as it was sure to. Her newsworthiness was guaranteed, and to every snippet from now on was attached that postscript, like a snake to Medusa's head. She had done something sufficiently horrible to become the notoriety she had always wanted to be, the power behind the throne. Outrage and success were one and the same. The Daily Express of 26 June had seized on the Hesselberg meeting, though wrongly attributing it to Heidelberg, and carried a photograph of her with Streicher. The Daily Telegraph also reported her as chief guest of honour there, complimented on her courage by Goering, and being presented a bouquet, and on 27 July its correspondent filed the story of the Stürmer letter. The Daily Herald and the Evening Standard followed suit. 'Peer's Daughter as Jew-Hater' ran the Daily Mirror headline, with a photograph. 'I wonder,' asked a reader from Kingston-on-Thames, 'if the Hon Unity Mitford were put in a kindergarten with a score of beautiful Jewish four-year-olds and then given a gun and told to wipe out that much Jewry, whether she would do it?' (Not much doubt how Unity would have answered the question, theoretically at least.) A self-declared Jewish lady wrote in, 'If she is rash enough to make such a definite and, if I may say so, incoherent statement embracing all of us, then she must be prepared to give her reasons.' The Jewish Chronicle of 2 August had a leader pointing out the obvious. 'Here was a scribbler so obscure that she begged Herr Streicher to "publish her whole name". She realized that without her title, which was, of course, a mere accident of birth, her vapourings could have been of no more concern to the public than those of any other irresponsible young hussy out to get her name in the papers.' Yet she had a title, she had used it to get her name in the papers, and there was no getting her out again.

Finally, in this season of raging anti-Jewish phantasmagoria, Unity, in the words of the *Daily Mirror* of Monday 11 September (about the events of the preceding Saturday), was a guest of honour at the Congress of Nazi Groups Abroad held at Erlangen, in Bavaria. 'She and her sister, says the British United Press, were given seats at the speaker's table, where Julius Streicher, Germany's Jew-baiter Number One was addressing the congress.' This Congress of *Auslandsorganisation*, foreign Nazi organizations, was a characteristic Streicher jamboree. Whether Unity and Diana were official BUF representatives is at issue – certainly Streicher treated them as such. A Congress of World Anti-Semites had been organized by him earlier, on 10 May, when Streicher had again thrown a friendly nod in the direction of Mosley's movement. Soap-box posing was in fashion. (On 28 October the *News Chronicle* was to report a mass demonstration in Hyde Park against German cruelties and persecutions. 'Mrs Guinness, daughter of Lord Redesdale, stood in the crowd on her own and recorded a lone vote opposing resolutions refusing business relations with Germany and declining to buy German goods ... Some of the crowd jeered, and others laughed. "I simply wanted to give my opinion like anyone else," said Mrs Guinness. During the singing of "God Save the King" while the crowd stood bareheaded, Mrs Guinness raised her hand in the Fascist salute.')

At Erlangen, at the evening gathering, or *Kamaradschaftabend*, in the local Colosseum, Dr Gross, the town's Burgermeister and leader of the Nazi *Rassenpolitisches Amt*, spoke on his subject, 'The Race Politics of National Socialism'. Following on, Streicher's speech was indistinguishable from all the others, though he told a story about a Jew called Meyer which may have failed to amuse another guest at the top table, the man on his left, Gauleiter Meyer of Westfalen Nord, on whose other side Unity was sitting, as in the photographs published in the *Fränkische Tageszeitung* on the morning of the 10th, along with a full and sycophantic report of the proceedings. Streicher, it was observed, had interrupted his speech to introduce to those present the ladies Leni Riefenstahl, Frau Troost, wife of Hitler's pet architect, and Unity and Diana. As if coincidentally, the issue of the *Stürmer* then current had a letter from a Mr F. Tong of Poulton-le-Fylde, Lancashire, expressing sympathy for Unity. An article on another page described Mosley now as 'this courageous man ... the Press is silent because Mosley has set himself the task of solving the Jewish problem'. Streicher was returning the compliment paid to him by the attendance of Unity and Diana at this Congress whose purpose, as he expressed it, was 'fruitfully to implement the work of Party members under different leaderships abroad'.

Unity and Diana, noted the *Fränkische Tageszeitung* reporter, had heard the Nazi message in their blood. 'Leni Riefenstahl and the two English fascist girls who had come together on the podium were greeted uproariously.' The evening closed with folk-festivities.

The Erlangen Congress had been intended as a curtain-raiser to the Party Day of Freedom. This began in nearby Nuremberg on the 10th, with Hitler's arrival at half past four at the airport, to be received there by Streicher, Hess, Gauleiter Wagner of Munich, Bormann and Himmler. The sisters had already moved into their hotel in Nuremberg, and had been travelling from there to the Erlangen Congress, a short distance. They had met up with Tom, and Mary. That first night, Hitler, accompanied by Streicher and Liebel, the Burgermeister of Nuremberg, attended Die Meistersinger at the opera, in a production of Benno von Arent's, Furtwängler conducting. (The cotton aertex shirts drama was not until the repeat performance the following year. Mary's diary for this year has, 'September 9th. To Grand Hotel – Unity and Diana there – hotel seething . . . September 12th. Unity and Diana invited to dinner by Ritter von Epp. September 14th. Left Nuremberg by train.') On the 11th, in an opening proclamation of Hitler's, Jews and bolsheviks were attacked, while in the afternoon the foundation stone of the Congress Hall was laid. Dr Otto Dietrich held a press conference, and so did Putzi Hanfstaengl, loftily juggling for the foreigners the names of François I of France, Napoleon, Bismarck, Hitler; Goebbels spoke too; and Rosenberg. The sisters were in the swim. And, part of the massed crowd, they listened to Goering on the need to safeguard the purity of the Nazi soul; they heard Hitler on the evening of the 14th read out the Nuremberg Laws which deprived German Jews of their citizenship, and segregated them without legal rights, the foundation stone of Auschwitz, Treblinka, and Belsen.

Did the nympholepsy which Hitler considered Streicher's one disease embrace Unity? Streicher had two sons, Lothar, born in 1915, and Elmar, born in 1918, by his first wife who died at the beginning of the war shortly after his downfall. Elmar Streicher consented to speak to me, saying, 'The Unity–Streicher friendship dates from 1934. I first saw her at the 1934 Parteitag, I went with my father and Lothar every year. It didn't take long to establish a lovely relationship, she soon belonged to the family. If one hadn't seen her for a while, she would take one in her arms, as an expression of friendship. Oberburgermeister Liebel had converted for the Gauleiter's use the Cramer-Klett Palace, once belonging to an old patrician family, but my father did not feel at ease in it, he liked simple food, Swabian-style, no banquets and so on. Down outside there was a skittle alley and Unity loved it there, playing out in the garden. She stayed at the Deutscher Hof Hotel, or else the Grand, I can't think she ever stayed with us. She preferred not to be tied down. She was a natural type in spite of her make-up and rouge. She could have stayed with us, we had other English girls in the house, one of them was Mary Crum, and she and Unity were rivals over my father. Unity was always a lady, she kept her distance, but not with my father. At their first meeting, she had stood up in front of him like a general. She wore dark suits, cut like a uniform, usually her black shirt, and always the party badge. She also always wore big gauntlets. She was a bit of a suffragette. She believed in uniting the Nordic countries and would be saying, Sooner or later we'll all be fascists.

'Mother was a hausfrau, unpolitical, she liked Unity, seeing she wasn't the kind of person to take a shine to Streicher, and make a play for him, as some did. She'd had an operation for goitre, which gave her a bad heart. Tante Eia lived with us, she'd been a teacher at school with my father and wrote him home-front letters in the Great War, thus becoming a family friend. Tante Eia was a second mother to us all, a spinster, very active politically in the party, leader of school-teachers in Franconia. There was also Tante Sophie, Streicher's sister. And Michel the dog. Unity was at home in this circle. Streicher bought his farm at Pleikersdorf in 1934 [disgraced, he lived on this farm from 1940 until 1945, when he was arrested there as a war criminal, tried in his own Nuremberg, and hanged]. Unity went out there too. We drove on expeditions in the region of Erlangen – Wachberla bei Forchheim is a mountain like the Hesselberg – and we also once went to inspect a work camp, an *Arbeitsdienstlager*, at Ebermannstadt.

'Unity could ring up my father direct, or contact him through König, the adjutant. We all owed him a lot. On big occasions, at the Hesselberg, or in Nuremberg, she came with us. From 1934 to 1937 I was at the NSDAP school for future leaders at Feldafing under the direction of Hess, so I saw her at home in the holidays. Lothar liked Unity, he had been in the Condor Legion in Spain, but by 1938 was working as a journalist on the *Fränkische Tageszeitung*. When he went to London that year, Unity gave a cocktail party for him. The year before, I'd been in London, where I made a speech for the proper English fascist movement, of Arnold Leese [leader of an extreme splinter group, the Imperial Fascist League, Leese was another string for the Stürmer bow, pulled taut when Mosley's movement slackened]. He was a straight-line anti-semite, and I wanted to experience it. The reds attacked us in the East End, we came to blows. I finished up in court. A police colonel told me that as a foreigner I'd been watched. We had a Leese fascist girl at the house, called Tommy Thomson, she wanted to fight for Germany but at the declaration of war she was bundled out of the country. Like Mary Crum, she was a rival of Unity's over my father. In England I never saw Unity, only

Diana and Mosley. Unity wanted us to support Mosley, but we who knew the movement would argue with her, we analysed for her how a fascist party could come to fruition only through its stand against the Jews. She adopted this opinion completely from us. My father had often warned Mosley that a political movement like his could achieve nothing without a deep understanding of the Jewish question. Unity was altogether fascinated by my father, but especially on the Jewish question as he explained it. No conversation took place without coming back to it. Unity always was telling us about her grand relations, how she was related to the Royal Family but they had Jewish kin, and that was printed in the Stürmer. We had to invite the Duke of Windsor to our home as at heart he was a Nazi.

'I was at that speech of hers on the Hesselberg. My father improvised it all. She was very happy about it, she laughed. Mind you, she could weep like a little girl. During the Abyssinian crisis, she absolutely had to speak to Hitler, but couldn't get access to him. She wept with rage. Unity can't be compared to Eva Braun, she had nothing to do with Hitler as a woman. Just a butterfly to a flower. She was a virgin to the day of her death, I'd put my hand in the fire to say that. As a woman she was very tall, she towered two heads above my father, you would have laughed to see it. She simply wasn't sexy.

'During the Party Day of 1937 she was lunching with us, and my father said to me that someone had to be fetched at the station. Unity saw our car and chauffeur had gone and told me to take her MG, with its hood down, right-hand drive. I thought it would fall to bits. She was the type to think that whatever she could do, everybody could.

'The SS men were anxious about her in case she was spying. I heard Himmler didn't like her. Mary Crum caught General Wolff's eye [Himmler's ADC] and he asked her to the SS tent as an Ehrengast during the Party Rally. My father felt responsible for Mary and these English girls – his relations with them were held against him at the Commission of Inquiry. He fell out with them in 1938, through Dr Martin, police chief of Nuremberg. Hans König had a soubrette at the opera, she was pregnant, the story was coming out and he shot himself. Oberburgermeister Liebel had a printing firm in Nuremberg and printed the Stürmer – he and Karl Holz died in the fighting at the end of the war. The Stürmer offices were in the Pfannschmittgasse. Unity knew them all, including Fips [whose cartoons were the paper's leading obscenity]. Streicher used to go to political cabarets in Munich, sometimes with Unity, to Schaiffer's near the Englischer Garten, and Platzl's. He was pleased she liked Germany, she was flattered by such company. She saw herself as an ambassadress, and my father opened doors for her. It was fatherly affection on his side, but they were of like minds.'

The Studentinnenheim period ended, and for the third weekend in October Mary invited Unity to the yachting school at Priem on the Chiemsee, where she rather single-mindedly sailed, and then they temporarily parted, Mary moving into the Pension Doering by herself on 21 October. Unity spent the best of the October days on an excursion in the mountains with sisters Pam and Jessica, and Erich, the tame SS man. On 20 October, she had left some money at the Vierjahreszeiten for a friend of Tom's, Janos Almasy, whose name she had misspelt as Almascy, and then she seems to have caught a late train to Berlin, perhaps with Lord Redesdale; a change of plan, it may be, for she had written to Michael Burn that she was planning to drive her father there. At any rate they were back in Munich on the 27th, meeting Janos and his friends Prince and Princess Kari Auersperg, in mid-morning at the Regina Bar. Mary's diary: 'October 27th. Unity had Lord Redesdale to Osteria ... they stay until Thursday.' Their last day before returning to England was spent in the same way, in the same places, though Unity took her father to dine at Platzl's, for the cabaret. Ten days later, in London, Unity was dining at Quaglino's with Diana and Tom, Lady Bridget Parsons (sister of Lord Rosse, who had been best man at the Guinness wedding) and Janos, whose surname Unity could now spell correctly. They saw The Informer at the Metropole, and went on to Eaton Square. The following weeks were spent in England, though with a flying visit abroad before Christmas, for Mary, settled in the Pension Doering, writes, 'December 21st. Unity came from Paris – has a room here.'

8

COMPLETING THE HITLER CIRCLE

Bavaria once strayed from the south. Baroque and rococo Munich echoed Italy, until the classical revival cracked down on it and drove gaiety from the air. Nazi architecture confirmed the citizen in his duty, especially in Munich, capital city of the movement, and also Hitler's home, in a way that Vienna, also with wayward Latin lights, never was. In Berlin Hitler was Chancellor, plagued by statesmen, diplomats and journalists. Berlin was bureaucracy, bad temper and few teas with young girls. In Munich Hitler was still the hopeful bohemian who would not drag himself off to bed, nor attend to business in the morning. In Munich he was the coffee-house maestro, out to harvest his due applause in person. His vanity, his fitfulness, created a vacuum around him, and Unity rushed into it, one might-have-been artist to another. Personality and place combined to give her a unique opening, and she seized it: that was her coup.

In Munich Hitler had to be wooed by his staff and officials, and the most senior of them established secondary but permanent offices there. Goebbels, for one, did not like it, but had no choice. Absence from Hitler was a form of extinction. Meeting Hitler, therefore, Unity met everyone. Mary's diary has the first mention of Goebbels as early as Saturday, 4 March, 1935. 'Lunch Osteria – Hitler, Brückner, Goebbels . . . Thursday May 9th. Lunch Flughafen [airport] Unity and Diana – on her way to Rome . . . June 3rd, Lunch at Hitler's flat. [This was to meet some English fascist who was in Munich, but not apparently Mosley, whose own memoirs My Life records, 'My first meeting with Hitler was in April 1935 . . . Hitler gave a luncheon for me in his flat in Munich, where a large company assembled, including Frau Winifred Wagner, the brilliant English wife of the composer's son Siegfried . . . Hitler had solemnly introduced me to Unity Mitford at the luncheon he gave me in April 1935, as he was unaware that we knew each other; in fact I had first met her at her coming-out ball in London, given three years before by Diana.'] In the evening, dinner Regina Hotel with Unity, Diana, Gordon Canning [an English fascist, for whom perhaps the lunch had been given], Brenda and Paul Willart . . . Thursday June 4th. Flugplatz to see Diana off.'

'I remember that dinner,' Paul Willart says, 'because she came in one of Hitler's vast cars. I'd been working in Germany for the Ullstein Verlag, but then was on holiday in Munich, writing for the *Guardian*. Unity was a good contact. Tom I'd known at Eton, and I used to go over to Swinbrook, as did my wife, who had been Brenda Pearson. I tried to argue with Unity on an intellectual basis, but she was a stupid girl, illiterate. She had mopped up everything in the *Stürmer*. Brenda invited her to stay with us at Hayling Island for a long weekend in the summer. When Unity arrived we were all out sailing. Father [Sir Arthur Willart, one of the old-school correspondents of *The Times*, a great Liberal] received her and went off to do some work. Then he heard the sound of shooting and found Unity firing at targets with her pistol. He asked her why. I'm practising to kill Jews, she said. Father almost left the house at once.'

It had become a life of sorts, a lop-sidedly Nazi life, with these interrupted too-brief snatches of Hitler at lunch or tea, with the big seasonal pinnacles of mass meetings, and the Mosleyite cause on the boil, and passing English friends and acquaintances to be shepherded, if possible, into the Nazi fold. Hitler's comings and goings now dictated hers. 1935, break-through year, set a pattern which was to last until the war. She never gave in, neither wearied nor disheartened. Such is fanaticism.

In the New Year she was at Rutland Gate on 27 January, writing to Robert Byron who had told her of his intention to write a book about the Great War, for which he was off travelling in Germany and the Baltic. She could help; she enclosed a letter of recommendation to Gauleiter Forster of Danzig. Unity was afraid that her name might not be remembered off-hand, as she had met the man once only with the Führer, in which case Robert Byron was simply to be pushing. A second letter of introduction for him to the Ministry of Propaganda would be sent from Berlin, where she was going the next day.

Mary's diary fills in the Munich news: 'January 19th, 1936. Diana came from South of France for a week . . . February 9th. Invited to Hitler's flat for tea with the Goebbelses. They left 6 and we stayed till 7.15 and came home in Hitler's car . . . February 14th. Unity gone to Berlin for weekend with the Goebbelses.' Longer than a weekend actually, for on the Tuesday, the 18th, the Berlin correspondent of the *Daily Telegraph* filed a despatch about the reception for the German motor-show. Hitler, he cabled, had been sitting at a table with Frau Goebbels, Unity Mitford and half a dozen other women. She was, therefore, taking up the leads of the previous year, and profiting from the powerful contacts of the Osteria and the Prinzregenten-strasse flat. She was consolidating.

Like all well-placed Nazis, Goebbels acquired property, whether through fees or sinecures due to him as a propagandist and editor, as a Minister, and Gauleiter of Berlin. Schwanenwerder, where Unity stayed, on an island in the Wannsee just outside Berlin, was the home which he bought after the Roehm purge, out of which he ran with a clean pair of heels, clinging to Hitler. It was done up for Magda and his children with the parvenu ostentation of which Hitler's Berchtesgaden and Goering's Karinhall were the most pharaonic examples. Yet Goebbels aspired to style. Like Hitler, he was fastidious about linen and finger-nails. Like Hitler again, he was that most frustrated of creatures, the man with enough of the artist in him to know the short-comings of his gifts, and suffer from it. His novel, Michael, is the egomaniac whine so often heard in bad literature, of the writer who pities himself for being insufficiently appreciated. There is no revenge for being mistaken about literary abilities, but Goebbels thought there was, as scribblers do sometimes, destructively, in a vendetta against real artistic achievements he could not dominate even by bonfires and guns.

Although not a lecher like Streicher, Goebbels was a womanizer, and one wonders what impact Unity made on him. Printed sources are little help. Mosley's autobiography states, in a passage about Hitler as a mimic, 'Such private occasions with relatively few people present revealed unexpected qualities, particularly if Goebbels was there as well. Diana was very fond of Frau Goebbels, who, with her husband, was often at dinner with Hitler. Goebbels, distinguished in public by his qualities as an orator and master of mass propaganda, had in private life an almost exaggerated sense of humour which, surprisingly, Hitler shared; it was one of the bonds between them. They also had in common a love of music.' This little circle of music-loving merry-makers might have been expected to leave evidences of geniality, but needless to say, what really they had in common was national socialism, its aims and its fruits. Die Gefährtin des Teufels, a biography of Magda by Erich Ebermayer and Hans Roos, describes a lunch at Schwanenwerder at which Hitler had the Mitford sisters on either side, attacking him for the appoint-ment of Ribbentrop as ambassador to London. 'During the double-pronged female onslaught Goebbels said nothing. He smiled. Lady Unity had already been staying a fortnight in his house and had been easily influenced. Hitler listened, but said nothing and soon changed the subject.' Not improbable, but beyond verification – like similar passages in Wilfred von Oven's auto-biography Mit Goebbels bis zum Ende (1949, published in Buenos Aires, as well it might be). Here long soliloquies are put into the mouth of Goebbels himself, reflecting on the past in the manner of *Hitler's Table Talk*. Unity, so Goebbels judged here, 'in point of fact through her exaltation and sledge-hammer methods was more harmful to us than helpful', an opinion which he also extended to Mosley. This book has been the source for an unproven belief current in the Goebbels' circle, that before shooting herself Unity wrote a letter of farewell to Hitler, 'putting on paper her whole love for him with an almost poetic rapture . . .' so becoming the first casualty of the war – which, of course, had been Lady Mosley's very phrase.

Helmut Heiber's penetrating biography of Goebbels traces the man's social insecurity in much of his behaviour, down to details like 'employing a prince to carry his briefcase'. Although not naming him, Heiber was referring to Prince Friedrich-Christian zu Schaumburg-Lippe, born in 1906, sixth son of a former ruling prince. Joining the party in 1929, the prince was an aggressive orator and publicist, with an axe to grind, that the nobility were not pulling their Nazi weight. Goebbels' adjutant from 1933 to 1935, the prince has also written *Dr G*, not exactly a *pièce justificative*, but which bends over backwards to show his old master as a hard-working minister. After a denazification trial, the prince served a prison term, and is today still a prolific author. I had also wanted to test out on him another of the denunciation stories, concerning another prince, a Lippe. Paul Wallraf, who had left Germany in 1924 and was therefore an *Auslandsdeutscher*, told me how he had dined, probably in 1936, with Lali and Freddy Horstmann, Berlin's most fashionable couple, in their house on the Tiergarten. (Lali Horstmann's book, *Nothing for Tears*, on their sad fate, should be better known than it is.) At this dinner party a Prince Lippe-Biesterfeld had openly railed against the Nazis to his neighbour, Unity, only to be arrested with his wife forty-eight hours later. 'Everybody knew that if you ran into Unity you had to be careful,' Paul Wallraf said, 'she was a very dangerous woman, I saw her afterwards at parties and kept well away.'

Prince zu Schaumburg-Lippe said: 'Unity was very often in the Goebbels circle at Schwanenwerder. Goebbels liked her though he used to stress that she was a friend of his wife's. With Magda, Unity was on the closest of terms, they used to go out shopping, to the cinema and the opera, and running around. She stayed for weekends or even for longer periods. She was extremely nice to the Goebbels children and played with them a lot. Full of jokes and wit, very much at home there. I don't remember her talking politics. Hitler used to drive out at odd hours to Schwanenwerder, unannounced, to put his feet up. I was only at Schwanenwerder on duty, but I went there very often. We went boating round the lake, that was a favourite pastime, she used to come along. On the photograph I have of her she is with an Indian prince and Goebbels. If we had known what role she would play, we might have paid more attention to her. As for the denunciation you've told me about, I wouldn't know, I shunned the Horstmanns. The Lippe-Biesterfelds were well connected with the SS. It might have been a Lippe-Detmold.' And there that matter rests, up in the air, ectoplasm of the period.

During the night of 6 March, Hitler ordered troops into the Rhineland, the final stage of wresting it back after the Treaty of Versailles; the rupturing, what is more, of political *démarches* with England and France. Among historians it is commonly agreed that this would have been the moment to take a position against Hitler, compelling him not to compel others. From now on, unresisted, he was to threaten force to get his way, gloating over his adversaries' reluctance to stand up to him militarily. Unity and Diana were reported in the press as entering Cologne in the wake of the German army, in the car of Field-Marshal Blomberg himself, the Heavenly B. An eye-witness account of the sisters at this juncture, and a photograph of them in front of lines of storm-troopers, is to be found in Ward Price's *I Know These Dictators* (published in 1937, in the freshness of events). Ward Price was a ponderous man with a monocle, a bachelor more blimp than roving correspondent, exactly suited to be the instrument of the *Daily Mail*'s curious two-step with Hitler, the extension into foreign affairs of its earlier endorsement of Mosley. Ward Price liked to tell the story of how he and his employer Lord Rothermere, and the latter's son Mr Esmond Harmsworth, were at Hitler's first dinner party in the rebuilt Chancellory on 19 December 1934. Ward Price became one of Hitler's favourites among foreign correspondents, Sefton Delmer not being amenable as originally hoped, while the Knicker-bockers, Sheeans, Shirers, Lochners, positively got under the skin. Towards the start of his book, after the account of the Chancellory dinner, Ward Price turns to Hitler's predilection for feminine society, and the Mitford sisters in particular. 'They are in frequent touch with him. Their arrival at the Hotel Kaiserhof in Berlin is generally followed by an invitation to go across to the Chancellor's Palace to take tea or dine, or see a film, an entertainment which is succeeded by lively conversation lasting till long past midnight. There is no more human trait in Hitler's character than the pleasure he takes in the light-hearted company of these typical young Englishwomen of today. I remember his delight when they paid him an unexpected visit in Cologne during the General Election campaign in April 1936. Hitler had not yet arrived when walking into the restaurant of the Dom Hotel, I found Mrs Guinness and Miss Mitford lunching there ... "The Führer does not know we are here, so it will be a surprise for him,' said Miss Mitford. While we were at lunch, Captain Rattenhüber, the head of Hitler's bodyguard, came to say that he had orders to drive me down to the station to meet the Chancellor's special train. "I wonder whether he would take us too," said the Mitford sisters when he had gone. I went after the officer to inquire. "I'm afraid I can't," he said. "It is the Führer's own car, and I have no orders to take any ladies in it, but I will arrange for them to have a window in this hotel, so that they can get a good view of the procession." "We don't want to watch the procession," said the Mitford girls, "but we do want to stand inside the row of guards in the hall of the hotel so that the Führer will see us directly he comes in . . ." As Hitler came into the hall, his expression was set and stern. He raised his hand automatically in response to the roar of "Heil!" that met him, and to the sudden upflinging of arms in the Nazi salute. Then his eye fell on the two sisters. His face broke at once into a smile. *"Was! Ihr beide hier!"* he exclaimed. "You must come and have tea with us."'

The comedy of the anecdote is rather blunted by Ward Price's comment on it, that the sisters 'keep free from all contact with German politics. By the natural charm of their good breeding and social training they have done much to enlarge Hitler's angle of vision upon Britain and the British character.' He was to return to this point in a long article for the *Daily Mail* on 3 January 1940, when Unity was arriving home on a stretcher from Munich. 'I used to think it a good thing that Miss Mitford should be in close contact with Hitler . . . In the morbid isolation which surrounds him, this beautiful and high-spirited young English girl was a unique figure . . . When there were any big entertainments at the Chancellory in Berlin, Frau Goebbels would be asked to have Unity to stay with her and bring her to the parties. I often saw Hitler and Miss Mitford in lively talk on such occasions. It was generally of a jocular, teasing kind. In fact the only joke I have ever heard credited to Hitler was made to her. Unity had expressed her indignation that some people had gone on dancing while the German national anthem was being played. "Perhaps they did it out of enthusiasm," was the Führer's rejoinder.'

'Wheels were set in motion,' writes Jessica in *Hons and Rebels*, 'for Muv, Boud, Debo and me to embark on a Mediterranean cruise in the spring of 1936.' Family antics were at their usual pitch through Gibraltar, Algiers, Athens, Istanbul, except at a stop at a Spanish port, from where the party drove to the Alhambra in Granada. Hitler had given Unity a swastika badge, the *Goldenes Abzeichen*, gold with his signature engraved on the back as special authorization for her, a foreigner, to wear it, as she invariably did, the outward and visible proof of inward devotion never relinquished. Spaniards spotted it. 'She was surrounded by a hostile crowd, shouting at her, clawing at her clothes, trying to tear off the hated symbol. Other cruise members hustled us back into the car, and we started the long, miserable journey back to the ship. On the way back Boud and I had a furious quarrel which ended in a fist fight and hair-pulling match, and my mother crossly sent us to the cabin as soon as we boarded the cruise ship.'

This ship, the Laetitia, was on a Lunn Hellenic Travellers cruise. Lectures were included in the evening as part of the normal programme. When the improbably fellow-travelling or 'red' Duchess of Atholl gave a critical speech against 'Modern Despots', Unity insisted on equal time and next day preached fascism, shocking some of the more elderly passengers by a vivid description of Hitler's dressing gown. An article in the Daily Express, 16 September 1938, reports this jousting between the two committed ladies, and it is a little suspect for being so late in the day. (Lady Redesdale, however, published a letter in the Daily Telegraph, 14 August 1936, taking the Duchess of Atholl to task and telling her that 'Nazism is from every point of view preferable to communism', her anger perhaps arising from shipboard confrontation.)

A party of schoolboys were on board, stowed somewhere down in the steerage, and they included Michael Farrer, Rudbin's younger brother, Peter Ramsbotham (now Sir Peter, British ambassador in Washington) and John Biggs-Davison (a member of Parliament). The cruise was organized by Sir Henry Lunn, founder of the travel business that bears his name; his grandson Peter Lunn was employed on board and he writes to me, 'It was Jessica whom I knew best, and what I learnt about Unity really came from her. She shared a cabin with her sister, who would lie on her bunk while she said her night prayers to Hitler, whose large signed photo would be propped up before her; at the end of her prayers, she would, still lying on her back, raise her arm in solemn Nazi salute. Unity was unabashed when I tackled her as to the truth of this story. I asked if she believed Hitler knew somehow she was praying to him and that he then interceded for her with God. Unity said she did not know how it worked; she simply knew that it worked.'

By June she was back in the Pension Doering, and according to Mary's diary, had arrived there on the 22nd in a Mercedes from Nuremberg, after the Midsummer Hesselberg meeting. She had returned with Streicher to the scene of her exaltation of the previous year, as indeed she was to do one more time yet, but never again was she to be handed the microphone. Anglo-German relations were now deteriorating, and she could no longer serve to embellish them. Early on the morning of the 26th she left for Vienna, to be met at the station by her host in Austria, Janos Almasy.

Just turned forty, Janos was sleek and groomed, handsome in his leisurely way. His dark hair was no more out of place than his smile. His wife, Marie Esterhazy, sister of Prince Esterhazy, head of the family, had been paralysed from the waist down by poliomyelitis in her childhood, and it was common gossip that Janos had been dowry-hunting when he married her. The Hungarian Counts Almasy were indeed rich, but Janos was only an aspiring relation of theirs, though not inclined to correct those who called him *Herr Graf*. He was very much a lady's man, attentive, and since Marie had been so prematurely restricted to her wheelchair, he granted himself a seducer's licence.

Bernstein, where he drove Unity, was then about two hours from Vienna, eastwards across plains at first, until into the Burgenland unexpectedly steep heights rise to dominate the approaches to Hungary. The village of Bernstein was unspoilt, ancestral, a Central European idyll, with some fifty or sixty peasant houses or smallholdings, all low buildings in the pale Habsburgian yellow and green and pinkish washes, with plaster and decorated casements; and doorways high enough to allow hay-carts into the enclosed farmyards. At the village centre was a pond, with geese, and chestnut trees, while nearby stood an outstanding eighteenth-century baroque building, the Hotel Post, the former coaching house. Of all this, the trees survive best – the pond has been drained, a modern café has replaced the Hotel Post. A drive still leads to the very summit of the slope above the village, and there the castle holds its own, an irregular fortress within buttressed brick walls. Its courtyard is shut in. At its far end is an external staircase, prettily overgrown with creeper, and painted on the wall is the horoscope which Janos cast for himself – on his way up and down from his study he would pass it and its motto in Greek, 'In life there is no luck, only harmony and order.' Here he had made his appearance to Baroness Bentinck with Hitler's dire horoscope as the war was beginning.

At the near end of the courtyard, under the portcullis entrance, is the main staircase, its sweep upwards decorated with coats of arms of previous owners back into the Middle Ages. Round the entire first floor runs an encircling corridor, with the bedrooms off it, first Marie's suite, then Janos's, and his study, Laczy's rooms, on round to the dining room and the main drawing room, a *Rittersaal* in its way, dark, heavily curtained, with the inscription 'Dracula' round the open fireplace, a joke typical of Janos.

Little has altered in Bernstein since Unity first set eyes on it. Floorboards creak and the plumbing groans as ever; blackened old canvases of ancestors or saints in the gore of appalling martyrdoms, to suit Marie's piety, still cover the walls. The electric light is dim as a candle. Bernstein is famous for its ghost, the White Lady, who is supposed to race down that one winding corridor to supplicate the Virgin on the wall outside Marie's room, as benign, really, as Asthall's Grey Lady. Women have not tamed this castle; these are garrison quarters for men-at-arms, an outpost against invaders. In 1945 the Russians swarmed into Bernstein, to be faced by a scared Janos, but not too scared to compromise as best he could. Every house for miles round was looted, the castles thoroughly sacked, except for Bernstein. Marie, on the other hand, blonde and placid in her wheelchair, was attacked by the Russians, hauled to her feet, and beaten when she could not stand. The resulting injuries hastened her death. Her brother, the prince, was to be arrested in Hungary, rigged into a show-trial along with Cardinal Mindszenty, and freed from prison only in the revolution of 1956. After Marie's death, Janos married Countess Pacetta Kuefstein, who today runs Bernstein as a hotel. She received me there, ushering me into Marie's bedroom (where, amid the gloomiest religious relics, including a framed letter of 1913 from Pope Pius XII commiserating on her illness, and a signed photograph of Bishop Mikes, I confess I did not sleep, my senses pricked for the White Lady). Along the passage is Tom's Room, the name on the door. Unity survives in the papers in the study which with true generosity Countess Pacetta allowed me to consult, especially Janos's pocket year-books, and invaluable they have been to this narrative.

On Janos's desk is a skull with a Jewish *yarmulke*, or cap, perched on it; also a piece of polished serpentine, a soft gem-stone usually glorified by being called jade, from the quarry on the estate which Janos had discovered and exploited profitably, this particular strip chiselled with Hebrew lettering, supposedly a curse in the form of an acrostic. And in the drawers lie folders of horoscopes, duly filed, neat and tidy, Tom's and Unity's among them, both cast after their deaths. How mad the books in the locked cabinets are! Vehlow's *Astrologie*, Eliphas Levi's *Salomonische Schlüssel*, Papus' *Traité élémentaire de science occulte*, *The Tarot of Bohemia*, the *Sephir Jezirah*, boxes marked Pentacles, Mithras, Stones, Months. Such was the man who now steered Unity into his life, not to budge Hitler out, for that was inconceivable, but rather to be his simulacrum: Janos too had created a world responsive to him alone. Countess Pacetta knew about Unity only what Janos had told her, and he had not been one to dwell on the past. He would have been off-hand to me, probably, behind a mask of flippancy, but he died in 1970, before I had heard of him.

As it was bound to, Bernstein struck Unity as the most beautiful and thrilling place she had ever seen. Also frightening. Janos introduced her to Marie, and to his sister Mädy, who was married to Anton von Gyömörev. Then he walked her round the garden, which he was redesigning in conjunction with a man after his own heart, Professor Kleiner, the title being as honorific as Janos's. Kleiner had a wife whom nobody set eyes on, he was a small-time artist, landscape gardener, astrologer, occultist, toady on the rounds of the country houses, earning his keep for months on end by undertaking commissions which might or might not be fulfilled. The new swimming pool at Bernstein was part of Kleiner's plans. Kleiner is the comparative of klein, meaning small, which translates into Hungarian as Kisebb, the man's nickname. They changed for dinner at Bernstein, a meal at which Janos's mother did not appear. Marie might also stay in her rooms, to save being carried up and down. Afterwards Janos and his guests would sit up in the library till the small hours, talking, on this first evening, as on many others, about national socialism.

For entertainment, Janos depended on his neighbours, the Auerspergs at Schloss Stein, the Erdödy sisters, known as the Countesses Jimmy and Baby, at Kohfidisch, Count Paul Drashkowitch at Güssing. House parties drove to and fro. This first visit of Unity's to Bernstein was unusually quiet in that Janos showed her only the estate, the farm, the small factory where the serpentine was hewn and manufactured into objects for sale. They paid a Sunday visit to Dr Smital, who ran a clinic in nearby Oberwart, often drunk and always a rabid Nazi – but he was out, and they had to make do with watching a village football match. That Monday, Janos and Kleiner had business in Graz, so Unity accompanied them, first sightseeing, then lunching at Reifs, the best restaurant in that charming town, and finally meeting up with Princess Auersperg, who drove with her to Stein. They dined at Kohfidisch with the Countesses Baby and Jimmy Erdödy, who returned the call on the Tuesday, bringing with them a journalist whom Unity found ausgewaschen, washed-out, for he did not respond properly in the late-night run over national socialism.

Janos drove her back to Vienna on Thursday, the summer heat breaking into a thunderstorm. As any tourists, they walked round the park at Schönbrunn, and drove up to the Kahlenberg, to dine out of doors there with a view of Vienna lit up below. Janos put her on the 10.55 Munich train; she travelled third class and sat up all night. What she could do for him by way of a bread-and-butter letter, on arrival in Munich, was to walk to Hoffmann's and reserve another complimentary ticket for the coming Parteitag. Mary in the Pension Doering received her: 'July 3rd. Unity back. Diana has taken Wootton Hall, near Ashbourne. July 4th. Unity gone to England.'

As Mosley puts it in his memoirs, 'I married again in October 1936. Diana was living in a remote country house at Wootton in Staffordshire ... My scanty holidays were spent at Wootton.' In the course of her visit there, Unity found time to write to Roy Harrod, at Christ Church, Oxford, giving the Wootton address and telephone number – Ellastone 22. She beseeched him to come to Germany some time; she would show him everything, and once he had seen it all he would not think her wicked any more. It sounds as if she was apologizing for a row, but Sir Roy has no recollection of this. To her love, she added a Heil Hitler, further decorating the tongue of the envelope with a swastika – envelope and letter alike were preserved for many years, almost as specimens, on the mantelpiece of Sir Roy's college rooms.

Diana and Unity, Mosley also reveals, were invited by Hitler to the Olympic Games in Berlin, which marked the Nazi zenith internationally. The regime had reason to congratulate itself on so beautiful and imposing an out-door exercise. To thousands of ordinary visitors, the country's order and discipline appeared to have been achieved at no cost. Other reasonably informed people were awed by the rampant militarism into believing that submission to Hitler's policies was the governing European reality. The foreign Prominenten, among them Unity, were dazzled at the receptions given on a Roman scale by Goebbels and Goering.

Leni Riefenstahl was with the Ehrengäste throughout, directing Das Olympiade, her film of the Games which earned her much recognition, and I had hoped that she would be able to shed light on Unity there, and elsewhere as we have already noted, but she said, 'I'm sure I never met her, never even saw her.' What about the published photographs, then, the evenings with Streicher, the Erlangen Congress, the columns in the Fränkische Tageszeitung, the snapshots with Diana and Mary and Michael Burn at the Parteitag, the gleam of her eyes in the lift of the Deutscher Hof? 'Photo-montage.' The blanked-up wall of her memory has been delineated tellingly and at length by Susan Sontag in the New York Review of Books, 6 February 1974.

'September 4th. Unity and Iris Mountbatten came to swim. . . . September 8th. Unity and I by train to Nuremberg. Hotel Roter Hahn. Herr FitzRandolph came for us – Grand Hotel – Putzi took us to the opera – Meistersinger. Hitler's box interval – everybody frightfully overdressed. September 9th. Opening of Congress. Unity and Tom came. September 10th. Lunch with Ward Price. Congress – Rosenberg and Goebbels long speeches. Dinner Grand Hotel. September 11th. Congress – Third row – Jean de Faucigny-Lucinge and Janos . . .' Mary's memory, to its credit, is confirmed by the diary. The opening, or aertex-shirt, evening of this Party Rally is already familiar. By the 11th, a Friday, Unity had lost her voice; she was in a dervish whirl of cheering and racing by bus or on foot from one gathering to another. To the joy of that third row, where Mary and Diana and Tom were also sitting, Hitler recognized them and smiled. He had arrived late enough to miss the first speech, but in time for Reichsärtzeführer Wagner. After lunching at the Grand Hotel, the party decided not to attend the Frauenschaft meeting at the Congress Hall, but to compensate, Diana, Unity and Mary stood in boiling sun from four o'clock until quarter past five to see Hitler driving by on his way back from the address by Frau Scholtz-Klink, the dour leader of the Nazi Women's Association. At half past eight they paraded again at the Zeppelin-wiese, for a review of the political leaders. Like a pantomine star, Hitler was produced under a tent of blue light projected by a hundred and eighty searchlights. A march past of banners. A speech by Robert Ley of the Arbeiter-front. Then Hitler himself speaking. And so back to the Grand Hotel, though Unity was beginning to feel ill, and preferred her room at the Roter Hahn.

Early next morning, at eight o'clock, the shuttle by bus between hotel and Congress Hall resumed, for the Hitler Youth Review. Hitler was not on display until half past eleven. Back to a hotel lunch, and in the afternoon Tom, Diana, Unity and Janos had seats in the front row of the Congress Hall, to listen to Hans Frank, the Nazi lawyer who was to become governor of Poland, Otto Dietrich, Amann the publisher of Mein Kampf and the Völkischer Beobachter, and Reinhardt. Once again, Hitler timed his entry to be late, but Unity enthused to see him smiling at her several times. Dashing to the hotel, they had barely time to prepare for the evening function, a bivouac dinner given by the SS. The special secret-police and terroristic role of this body was already clear, and symbolized by their encampment separate from all other units. The SS and their guests dined at long tables in a huge tent, while their band played and the men sang. Unity talked to the official host, Himmler, to Streicher, Graf Helldorf the chief of the Berlin police, Gauleiter Wagner, and many others. Hanfstaengl arrived by himself in time for the Zapfenstreich, or 'taps', after dinner. 'Putzi does handies' was the phrase to describe how he over-demonstrated his pleasure in Unity's physical presence, or perhaps he was hoping to reward himself for having hustled them into the opera.

The Sunday start was even earlier, at six, for a bus to the Luitpoldhain for a march-past of massed Nazi formations, Hitler taking the salute. He spoke again. Afterwards the Mitfords walked home slowly in the milling crush, but had strength to spend the evening in the Congress Hall, where Mary and Janos joined them, in the second row. Hitler entered at half past six, and duly smiled several times to his English friends. The day may have been too long, or its emotions may have driven out all sense of perspective, but whatever the cause, Unity was no sooner back at the Grand Hotel than she had a flaming row with Mary whom she accused of taking the place of Tom and Janos at dinner, 'which was awful of her'. Mary answered back, and summed the incident up that day in her diary, 'September 13th. Tea with Janos. Back to Grand Hotel. Unity is sometimes intolerable. "You can't sit there, there is no room".' While Mary and Janos had been having tea tête-à-tête, Unity had been jostling homewards, and perhaps the sight of them comfortably alone had fired her jealousy. At any rate, something snapped, the quarrel was not dispelled. Mary was good-natured enough to lug Unity's trunk back to Munich, but the more and more fragmentary diary references from now on tell their own story of friendship declining.

On the 14th, the whole Congress came to an end. At the Zeppelinwiese, the Wehrmacht columns were marshalled for a farewell taunt of cannon-fodder. The Daily Express picked Unity out among onlookers at the immense march-past. And it was at this point that Hitler, hitherto so smiling, chose to play a thoroughly Mitfordesque practical joke on Unity, by seating her in his reserved stand next to Eva Braun, an angled introduction which Mosley in his memoirs finds 'highly individual'. Eva Braun did not varnish her dislike and jealousy of Unity. In 1932, as Hoffmann's sales assistant who had caught Hitler's fancy, but been dropped, she had attempted suicide. Hitler was appalled. His niece, Geli, had killed herself in the previous year, and Eva Braun's thoroughly self-controlled gesture stretched taut his guilt. He came to believe that his attentions to women brought them malign luck. As much as a woman could, Eva Braun had snared him; she too had her rabbit-run of tea at the Carlton and the Vierjahreszeiten, her palpitating half-hours with the dream-lover, the afternoons wasted by the telephone, the frustrated appointments at Hoffmann's house, when he – both she and Unity used this third-person figure of speech, flatly, as though for a deity – did not show up, chucking her without a word. On 10 May 1935, when Unity's drive at Hitler was at its most startling freshness, Eva Braun put on paper a pure feminine outburst against her new rival – the loose diary pages survived and have been published conveniently in Nerin Gun's Eva Braun: 'Herr Hoffmann lovingly and as tactlessly informs me that he has found a replacement for me. She is known as the Walküre and looks the part. Including her legs. But these are the dimensions he prefers. If this is true, though, he will soon make her lose thirty pounds, through worry, unless she has a gift for growing fat in adversity.'

By the 1936 Party Rally, Eva Braun was feeling more secure, installed in the Berghof at Berchtesgaden, the maîtresse en titre. Frau Hess, for instance, explained to me, 'We were so often at Berchtesgaden, my husband always liked Hitler. At receptions for Lloyd George or the King of Bulgaria, or whatever, Hess would say, Ilse, you don't mind if you're here, do you? So look after Eva. And the two of us would go on a walking tour in the moun-

tains or something. Hess always treated Eva Braun with the respect due to
the lady of the house. After 1933 she was his mistress but it must have been
terribly hard for her being kept out of sight. We knew Unity as a nice
young girl, I met her in Elsa Bruckmann's house on the Karolinenplatz, or in
the Osteria Bavaria, but never at Berchtesgaden. I tell you who she looked
like, Geli, she was the Führer's type.'

All the same, that seating arrangement may be considered the knocking
together of two like heads. For in the evening, at the Congress Hall for the
closing ceremony, Unity was no longer in the place earlier allotted for her
by Hitler in his reserved stand, but back in her own third-row seat. Hitler
made his entrance at a quarter to eight, to the overture of *Die Meistersinger*.
Unity seems to have been more than usually overwhelmed by his speech, by
the singing of *Deutschland über Alles* and the *Horst Wessel Lied*, which made her
cry. Hitler, she again observed, looked at her very seriously going out – it
is a wonder how, after all, behind the shattering public performance, this
little private comedy of his had been signalled.

During the loose ends of packing up in the hotel, a man came to photograph the Mitfords for a book on race – there are many rumours, all un-
traceable, of what became of this project. Were posters subsequently made
of them as Aryan types? Did Goering really make a much-quoted remark that
his wife and the Mitford sisters were the most beautiful Aryans he had ever
seen? Anyhow by mid-morning they were finished, and Janos drove Unity
and Tom to Munich, happening to spot Baldur von Schirach's car, and trying
to outpace it. To reach Munich was to head for the Osteria, where Mary had
been imprudent enough to be lunching with *Das Kind*, her fiancé, in order to
pour out everything that had happened – so Unity and the others moved on
to Walterspiels, the famous gourmet restaurant in the Vierjahreszeiten,
emphasizing, so it appears, the new rift. Unity took her rolls of film to be
developed, and then, with Tom in tow, was headed off by Janos on to the
Salzburg autobahn, to spend the night in the Hotel Elizabeth at Ischl, as a
preliminary to a spell of recuperation.

Acquaintance with Prince Jean-Louis de Faucigny-Lucinge, it will be recalled,
dated back to Biddesden. Now my aunts and uncles have known him since
that time too, he has a house close to Royaumont, and it was there that I
called on him, to learn that he had flushed the 1936 Party Rally out of his
system by writing a journal. This document of seventeen typed pages he was
kind enough to offer me; not all of it concerns Unity, of course, and I have
amalgamated below his spoken and written evidence. Unity, as he remembers, had first come to Paris with her mother, and he had been asked to do

what he could for her. 'She came to the house in the Avenue Charles Floquet dressed in a grey suit like any other young Hitler girl. She had come from attending a session in the Chambre des Députés, someone had given her a ticket to the visitors' gallery. She was terribly proud of herself for having worn her Nazi badge there. I told her that it had been foolish and could have ended badly. She told me that I had to see Germany for myself. Curiosity was aroused, and when in the summer of 1936 I was going to Venice, I decided to stop off in Nuremberg. I had Bobo's Munich address, and sent her a telegram, which received the laconic reply, Expecting you. So I made up my mind to reach Nuremberg early in the morning of the 11th, and if I failed to find a hotel room, to return to Munich. Count Wilczek, the German ambassador in Paris, had told me that he could do nothing to gain admission for me anywhere. At the Grand Hotel I asked if there was a reservation for me, but nothing was available. Hearing my name, the concierge handed me a note from the sisters to say that they would be back in the evening. Annoyed, I was hesitating whether to return to Munich, when in the hotel bar I bumped into Prince Henry XXXIII Reuss, who spent part of the year in Paris, and before I could explain my predicament, we were joined by Comte Jean de Castellane, formerly Président du Conseil Municipal de Paris, married to Prince Fürstenburg's widow and strongly pro-Nazi, with Jules Sauerwein, the eminent political journalist. They were taken aback by my presence as an ordinary spectator, but Sauerwein led me over to a chubby young man in charge of French visitors, and Otto Abetz, for he it was [later ambassador in Paris], got me a room at once, and told me that everybody would be meeting up in the hotel dining room at one o'clock. Fifteen minutes later, I had a programme and invitations to all the organized meetings and receptions. More than that, a young Count Alvensleben with an official car was attached to me.

'In the dining room, there were tables for the English delegates, about seventy of them, for the Italians, the Belgians, the French. At one table were Guy de Pourtalès, the writer, Raymond Recouly and Emmanuel d'Astier. The Belgians were principally Rexists [Belgian fascists], the most prominent being Pierre Daye. We were waiting for Ribbentrop. When he came in, he shook everybody's hand and said something banal. Suddenly I caught sight of the Mitford girls recognizable at a distance, in spite of their grey suits, because of their height and their make-up. Astonished to see me in the thick of it, they had to make do with a little wave of studied detachment. After lunch they rushed over. "What a relief," said Bobo. "We didn't know what to tell you. The Führer's staff hates us. We can't get near him here, and if we'd asked for a room for you, that would have been enough to dish you." To tease them I did not bother to explain how I had managed. We went for a short walk and Bobo explained how during the entire rally, Hitler was too busy to be able to relax, and so she could not see him. She added that in intimate surroundings, he was as jolly as could be and that time flew by in telling scabrous stories. Ribbentrop in particular loathed her as he set himself up as the one and only intermediary between the Führer and Great Britain. Bobo also assured me that Hitler had no sex life, he abstained completely.' There follows a lengthy description of Hitler, with Goering and Hess, at a five o'clock reception for the delegates. Escorted afterwards by Count Alvensleben, the prince found himself in that third row of the Congress Hall, with Mary and Janos, for the speech of Hitler's, and his smiles. He continues: 'I saw for myself Hitler's powers of incantation, like an African witch-doctor. We returned, some of us deeply depressed, some shrugging it off, others convinced. Diana and Bobo were beside themselves with enthusiasm, and I went with their party to have a beer in a beer-hall. Diana and Bobo spent some of their days, they started to say, going to morning classes for Nazi youth, "We're going to do our lessons." But we felt we were being criticized there, the atmosphere worsened because of the girls' make-up, and after ten minutes we left. Bobo found it nasty, she was embarrassed for the rest of us, and left for her hotel.'

On the 12th he lunched with them all, but was not present at the SS bivouac supper. Next day he and Pierre Daye relieved the tension by sightseeing in the nearby medieval town of Rothenburg, and on returning to Nuremberg he found he could stand no more, and beat his retreat that evening to Venice.

At Ischl, on the 16th, Janos acted the guide round the Kaiservilla, where the old Emperor Franz Josef had slumbered away half a century's summers; then on to Graz for another lunch at Reif's. Janos's country gentleman routine was unchanging, and it says something for the force of his peculiar personality that voiceless, aggressive Unity complied with it. Two days sped by at Kohfidisch with the Countesses Baby and Jimmy Erdödy. The house, whose low central block has supporting wings, was one of the prettiest examples of eighteenth-century baroque until the Russians pillaged and ruined it in 1945, using the period bound books in the library as deep litter for their livestock. Punctually on cue Kisebb joined them there, for a shoot, and for wine-tasting at Janos's *Weinberg*, or small winery, this corner of the Burgenland producing some of the best of Austrian wine.

On a quick sortie to Bernstein before the weekend, they passed through Oberwart, calling on Dr Smital, who this time was in his clinic, in the process of cutting off a child's finger. Unity watched, and afterwards was still able to eat sausages for lunch, rounding the experience off with a visit to Dr Smital's pigs and a session with his cognac. At Bernstein Unity wrote to Hitler, presumably to thank him for the reserved seats, and she had a refresher course round what were called Janos's 'anti-Jew and Freemason books', taking some of them back to Kohfidisch for evening reading and some 'pornographic Yiddish jokes', which, whatever they were, made Tom cross.

Sunday was hot and sunny, the perfect harvest weather for Hungary, where the partridge season was open. Country houses were still maintained there with a lavishness already a fable elsewhere in Europe. Budapest was in its closing years as the Sleeping Beauty among capitals. The Almasys had a flat in a house at 29 Horthy Miklos Körut (now Bela Bartok út) close to the famous Gellert Hotel by the Danube. Janos was in the habit of spending a regular week or two there, discharging himself from rural Bernstein. His younger brother Laczy, whom Unity among others called Teddy, made his home in the Horthy Miklos Körut, in so far as he was not away on African explorations. A dare-devil, he had been a pioneer pilot in the manner of Saint-Exupéry; he had accompanied Karl, the last of the Habsburg rulers, in the ill-prepared attempt to recover at least the throne of Hungary in 1921. With a Count Szechenyi and a Count Esterhazy, Laczy had also driven across the Sahara, acquiring expert knowledge of the desert, of the nomads and of Arabic, earning for himself the honorific sobriquet of Abu Ramleh, or Father of the Sands. He wrote up his travels in several books which are available only in Hungarian.

This remarkable adventurer had been ill that summer with one of the nameless Egyptian bugs which were his occupational hazards (he was to die of amoebic dysentery in 1951) and he had been in hospital at Szombathely, just inside Hungary from Bernstein. Unity and Baby Erdödy left Kohfidisch to collect him there and, after a delay at the frontier, they all lunched at Györ, reaching Budapest in the evening. Laczy typically went straight to the boy-scout school of gliding, to show the others an Olympic machine, and to arrange a flight in it for Tuesday afternoon out at Gödöllö, the flying field. Then he took Unity to the family flat where she was to spend the next five days, and as Janos had not yet arrived, he gave her dinner at the Ritz, with Baby Erdödy and a Countess Zichy.

Everything Unity did was in pursuit of pleasure in the sense that nobody and nothing compelled her but her own inner motives. To herself, she justified her life as voluntary dedication to Hitler, as though that were self-sufficient cause, and of course to most people she was therefore boring to be with, if not repulsive and worse. With Janos she could relax, among like-minded people, though they did not have her urge for emotional exposure. In Budapest she was for once able to enjoy herself and leave it at that, at the hairdresser, and the dress-shops, as a tourist, lucky enough to be introduced to a foreign city by its residents. True, on her first afternoon, after seeing the Gellert Hotel and having tea in the Zichy palace, she had an argument about national socialism with a Prince Lippe (a resonance of the denunciation story?). That evening she dined at the Kis Royale with Janos and Laczy, Baby, and Hannah Mikes, all of them going on to the Café Ostende to hear a gypsy band, and finally to the Arizona Bar – turning night into day, as was the done thing in Budapest.

Hannah Mikes, now Mrs Van Horne of New York, is the younger sister of Princess Auersperg. At one time she was to marry King Zog of Albania. Her uncle was Count Mikes, Bishop of Szombatheley, who died in 1945 on his front-door step trying to save some girls from being raped by Russian soldiers. Bishop Mikes was the object of one of Unity's typical inquisitions, for some time in the following year at a party in London she met the photographer Costa Achillopoulo who had just returned from Roumania, and she informed him that she had been asked to stay with a bishop in Transylvania, but was afraid he might be a camouflaged Jew. Hannah Mikes said: 'The Kis Royale had excellent food and a gypsy band. I often saw Unity at Bernstein or Stein with Janos, who was amused by her and interested in news of Hitler. I knew him all my life, he was intelligent but overwrought. A skirtchaser, but there was nothing between him and Unity, no sex. Marie was good natured, she told me how amusing it was to have Unity about, she thought nothing of it. Laczy had a flat in Cairo and I was in Egypt with him and Janos when the Germans invaded Austria. The Egyptians were delighted. Taher Pasha took us round, an uncle of the king's, a bachelor, German-speaking, and a very strict Moslem. Tom was Janos's friend. Tom had been to stay with us at Zabola in Transylvania. My uncle, the bishop, was only about twenty kilometers from Bernstein, so Janos went often. As for being Jewish, my grandfather's father was a Swiss called Moser, which in Hungary is usually a Jewish name, that is the source of the remark. I disliked Unity strongly, she went against the grain. We called her the Danish cow because she was big, strong and stupid. After she shot herself, Janos came to me in Budapest and asked me to hide her diaries, making me promise not to read them. I wish I hadn't kept my word, but I did. After some months he took the parcel back.'

Her sister, Princess Tima Auersperg, whose husband is now dead, played a more important role in the life of Janos. She says, 'We often had Unity here at Stein. She was quite simple and nice so long as you didn't speak about

Hitler, for if you did, she became hysterical. That supper in Munich with Lord Redesdale which you mention, on 28 October 1935, was when I first met Unity. In the middle of it she stood up to say that the Führer was arriving on his train and she had to meet it. I was sitting next to the father and he said to me, I'm normal, my wife is normal, but my daughters are each more foolish than the other. What do you say about my daughter, isn't it very sad? Unity was not much in love with Janos. Hitler was her one God. When she wanted to kill herself and was in hospital, I visited her just before her departure and she said over and over again, Now please tell me who I am. I tried to talk about the old days but couldn't. It was awful.'

Among those who turned up during the week in Budapest were Prince Kari Auersperg and Taher Pasha, with Laczy, at the Ritz. The revolve of lunch, tea and dinner, with plan-making in between, left little time. After the glider experiment, everybody fitted in a cocktail party at Countess Szapary's. Next day was spent at the shops and the sights, such as the view over the city from the ancient citadel. On Thursday Unity and Janos packed up to return to Bernstein, their car followed by Prince Kari and Baby Erdödy in theirs, in a procession, with halts at Szombatheley and Kohfidisch. Home again, Janos and Prince Kari recorded a wireless talk, on the recent Party Rally, an airing of Nazi views for the Germans, probably, as the Austrians were to hold their own for a year or so longer. Tom had greeted them at Bernstein. Much of the remaining week of the holiday was spent indoors or on the usual drives to the neighbours, for the weather was changing. On the Saturday, two English guests arrived, Christopher Hohler and Pamela Tower. Pamela Tower became vice-consul in Innsbruck. Her stepfather, Sir Patrick Ramsey, was minister in Budapest. She said: 'Through Hannah Mikes, I knew Tima Auersperg and all of them. I was much taken with Tom. He was delightful. I remember Unity swallowing all the stones in her compote of plums at lunch. She showed me her photographs of Hitler. In order to get them through the Hungarian customs she had pasted pictures of saints all over them.'

An expedition on Sunday to Schloss Hainfeld, where Freiherr von Hammer-Pugstall had a celebrated collection of oriental art, broke the monotony. Kisebb also arrived to entertain them, and so did Herr Pohl, Janos's factor from the nearby small town of Grosspetersdorf; he travelled on the Wednesday with Unity and Tom from Grosspetersdorf to Oberwart, a stretch of the branch line to Vienna. With a pause for buttered eggs at the station, they caught the same 10.55 connection to Munich, travelling third class as usual, which meant sitting up for a miserable and crowded night, arriving in the cold dawn of Thursday, 1 October.

The following week, Diana married Sir Oswald Mosley in secret. Unity was of the very small number of people in the know, though as we shall find, her mouth was not kept quite shut. The public at large heard nothing, until, after a long lag of two years, the *Daily Telegraph* and the *News Chronicle* simultaneously broke the story on 28 November 1938, and even then the dating and the details were inaccurate, claiming that the wedding ceremony had been solemnized in Hitler's private offices in Munich, with Hitler himself as best man, and Lammers, the *Reichsnotär*, or Head of the Chancellory, as witness. The *New York Times* also published this news. Lady Ravensdale, sister of Mosley's first wife, stated in her memoirs *In Many Rhythms* (1953) that reports of the wedding were circulating in the summer of 1937, thanks to Ward Price and others, and that 'the Führer and Goebbels had been witnesses'. ('My heart stood still, though he denied it to all of us and his children.' Nor did she care for the portrait of Hitler hanging at Wootton.) Blackshirt newspapers prevaricated, and it was not until the birth of a son in December 1938, that Mosley issued a statement admitting that his marriage had taken place 'just over two years ago'. His memoirs explain that secrecy was in order to spare Diana possible violences. 'The only answer appeared to be Germany, where by a reciprocal arrangement English nationals could be married by a German registrar instead of at the embassy, as is necessary elsewhere. Frau Goebbels, who was a friend of Diana's, helped to arrange the marriage, and after the ceremony she gave a luncheon for us at her villa near Wannsee. Hitler was a guest. From this incident arose the rumours that Hitler had been my best man, while in fact this duty was performed by an English ex-officer of the 10th Hussars who accompanied me.' In his book *The Fascists in Britain* (1961) Colin Cross has yet more information from Mosley himself: 'The marriage took place before a registrar in a house near the Reichs Chancellory with everyone present sworn to secrecy. The gathering consisted of the bride and groom; Josef Goebbels, the German propaganda minister; Frau Goebbels and two British witnesses [the Hussar officer and Unity]. A few hours later Hitler marked the occasion by entertaining the newly married couple to dinner, with the Goebbelses and other members of the Nazi hierarchy among the guests.'

On 4 October, the Sunday, Mosley had led a march of fascists from Tower Hill to Victoria Park. Inhabitants of the East End had been advised to remain indoors. 'East London,' Mosley declared, 'will be asked to choose between us and the parties of Jewry.' The result has come to be called the Battle of Cable

Street: in fact the unprecedented provocation and violence offered to the
East Enders permitted the government to legislate, and the Public Order Act
tardily but appropriately clipped the wings of fascists and communists alike.

Sefton Delmer, with the sixth sense of good reporters, was on the scent, but
the scoop eluded him. In the Sunday Express of 11 October, he wrote, 'This is
the story of a secret visit to Berlin which Sir Oswald Mosley, leader of the
British Union of Fascists made last week. He arrived unannounced on Monday
[i.e. 5 October] and slipped away quietly on Thursday. His stay in Germany
was devoted to studying the organization of the Nazi party. He met Dr
Goebbels, Germany's propaganda chief, who told him, I understand, about
Nazi organization and the holding of its vast mass meetings . . . Last Tuesday
night Sir Oswald listened to Hitler's speech to 20,000 cheering Nazis at the
opening of this year's winter help campaign in Berlin. In this speech Hitler
made a violent attack on European democratic government.' The Daily Telegraph correspondent had also been there, and he reported how 'Hitler delivered
another attack on Bolshevism and democracy. He classed them together as
destructive elements in international life. Like Dr Goebbels who spoke before
him, he used bitter words about the foreign Press, and declared that "these
ridiculous newspapermen could squirt their poison" for all he cared. One
surprise was caused by the presence of Count Preysing, Catholic Bishop of
Berlin, in the front row of the audience. Just behind him sat the Hon Unity
Freeman-Mitford. Both distinguished themselves by giving the Nazi salute on
every possible occasion . . .'

This Winterhilfe rally should be looked on as something of a stag party,
for obviously Hitler was not free that evening to give a dinner. Since Mosley
was already off on the Thursday, it follows that Wednesday, 8 October, was
clear for the wedding and the entertaining, though the date has never been
confirmed by bride or groom.

Of all the German Prominenten at that wedding, none have survived, except
Henriette Hoffmann, known as Henny, daughter of Hoffmann the photographer and purveyor of complimentary tickets. Hoffmann was a drinker and
raconteur, a court jester. In Hitler was my Friend, a rather disappointing book
from someone who had been so much in the know, he describes how Hitler
raved over Unity's personification of perfect German womanhood, 'a fact
which drew from Eva Braun many acid comments, which were zealously and
faithfully repeated to him . . . but he was even more aware of the value, for
propaganda purposes, of Unity and her blind devotion to him . . . with every
fibre of her being she yearned to see Britain and Germany closely united. She
often said to me, she dreamed of an impregnable and invincible alliance
between the Ruler of the Seas and the Lord of the Earth; the land of her birth

with the country of her hero could, she was convinced, achieve a world dominion ... the declaration of war was the final, cataclysmic explosion which shattered for ever and beyond repair everything that she had hoped and lived for ...' This dream of Unity's passed for *realpolitik* in such Nazi circles, on the grounds that the immediate expedition of a nation's power is its one and only imperative, an intolerable simplification as well as a misreading of democracy. Hoffmann was not intelligent, but quick on to the main chance. He lived in Schwabing round the corner from the Osteria. His first wife had died young, so he took his daughter Henny with him everywhere. Hitler called her 'mein Sonnenschein' [my little sunshine]. A year younger than Unity, she was only seventeen when in 1932 she married Baldur von Schirach, leader of the Hitler Youth, with Hitler and Roehm as her witnesses. In the war, von Schirach became Gauleiter of Vienna, and afterwards served twenty years in Spandau as a war criminal. His memoirs, *Ich Glaubte an Hitler*, repeat the standard stories about Unity in the standard tone of wonder, though as Henny Hoffmann points out, the work was ghosted with even greater disregard than in her father's case, from tapes recorded after his release – 'That was a book Baldur neither wrote nor read.' In her own book, *The Price of Glory*, which is mostly about her days in Vienna and the end of the war, she mentions Hitler at the Osteria and how 'the Mitford sisters, two pale blonde English girls wearing sky-blue sweaters, came to his table. Hitler was fond of explaining why English girls had peach-coloured skins; it was due to the rain, he said, the walks in the English rains.' Which opinion seems easily derived back to source. Frau Hoffmann, as she now is, was writing about the women in Hitler's life when I contacted her. To show me exactly which tables Hitler and Unity had occupied, she led me to the Osteria, with a pause for the broken Nazi emblem over the lintel of what had been her father's studio – Eva Braun's work-place and trysting-place – fifty yards away. In the Osteria, she was greeted with a perfect blend of manners and regret by Frau Salvatori, who has been there for a lifetime. Unity, she said, 'always parked that little car of hers illegally outside in the Ramburgstrasse, but the police knew it and never did a thing'. Himmler used to come in by himself, and he had been the one to make the knees tremble.

Frau Hoffmann said: 'She used to go to a hairdresser in the Ismaningerstrasse in Bogenhausen, and he first advised her to meet Hitler in the Osteria. We all used to go on picnics, and she was on one of the biggest of these. We'd set off towards Austria, we sat on the ground, five or six girls, the daughter of Müller of the *Völkischer Beobachter*, and Frau Brandt, and my father and Hitler more to one side reading the papers. In 1936, I think. She used to be driving right across Germany in her own car. She seemed rich, rather too much the lady for me. She had her books, the back of her car was a jumble of books and pullovers any old how. Her German wasn't too good, she carried a dictionary round. She had great liveliness. The royal family were only puppets, she told me once, and she'd boast how she had carried a little pet rat into Buckingham Palace for a garden party.

'Hitler used to say, Unity talks so much that whenever I have anything to announce to the world, I have only to tell her. Her influence? Here comes this young girl out of the blue and persuades him of all the things he wants to believe, she strengthens his feelings about England, and they sit saying Yes, Yes, to one another. My father said that she was a figure from antiquity, riding in triumph in Hitler's chariot. There was nothing special about my father getting her complimentary tickets, he was responsible for that, it was the regular way of going about things. Once he got her an invitation to some select fancy-dress ball, and she had a costume made by Inge Schröder.

'At that wedding party for the Mosleys, Hitler said to me, This is an occasion which we must not speak about, it is a secret and we must ensure the news does not get out. Baldur and I and Hoffmann were there. There was a room for receptions, wonderful flowers and a meal. But Hitler kept his distance from Mosley and it was so obvious that I asked him why. He answered that if he joined forces openly with Mosley he would lose his prospects of manoeuvring with other politicians, like Lloyd George. Mosley, he said, had imitated him, and that was why he did not approve of him.

'Baldur liked Unity, though we had our disagreements over her. Magda Goebbels was particularly kind to her, inviting her to Berlin, introducing her to all the opera singers.

'The gun she had was a 6.35 Walther. We girls all learned to shoot, we had to swim, ski and ride too. To Hitler sport was all-important. I'd learnt to shoot a revolver of this calibre at the Foehring shooting range, where she had also learnt. We were taught to handle guns, to load and clean, and we practised target shooting. Whether Hitler actually gave her the gun I don't know, and it would be dangerous to say so, in case it created the impression that he was trying to get her to do away with herself.

'My father was telephoned by Gauleiter Wagner when she shot herself, and he insisted that Hitler be told, they were away on the Polish campaign. Hitler was very upset, and he also worried about her dog, asking everyone what should be done with it. Hitler gave orders that someone be with Unity all day and every day. Frau Schaub visited her most. I went two or three times but I saw her only when she was completely unconscious. Quite without a scar. No blood.'

•   •   •   •   •

It had struck me that St. Clair Gainer, the consul in Munich, would have been bound to play a part in preliminaries for the Mosley wedding, if only to steer through red tape. Gainer had been in Munich first from 1925 to 1928, and was posted back to this sensitive post in 1933. He spoke good German, he saw eye to eye with Sir Eric Phipps on the Nazis, and his despatches stand up excellently today. When Sir Nevile Henderson became ambassador, he had Gainer shuffled on to Vienna, as an act of appeasement.

His widow, Lady Gainer, said: 'Diana was to have married Mosley in Munich. Witnesses were to have been Hitler, Goebbels and my husband. He had been dreading it, prevaricating as best he could, and he was very pleased when they switched to Berlin. Why keep the wedding secret? I asked Unity, and she said, They're crazy. After the wedding she came back to Munich, and when she described it she said she could not imagine why it was all so secret.

'Lots of English girls got tied up with SS men, you know, the boots, the red leather in their cars. We had a lot of trouble. Unity was a dumb blonde. She came quite often to see us at home in the Mauerkirchestrasse, but was at the consulate more often still, turning up without an appointment. Once her father came and said to my husband, Can't you persuade Unity to go away? She was persuaded to go to Paris, but stayed there for only two weeks. [This was during Lord Redesdale's Munich visit of October 1935, and chimes in with Mary's diary entry for 21 December that year, 'Unity came from Paris.']

'She used to tell us in a spirit of amusement how she had met Hitler for the first time. Diana had Mosley, she had nobody to look up to until she found Hitler. It was as simple as that. Diana and Unity at the Nuremberg Party Rally had come up to me with stars in their eyes and said, Wasn't the Führer divine today? She liked to drop remarks about Hitler. In 1937 she told us, Hitler is banting because he wants to look well for Mussolini's visit. After that famous encounter, that same day the Duke of Windsor was coming through Munich. It wasn't easy for us. A day or two later Unity came and said, If there hadn't been the Abdication the Führer might have been greeting the King of England today. Hitler lent her a car whenever she wanted one, and she liked to turn up to us in it. She had nothing to do with the British colony here. She liked to argue with my husband, but it was water off a duck's back to him, he used to laugh at her.

'Afterwards when we were in Vienna, she dropped in from the Burgenland somewhere to tell my husband, When you warn British subjects to leave, don't warn me, because I intend to stay. They had taken a lot of Jews to an island in the Danube and stranded them there to die, and she said, That's the way to treat them, I wish we could do that in England to our Jews.'

Not even subsequent, more gigantic atrocities diminish the horror of this outcome of the *Anschluss* in the Burgenland. Louis Golding, in *The Jewish Problem*, described it at the time: 'Either because this is a frontier area, or through the zeal of some local leader, it was determined to make a clean sweep of the Jews from the entire province ... The Jewish population of the Burgenland was about 5,000 souls ... all were rounded up and forced to sign a declaration that they would leave the country within a month. Without waiting for the expiry of this period of grace, a large proportion were literally thrown over the frontier but the neighbouring countries could not risk the dangerous precedent of opening their gates. Fifty-one were put on a breakwater in the Danube, near the Czechoslovakian border, without food or money (the Storm Troopers had relieved them of these unnecessary trifles). Czechs rescued them and provided them with temporary shelter and food; but they could not venture to let them have permanent hospitality, and so despatched them to Hungary, who in turn sent some back to Austria; others were shipped on a barge and were afloat for weeks on the Danube, a human flotsam and jetsam, until at last they were allowed to anchor outside a Hungarian river post.'

Corroboration of Lady Gainer's memory is to be found in her husband's despatch Number 97, 27 September 1937, from the Consulate General, to the Embassy, and forwarded thence to the Foreign Office. 'I have the honour to report,' wrote Gainer, 'that towards 10 p.m. I went to the station to receive HRH The Duke of Windsor and the Duchess of Windsor who were on their way to Paris. At the station I met the Hon Unity Freeman-Mitford who told me that on Friday the 24th instant she had been at tea at Herr Hitler's flat in the Prinzregentenstrasse together with Dr Goebbels and several of Herr Hitler's suite. The conversation had turned upon the coming visit of Signor Mussolini and upon his personality. About this opinion was divided; Dr Goebbels and several others maintained Signor Mussolini's essential greatness and declared their confidence in him and his country. Herr Hitler himself had expressed doubts about both and had not concealed his personal dislike of the Duce. He had said that he did not intend to run Mussolini's errands in the Mediterranean or elsewhere but that the visit was useful as showing "certain other countries" the strength of the Berlin–Rome axis.

'Miss Mitford told Herr Hitler later on that the Duke of Windsor was arriving on the evening of the 25th. Herr Hitler replied, "If Mr Baldwin had not turned out King Edward VIII I might have been receiving him today instead of Mussolini", and evidently regretted that this was not the case. Miss Mitford then said that she had heard it stated that His Majesty's Government had asked Herr Hitler not to receive the Duke of Windsor to which Herr

Hitler had replied that he knew nothing of this and would gladly receive the Duke of Windsor any time.

'I cannot of course guarantee the accuracy of Miss Mitford's statements but I know that Herr Hitler is on familiar terms with her and talks freely to her. It is, however, possible that Miss Mitford who is a fanatical worshipper of Herr Hitler, puts words into his mouth which he may not have uttered or which she may have misunderstood, but subject to certain reservations I have little reason to doubt the accuracy of what she occasionally tells me of her conversations with the Chancellor.' (F.O. 371/21176.)

Here is a crystalline example of how Unity served as a mouthpiece for Hitler, in exactly that ploy which he had confided to Henriette Hoffmann. Were Goebbels and the others conniving, winking? He spoke, she trumpeted. There were conclusions for 'certain other countries' to be drawn from these events. The version of Hitler's attitude towards Mussolini which suited him had been planted on the Foreign Office, via Unity's gossiping to Gainer, as it was certain that she had the chance of doing, not as a deliberate agent, but revelling in self-importance. If Hitler was so tepid towards Italy, then England's commitment to that country could be advanced and tested. At the very least, English policy-makers, anyhow known for indecision and squabbling on this point, would have something else to stumble over. It worked to this extent, that on 18 October Gainer's despatch was minuted, 'If this is true, Hitler will not have committed himself to Mussolini in Berlin,' and initialled 'A.E.'. Just four months later, Anthony Eden resigned as foreign secretary, pincered by the Berlin–Rome axis, to the considerable pleasure of both Hitler and Mussolini.

Home for Christmas in 1936, she was in time for the final spasm of the Abdication crisis, in on the kill of her ambitions to link her actual and her adopted monarchs in joint-ownership of the world. The Abdication speech was read to Parliament in the afternoon of 10 December, and Unity took advantage of her right as a peer's daughter to a place in the House of Lords gallery. Unity whispered fiercely to her neighbour (the sister of someone in this narrative, but who wants her name kept out), 'Oh Hitler will be terribly unhappy about this, he wanted Edward to stay king – I think I shall have to make a demonstration against this,' but for once, she thought better of it.

On the 15th, she was at the customary London banquet of the Anglo-German Fellowship, the only organization which endeavoured with some success, and even social respectability, to present arguments for surrendering to Hitler on all possible occasions. In the main speech of the evening,

Ribbentrop demanded the return to Germany of the colonies lost after the First World War, and this was also one of Lord Redesdale's favourite hares, which he chased in several speeches in the House of Lords. He and Lady Redesdale were seated with Unity at the top table. So were Lord and Lady Rennell, Nancy's parents-in-law. It is a matter of curiosity that masquerading among the more anonymous guests was the spy, Kim Philby.

9

MITFAHRT

Lank and leonine, Putzi Hanfstaengl is to be bearded in his lair on the Pienzenauerstrasse in Munich, as though a mist of forty years had lightly evaporated. His lantern jaw is as firm as ever, he roars, he subsides, his papers avalanche from every flat surface. In this very place, this disordered library-cum-smoking-room of his, Hitler whiled away anxious time before he came to power, and there on the carpet he fell lovelorn to his knees before Putzi's first wife, who reported afterwards, 'Das ist kein Mann'. On this piano Hitler heard – as I will – the *Appassionata* and the *Liebestod* from *Tristan*, played with pedal and barrel-organ gusto. Dr Pienzenauer, Hitler called him, and Hänfl, and other such endearments, all of which ended abruptly on 11 February 1937, Putzi's fiftieth birthday, in a weird attempt at murder. He was to have been thrown out of a military aircraft over the Spanish lines, and officially posted among the roll of heroes – but the pilot spilled the beans and by the end of the day Putzi was in Zurich instead.

The Night of the Long Knives had already set the Borgia pace for the *Prominenten*. In the August 1934 number of *Collier's*, to a wide American audience, Putzi had thought it wise to affirm loyalty in a piece entitled 'My Leader'. He believed what he wrote. Efficiently he collared foreign correspondents and he sponsored dignitaries, in that murky zone where fact-finding and opinion-making and free-loading wallow together. Unity was an unsolicited publicity hand-out, and Putzi's bandwaggon accommodated her: he looked after her and Diana at party rallies and Brown House functions right up to his downfall.

It is his contention in his memoirs that 'a remark of Unity Mitford started the chain of events. We had continued to see a lot of her in Munich, and she became a close friend of Erna. She was always gadding in and out of the Brown House ... I suppose she had some idea that, with her sister married to Sir Oswald Mosley, she might always go one better and end up as Hitler's wife. Because she was so much *persona grata* I made a point of keeping in with her, and tried to put over my own ideas in the hope that she would repeat them ... I may have gone too far one day. We were out on the Starnberg Lake with Egon [his son] in my yawl, and I must have been railing away in my usual fashion when she turned on me and said: "If you think this you have no right to go on being his foreign press chief . . ." The fatal remark of mine she repeated was one I had made criticizing the crazy militarization and soldier-cult of the party.'

From Zurich, Putzi moved to London, to a cottage in Maida Vale. Egon joined him. Efforts to entice him back continued sporadically until the war, some of them potentially lethal like those of Goering's, others well intentioned like those of Erna's. A document in the Foreign Office archives (F.O. 371/23089) 20 April 1939, for instance, succinctly states on the question of his residency in England, 'You will, I think, be interested to know that we have heard from a secret source that Putzi Hanfstaengl who has been resident in this country for some time may once again be received back into the Nazi fold. It appears that some sort of negotiations are going on with a view to his return to Germany.' In these negotiations, which Hitler alone could have resolved by pardoning Putzi unconditionally for whatever might have been said, Unity played a part with enough application to suggest guilt and a wish to make amends. If indeed she was responsible for this backstairs denunciation, then she had frivolously and hideously staked a friend's life on her own ideological purity, as a Nazi ought, though the consequences were not as foreseen, stranger ironies being in reserve. Because he had fled Germany in good time, Putzi spent the war in England and America, escaping retribution, and thus against the grain Unity may well have been the unwitting instrument of his prolonged old age safely in the Pienzenauerstrasse.

Putzi Hanfstaengl said: 'In 1933 I was in England with old William Randolph Hearst, we went to St Donat's for a house party including Elinor Glyn. I was on good terms with the Guinnesses, and met Unity through them in London – she was very much second string to her sister, tagging along. Otto von Bismarck contacted me as foreign press chief, with the request to introduce the two Mitfords to Hitler, and after that I had Unity on my hands, I didn't know what to do with her. I took charge, I acted as their bodyguard at Nuremberg. I sent her to my sister's house. Unity was meant for bed and children, but she had none, and I don't know whether she ever went to bed. What about "Putzi does handies?" It's my manner [he gives my thigh a tremendous horse-bite], that's all I did to her. Unity came to this very house much too often. She was good looking but not my type. She didn't come to my office which was opposite the Reichskanzlei, she considered me second rate, *abgetan*.

'These maidens stretching their arms to Hitler had *salutitis*, an inflammation of the arm-pit. I had extended jokes about their needing massage for it at Nuremberg. Hitler never talked to me about Unity, she could just as well have been a bath-tub with the water overflowing. He told me, The crowd is a woman and has sexual appeal, after a speech I feel as if I had had sexual release. To Hitler she had snob value. She spent her time snooping. She hated Americans, and she was a fanatical Jew-hater, always on about it, boring me with the Jews. She corroborated Hitler in his asininities, that was her chief failing at a critical moment. Her importance was that she fed him all the gossipy stories, but her influence was erratic. The English are thorough cowards but there comes a point when they will fight, that was what Hitler did not wish to know, and she fostered his delusion. I told her that Hitler did not listen to me any more and that she had to insist to him on the urgency of coming to some accommodation with the USA. Did she tell him? Of course not. She had fallen in love with the man. She wanted to marry him, not educate him. I remember her saying, Hitler is going to be the Emperor of Europe. She wanted to preside over the Nazis. That's what women want above all else: power.

'Only that once I went sailing with her – once too often. Through her Hitler heard that I had criticized him. When I reached London, she came to my house. She also invited me to a discussion with her in what she called The Garage, though it was fashionably decorated. I got the whole story there. She had a bad conscience, she knew she was to blame. They wanted me to go back, they wrote to me. I replied to Hitler, that either it had been pre-meditated murder, or a joke, and if the latter, then it stank. Without his written letter of apology, I could not go home. Unity said that Hitler was prepared to grant me a pension in Switzerland, and Erna would collect the money for me. They kept on at Hitler. Unity assured me that everything would have come right except for the proposal to transmit the pension in this way. Erna ruined it all, she told me. Erna would be a wonderful witness – they had liked each other, after this they hated each other – quack, quack, quack, this is very good tea, women say, very good jam, very good cakes, and a man's life is ruined.'

After the last of several absorbing conversations, when the Nazi leaders had been called up as at a phantom seance, a visitor's book is produced, and he writes under my signature, 'Poor beloved Unity'. And to the gawp-eyed young taxi-driver waiting in the street he speeds my departure with a huge piratical example of salutitis, laughing like an earthquake. (One year more, and it would have been too late. He died in November 1975.)

Erna is a year or so older, rising ninety, alert and imperious, with the command of a Queen Victoria whom she somewhat resembles. She can refer to herself in the third person as Miss Hanfstaengl. No better conduit into the Munich haute-bourgeoisie could have been found for Unity. The circle of Erna Hanfstaengl's friends had to come to terms with the Third Reich as best they could, the enthusiasms and the distastes finely graded, for they were after all German citizens and had families, professional people for the most part, with property, in business or associated with the arts. Erna entertained a good deal. Those closest to her included Eberhard Hanfstaengl, a cousin and director general of the Pinakothek art gallery, Arno Rechberg, a manufacturer of chemicals who died at the end of the war in an American camp where he was being screened, Sauerbruch the famous surgeon, Baroness Redwitz, Bobby Schrenk a writer, the Bruckmanns who were publishers, Frau Bruckmann being a Princess Cantacuzeno from Roumania and a Hitler-devotee of long standing, although she broke with him in the end. Unity could pick and choose among them. Erna's *dame de compagnie*, Pinky Obermayer, intelligent if sharp tongued, had been crippled by polio like Marie Almasy, and although she kept a flat of her own, she was a welcoming figure in the background at Solln, only eight years older than Unity. Besides Unity, Erna also took under her wing Rudi Simolin, only child of Baron Simolin, a friend with a fortune from aniline dyes, whose country house was at Seeseiten on the Starnbergersee.

Solln was bombed in the war, and the country house at Uffing has long been sold. Much has been salvaged, however, not least will-power. Erna plans to write memoirs from her copious diaries. Josefa, her maid, has been with her fifty years and more.

Erna Hanfstaengl said, 'When she stayed with Baroness Laroche I did not know her. She had learnt some German but it was rather poor, she improved a lot with me. The Braun Haus *Hausmeister*, a nice straight old officer, a major, one day came to me through Putzi and said, Miss Hanfstaengl, please help me place these Mitford sisters because I can't speak English and I am at my wits' end. Send them to me, I answered. I was running my shop. Right at the beginning they came there – they used to tease me afterwards about it, saying that they had seen my dress shimmering but since I had not come over to talk to them, they knew I didn't like them. I was having a party, a big lunch, they were bright so I invited them, and soon they came again with Tom. I had ducked out of sight from Nazi society. It was difficult to camouflage the English girls, they were so crazed for Hitler, with not the least idea how dangerous it was.

'On and off Unity lived with me practically the whole Nazi time. Her clothes were left in her room at Solln, with her books and photographs. In the winter she would come to Uffing. She was away in England or travelling of course, and she moved into the Pension Doering. She needed a room in the centre of Munich, she told me. Every summer, at least until 1939, she was my guest, not *en pension* either, I was a rich woman then. Tom used to drop in regularly, he wanted me to go with him to Cyprus where he was judge or advocate in a military court. Before the war Randolph Churchill came there three or four times – he introduced Sefton Delmer to me – and he was on the best of terms with Unity. I told her that she looked like his sister, and she answered, You know my grandmother was a very naughty woman.

'To be coming and going from my house was conspicuous and I told Lord Redesdale that Unity should not be running around like that. His response was to give Unity her car so that she would not have to depend on SS cars. Max, that SS man, took her out regularly. They were using her, exploiting her. The whole of the *Bund deutscher Mädchen* was against her, and could well have thrown acid in her face, I told her father that too. I know how deeply hated she was by the party. Jealousy of course. She was more prominent than some German leaders and they could not forgive that. Frau Himmler came into my shop and in the course of conversation she remarked on "that good-for-nothing Unity" – quoting what Himmler thought of her too. Himmler didn't like her. She had no idea of the implications. I told her, You can't laugh openly about Frau Himmler, you ought to be smacked. I apologized on her behalf to Himmler, to get off, so to speak. Frau Himmler was a poor wretch, who'd been through the First World War as a nurse, and nothing was left of her.

'I felt responsible for Unity and tried to stop her seeing so much of Hitler. With me she was on an island of safety, but all she did was telephone after Hitler and write to him and rush about. She hardly had time to read. Through Professor Hönigschmitt of the Technische Hochschule I arranged for her to have mathematics lessons, and the teacher said she was a good student, quick witted. She had singing lessons with Raventos [a Spanish tenor who married the grand-daughter of Grieg], she had a beautiful voice and Raventos said she would be able to sing Elsa in *Lohengrin*, her heart's desire. She was *intime* with Hitler and of course it was incredible that the top man of Europe should take her up and receive her at home. Because of it, they ran after her, she was at all the party occasions. She used to laugh at party women, how frumpy they were, how plain. I told her, You're acting as if the party were an operetta, but it is not funny at all. Everybody paid her fares and tickets, because they never knew when she might come in useful. Somehow she always seemed to come back from England. Lord Redesdale did not keep her short, and I wondered if there were political strings, whether open or secret. An English friend once told me that Unity did not have to belong to the secret service, she was doing her job well enough outside it. All she had to do was report to her friends what she heard and that set the picture. Rechberg was of the same opinion, she often went out with him – just reporting the gossip, said Rechberg, makes it ridiculous to some and impressive to others, and they're all equally pleased to let her carry on.

'She was English to the core, transposing her feelings on to us. She was sure Nazism would spread everywhere. She told me once she was going to become German; I told her not to be such a fool. She took up anti-semitism as breezily [mit Luft] as everything else, talking about Jews with her usual exaggeration; she wanted to have them all burnt. Burn the Jews, that's the thing for them, she would say, it was the fashion to chatter on like that. She treated Streicher like an amusement arcade. Her education forced these attitudes on her. I was trying to make changes in her. Only her education as a lady was perfect, and that appealed to Hitler, she didn't make love to him or fall on her knees and make an exhibition of herself as other women did.

'She went to Bayreuth without me. Hitler offered me his box for the 1939 Salzburg festival but I answered that I had my seats already. Unity did not talk to me all that much about Hitler but once reported that they had been discussing me and Hitler had said, What a great pity it is that Erna is such a cosmopolitan.

'Putzi's downfall would have been impossible unless Goering and Goebbels had wanted it. Putzi never much liked Unity, but that is no final standard to judge her by. She wore these people like a new hat – it was exciting for her.'

It was time for lunch, to which I had been invited. Josefa was with us, and Erna continued, 'When she came to me, she brought Ratular in a cardboard box. I had to be tolerant, telling myself that animals have their rights too. She used to put the rat into her handbag and sometimes it escaped. What happened to it in the end? We also looked after Boy, her dog, and Hannibal too, both English dogs.'

Josefa said, 'I rode on Boy, he carried me round and round the courtyard. Er war mein Pferd, my horse. I liked Unity, she was no trouble to me, and tidier than some we used to have. One Sunday morning when everyone including Miss Hanfstaengl was in church, Unity and Rudi came down and collected all the radios in the house, half a dozen of them, put them in the courtyard and turned them up full blast, each on a different wavelength. An orchestra of radios. I came down and sorted them out. On a Sunday morning, I ask you. That was Unity. We had cats and dogs in the house. Miss Hanfstaengl had a little dachshund with a bell round its neck. Rudi used to be up early riding and so had a siesta after lunch. Unity too. The dachshund's bell would wake them up and Unity would shout, "Horrid little dog!"'

·   ·   ·   ·   ·

One extremely penetrating observer in the Hanfstaengl circle was Friedrich Reck-Malleczewen, who refused all compromise where brutality and idiocy were concerned, an upright pessimist who went to his death in Dachau in February 1945. The fine cast of his mind is to be found in his moving journal *Tagebuch eines Verzweifelten* (1947). Of Hitler, glimpsed in the street, for instance, he notes, 'the scorified, doughy moon-face, in which are stuck a pair of mournful black eyes like raisins. So sad, so insignificant among the masses, so profound a failure, that even thirty years ago in the gloomiest times of Kaiser Wilhelm, this visage would already have seemed improbable on physiological grounds.' By chance seated next to Hitler in the Osteria Bavaria, he saw in him the petty clerkly official standing on his rights and his money's worth. Under an entry in this journal dated May 1937, he wrote up the fall from grace of Putzi, whom he considered the *enfant gâté* of Hitlery. 'Arno Rechberg and I were having breakfast with Putzi's sister Erna,' he began. 'Now she is foaming with rage, throws the entire blame for this scandal on to Goebbels, whom she reproaches for his sheepish envy, personal malice ... At Erna's breakfast with us was also a young English girl of that type midway between a soap advertisement and an archangel. She is called Unity Mitford and pays court to Herr Hitler at Obersalzberg, intending to become Empress of Germany and to avert the great confrontation between Germany and England. This overweening lady and he, the Lord Almighty, so be it: bon voyage ...'

Clemens zu Franckenstein, the musician and director of the Munich opera was also a friend of his (and of Erna's), and he relates how in the summer before the war Franckenstein was conducting a concert at which Churchill was present. So was Unity, but when she was introduced to Franckenstein, by his own account he turned his back on her, 'which was really the only decent thing to do'. And finally under an entry for January 1940, he wrote up how Unity had shot herself. The details are incorrect, which is hardly surprising as he can have gathered them only on the grapevine (though Erna could have filled him in), but his judgement is firm, nonetheless, that England has gained through the loss of this thwarted archangel.

It remains to be said only that Erna would hardly have invited Unity to breakfast three months after Putzi's flight if she had thought her really incriminated in it. Putzi, however, sees no exonerations anywhere.

'February 15th 1937', reads Mary's diary, 'Unity and Baronin [Laroche] came at 6. February 17th. Unity and [her cousin] played my piano. February 20th. Lunch Frau Bermann and Unity. *Sie redet zu viel.* ["She talks too much" – meaning that Jewish Frau Bermann ought to have known better and kept her trap shut in such company.] February 24th. Lunch Unity and her cousin. Decca gone to Spain with some crazy man. Unity and her cousin are going back to England.'

Unity's cousin, Clementine Mitford, had been a contemporary at St Margaret's. In the winter of 1936 she was learning German in Berlin. She said, 'Early in 1937 Unity telephoned to say she would be in Berlin and would I like to come to the Kaiserhof Hotel where she was staying with Diana. They were going to the Reichskanzlei for the anniversary of the seizure of power by Hitler [30 January], and they took me along with them. Then Bobo said, Come and spend the summer holidays with me in Munich. So although I went back that March to London, I returned in July to Munich with her, sightseeing all the way, we both loved that. At the Pension Doering she got me a room. Our two lunches with Hitler were in the Osteria Bavaria. Hitler sat in his alcove. Bobo said whatever came into her head, and spoke to him as she might have done to anyone, and he loved it. The name of Lord Londonderry [who had been in both Macdonald's and Baldwin's National Governments, the only minister of the period to have admired Hitler simply for the dictator that he was] cropped up and Bobo said, Everybody knows he's a joke. The point of that was to show up his friend Ribbentrop as a bad judge of character. She would stand on street corners, saying, The darling Führer is coming past, let's go and waggle a flag.

'That summer we went to Bayreuth on Hitler's train, which stopped at Nuremberg and there was Streicher on the platform to pay his respects. Bobo rushed out to him. For some reason Hitler did not want to see him, but she tried to stage-manage their meeting. I remember Streicher's shiny pate outside the window. Frau Winifred Wagner did not like having two young girls around, she was unfriendly, she would not speak English to us; Bobo liked to tease her. We stayed in lodgings in a tiny house and went every evening after the opera to Wahnfried to dine with Hitler. That I know, Bobo was never alone with him. One sensed she was not happy, a lonely figure, very eccentric though full of affection. In no way was she a person who wished to escape her background. I think she would always have come home.'

Esmond Romilly was the 'crazy man' with whom Decca had gone to Spain, in the Mitford upheaval of the season. Unity was dispossessed from the headlines. Hearing the news in Munich, she came scramming back at once, as she put it. Before she left she had seen her friend, as she was writing without further ado to Decca from Rutland Gate on 4 March, and he had been a perfect angel and comforted her like anything, though he was terribly sad himself about it. Boudledidge boomerangs such letters of Unity's high over the head of politics back to childhood: Hitler is cocooned in sentiment more appropriate to Nanny Blor. Still, Unity fell into the atmosphere of consternation, as though eloping to Spain was the equivalent of a death in the family, with condolences, flowers, Farve making tea for Muv in their sleeplessness, and vile Aunt Weenie remarking that it would have been better if Decca were dead. Mrs Hammersley, Unity reported, used to come to the house about five times a day, consulting each person, one by one, for individual slants on the affair, thoroughly enjoying the crisis. At a family conference it was proposed that Unity should fetch Decca back from Spain, an idea rightly scotched on the grounds that it might do more harm than good; the comrades at Bayonne would scarcely be welcoming.

Instead, after three weeks of distraction, Unity returned to Germany in the new car (black, with room for four people) which her father had just presented to her, and lovely she found it, henceforward being able to scram up and down the autobahn with that total freedom of movement which had so flustered Erna Hanfstaengl. By 24 March, she was with her lovely Streicher – as she could not resist trailing her coat to Decca – for two days before reaching Munich on the 26th, Good Friday as it happened, for the weekend. The Tuesday after Easter, the 30th, she had tea with Mary, the only moment they seem to have spent alone together since their row. Nor did it last long. Leaving Mary, she had the great good luck to be driving along in her car when her friend was driving in his, and they met at a street corner. He got out to speak to her, everyone rushed up from all directions shouting 'Heil!' – he had not known she was back, he seemed pleased to see her and she followed his cars back to his flat, to sit with him for two and a half hours, alone, chatting. He wanted to hear about Decca. As a favour, he had suppressed all mention of the dash to Spain from the newspapers. Clocking-in and debriefing thus, she had something to offer. And next day Mary's diary shows the old form, 'March 31st. Lunch Osteria. Hitler asked us to join him – Werlin, Brückner. Pleased to see us.'

In long letters to Decca on 3 and 11 April from the Pension Doering, she showed herself to be rather impressed by the derring-do of the elopement, and the congratulation wrested out of her is stronger than any reproach for hurting the poor Fem and Male – though on that charge she was herself in the weaker position. Therefore a little trumpet-blowing about her lovely Streicher and her friend who needed no further naming was in order; the DFD lines were fully manned, after all. She hated communists just as much as Esmond Romilly and Decca hated fascists, or National Socialists as she preferred to be called, and would naturally not make friends with them without a reason. Just as she would not hesitate to shoot Esmond for her cause, so she would expect to be shot by him, but meanwhile that was not necessary and they could be good friends personally. Family ties made all the difference, she argued lamely, for at the same time she stressed how much she despised that democratic-liberal-conservative English idea of walking about arm-in-arm with one's opponent as though politics were a business or a hobby. Because family loyalties were so powerful to her, one realizes, she resorted to the utterly unreal figment of them having to shoot each other, which was only an image expressing the need for both the old Boudledidge ways and the new Nazi life, or once again having her cake and eating it.

The plan had been to return home for the Coronation, which Mary's diary confirms on 28 April, 'Unity went back to England.' The Redesdales were in The Garage, having let Rutland Gate for the summer to the banker Helmut Schroder, whose wife Margaret had stayed at Asthall as a friend of Nancy's, and was also a cousin of Sir Oswald Mosley's, though he was not allowed into her parents' house. Mrs Schroder said: 'Lady Redesdale had shown me the house and when we came to Unity's room she said, You can't have this, it mustn't be disturbed – swastikas in flower-pots, Hitler's photos, and maps all over the walls. So I said we had to have it, and that was that. We gave a terrific party for the Coronation [on 12 May] and asked the Mitfords over from the mews. One of our guests was N. A. Bogdan, known as Boggie, vice-president of J. Henry Schroder Corporation, and I had warned him, Don't say anything to Unity. The conversation did turn on Hitler, Unity sat up in her chair and said how much she admired him. Boggie rounded on her, Who the hell are you and who the hell do you think you are? She answered, Don't you realize I am Unity Mitford. There was a crushing silence.'

The Coronation had been very swell, Unity reported to Decca on 16 May from Old Mill Cottage. She was looking forward to the Naval Review, to which Farve was taking her, to spend two days on board a liner. In the event, the Naval Review was heaven, the illuminations fairy-like, and best of all they had been guests of the government, not a penny to pay, and flowing champagne too. Did she really think that she had seen the Wehrmacht's partner in world-dominion? It had been one huge party on board, members of the Houses of Parliament, ambassadors and foreign delegates including her old acquaintance-in-arms Field-Marshal Blomberg, the Heavenly B, who was on this occasion replaced by the heavenly Terence O'Connor, the solicitor-general, who even promised to visit her in Munich. By then Decca had been married and Unity wanted to hear about the presents garnered in, for instance the gramophone she and her cousin Tina had clubbed together to give, and the amethyst necklace from Diana.

At the end of May Unity returned to Munich, and Muv either accompanied her or soon joined her, for by 13 June they were sending wish-you-were-here postcards to Bayonne from the Café Luitpold – where the dashing looks of Géczy the band-leader were a by-word in the family. Joy-riding off in the new car, Unity then drove her mother to stay with the Heskeths, who had taken Princess Starhemberg's villa at Ischl. Peter Hesketh said, 'In the early stages the Redesdales hated all this Hitler business – they wanted a happy family and nothing more. I travelled home from Munich with Farve and Unity, he'd gone to fetch her back and she was obviously not well [the October 1935 journey?]. We met at the station and stuck together. Not long after that Farve changed his attitude. Once at Rutland Gate I said how dreadful the Nazis were and Muv showed considerable interest and seemed rather pleased, saying, I hear only the other side and your point of view is so different. When they arrived at Ischl, Unity's car had swastika flags on it, and one long banner given to her by Hitler. We had English servants and the loyal Starhemberg servants who were strongly opposed to Hitler. Muv and Unity spent a few days. My mother took them over to Engleiten, a charming little castle not far away belonging to Lucy Goldschmidt-Rothschild, married to Baron Spiegel. When Unity was asked to sign the visitors' book, with a flourish she put a huge swastika opposite her name. Lucy picked the book up, hugged it and said something to the effect that it was her first swastika. When the day came for Unity to leave, and the car had been packed, her banner was missing. In tears, she had to set off without it. After the *Anschluss* our things were crated up and arrived at Liverpool a week before the war. Under the lid of the first box was Bobo's flag, hidden by the Austrian servants.'

In fact Unity had hurried back to introduce her mother to Hitler at a tea party in the Prinzregentenstrasse, which was none too successful as Lady Redesdale could speak no German, though this did not stop her insisting on telling Hitler all about bread. The Engleiten visitors' book has survived. Lucy Spiegel was the sister-in-law of Baby Friedländer-Fuld, Unity's one-time aunt, so possibly the swastika had personal malice in it too. When I discussed this episode with another of the Hesketh sisters, Joan, who had been present, she had staying with her, by chance, Mrs Janet Home, who like scores of other people had registered Unity simply as one of the tourist attractions of Munich. 'I was at Anna Montgelas's, who was Hitler-mad herself. Unity telephoned, then popped round. We used to go to the Carlton Tea Rooms for Sunday afternoon concerts. Hitler frequented it. The waitresses came round with a big tray of cakes including pink ones which the Montgelas girls chose, but as they were receiving them, Hitler beckoned and these very pink cakes were put on his plate. Unity had on a thick tweed skirt, a fur coat on top, thick shoes, a string of pearls. I saw her several times at the opera in Hitler's box.' Diana Quilter, now Mrs Tennant, was someone else introduced to Unity by Anna Montgelas. She had been staying with her at Oberau during the Winter Olympics in February 1936, she says, when 'Unity burst in to return a book, saying, I'm in a hurry because I have the entire government waiting outside. I didn't believe her and went to the door to see her get into the back of the leading car with the Goebbelses. Every year I went back to Anna Montgelas, and she arranged for me once to share Bobo's flat. We had a thundering party, with bodyguards in uniform, they got drunk, their ties came adrift early I think we started at the opera, in any case we ended in an all-night café with Bobo dancing on a trestle table in that camel-hair coat with a belt at the back which she wore. In London she sent me a card to a cocktail party she gave in honour of Lothar Streicher, but it was going too far to accept. Anna Montgelas told me, Unity says the happiest moment of her life was sitting at Hitler's feet and him stroking her hair.'

Without Lady Redesdale, who appears to have left for England by herself, Unity fell in again beside Streicher for the midsummer parade on the Hesselberg on 19 and 20 June. The mixture was as before. Streicher was accompanied by the leading personalities of his Gau, noted the Fränkische Tageszeitung, with General-leutnant von Roques of the Reichsluftschutzbund as principal guest of honour. After a final speech, and Hitler youth songs such as Im Frankenland marschieren wir, Streicher presented the Gold Hesselberg badge to Fritz Schöller, his deputy in charge of organization, 'and to the English Lady Mitford, who has already participated in past years in these rallies in Franconia, Julius Streicher handed the Silver Badge of the Hesselberg, as he did also to General-leutnant von Roques.'

From the Hesselberg Unity drove up to Berlin, to stay with Mary Ormsby-Gore, then married to Robin Campbell, and expecting a baby, or 'in pig' in the Mitford slang. Their flat was large and Comfortable, Unity informed Decca, and they had talked about her to amuse another visitor, Jakie Astor (Major J. J. Astor, one of Nancy Astor's sons), inventing stories in order not to disappoint him. Best of all was a whole evening with the Führer, who happened – once again – to spot her in a crowd outside the opera where she had placed herself. A message was duly sent, she climbed into the second car in his cavalcade and went to the Chancellory to sit chatting, quite alone (which two crucial words, of course, she was investing with whatever mystery could be inferred). Contact had been established, and the following night too she went with Hitler to Aida performed by the Scala Company.

Robin Campbell was a Reuter's correspondent in Berlin from February 1937 until early in 1939. He and Mary had a flat in Charlottenberg, in the

Flensburgerstrasse. Mary Ormsby-Gore said, 'Bobo had made her corner in Hitler. In her he liked what he called *dieser Fanatismus*. They both used to comb through the *Tatler* every week to mark the names of those who might come over to them when he occupied England. Several rather dizzy lords. They had great lists, the Nazis. Mosley was treated seriously but not intimately. I knew about the wedding at the time, Bobo said it was a great secret. That July I was pregnant. Bobo said to Hitler that she was staying with us, so we were invited to dine with him. He adored pregnant women, Bobo told me, He'll put his hand on your stomach and feel the baby. I didn't like the idea and refused. Bobo spent hours getting ready, trying on a frock and making up. Someone so insignificant called for her that I stuck him in the kitchen. Oh Dr Dietrich, Bobo said, when she came out and saw who it was. She adored children and marrying, and thought it awful of me to go back to London to have the baby. When Magda Goebbels had her sixth child, it was all of a sudden, a *stutzgeburt*, Bobo was in the next room – she told me how the sofa had to be re-covered.

'Ringing up the Chancellory, she could speak to Brückner but then "that horrible Brückner won't let me get through". Though she was at the Chan-cellory with Hitler a lot. She knew he was going to the first night of something and said to me, Let's go and look at the Führer in his sweet mackintosh, so we stood waiting, though as he came charging out with his heavies he didn't smile at her or anything. Did you see his marvellous blue eyes? she asked, and I said, Did you see his marvellous cruel eyes? Streicher rang up the flat once, I put the phone down. She found that out later from him and asked, How could you be so nasty to darling Streicher? She had the anti-Jewishness just by believing the Nazis. We were rather ashamed of her. We were giving a cocktail for the journalists, the Shirers and all, she was all dressed up with her badges and we told her she couldn't stay. She had Erich, but I was never allowed to meet him. Brian Howard used to make her pimp for him. At these *faschings*, we were all got up and he'd say, Go and get that boy. Then she became cross, saying, I didn't have any fun just pimping for Brian. She always had that pistol, very small and pearl-handled. The sisters had their running-away money, her form of it was that pistol.'

Robin Campbell added: 'I see her as a solitary figure in a mackintosh entering a room. Everyone attempted to keep her away from Hitler and her main trouble was to get access to him. She had to sleep with the ADC, she used to say, if she wanted an appointment. The pistol was to defend herself with against attacks by Jews, communists or whatever, she was in the flat boasting about that. I used to say, Would you really contemplate persecuting and torturing a Jew? but that was as far as I allowed myself to go, and she would turn questions away, saying, Streicher says they're so wicked. Her eccentricities were very violent. Everything came back to the obsession, she could not talk, to me at least, about anything else. She talked about Hitler as though about that rat of hers, in the tone of flat enthusiasm the Mitfords manage, and those with no conception of the mentality must have been scandalized. The more outrageous it was, the more she embraced it. The easiest way of avoiding the criticism of ordinary people was to exaggerate admiration of what was totally unacceptable and repulsive. I did mind her, because she maddened me.'

Berlin to Aachen is four hundred and fifty miles, which she covered in a single day when she left the Campbells, through Hamelin, where the river Weser reminded her of Asthall and of Ratulars. She left her car at Ostende and caught a boat-train. By 3 July she was at Old Mill Cottage with Tom, who was writing to Decca to describe a summer's day on which they were too hot to move off the lawn; though, Unity added, playing the sad tune, 'Somebody stole my Boud.' (A parody of 'Somebody stole my girl'.) In revenge Decca remembers a song she used to sing with Tom to annoy Unity, to the tune of a marching song:

> Wenn am Samstag Abend, Der Reichskanzler spricht,
> Eintopfgericht, Eintopfgericht, Grünkohl,
> Macht der alte Goering ein langes Gesicht,
> Eintopfgericht etc*

Like an object in a disturbed magnetic field, she was gyrating between England and Germany, between Hitler and family and friends. Pointless movement. Restlessness. Stridency. She had chosen the cage, but it had bars. By Friday 11 July she was back in Munich, writing a bright account of her journey with cousin Tina. They had left London on the Monday, retrieving the car in Ostende, to have six breakdowns in Belgium, with a wonderfully handsome Belgian mechanic to the rescue. She and Max had been to hear Géczy the band-leader – she was always foisting this Max on to Decca, transmitting his love, reminding Decca how once on a tram she had said German beds were uncomfortable and everybody had roared. She was unable to leave well alone. In the middle of July, Decca gave her the news that she was 'in pig' and Unity, rejoicing genuinely, mentioned a plan of hers to have eight darling little bastards, all with different fathers: Farve was literal-minded enough to

---

* On Saturday evenings when the Chancellor speaks,
  It's a one-dish meal, a one-dish meal, cabbage,
  And old Goering pulls a long face,
  It's a one-dish meal etc.

draft a new will with Probyn Williams, his solicitor, disinheriting any illegitimate grandchildren he might have.

The summer reached its peak, as we know, with the ride on Hitler's train to Bayreuth. It had been heaven to see a lot of the Führer, she was telling Decca on 10 August, but now he was back at his mountain for a bit. Among friends at Bayreuth had been Kukuli von Arent who had not heard of the escape to Spain, and was as amazed as two SS men there who apparently had called her *die lustige Kommunistin*. In that same letter she made fun of some Buchmanites who had invaded Old Mill Cottage, and even moved on to badger Diana at Wootton. What they had wanted was an introduction to Hitler, and Unity was not to oblige. In Munich the weather had been so boiling, she added, that she had found a secluded spot in the Englischer Garten for sunbathing with no clothes, until suddenly it had crossed her mind that Muv, with her second-sight, *knew*, and she had laughed aloud, though luckily nobody had come along to think her mad as well as indecent.

Kukuli von Arent's father had been naturalized English, a China merchant for thirty-five years, so that she was actually British-born in Shanghai. In 1927 she had married Benno von Arent who soon won a reputation as one of the leading young German stage designers. As a couple they had known Magda Goebbels during her previous marriage, as Frau Quandt, and this was to be their entrée to Nazi circles. At the Goebbelses one day, Benno had a long conversation with Hitler, whose views on politics and the theatre he shared. Benno worked at Linz, the Salzburg festival, the Deutsche Operhaus, acquiring the spurious title of *Reichsbühnenleiter*. Their house in the Bismarckstrasse in Wannsee – with the Goebbelses as close neighbours – had been sold to them by Baldur von Schirach because Henriette had not cared for it. From this house in 1945 Benno was arrested by the Russians in his reserve officer's uniform, and spent nine years in captivity, working in Stalingrad as a theatre architect. Eighteen months after his return, he died. His work was destroyed though Kukuli has his diary. She found in it, for instance, 'Führer sitzt lang und unterhaltet mit Kukuli' [Führer sits and talks to Kukuli for a long time] though what they sat and chatted about has left no trace. Unity's letters to her did not survive the war.

Kukuli von Arent said: 'I got to know her at the Winter Olympics. She and I were invited by Frau Goebbels. We stayed together for several days in the Hotel Vierjahreszeiten. I think she moved into the hotel with us. Magda was certainly there, so was his sister Maria Kimmrich. Every day cars came to fetch us for the games [it was one of these processions which must have stopped for Unity to return a borrowed book to Anna Montgelas, with Diana

Quilter watching]. As we had taken to one another, I invited her whenever she was in Berlin, and I saw her if I was in Munich. Unless she was with the Goebbelses, she would stay with me. Diana too. Goebbels did not like Unity much, he kept his distance because she was a foreigner. Nor did Benno, he sensed her as someone rather apart. Most men did not care for her, they were also a bit jealous of her access to Hitler, she was needlessly in the way. Though as a woman when you talked to Hitler you felt no physical attraction. With Unity he was the same as with any other pretty woman, politeness itself. She was like the Wrede twins, or Sigi von Laffert, one of the circle.

'In the Reichskanzlei I saw Hitler and Unity together a lot. You would be rung up during the course of the day and asked to dine, and Unity would be there, though not with other foreign guests. What also happened was that Benno would be at lunch at the Reichskanzlei and would ring round about two o'clock to say that the Führer was on his way. There was hardly time to lay the table for tea. If Unity was staying, she would come obviously. Hitler would just arrive with General Engel or Colonel von Below, one or two of his private adjutants, just like that. Hitler did talk to me about Unity, he used to say how typically English she was, far too susceptible. But he was pleased to have her around, she was his ideal, he loved tall women, not too slim, those with something to them. Eva Braun was very jealous, she was jealous of everyone. Schaub and Frau Schaub would have helped your quest, they knew Unity well. Unity *was* British, not as German girls are, she was a bit too cool, not to be flirted with. Goebbels of course didn't like women who were taller than him. I always ask myself whether she had no friends besides us. I remember her at Schwanenwerder in the Goebbels boat. We all used to make rude remarks about women like Frau Himmler. Magda thought it funny, the wives were sometimes so unpresentable. About politics Unity was exalted, but not in other things. With Hitler, in public, she didn't speak much.

'I used to go with her to Nuremberg meetings, to the Sportpalast if Goebbels was speaking. I took her off to the theatre and the opera. She would get up late, have breakfast in bed, and we'd go shopping around town, calling on Magda or friends. She had not much money and although she was well dressed she was thrifty. Of course whenever we went somewhere the men always paid. Benno didn't work in Nuremberg but Hitler invited us there, to seats in the *Ehrenloge* with him. We knew Frau Winifred Wagner and were asked to Wahnfried with Unity and the Goebbelses. Unity, like us, was in a private *pension*, but she'd spend the day with us.

'After the summer, in 1937, I went with her to London from Berlin. Unity said, Why go first class, it's much too expensive, we can save the money and I'll buy a dress with it in London. So we were third class. Under her arm she carried a huge photo in a silver frame, signed *Für Miss Mitford, Freundliche Erinnerungen von Adolf Hitler.* In the train she had it openly beside her. Unity you can't, I said, put a bit of paper round it. We reached Calais late, the boat had gone and we had to sit out of doors at a bistro to eat a meal – she had her picture out still. On the boat we just lay down somewhere, it was hours before we reached Dover, and then Victoria Station where her father fetched us. I stayed with her parents.

'Unity showed me round Oxford and Swinbrook, and then drove me to Diana's house in the country. I knew the secret of the Mosley wedding. I had a four-poster there and was very frightened, Unity had told me there were ghosts, and I had lived in China where ghosts were very much part of life. Her bedroom was next to mine, I heard noises in the night and got into her bed. In the early morning I went back again. Next, the door opened without a knock and there was a woman, so fat and short – who put an English breakfast on my bed without a word. I heard shooting and asked what it was. That's Sir Oswald shooting a hare for our supper, they said. On the way back Unity was at the wheel and Diana and I sang German songs. They didn't know *"Andreas Hofer"* and I had to repeat it just one more time for them. Unity knew more Nazi songs than I did. She had read *Mein Kampf* which I hadn't. In London her parents gave parties, especially one dinner – Unity wasn't there – when I had to tell the guests about Germany and Hitler. After that we returned home. Magda Goebbels told me about the suicide letter Unity wrote to Hitler, in which was the phrase *Verschönen Sie mein Volk* [be merciful to my people]. Magda usually knew what went on in the Reichs-kanzlei.'

Gerhard Engel, whom Kukuli von Arent had mentioned, had then been a major, the adjutant representing the Wehrmacht on Hitler's staff. His pub-lished diaries, *Heeresadjutant bei Hitler* 1938–43, contain one or two insights which he was able to amplify – the other adjutants, Colonel von Below of the Luftwaffe, and Admiral von Puttkamer of the navy, had known Unity more cursorily. 'The great enigma,' said General Engel, 'was what did Unity Mitford want? Did she have an assignment from the Secret Service? Or from Winston Churchill who was after all her relation? Was she really im-passioned for Hitler as she confessed, or for Nazism in general? We called her *Mitfahrt* [untranslatable punning on the idea of fellow-travelling]. We always sought information about her. In our circle we had to know. She had a shadow on her [Erich? Max?] but nothing else, and Hitler did not even want that much. Not from the Gestapo, they wouldn't have dealt with a foreigner, but the Abwehr, Canaris's men. But he told her a lot of political and military secrets because he thought he could rely on having them passed on to the right people by that means. He was sure she would hand on to the English, especially Churchill, whatever information he pre-selected. Also everybody knew that she was the sister of Diana and had great English connections.

'We thought frankly in our circle that she must be an agent and we were put on the spot. There were sound reasons for our belief. She was too thoroughly briefed about Hitler's life, and in particular his time-table. We might be in the dark, for the sake of security, but she knew everything about his meetings, conferences, intentions, private life. For example he would decide to have five o'clock tea in the Haus der Kunst and lo and behold! five minutes before he turned up, Unity was there. Hitler would be flabbergasted. She had her sources. We tried to find them and to this day I have never learned how she did it.

'We would set off at night from Berlin to Munich – she would be in Munich. When we drove from Munich to Vienna, Lady Mitford [as sometimes he calls her] was already in Vienna. Once it went so far that she was in Vienna because she had heard about Hitler's movements in Bernstein [he knew about that]. Someone must have telephoned to her out there.

'She spoke quite openly to Hitler, it amused him. He was an innocent party to it, he took it lightly, enjoying her company. He didn't think she was a paid agent. Hitler strongly distinguished his private life from his duties. Besides he always had a friend in Eva Braun, she resided at the Berghof and set foot in the Reichskanzlei only towards the end of the war. He had women as guests, of course, but avoided intimacy. I remember Unity staying in the Berchtesgadenhof, the hotel in the neighbourhood, but not in the Berghof itself. She saw him at the Osteria, the Haus der Kunst, with the Goebbelses, the Bayreuth festival. At Wahnfried we would sit down ten or twelve at table, with Frau Winifred and her daughters. In 1938 and 1939 Unity was there with her sister Diana, and very interesting conversations developed about England and the English fascist movement. At one lunch in particular [the occasion is also recorded in his diary under the date, 28 July 1939] Lady Mosley launched out into optimism about the movement's future. She believed that anti-semitism had at last taken firm hold. Hitler answered that fascism did not lie in the English character, and that although Mosley might be a fine person and had grasped the weakness of English politics, he could not seduce a whole nation. But throughout the war, there was a plan to spirit Mosley away. At that lunch, Unity was babbling on about the scandal of England's armaments; the approaches to London had only eight anti-aircraft batteries for total protection – this information she had from a cousin of hers [Randolph?]. The army had outdated equipment, hardly enough for two divisions, and England was in no position to wage war. Only the navy came in for her praise. She spoke in absolute innocence but Hitler was struck by the remarks, we had to check them out, finding out that this was more or less the truth. Of course we then became more suspicious than ever.

'Unity addressed Hitler as Mein Führer and put questions to him about art, castles, Munich life, the theatre in Berlin. Her opera and theatre tickets were arranged through us, so she was Hitler's guest. She would just ring up and we booked her seats. The two of them might discuss anything. But she had no political influence at all. She wanted it, she thought Hitler a great states-man, a gift from God to save the situation. I often spoke to her, here and there, in ante-chambers, once she gave me a description of London, being proud of English traditions. She told Hitler he ought to get to know the Burgenland, she pressed him to visit it. She had no great opinion of Italy. When she returned from a short Italian holiday, she was contemptuous of it.

'She was never Hitler's mistress. Absolute nonsense! She was never alone with Hitler that I am aware of. To have allowed such a thing would have been far too trusting of us – he might blurt out anything to her. So we had to invent pretexts to fetch him to the telephone, for some family matter or something, just to get him away.

'That same evening she shot herself, Hitler was told the news and he ordered immediate best treatment from the best doctors. He felt her fate was close to his. His whole entourage formed up in front of him to ask forgive-ness for having been so suspicious of her, and his eyes watered and he said, You see, she was nothing but an idealist. She couldn't have put off the war. He did get messages through to her, via Switzerland and Portugal. He also had flowers sent to her after her departure. He suffered for her. At first a lot, then less. Sometimes her name came up by accident later, mostly when he was complaining about the English.'

In Hitler's Table Talk, preserved at the time on Bormann's instructions, there are frequent, ever more preposterous daydreams about possible roles for Mosley and his imprisoned supporters. The entry for 16 August 1942 runs, 'Churchill and his friends decided on war against us some years before 1939. I had this information from Lady Mitford; she and her sisters were very much in the know, thanks to their relationship with influential people. One day she suddenly exclaimed that in the whole of London there were only three anti-aircraft guns! Her sister, who was present, stared at her stonily and then said slowly: "I do not know whether Mosley is the right man, or even if he is in a position to prevent a war between Britain and Germany".'

General Engel is right that Unity was not in Secret Service employment, and in his perspective Hitler was also right to have considered her an idealist. She was what she seemed to be. I took such meagre steps as I could to check this, and learnt that an approach to her had been vetoed on the grounds that her activities, as such, superbly condemned the Nazis: if their English supporters were upper-class girls struck blind with calf-love, then the ordinary citizen would see the ridiculous side, he would shrug, he would have none of it. Unity had only to carry on regardless. With hindsight, it was possible to admit that an opportunity had slipped through MI 5 fingers, in other words that Hitler's treatment of Unity as a handy megaphone might have been reversed and information, whether true or false, plugged back to him that way. That he endowed her with grotesquely disproportionate influence is as evident as her blabbing of whatever she picked up, whether about the Mosleys, or Decca in Spain, or anti-aircraft defences. What she received from Hitler looked like tablets of Nazi law to her. What she passed on to him were random gleanings. They could cook up as many *Tatler* lists as they liked, but her prejudices were valueless to him because they were formed in Germany and unrelated to English realities – though who can assess the extent to which the man's tortuous instincts and mental attitudes were thereby confirmed or altered? If nonsense was palatable, he swallowed it whole.

Canaris's men in the Abwehr, however, did a thorough sifting to have reached out to Bernstein, a holiday with Janos in Italy, and the name of the dog. We know what Janos thought of Hitler. What did Hitler think of him?

'19th August,' Mary's diary reads, 'Diana came – they have three invitations to Parteitag, she said.' But by Thursday 26 August, Unity had completed another of her mammoth drives, to Bernstein. The next ten days of summer slipped idly by. Tom was there as from Friday onwards. So were Marie-Eugenie Zichy, Kisebb, Baby and Jimmy Erdödy. Herr Pohl, the factor on the estate, was misguided enough to take the Bernstein party to a service in the Szombathely synagogue. A plan for Janos and Unity to visit Yugoslavia was shelved with the discovery that visas could not be obtained in time before the Party Rally. The quake of the holiday, however, broke after dinner on Monday, when Janos went to fetch a book from his study and in the corridor saw the White Lady, her one and only apparition to him. ('*Abends Erscheinung Weisse Frau,*' is the laconic remark in his diary.) Although Marie and Marie-Eugenie Zichy took this in their stride, Unity and Tom and Janos sat up in the library till midnight. Next day, she had a furious row with Janos, perhaps on the subject of psychic manifestations. Jimmy Erdödy drove her into Vienna for relief in the shops and at the hairdresser's, returning to Kohfidisch.

There Jimmy arranged for a local SA Stormführer to come for a morning's discussion with Unity, and that afternoon was so harvest-hot that she, Unity and Marie-Eugenie Zichy lay out on the fresh-cut hay. For the weekend David Streatfeild arrived, but by Saturday it was time for Unity and Tom to be off to the Nuremberg Party Rally.

Countess Johanna Palffy-Erdödy, otherwise Jimmy, and sometimes Jenny, lives in a house on the Kohfidisch estate. When she drove me round, she pointed out Janos's *Weingut* in the village. Baby, her sister, died some years ago. Countess Jimmy wrote me a memoir, and I have fitted parts of it into what she told me on a spring-scented morning at Kohfidisch. 'From 1934 on I saw them all in London, with that cranky mother and her Good Body. I stayed at Swinbrook several times. We were fond of Unity, she often stayed here; she was childish, a pretty, tame pussy cat. Tall, on the heavy side, with an utterly expressionless face. When seated, she always held her hands loosely folded, palms upwards, in her lap. She was dreamily relaxed, to the point when one could not imagine her making a hasty movement. After dinner she was likely to nod off to sleep. So was Tom. In Budapest Baby had an apartment in the Erdödy palace. The Zichy palace, with Marie-Eugenie, was next door. I think the Lippe who puzzles you on that journey in 1936 was Freddy Lippe-Biesterfeld, a cousin, therefore, of Prince Bernhard of the Netherlands. Taher Pasha was anxious not to eat pork, he'd always ask, and we'd say it was veal.

'Now the young SA Stormführer who came on that morning of 3 September was Lajos Mezriczky, son of the Mischendorf head schoolmaster and a student of agriculture in Vienna – a singularly nice local boy, though he had done a *Fememord*. And as I knew he was a Nazi, I must have thought it would give them pleasure to meet. Nazis were still illegal in Austria. They were closeted together all morning. He was killed at Stalingrad.

'God only knows how she came to worship Hitler. The sophisticated Kohfidisch and Bernstein crowd teased her about it, asking her to tell what he was really like. He had marvellously silky hair, we were told, loved chocolate éclairs, and was utterly wonderful. Janos was only a Nazi hanger-on. Kisebb, Professor Kleiner, was a botanist and as such he was passed on from one château rock-garden to another. He was also a racial fanatic, Gobineau, Houston Stewart Chamberlain and all that, and an astrologer to boot. His Hungarian wife lived at Szombathely. He lived here for years, and also with Prince Yusuf (of the Khedivial family). Dr Smital and his wife, an eye doctor, had some functions in the party. My family had built the hospital in Oberwart and we could go in as we liked. Beside Herr Pohl the factor, there was a Jewish lawyer, Zoltan Szeghö, a wobbly-headed lady-killer, he condescend-ingly patted Unity's cheeks and stroked her arms in a fatherly manner when one evening after dinner over coffee in the library she could not elude his advances.

'Baron von Kottwitz used to be here often, he was violently anti-Nazi, with a great sense of humour. He remembers how one day the SS guards dis-covered in her luggage a book about the Roehm purge, and warned her that if she mentioned its existence to the Führer, she would never see him again. Once there was a fearful storm and Konrad von Kottwitz said to her, You must have been frightened, lightning struck the tree outside your win-dow. Oh yes, she answered, but I took the Führer's picture to bed with me and then I felt quite safe.

'It was a harlot's pistol she shot herself with, very small calibre, a baby-Browning [but see Frau Hoffmann earlier, for a different make]. She carried it around with her. Afterwards she had to learn to speak and write again, and she had to wear nappies, she could not control herself. I was living in England, Janos must have given me the address, and I received a pitiful letter from her, I have such a sweet little goat, I love my little goat, love and kisses. I suppose I ought to feel ashamed of myself for neither answering nor going to see her. But enough's enough.'

Both Countess Jimmy and David Streatfeild are convinced that Unity never went to bed with Janos. Hannah Mikes had said the same. The plain-as-a-pikestaff assumption, therefore, that she was his mistress, must be looked at with circumspection but not necessarily dismissed for all that. The Hanfstaengl circle, for instance, did think that they were having a straight-forward affair. Keyhole peeping into the past has a beastliness; the dead, at least, deserve to be no longer troubled by the flesh. So perverse a man as Hitler, on the other hand, is wide open to psychosexual theorizings, and in-credible, indeed prurient, stuff on this topic had been spewed from overheated professorial brains. Unity's love for Hitler had its point of departure in the mind, but she would have wanted to express it physically; she was hipped on the bearing of children; her maternity was blocked. She could not marry Hitler, it was out of the question; she had fixed on a man not for the having. Hitler was barricaded in by his inhibitions, let alone by his staff. Unity was frustrated. Some of those who seek to turn the quirks of the human spirit into dogmas would assert that irresistible inner compulsions governed her choos-ing to love Hitler, a man who, by every definition, could give her no satis-faction; likewise him, in his choice of her as an adoring neophyte. Common sense dictates that Erich, or Max, the adjutants, the one mentioned by Robin Campbell perhaps, even 'the darling storms', or Streicher, entered her emotional life. Moreover, one of the witnesses already quoted, but on whom the onus of speaking about this should not be placed, said that Unity had confessed to sleeping with Stabschef Viktor Lutze, who became the leader of the SA after Roehm had been murdered. Lutze had a glass eye, and Unity joked about how he took it out beforehand. She was going to have lunch with Hitler the very next day and became afraid that 'the Führer will be able to read it in my eyes'. (Another caution: the better placed a German was, the more he would have hesitated to make an advance to a girlfriend of Hitler's, taking it for granted that Canaris's men were on the watch. Another pointer: she had been for advice about contraception to Dr Beckett Overy, the family gynaecologist, whose name pleased.) Was she then telling the truth about herself? Probably, though there remained about her something not exactly virginal but rather a-sexual. It seems likely that she did not have the capacity to identify sufficiently with other people in order to have a genuinely fulfilling emotional life. Her own imaginings and fantasies gripped her instead. Janos, if anyone, could offer a relationship without much guilt, allowing for Marie. Janos knew how to handle these things and although not boastful, he made no secret of his conquest. He did not claim to have seduced Unity.

This emotional limitation in Unity was summed up with insight by David Streatfield in a letter to me. 'This business acquires significance in connection with Hitler to whose character and career it is the key. There is often a powerful and subliminal connection between such people, but only in the rarest cases do they understand it. It's most conspicuous between people of opposite sexes, and it explains the fascination he had for Unity (among many others) and the success she had with him. I have the impression that he wasn't just playing her up – in fact that he paid her far more attention than was called for, or even advisable from the political point of view. In such cases each partner performs a service for the other – almost invariably unconsciously. Yet they are aware of their need for one another. It is chastity, abstinence, which is the cause of this psychological integration.'

David Streatfeild knew Janos better than anyone else. His own interest in metaphysics was fired by Janos; he is the author of *Persephone: A Study in Two Worlds* (1961), a book grounded in the learning and general literature too easily dispensed with at Bernstein. He has made his home in Austria. He said: 'When I came to Bernstein in the summer of 1931 the place was derelict, Janos was on the rocks. Having me as a p.g. and teaching me German for eighteen months were unprecedented riches for him. At four remote points in the house were his mother, the old servant Burschen Franz (Boy Franz), so called to his face, Janos and me. As a joke, he used to call me his son, and I brought Tom who became his grandson. A whole paternity. David Lloyd was the great-grandson – all the English friends one after another. I'd been at the same house at Eton as Tom.We ran into each other in Vienna one day, and I took him out to Bernstein, that was how the connection began.

'Janos was a peculiar inverted type, he wanted to love women he couldn't marry. Marie was head over heels in love with him, and he also needed her money. Most years I went back for the summer holidays. I coincided twice with Unity, whom I'd met at Swinbrook with Tom, and at a party of Diana's in London. She sang us what she said was Hitler's favourite song,

> Es war ein Jäger mit seiner Lola
> Als der Mond am Himmel stand.
> Liebe Lola, lass das Weinen,
> Lola, lass das Weinen sein . . .
> und der Jäger zog von danen
> Kämpfte für sein Vaterland.
> Manchmal dacht' er an seine Lola
> Als der Mond am Himmel stand.*

'Unity was a curiosity in his life. He took her to Switzerland when she shot herself because it was a distinguished thing to do, it looked well. She was very remote indeed. I was intellectually snobbish and a few years older than her and she didn't interest me. I saw an overgrown schoolgirl with a crush on Hitler. Janos talked of her pityingly. He was the clever one. He was a rabid Nazi at the time – they'd impressed him at Nuremberg. A nation which can organize something like that, he said, must be victorious. I answered that the Coronation was as well organized, and he talked of the *Kraft der Idee* [the strength of the idea] as if that meant anything. The funny thing was that he liked Jews. At his school in Debrecen some colleagues had been orthodox Jews. He even learnt the Hebrew alphabet and a certain number of words, and he'd read German books on the Cabbala, and was keen on the numerological side of it. He was one of those people able to divide their minds. He had

---

* There was a huntsman with his Lola,
  When the moon stood in the heavens.
  Beloved Lola, stop your weeping,
  Lola stop your weeping . . .
  And the huntsman went his way
  to fight for his fatherland.
  Many a time he thought of his Lola,
  when the moon stood in the heavens.

intuitive gifts, he took the occult literally and was convincing about it. He hadn't sufficient general education in history or psychology to gauge it or to produce anything worthwhile. The main purpose was to produce himself, to get a circle around and explain things, being confirmed in other people's eyes. After the war he had no remaining view of himself. He had an inability to visualize the sufferings of others. He'd make a point of quoting from *Tartarin* the bit about "*épater les gens et faire marcher les invités*" [how a man needs to make a good impression and get the guests moving].'

The year's Party Rally opened on Monday 6 September. The *Daily Express* and the *News Chronicle* reported the presence of Diana, Unity and Tom, with their aunt Lady Helen Nutting, who had remarried after her husband, Clement Mitford, Lord Redesdale's elder brother had been killed in the First World War. She was the mother of Rosemary and Clementine Mitford. A reader's letter, from George Brown of Glasgow, voiced in the latter paper on 9 September what had become a question of popular interest. 'Once more members of the Mitford family are attending the Nazi Congress at Nuremberg. Why are Lord Redesdale and his children so interested? Why are they Britain's Fascist Family Number One?'

Blood and Banquets (1943), a vivid diary published by Bella Fromm, diplomatic columnist of the *Vossische Zeitung* before she fled to America, has this entry under 16 September 1937. 'Unity is most unpopular with the Nazis. Ribbentrop dislikes her. Hess is jealous and suspicious. He repeats, where it will do the most good, the late Roehm's remark about her: "She pinches her lips so tightly because she has crooked teeth." But Hitler seems to like her, and that's all anyone needs around here. Evi Braun, former assistant to Hitler's court photographer, Heinrich Hoffmann, has given Unity some rather bitter moments. She is terrified that Evi might make headway into the sanctified heart of Hitler.' The remark about the teeth is the more malicious for being true, but Roehm had been shot before he could have made it. Nor could Frau Hess, when confronted with this passage, recollect her husband having any such reaction of jealousy and suspicion; she thought it most improbable. The contemporary vibrations around Unity, though, were there for an acute ear.

'16th September. Unity came.' Mary's diary pins down movements. 'September 25th. Unity phoned 8 – Mussolini Day – with her and Ward Price and Randolph Churchill to the show – too many people – couldn't get home.' Consul Gainer, we know, caught up with Unity at this point. The arrival of the Duke and Duchess of Windsor was news, and William Shirer was among those who rushed to Munich to latch on to it. Under an entry by-lined

'Munich, October' in his well-known Berlin Diary, he recorded his encounter at the time with Randolph Churchill, 'who looks like his father but does not think like him – at least, not yet'. Randolph Churchill had sniffed out the Mosley wedding, incidentally, and was beseeching Unity to confirm it, which she refused to do, much to his disgust when the story did break. An article of his entitled Hitler, The Man in the Evening Standard, 25 February 1938, could well have been dictated in some respects by Unity, for instance in its eulogies of Hitler as lover of chocolate cakes in cafés, as cinema enthusiast, admirer of the English, 'very much a human being'. She herself was complimented as Hitler's friend whom he had met casually three years earlier, for 'Her company and conversation contrast refreshingly for him with those of his associates.'

Janos sent her a telegram on 2 October, having just received a furious letter from her, and he followed it up by arriving in person on the 7th, with Baby Erdödy and Kisebb in tow. The row must have been smoothed over, as they plunged into the social round of the Luitpold and the Regina Bar and the Osteria, Walterspiel and Platzl's, and Janos's favourite restaurant, the Franziskaner (still unchanged today). Baroness Redwitz gave a cocktail party; Iris Mountbatten was there. Kisebb enlivened them by being continuously drunk. On the 8th Unity and Janos had tea with Erna at Solln, but the foolish Kisebb was no more sober by that evening. Next day Janos and Kisebb left, Unity driving by herself, for Stuttgart, where one of the Bernstein regulars lived, an amateur pianist called Hubertus Giesen, or Hubsie for short.

In November Unity was in England, but before the year turned into the dooms of 1938, she was once more in the news. To judge by her statements at the time, Unity had just joined the Council of Emergency Service. She said to the papers, 'I did a week's course with them – drilling and listening to lectures morning and evening.' The council had been formed to train women to take over jobs in a national emergency. Its chairman was Dame Helen Gwynne-Vaughan, professor of botany at the University of London, and somehow she got wind of Unity's tentative steps to become a German citizen, steps which were never to come to anything. Dame Helen sent for Unity. It was Miss Boys all over again. Unity was asked to leave. 'I have had an interview with Dame Helen,' runs Unity's version as given in the Daily Telegraph, 13 November 1937, 'at which she told me that she understood I was about to become a German citizen. She said it was considered undesirable for a future German citizen to belong to an organization for the furtherance of British interests in war time. I told Dame Helen that, although it was true that I had contemplated becoming a German citizen, I had as yet taken no steps in the matter, and until I had done so I regarded myself as an ordinary

Englishwoman.' To the *Yorkshire Post* reporter she added, 'Of course, had I become a German, I would naturally have resigned, but so far I haven't taken any steps to adopt German nationality. In fact, I haven't been worrying about it. There is plenty of time. It is true that I spend much time in Germany, but, at the moment, I am on a long visit home. I shall be returning to Germany after Christmas.'

The fear was that Unity would be spying out the council's work for the Nazis. Had she actually been making a small effort to conform, nobody would have believed her by then. Here was just one more of the rejections she had inevitably engineered for herself in the self-injuring pattern all the way back to childhood.

One last tableau of the year comes from Lord Longford, who says, 'We were both guests one weekend of Sir Alexander Spearman, Conservative MP for Scarborough. We got on very well. She was kind enough to motor me back after dinner on the Sunday, and I spent the night at Old Mill Cottage with Lady Redesdale. I dimly remember being lent Houston Stewart Chamberlain's book for bed-time reading. At nine o'clock on the Monday I had to be in Oxford for a meeting of the City Council to which I'd just been elected. Up early, Unity and I set off for Oxford in her car. Not until we were drawing up outside the Town Hall did I rouse myself to notice the swastika flag on the bonnet. I saw my colleagues drawn up outside the Town Hall – we were a very left-wing Marxist party – I gave a terrified whisper that I'd left my papers in my rooms at Christ Church and could she drop me there.'

Sir Alexander Spearman's house was Rolls, near Chigwell, fifteen miles from the centre of London. Nancy and Diana had stayed with him often, he told me, and sometimes would ask if they could bring another sister; Unity had been three or four times. His diary showed that his guests for the weekend of 4 December 1937 had been Unity, Lord Longford (Frank Pakenham at the time), W. J. Brown, a trade unionist Labour MP who had stuck with Mosley as far as the New Party, Amabel and Clough Williams-Ellis (the architect of Portmeirion) and William Aitken, nephew of Lord Beaverbrook.

MISSIONS ACCOMPLISHED

The sophisticated Bernstein set were not to know that the New Year of 1938 brought with it the final few weeks of their independence. In so far as they were able to guess at their fate, they mostly welcomed it, not realizing that the Nazis sealed them inescapably into a conflagration from which they would be lucky to save their skins, let alone their possessions and that *ancien régime* tranquillity which they had been almost the last Europeans to enjoy. Unity telephoned Janos from Munich on 8 January, a Saturday, to learn that he was in bed ill, and she postponed her departure until the Tuesday, putting up that night in Vienna at the Hotel Maissl und Schaden, an old-world haven now no more. Next day at Kohfidisch she found Baby and Jimmy, and the latter's friend, Lady Patricia Russell, a daughter of the second Lord Dufferin. At Bernstein, on Friday, she arrived only a little before Count Tassilo Almasy, of the main branch of the family. He had been imprisoned by the communist regime of Bela Kun in 1919, and his stories were so many after-dinner shudders. Whether recuperating from his illness or for some other reason, Janos left Unity to her own devices, to walks with Uncle Tassilo or her dog Rebell (its names, Rebell, or Rebelly, and Boy, were interchangeable). On the 16th he abandoned her at Kohfidisch while he spent a week by himself in Budapest; he was finalizing plans for a long trip with Laczy to Egypt. At Kohfidisch, she caught up with her correspondence, for instance writing to Robert Byron that a letter from him had been following her round as she had been motoring out by slow stages from England. She was sorry not to have lunched with him before she had left, especially as she wanted to hear about a visit to the Baltic countries and to Germany, for which she had primed him with introductions. She hoped that if he was still intending to write about the Great War, he would do this most fascinating subject imaginable the justice which had not been done to it. In fact he wrote no such book.

The great excitement of the neighbourhood was the sight of the Great Northern Lights on the 25th, blazing to turn night into day. At the very end of the month she was at Kohfidisch again when Janos drove there to say goodbye, on his way back to Budapest on the first leg of his travels. According to his diary, he was in Brindisi by 7 February, and lunching with Taher Pasha at the Mohamet Ali Club in Cairo by the 11th. Among the people who entertained him in Egypt were Sir Walter and Lady Smart, and Russell Pasha, celebrated pillars of Anglo-Egyptian society. And also Victor Simaica, known to me as Simaica Bey, another long-standing friend of my family's. Not till 4 April was he back in Budapest, by which time Unity was in England again, the *Anschluss* was a *fait accompli* and Bernstein belonged to the Greater German Reich.

Born in 1894, Janos was two years younger than his sister Mädy and two years older than Laczy. Mädy had married a Hungarian, Anton von Gyömörey, and they had a dower-house on a hill looking towards Bernstein. Their son has become a Catholic priest, Father Lorincz Gyömörey, and their daughter Zita – named after her godmother, the last Habsburg Empress – is now Baroness Stoerck. They had both accompanied me to Bernstein on my first visit there.

Father Lorincz: 'I remember the Northern Lights very clearly, we all stood out on the terrace in admiration. That March, when the Germans occupied the country, a great swastika flag flew on the tower of the castle. My parents were arrested by the Gestapo and were freed to Hungary only in May. We had an estate called Mezökeresztes, near Miskolc, and lived there till 1944, when we went to Szombathely, and then to the castle of Bozsok quite close to Rechnitz. That October my parents and sister were arrested and taken to Komarom concentration camp, which was dissolved in December, its inmates driven to Mauthausen. They released my mother and sister, and a friend saved my father. We were united in 1945, and while waiting for the Russians we moved to Bernstein.

'As a Hungarian Janos could not be more than an *Ehrenmitglied*, or honorary member of the party. Like Unity. We often discussed his character. My grandmother was very sad about the development of his life, Bernstein was entailed, so he was the heir, but he had an inferiority complex towards his brother and sister. My mother spoke Russian fluently, and under the pseudonym Georgina von Althaus had published a novel *Kurgan* (meaning a Tomb, in the Kirghiz language). Laczy was a Don Quixote, the only officer of the Hungarian army who was taken into the German army with his rank unchanged. He became Rommel's desert adjutant, and his memoirs of this experience were published as *Rommel seregénél Afrikában* [with the army of Rommel in Africa]. But Janos did nothing seriously. I never thought he would even be able to make a good horoscope.'

Baroness Stoerck, his sister, said: 'My childhood was at Bernstein. Although then not more than twelve or thirteen, I remember Unity very well. I had to do a little curtsy to her. We met in the village or during the visit I made every day to my grandmother, who didn't approve of her and didn't want to talk to her. One summer Unity wore a red suit, there were photos of her in local costume. In the village there was a May-tree for May 1st, one for the socialists, one for the Nazis, Janos and Unity were round the latter, singing the Horst Wessel song – there was a scandal, the gendarmerie arrived and removed the swastika from their tree. [By 1938 the socialists had been outlawed, so this incident must be before then.]

'A few months before the *Anschluss* my parents' windows were broken. In the village Herr Angelus had a small store where he and his wife sold everything – it stood just on the corner as you turn to go up to the castle, on the left where the shop selling Bernstein serpentine now is. Herr Angelus was Jewish and on All Souls' Day he stood in his door when the village procession went by and took his hat off. Everybody loved them. He and his wife were both about eighty. They had a son who went to England and a daughter who married a man called Amin, in Bombay. Two or three days after the *Anschluss*, this old couple were expelled, driven to Hungary. A lorry came to take my parents to prison. The village communist, Herr Beigelböck, was arrested too. Besides the Angelus couple, the only other Jews in Bernstein were Dr Sarlai and his wife. Hungary didn't want to take them in, so they stayed in No Man's Land, in that horrible to-and-fro [quoted already from Louis Golding's description]. The Angelus couple lay down in the ditch there, they were old and could walk no more, and died. Dr Sarlai and his wife could go to Szombathely, and they were to die in Auschwitz. My aunt Schmitburg had their daughter Ilona in the war – she had played with Janos and Laczy as children. My parents were kept in prison at Oberwart for two and a half months. They had a lawyer in Oberwart, Dr Sebestyeny, he was beaten to death in the cell next to theirs, as he was actually Austrian, while my parents were Hungarian. My father got word through to Count Kanya, the Hungarian foreign minister, and they were expelled to the frontier. Janos used to say there was nothing he could do.'

The *Anschluss* thrilled Unity. The *Evening Standard*, 14 March 1938, reported from Munich, 'When Hitler arrives in Vienna this evening his most ardent English admirer will be there to greet him. Miss Unity Mitford ... had a special pass valid for two persons, given to her yesterday by the wish of the Führer and she and Mrs Victor Cochrane-Baillie left for Vienna last night.' The occupation of the Rhineland was to be repeated, with its '*Was! Ihr beide hier!*' Actually Mrs Cochrane-Baillie, who became Lady Lamington when her husband succeeded to his title, was more interested in music and entertaining than in politics; I used to go to chamber-concerts in her house but had no idea how I would come to regret her death several years before this quest for Unity was conceived. A week later, on 21 March, the *Daily Express* had a further instalment, entitled, 'Home to England from Vienna, by train, third class: The Hon Unity Mitford.' '". . . I was heartbroken that I did not see [Hitler] when he arrived near his birthplace at Linz," she said. "Another English friend, a man who was with him then, said it was the most wonderful experience of his life. But I saw his entry into Vienna, and perhaps after all that was best. Afterwards I saw him for a few minutes in his hotel. He was tired, but seemed very moved by it all. I think it was wonderful." She returns soon to Munich.' Simultaneously the *Evening Standard* retracted the detail about the special pass, but added that Unity had tonsillitis due to the strain she put on her vocal chords shouting 'Heil Hitler'.

The English friend she referred to was Ward Price who wrote a sickening description of the entry into Linz in his book *Year of Reckoning*; and no doubt he had had a wonderful experience. Once Hitler was ensconsed in the Imperial Hotel in Vienna, the guttersnipe thumbing his nose from this citadel of privilege which he had crashed, he telephoned instructions to Eva Braun to join him, bringing her mother and sister. 'A few minutes' was all that Unity had been able to cadge.

So much for the stories which burst through the grapevine at that very moment that Hitler was contemplating marriage with Unity. *Ken*, an American magazine which aimed to be both anti-fascist and glossy, in its opening number that April produced an article about the women in Hitler's life, and in spite of the knowledgeable air about it, much had been fabricated. Hitler's deficient or invisible sex-life was a red-hot journalistic topic. Unity was angry, mostly for fear that Hitler would assume this article to have been inspired by her, and she set about issuing a writ (as reported in the German émigré magazine *Pariser Tageszeitung* at the beginning of May), though nothing came of it, as *Ken* folded after only a few further issues.

In the *Sunday Pictorial* of 24 April Lord Redesdale did what he could to scotch the story. 'There is not, nor has there ever been, any question of an engagement between my daughter and Herr Hitler. The Führer lives only for his country and has no time for marriage' – which purely Nazi formulation shows how Unity's bees were buzzing in his old bonnet. In public relations style, he was now devoted to the Anglo-German Fellowship, and active on the council of The Link, founded by Sir Barry Domvile in 1937 as a Nazi front organization, with no pretences to be anything else. He made plentiful speeches about the supreme ideals of Hitlerism and the need for Germany to liberate Austrian or Czech brethren or recover her colonies; not only dundering in his own right, but an unusual example of a father visited with the sins of his children.

These wild marriage rumours coincided with Unity's most serious brawl so far. Her lengthy neglect of English fascism was recouped spectacularly on 10 April, when – the tonsillitis cured – she attended a 'Save Peace, Save Spain' rally organized by the Labour party, in protest against the policy of non-intervention. A large crowd had been anticipated, therefore separate platforms had been specially erected to provide manageable focal points for simultaneous speeches. Attlee, Greenwood, Dr Edith Summerskill, Lord Strabolgi, and Stafford Cripps, were among the twenty-four billed speakers. The Spanish Civil War had been of secondary concern to Unity, merely a foretaste of German arms conquering in the field against bolshevism, its outcome ideologically and physically certain, therefore a matter of time, not personal involvement. But it was the one scrapping-ground available.

A bugle call at half past three was a prelude to the speeches, and a challenge to the pacifist elements of the Labour party. A small group of BUF members collected opposite Stafford Cripps's platform, hoisted a swastika banner and gave the fascist salute. 'Five were injured in the general scuffle,' to quote the Daily Mail next day, 'and taken away by ambulance. Two, Eric Steer and George Curzon, were detained in St George's hospital ... Miss Mitford, bareheaded, smartly dressed and wearing a swastika brooch was listening to Sir Stafford Cripps ... when the trouble started ... she said, "I did not say anything and was standing on the fringe of the crowd when someone snatched my swastika badge and threw it to the ground. I was then surrounded by a pushing crowd of men and women, who screamed insults at me, threatening to duck me in the Serpentine. They started to push me in that direction when three police officers came up and escorted me, followed by the crowd towards Park Lane. I was kicked, and when I got to the bus some of the demonstrators tried to follow me."'

In fact, had the police not formed a protective cordon round her the whole way to the bus on which she escaped, she risked being lynched or drowned. 'Cries of "Kill", Stones Hurled at Girl Who Admires Hitler' ran the Daily Sketch headline, and Unity was quoted there as saying, '"The crowd got very angry and started saying insulting things. A man tore off my badge and threw it on the ground. I hit him in the face. Then a woman said something insulting about Hitler. I hit her too ... A Mr Warburton came to my rescue and the police helped us to get away. I was not really frightened, just very excited." Mr Edward Warburton, of Clapham, told me: "A woman shouted 'Go back to Germany', and Miss Mitford hit her. The crowd closed in. Two or three policemen and myself cleared a space. People hit out at her and at me. Some stones were thrown. In Park Lane we got on a bus, and three police-men got on after us to fend off the crowd. I think 200 or 300 people were in pursuit, but they had to give it up when the bus got going."'

The newspapers had a field-day. Unity put a bold face on it, and whatever else may be thought, the courage of her convictions is not in question. 'My badge was trampled underfoot,' she told the *Daily Telegraph*, 'and I am afraid I have lost it for good. I do not think it can be said that I did anything to irritate,' a very Mosleyite conclusion in its self-righteousness – as though anything else could have been expected from giving the fascist salute in those circumstances. To the *Evening Standard* she said, 'The Führer does not mind men getting mixed up in "shindies" but he does not like women being involved as he thinks it undignified. I'm afraid he may be cross with me for becoming so conspicuous.' And of course she had to raise the stakes, confiding to the *Daily Mail*, 'I am looking forward to becoming a German citizen as soon as possible, but I can't tell you when that will be.' Criticism of her was obvious, with this proviso, that she incurred it less for what she had done than for being who she was. Other fascists at this demonstration were allowed to relapse into their natural obscurity; they had neither social status nor notoriety.

All the same, Unity was shaken, more than she liked to admit. To assume, with the gayest of Mitford airs, that the greater the outcry, the more spirited the tease, lacked truth where mob-hatred had been released. She could argue that they were all wicked, all communists, all Jews, but nevertheless had had her own aggression turned on herself, as was certain to be the case with a gesture of such defiance. She was promising self-destruction again, using the mob against herself quite as surely as if it had been the pistol in her hand-bag. To everybody who would listen in the months to come she recited the Hyde Park saga. To have diced with death also closed off retreats. Full-steam ahead, she forged back to Germany after Easter, all the more hyper-agitated for this back-wash English lick of the mass degradation now commonplace there, but still she was unable to see through to the process of its spon-taneous generation around her and through her – not even when the most accusing example stared her in the face, for she had passed that small shop in the village of Bernstein scores of times; old Herr Angelus and his wife addressed her humanity, and so did the manner of their dying, and she was not touched.

She was in the Pension Doering with Mary on 28 April. Two days later, a Saturday, she drove from Munich through Leoben, Graz, Güssing, to Kohfi-disch, to Baby and Jimmy and Lady Patricia Russell again. (Unity was

laughable, says Lady Patricia, but laughter-creating too. She remembers telling
Unity that if she were to insist on killing herself one day, such a silly little
pistol would not do; just as Jimmy Erdödy remembers telling her that bullets
fired into the temple can easily be deflected.) There she pasted the amassed
press-cuttings about the man-handling in Hyde Park into her albums; she
drove into Oberwart, to Dr Smital, idling until Janos turned up during the
evening of 4 May. Next day he returned to Bernstein, where Unity and Baby
lunched, though they drove on afterwards to Vienna. The impression is
created that Marie and Janos were less than welcoming, and Kohfidisch was
being used to make the point that she had other friends. At any rate, after a
long weekend in Vienna, she was back in Munich by 10 May.

The *Anschluss* had fatal repercussions upon Czechoslovakia. While Unity was
demonstrating in Hyde Park, Henlein, Hitler's chosen spokesman for the
Sudeten Germans, was rejecting Czech proposals for compromise and putting
forward his own 'Carlsbad Programme' for a Nazi state within a state, as a
prelude to more territorial demands. The Czechs relied upon their mutual
treaty of defence with France, and the pledges of the British government to
assist them in the event of an unprovoked German attack. Chamberlain and
Halifax. however, handled matters in a way which suggested that the British
government would back down and surrender if German threats of war offered
a suitably alarmist pretext for doing so. Whether intentionally or not, their
supine and obfuscating approach encouraged Hitler to adventure. England
might not march, but then he would. Elections were to be held in Czechoslovakia on three successive Sundays beginning on 22 May, but before then, on
the 19th, German troop movements were reported on the Czech border.
Next day, the Czechs partially mobilized their army, with England, France and
Russia ostensibly resolved to stand firm with them. Although German
intentions had been correctly read for once, the troop movements were scare-
mongered, and this offered the kind of initiative displaying solidarity with
friends and contempt for enemies in which Unity excelled. On 28 May, in
his rage, Hitler decided to smash the Czech state by the end of the year, at
the risk of war, and he issued directives to his chiefs of staff to that effect. As
though picking up the sound-waves of these directives, on that very day
Unity set off for Prague, the tension still explosive.

Sefton Delmer was the first to spot her. In a cable date-lined Prague,
Sunday, and published in the *Daily Express* of Monday 30 May, he wrote, 'Just
to make us all feel thoroughly comfortable in these exciting circumstances
the Hon Unity Mitford walked tall and blonde among the crowd, a forbidden Hitler swastika badge in her button-hole. "They booted me in

London for wearing it," she said to me, "I'd like to see them try it here."' In *Trail Sinister*, his memoirs, he adds the detail that their talk took place on the terrace of the Esplanade Hotel.

Next morning she set off for Karlovy Vary, or Carlsbad, as that once-tranquil Edwardian spa is called in German. Basil Newton was in the British Legation, no friend of the Czechs either, but at least familiar with Unity at first hand since her debut on the Hesselberg. His telegram dated 1 June (F.O. 371/215 81) tells what happened next. 'Miss Mitford rang up Legation yesterday afternoon to say that she had been arrested at Kamenne Zehroviče with an English and American friend on her way from Prague to Carlsbad and that a considerable amount of property had been taken from her. She said she did not know why she had been arrested. As it appeared that she was on the point of being released she was merely advised to send in her story in writing. British Vice-Consul then rang up the gendarmerie station at Kamenne Zehroviče and was told that she had been detained but had already been released and allowed to proceed to Carlsbad. Certain documents had been taken from her and handed over to the military authorities at Kladno. The gendarmerie stated that she was in the company of Sudeten German Senator Wollner in addition to the two foreigners. British Vice-Consul has been promised more detailed story from competent officers. I should add that Miss Mitford had been causing great anxiety to Czechoslovak government by parading the streets of Prague wearing swastika emblem, a clearly provocative act at this juncture. Legation endeavoured without success to get in touch with her while she was in Prague in order to give her warning. Warning was conveyed when she telephoned about her arrest.' A copy of this was forwarded from the Foreign Office to the embassy in Berlin. 'She was probably asking for trouble' minuted J. H. Roberts with a caution which R. L. Speaght threw to the winds when he added below, 'and deserved what she got.'

Next day the British Legation presented their compliments to the Ministry of Foreign Affairs of the Czechoslovak Republic, to inform them of Unity's complaint that she had been stopped for no apparent reason thirty kilometres from Prague; held for four and a half hours; had her luggage searched and many things confiscated. The Czech reply was immediate and restrained, pointing out that she was known to them as a Nazi (*admiratrice de certaines tendences politiques étrangères*); she had been warned at several roadblocks not to drive through the area at this moment of electoral fever; and finally, everything confiscated had been handed back to her two days later. Formalities had been observed, and both parties were thankful to leave it at that.

Sefton Delmer picked up the trail on arrival in Carlsbad. Unity, he cabled, had been indignant to find detectives outside her door when she woke up on the morning after her arrest and release. '"As I got into my car to drive away," she said to me, "several men jumped into another car and followed me through the town. After about ten minutes of this I turned sharply into a side street and gave them the slip."' Among the items confiscated, apparently, had been a Nazi dagger, swastika emblems and a portrait of Hitler. *Narodni Politika*, then a leading independent paper in Prague, on 3 June confirmed that her belongings had now been returned 'with the exception of her camera and some films, which were sent to Prague for investigation ... Unity Mitford promised to leave Czechoslovakia at once, and has now gone to Germany. She travels on a British passport, issued in Munich, where she used to live. An English student named Spranklin and an American, William Rueff, had been detained together with Miss Mitford. Both were released after questioning.'

She might also have been deprived of the special Nazi badge which she had been wearing as usual, but apparently it had not been perceived by the Czech police until proceedings were almost over and done with – or so she told Ward Price in an exclusive interview. Faithfully at her heels in Carlsbad, he had returned to Prague to report her version at some length in the *Daily Mail*. She was quoted there as saying about the badge, 'I should have been sorry to lose it, as it is the second one that the Führer has given me. This one was to replace the badge that was torn off my dress by the Communists in Hyde Park at a Save Spain meeting a few weeks ago. At the police post to which we were taken, I was very thoroughly searched. A woman was brought into the police station and took me into a side room, where I had to undress completely, even taking off my stockings, while she minutely examined all my clothes to see if there were any papers hidden in them.' (At least it is clear that her fears that Hitler might be cross with her for being so conspicuous were unfounded. The unrecovered camera was also made good by him that Christmas, when he ordered Schaub to present her with a new one, which had cost fifty pounds – a snippet of intimate news in turn handed to the waiting press.)

The *Fränkische Tageszeitung*, however, sprang to arms with a headline 'Czech Gibes. Police Hoaxes against English and American'. The trouble had begun, its article stated, when officials arrogantly inspected the boot of Unity's car, to unearth a portrait of Hitler, which was snatched to and fro in the ensuing argument, and damaged. Although the writer of the article did his best to gnash teeth, especially over the body-search to which Unity had been submitted, he was constrained, more or less, by the impossibility of concocting an atrocity out of these thin facts, although his climax is horrible humbug, 'nothing of this kind had ever happened to them in any other country'.

On the road home from Carlsbad to Munich, Unity and her two companions stopped off at Nuremberg, to be photographed posing with Streicher, for the *Fränkische Tageszeitung* (3 June). The caption related how Jews had attacked her in her homeland, a reference to the Hyde Park battle, while now she had been 'most revoltingly molested'. German mobilization was alleged to be a fiction of the British Secret Service, and therein lies the clue to this episode. Once before, at the Hesselberg meeting of 1935, it had suited immediate German ends to claim English friendship, and Unity had been the available means of display. Now again she was being exploited for a similar purpose; the implications were that the Germans had nothing to hide; the devious British had invented a tale of German militarism and Czech self-defence, very well then, they would soon see what sort of reception an innocent English girl had from the hands of the Czechs; moreover, if foreigners circulating peacefully in Czechoslovakia were so roughly treated, then Sudetens and Germans must be thoroughly victimized; German attitudes were justified as that very self-defence the Czechs were claiming. That Streicher should again have been conveniently handy for a photograph on the journey home is quite beyond coincidence. As with the Hesselberg meeting, this must have been a political contrivance – if not pre-arranged, then astutely grasped in the moment, a miniature but perfect example of how Nazi propaganda processed non-events into politics. Unity served this eye-catching purpose exactly. Mission accomplished. That Unity had calculated the risks she was running is clinched by the fact that she took out an insurance policy in the form of the Sudeten Senator Wollner. Alone, she might have been a hostage to fortune. With him, she had immunity. There would have been drastic German reprisals if they had been really abused.

The British press performed obediently by spreading this newest cliff-hanger of Unity's across its pages, with photographs of her and Streicher. The energy with which they plunged into the trap must have gladdened the watching Germans. The *Daily Mirror*, in particular, gave almost half a page to a tongue-out article, 'Stay Home . . . That's a Good Girl!', a neat reversal of the 'Go back to Germany' line taken only two months earlier after the Hyde Park demonstration.

The way to snap her fingers at the Czechs, to show that they counted for nothing in the Nazi equation, was to cross their borders again, and this she did in the third week of July, by which time the Czechs would have turned a blind eye to any outrage she might have foisted on to them, so apprehensive had they become about their imminent betrayal by England and France. Lord Boothby, in his *I Fight to Live*, describes leaving England on 16 July, to motor to Marienbad, and then to Eger in the Sudetenland, for the annual Wallenstein celebrations. He was on a platform behind Henlein, no less, who, 'flanked by an aide-de-camp and a flaxen haired Brunnhilde, with a swastika brooch pinned to her bosom, took the salute . . . none other than Miss Unity Mitford.'

Senator Wollner, although parliamentary deputy for Carlsbad, was a small-fry Sudeten Nazi, long since dead. I had hopes that Unity's other companions, Phillip Spranklin and William Rueff, might have been able to confirm the extent to which this Prague jaunt had been a put-up job. Spranklin's name was familiar from Munich Playground (1941), a breezy, rather too chatty round-up of a stint as a Reuter's stringer in Munich by Ernest R. Pope, then a veteran American journalist. In a chapter on the hazards of news-gathering among the Nazis, he wrote, 'I also made occasional use of the British Fascist, Phillip Spranklin, Munich correspondent for Sir Oswald Mosley's Fascist newspaper, Action, a close friend of Unity Mitford's, and wearer of Heinrich Himmler's SS badge for privileged Nazi sympathizers from abroad. In return for lucre or liquor, Spranklin would lift the veil off Unity's love life with Hitler, or other goings-on within the walls of inaccessible Nazidom. Young and beautiful, Phillip enjoyed proving how close he stood to the Nazi leaders.' (Quotations are from the fuller American edition of the book.)

'Tea for Two' is the heading he gives to a chapter about Unity, and a spirited portrait it is too, though minor details, such as the name of the Pension Doering, are wrongly given. He establishes their friendly relationship by opening with an account of bumping into her outside the beauty parlour of the Regina Palace Hotel as she was hurrying off to tea with Gauleiter Wagner. The point is well made that by becoming a German citizen she would no longer have been entitled to change her English pounds into reichsmarks at the tourist rate, which was double the official rate. 'She could run important errands for the Nazis as she travelled round Czechoslovakia and other adjoining countries in her British car, with British licence plates and British papers . . . and have her talks appear in the German newspapers the next day as representing "the British attitude".' He asserts that she was known as 'the most dangerous woman in Munich' whose several denunciations landed anti-Nazis in concentration camps, but supplies no examples.

It was good wartime sensationalism to say that had England agreed to an entente with Germany, leaving her a free hand in Eastern Europe, 'it is quite possible that Hitler might have embraced Unity before the altar . . . England spurned Hitler's advances so the Führer's love for his Blond Britain [sic] cooled . . . Unity has spent anything from an afternoon to several days at Berchtesgaden appeasing Adolf and also clinging to his every word. Spranklin once showed me a photograph of the would-be Mrs Hitler with Adolf in a very informal tête-à-tête over some tea in the Führer's home on the Obersalzburg. Phillip had obtained this candid-camera shot from triumphant Unity herself, who wanted to prove to her sister that she too could snare a Fascist leader.'

So far so good (although the phrase about spending several days at Berchtesgaden is untrue). But here is the account of Unity's return from Prague. 'The British Nazis headed straight for Nuremberg, where they were received by Julius Streicher. The Franconian Gauleiter put them up at the Deutscher Hof, the hotel reserved for the Führer and his retinue whenever he visits Nuremberg. Spranklin, in an unguarded moment, later told me the following story about Unity's adventure at the Deutscher Hof. The Führer's blonde came down to breakfast the next morning looking very pale and upset. She complained to the management that a man had come into her room while she was sleeping, and that she had struggled with him in the dark. She did not reveal the outcome of the fight. The Gestapo manager of the hotel apologized profusely, and promised an immediate investigation. But his sleuthing ended as abruptly as it had begun. Poor Unity's midnight visitor turned out to be "a very high official in the Gestapo". Heinrich Himmler is a fanatic worshipper of blonde Nordic womanhood.'

Lucre or liquor must have been too hard at work. Himmler was unlikely to have coincided with Unity at the Deutscher Hof in Nuremberg on 2 June; if he had, the manager would have known and not been promising investigations; not even Himmler would have dared to pounce on Unity in the night, given her protection from Hitler; in any case he would have known about the Abwehr men on her trace. The possible interpretation that Himmler had sent another high official to kidnap her for him need not detain us.

To trace Phillip Spranklin became an investigation in itself. Officially he had worked in the Munich Foreign Press Office run by Hoffmann under the aegis of Goebbels's Ministry. Mrs Beckett, quoted earlier, had known him in Black House days in London, as one of the wilder young men on the publicity side, still in his late teens, 'pleasant, very fair, not very tall, quite clever but mischievous'. One of his BUF friends had been E. D. Randall, just out of a Catholic public school, who himself went to teach in Germany in the mid-thirties; another was the son of W. J. Leaper, a leading Mosleyite journalist. All leads proved cold. As luck would have it, I came upon information about him as a result of systematically contacting Hitler's attendants. His chauffeur, Erich Kempka (who had been with him right to the very end in the Bunker, when he had broken out with Bormann, Axmann and Stumpfenegger), had seen Unity but before the war had been too junior to drive her. The secretaries, Gertraud Junge, Fräuleins Christa Schröder and Daranovsky, might have been able to shed light on the Hitler–Unity correspondence, which of course has vanished, but although they knew nothing personally, one of them put me in touch with a friend of hers, Frau Sakalarides. Her maiden name had been Elsbeth Seifert, and originally she was from Leipzig. We met in the Osteria Bavaria.

Frau Sakalarides: 'In 1938 and 1939 I knew her in our student circle. I'd come to art school in Munich, and lived in the Königinstrasse, in a private student house. Bill Rueff, a very nice American from Chicago, was in the same lodgings. He was at art school too. A good friend of his was Michael Heron from Manchester, here as a salesman or representative for his father's textile firm. Phillip Spranklin, a blond boy, blue eyes, a small nose, was very lively. Unity had a wonderful MG and her big dog in the back, one day it came over my shoulder and licked my whole side. We played tennis and rode and swam in the Prinzregentenstrasse pool. I was twenty, quite unpolitical, but the atmosphere was Nazi. Our clique was international, we enjoyed ourselves at our lokals, the Hopfenperle in the Ohmstrasse, and the International Student Club on Hess-strasse which held evening dances. There was a Peruvian, a Greek – another Englishman called Jeff Goffrey and his Dutch girl friend, Masha ter Porten. They couldn't bear to leave Germany. By 1939 Michael Heron was saying that they had to go, and that spring I ceased to see them. I took Bill Rueff to Stuttgart, he had to catch a plane, he bought us orchids. Unity was very reserved. She rarely came out of herself. When I last saw her, she had been invited to the Obersalzberg and was thrilled, she said she could not be invited there because of Eva Braun.'

Months later, more luck finally led me to Mr D. H. Spranklin, Phillip's younger brother. From him I learnt that Phillip had been born in 1917, and left Felstead school at the age of sixteen, already politically committed as an anti-communist. He had made his mind up for himself. He joined the BUF without delay. In 1935 he was teaching at the university of Westphalia, learning to speak German like a native, identifying with Nazism to the point of losing his British nationality. As a fascist journalist he had become a friend of Ward Price's, and when he returned to England he also spoke a good deal about Unity, always admiringly. In the Czech incident, he had complained of the disadvantages of being a foreigner shot at by both sides. Caught in Munich at the outbreak of the war, he had banked on a rapid German victory, and so stayed there under cover, passing himself off as a German, being looked after by a kindly couple, a dentist and his wife. After nine months, this became too risky, so he made his way on foot into Italy, then on by boat to Spain, returning to England in 1941, to be interned for a couple of months. The Home Office confiscated his papers, including material about Unity, and none of it was ever returned. In 1944 a flying bomb hit his flat in Brixton, and so the Germans had been the death of him after all.

After the Czech foray, Unity had a post-Hyde Park spell in London, collecting accumulated press-cuttings and attending Debo's coming-out ball. Lady Dorothy Lygon dined at Rutland Gate for the ball and remembers arguing with Unity about the *Anschluss*, at which she had been present by accident, and was punished for her opinions about it when Unity ordered that no more champagne be served to her. She went to a cocktail party of Robert Byron's on the 23rd, discussing with him the plans to attend the coming Party Rally. At a supper for one of this season's dances, she and Diana were sitting on either side of Philip Toynbee, then a communist as well as a close friend of Esmond Romilly and Jessica, and in his book *Friends Apart* he has recorded how he was snubbed: '"We don't mind talking to you," said Unity, "because we, after all, are on the winning side".' During Unity's absence from the Pension Doering, Mary moved into her room, on 14 June, and that September she actually settled into a flat of her own. By July, when Unity was again in Munich, she had missed her midsummer appointment on the Hesselberg.

In the Bundesarchiv, in the *Führer-Adjutanten* files (NS 10/38) there is a document generally referred to as Bormann's notebook, and dullish it is too, a secretarial calendar. References to Unity are scanty. On 10 July, though, after Hitler had opened an exhibition in the Haus der Kunst, he returned home and Unity must have been on his mind. 'The Führer gives orders for Lady Mitford to receive tickets for the Tag der Kunst [that annual festivity of Nazi art and folklore held in Munich over several days towards the end of July, a civic or cultural equivalent of a Party Rally].' On the 11th, Ernest Pope, among others, had also reported her busy with her camera, in spite of the rain, at the Haus der Kunst exhibition.

Sunday 17 July, according to Bormann's notebook, began when Schaub laid before the Führer the guest-list for the coming Bayreuth festival. At 11.15 he agreed to Otto Dietrich's leave of absence, and heard that General Engel's aircraft was now available. Lunch at the Osteria was at a quarter past one, with Minister Wagner (of the Health Service, not the Gauleiter of Munich), Professor Gablonsky, and Lady Mitford – as Bormann fell into the usual error of over-ranking her. After the customary film, on this particular evening *Nach der Scheidung*, Hitler gave orders, 'Lady Mitford für Dienstag 16.30 zum Tee.' Sure enough, on Tuesday the 19th, Bormann noted, 'Lady Mitford to tea at 16.35.' Five minutes late maybe, but this is the first firm evidence of Unity on the Obersalzberg as a guest of Hitler's, rather than peeping through the wire as a tourist. Unfortunately Bormann did not specify how Unity had done the journey out from Munich, but had she arrived with Hitler, or been staying in the house, his standard procedure would have been to record it. Probably a special car fetched her.

The day, however, had some importance in the *dénouement* of one of the minor diplomatic flurries spawned by appeasement. In his preparations to dismember Czechoslovakia, Hitler spared no effort to neutralize England and France, instinctively and correctly sensing that their governments, simultaneously baited by carrots and menaced with sticks, would concede him his territorial ambitions. Fritz Wiedemann had been Hitler's company commander in the First World War, a stolid, regimental type who promoted himself by means of old-comrade tales of Hitler's soldiering. On 18 July, Wiedemann was on a secret mission to Lord Halifax to assure the British government of Hitler's goodwill, and his desire to solve the Sudeten question peacefully. This elementary piece of deception was soon exposed to all but the cabinet. Wiedemann himself has described in his memoirs, *Der Mann der Feldherr Werden Wollte*, how he hurried on the 19th (to and fro in that aircraft made available by General Engel), from Lord Halifax in the Foreign Office to Hitler at Obersalzberg, landing at five o'clock, only to be kept kicking his heels. 'The Führer was said to be out walking with Unity Mitford and was expected back only by supper-time. The success of my mission did not seem to carry much weight with him. Shortly before seven he returned, saw me and summoned me in, "Now tell me about your trip!" ... Hitler's attitudes towards England were always greatly insecure, and once more he had turned over a new leaf. Whether Unity Mitford had been whispering in his ear ... I do not know.'

From Bormann's schedule, the tea party was over after a couple of hours, for at a quarter to six there was an inspection of the Führer's new car, and orders to be given to the chauffeur Erich Kempka. '18.00 hours, Captain Wiedemann reports back to the Führer. Walk to the Tea-house. The Führer gives instructions that a car be reserved for Lady Mitford in Nuremberg, which will then bring her on to the Obersalzberg. 19.50 hours, Captain Wiedemann's statement (England). 20.30 hours Dinner: taking part: Minister Wagner, Reichsleiter Bormann and wife, Director Werlin.'

Unity, then, did not stay to dine, nor is her presence on the walk to the tea-house stated in so many words but it may be reasonably inferred that the request for a car to bring her back to the Obersalzberg had arisen from plan-making during the walk. Undoubtedly Wiedemann had been obliged to wait. It is striking that at a moment of major crisis when a personal overture on

Hitler's behalf was being made to the English government, an English girl should have been with Hitler. What she whispered into Hitler's ear, whether they were drawing up further *Tatler* lists around Lord Halifax, cannot be known, though it is not beyond guessing that she will have encouraged him to believe in the lack of British resolution, and the consequent rewards of invading the Sudetenland as planned. As for Unity, she cannot have failed to have seen that if Wiedemann believed in his mission, nobody else on the Obersalzberg did. For Hitler to stroll out as soon as his deputy appeared was the purest cynicism.

The Bayreuth festival blocked off a fortnight in the diaries of Nazi *Prominenten*; Unity's attendance has already been mentioned by Mary, Kukuli von Arent, Albert Speer and others. She was there regularly, to catch Hitler at his most informal, the art-lover communing with the higher Teutonic spirit. Wahn-fried, where Hitler lived during the festival, had been built by Richard Wagner, a gloomily bombastic house and shrine to megalomania. Here the maestro had pickled his genius for coming generations, though he could never have imagined what blaspheming rites would grip the place in its Nazi incarnation. The Wagner family was then, as now, masterfully repre-sented by Frau Winifred Wagner. Once Winifred Williams from south Wales, she had been sent as an orphan to Germany before the First World War, during which she married Siegfried Wagner. The association with Bayreuth worked upon her as it had upon Houston Stewart Chamberlain. Although far more intelligent than Unity, she too transferred her allegiances to Hitler in his early days, and then to his Reich, with such personal steadfastness indeed, that a romance between her and Hitler was constantly being forged in the news-papers, though with no greater truth than in the parallel case of Erna Hanfstaengl. Left a widow before Hitler seized power, Frau Winifred ran the festival single-handed. Her sons, Wieland and Wolfgang, were later directors; one daughter was too young to help, while the other, Friedelind, escaped to America before the war, and lives now in England.

The *Royal Family of Bayreuth* is Friedelind Wagner's reckoning with a heritage oppressive to her, and a useful, bright book in its own right. Already in April 1935, during Mosley's visit to Hitler, Frau Winifred had met Unity, picked up the gossip and 'thought her too naïve for the position of Hitler's wife, and doubted if such a marriage would improve the relations of the Third Reich with England'. When Unity arrived for the 1936 festival, Frau Winifred asked the Führer if he would like her invited to lunch. To quote Friedelind, Hitler replied, 'It would make me terribly happy. You know Unity lives on little more than a mark a month. Her parents have cut off her allowances to force her back to England. She has returned once or twice but she always runs away again.' (The truth was the opposite, as we know, for the longer Unity was in Germany, the more her parents became her subordinates, until they may be said to have run away with her. That new car of hers was a symbol as well as a gift.)

Unity's teeth spoiled her appearance, according to Friedelind, who thought Diana was truly beautiful. 'The low-necked dresses of the girls and their lipstick made the Führer's party stare.' She goes on, 'The idea that Unity was performing a sacred mission by bringing about a German–British understanding was without foundation – quite the contrary, for the girl tried to prejudice Hitler against England by giving him the idea that most of the English were stupid.' By the 1938 festival, Friedelind judges, Unity 'was no longer Hitler's shadow. She did not walk through the cordons of SS guards but saw the Führer only when she received an official invitation and was conducted to his table during the intermissions by an aide-de-camp.' After Hitler had left, Unity fell ill, was discovered in her night-dress pouring her medicine out of the window, and had to be sent to the clinic. 'One night, or rather morning at four o'clock, we were awakened at Wahnfried by a violent ringing of the bell. The urgent caller was Hitler's physician looking for Unity . . . we sent the doctor to the clinic and he attended Unity constantly until she was well. Hitler paid the bill and also sent autographed pictures of himself for her to give to the nurses. When Unity was able to leave the clinic, Lord Redesdale took her to Obersalzberg where he gave Hitler the amount of his daughter's bills.'

Frau Winifred Wagner lives in the extension of Wahnfried which she built in 1933 for guests. Erect, strong-willed, she does not look her age. She said, 'My connection with the family was via the grandfather Redesdale, a great friend of my husband's. After the war Unity's parents came to collect her belongings in Munich, they visited me and said she was riding a bicycle and getting about, but was not really well. I never saw her in Munich. Diana and Mosley used to come to the festival, I'd met them when I was asked to interpret for him and Hitler in April 1935. I knew Hitler much longer than Unity did, and much better too. Hitler often invited me on his private train, in the so-called *salonwagen*, a comfortable sitting room. She was always hanging around Hitler. When she was here, she never stayed with me as Hitler did, or the Goebbelses and the Goerings. I would just shake hands with her, he had invited her and given her the tickets – he bought them. We were together in the intervals but she never sat in the box with us, not in the Führerloge. Hitler knew that if he wanted something broadcast he had only to talk in front of Unity – that he told me himself. Unity looked like a baby, such an innocent look. Hitler liked to have youth about him. But in a way she was such a bother. Marriage? Quite impossible. She might have hoped for it, he was kind and polite, they got on well together, but he used to say he could never marry anyone. I can't say much, she wasn't interesting enough to me.'

Frau Winifred then introduced me to Dr Helmut Trauter, into whose clinic Unity had been despatched at the end of the 1938 festival, in the early part of August. The Clinic am Hofgarten, as it was called, adjoined the Wahnfried gardens, in the Lisztstrasse (where Hitler had lived in 1925). The doctor calling so post-haste at four in the morning was Dr Morell, the sinister and quackish personal physician at the Berghof. Dr Trauter said, 'I was telephoned by some official. She was brought in with pneumonia, inflammation of the lungs, running a temperature. Mine was the only private clinic in Bayreuth, it had thirty beds. Before she came, I had no idea she even existed. *Prominenten* were always coming to the festival, I confined myself to a medical view. My files were lost in the war. After two or three weeks she had recovered, her mother and father were near by in a hotel and they took her away.'

For the remainder of the month, as we shall learn from Rudi Simolin, Unity and her parents were guests of Erna Hanfstaengl at a farm which had been lent to her for four weeks by Frau Stöhr, a friend of hers. This mountain house was on the Untersberg, opposite Obersalzberg, conveniently close to Hitler, and it was from there that Lord Redesdale set off to repay Hitler for having settled the doctors' bills.

Unity, honorary princess of the party rallies, had an unbroken record of attendance at Nuremberg since Hitler had seized power, and on 5 September she enjoyed some sort of apotheosis by arriving there with her parents, who had been bound hand and foot to Nazism by her. This was in fact the last such rally to be held, for the war put an end to these performances for good, and Hitler's determination to pulverize Czechoslovakia lay heavily over it. The Runciman Mission had already done its worst.

'All week long Hitler had appeared grave and preoccupied. He had refused to receive foreign diplomats and even to talk to his advisers,' wrote Virginia Cowles in *Looking for Trouble*, about her experiences as a roving correspondent. On the Saturday, the 10th, she continues, Hitler appeared at the Deutscher Hof Hotel for a tea in his honour given by Ribbentrop, with some seventy select guests. 'Most of the leading German officials were present – Goering, Himmler, Heydrich, Hess and many others. Unity Mitford was there, surrounded by officials who kissed her hand and bowed and scraped. She seemed rather embarrassed by their attention, left the group and joined my table . . .

Hitler took his place at a table across the room at which there were about a dozen men, including two English peers: Lord Stamp and Lord Brocket. There was also Ward Price, and Herr Henlein . . . When everyone was seated, Hitler's gaze wandered over the gathering and his eye suddenly lit on Unity. His face broke into a smile, he nodded and gave her the Nazi salute. She saluted back and a few minutes later Captain Wiedemann, Hitler's ADC, came over and whispered in Unity's ear, "The Führer would like to see you. When tea is over he would like you to come to his suite." Unity nodded. I couldn't help thinking how odd it was that, on the brink of war between Germany and Great Britain, the only person that the Führer would condescend to see was a twenty-four-year-old English girl . . . After the reception Unity had her talk with Hitler and came back to the Grand Hotel just before dinner. I hastily cornered her and asked what he had said and whether or not she thought there was going to be a war. "I don't think so," she smiled. "The Führer doesn't want his new buildings bombed".'

That evening Virginia Cowles dined with Unity, Robert Byron and Ward Price. 'It was difficult to get across the town, as the Storm Troopers' parade was scheduled to begin at nine o'clock and no cars were allowed on the streets. Unity, however, arranged for one of the SS cars to drive us to the restaurant; and we soon found ourselves in a long, sleek, black car racing through empty streets with crowds on either side . . . Unity sat in front with the black-uniformed chauffeur, her blonde curls streaming in the wind . . . She had a straightforward friendly manner and a lively sense of humour . . . She claimed that if Hitler were not the Führer of Germany, he would make a hundred thousand dollars a year on the vaudeville stage. He often did imitations of his colleagues – Goering, Goebbels, and Himmler – but, best of all, he liked to imitate Mussolini. This always provoked roars of laughter. "And sometimes," added Unity, "he can even imitate himself." How Mitford are those "roars of laughter!" No less Mitford, either, is a hilarious glimpse of Lady Redesdale, "who spent most of her time (when she was not at one of the reviews with Unity) in a corner of the hotel lobby sewing," while Lord Redesdale helped her to find her needles or "wandered about with a bewildered air as though he were at a rather awkward house-party where (curiously enough) no one could speak any English".'

Hitler's jovial tea party was reported in the English press. So was the usual SS bivouac reception, and the Daily Telegraph on the 12th observed that the ambassador, Sir Nevile Henderson, had sat between Frau Himmler and Unity. In one of the many private letters to Lord Halifax which sought to by-pass the permanent officials in order to urge appeasement, Henderson wrote that the SS camp supper had not been very inspiring on account of the rain, but the Germans had been friendly.* 'Were they thinking to pull the wool over my eyes, to detach Great Britain from interference in Czechoslovakia? ... Incidentally I met for the first time the notorious Unity Mitford at Himmler's party. A lady introduced me and when she squeaked out "Heil Hitler" to me, I was so dumbfounded that I forgot my usual retort which is "Rule Britannia". Except to shake her by the hand I didn't speak to her.' In a similar confrontation, his predecessor Sir Eric Phipps had done better, as usual.

Robert Byron, it should be explained, had tagged along with the Mitfords in order to spy out the land. A man of the world, he was already the author of successful travel books about Greece, Russia and Persia. Churchillian in outlook, an out-and-out opponent of the Nazis, he was not someone to restrain his temper or his tongue on the subject, but he did have the wits to use Unity as a valuable contact. He had been stringing her along with his plans to write a book about the First World War, as we have seen, and he had extracted introductions from her which otherwise would have been hard to come by. Since that June, he had been determined to see this Party Rally, to have his fears confirmed that war was unavoidable. Tom had intended to be his escort and to obtain the necessary tickets through Ribbentrop, but duty with his territorial regiment prevented him at the last moment from doing so, and Unity had to do the honours. After the rally he went to stay with his sister Lucy in Berlin, where her husband, Ewan Butler, was then *The Times* correspondent. She wrote to me, 'Unity came to see us just after Hitler's birthday, 20 April 1939. They had been looking at Hitler's presents together and she described him in fits over a life-sized picture some admirer had sent him. It was a portrait of him in the nude, standing upon a vast flashing faceted diamond holding a sword which he was waving above his head. What this represented I have quite forgotten. Unity also described to us how funny he was imitating Chamberlain, we had heard from other sources that this was one of his star turns ... In a way Unity was terribly smug about him. I remember she came to dinner with us that May and infuriated my first husband and myself by refusing to smoke or drink what was then pretty good hock. "The Führer doesn't like me to." I have found a letter I wrote to Robert at the time which I quote for you, "We had dinner with Unity the other night, I must say it wasn't a very gay evening, somehow in Berlin she seems a bit too close to reality, specially when she talks about England being taken over in 1942 as part of the programme. I think she is really very unhappy and has to cling to all the nonsense to keep herself going, I can't

---

* Documents on British Foreign Policy 1919–1939, Third Series, Vol. II, Appendix 1, pp. 653-4.

think what pleasure she got out of seeing us, as we are neither of us the sunny-tempered pair we used to be." It was difficult to take Unity in the near-war atmosphere of Berlin at that time.'

At the very moment when Unity was passing the message on to Virginia Cowles, Hitler may not have wanted his new buildings bombed, but he did want to pull the wool over Henderson's, and everybody's, eyes; and Unity could be pressed into service once again. The message she relayed might even cosset those who heard it. So long as Britain abstained from interference, Germany would carry off the spoils, and the anti-Czech vituperation of his speeches rubbed at the sore. From Hitler's point of view, speculation about war had immediately to be whipped along. Mary's diary is to the point. 'September 14th. Unity says Führer advises all Ausländer [foreigners] to leave. She is staying.'

On the 15th Chamberlain made his first dramatic visit to Berchtesgaden to receive an earful in the same vein: the fact of the flight itself had indicated to Hitler that the Czech–Franco–British front of May and June had shivered to bits, and he had only to be as unreasonable and bellicose as possible for the Czechs to be handed over to him. Hitler was master of the artificial tantrum, a self-parodist, and Chamberlain flew home on the 16th with the strengthening conviction that Czechoslovakia really was a faraway country. Hitler was also playing from strength in that his troops were anyhow under orders to enter Czechoslovakia at the end of the month.

The despatch which Gainer, now consul-general in Vienna, sent on 20 September (F.O. 371/21780) to Ivone Kirkpatrick in the embassy in Berlin was therefore opportune. 'It may be of interest to you to hear that Unity Mitford has just been in to see me and has told me that she saw Hitler privately after his Nuremberg speech, when he advised her to leave Germany at once, and to tell "all her English friends" to do the same, as he "felt certain there would be a war". She says he has now changed his view, but I don't think she has seen him recently. She is staying in Burgenland and said I need not bother to warn her to go, as if war broke out she would of course stay in Germany.' (Henderson had forwarded this to the Foreign Office and the resident clerk had scribbled on it, 'Good riddance.')

The bravado was Unity's alone, a repeat of what she had told Mary six days earlier. But this was the tune to pipe to the Foreign Office at this juncture; it was sure to needle; Gainer had been an intermediary before and he was known to be considered trustworthy. It could not be decisive of course, but coming straight from the horse's mouth, this despatch was well timed while the Munich Agreement was in the stew. If war really was imminent,

Hitler would certainly be advising Unity to be out of harm's way; it would be only responsible of him, gentlemanly. Here was one more example, fortuitous or not, of Unity broadcasting Hitler's up-to-the-minute bulletins.

On the 12th, she had swooped upon Munich to find Frau Smital and a delegation of twenty-four girls from the Burgenland and escort them back to Nuremberg, to the Deutscher Hof Hotel, for an official audience, in the hopes of one of those syntheses to which she aspired, between Hitler and Bernstein. The Redesdales went their own way, and by the 15th Unity was turning up without forewarning at Bernstein, arriving at half past one in the morning, rain-swept and exhausted, with Janos away, and only a servant at last to open the big bolted door. Next day she paid her respects to Marie in her bedroom, chatted to Kisebb, and moved on to Kohfidisch, to find other guests, first the de Rutzens, and then at the weekend an old friend of Janos's called Jules Mertz. Everybody oscillated between Bernstein and Kohfidisch, with an outing on the 19th to Szombathely to fetch dresses for Baby Erdödy, and an expedition early on the 20th to Vienna, taking in the de Rutzens because they needed new passports from the consulate, which was Unity's chance to collar Gainer – he wasted no time about getting off his despatch. She was also planning a holiday in Venice with Janos, so after lunching with the de Rutzens at the smart Drei Husaren restaurant, she collected Italian money at the bank, and returned to Bernstein by herself.

John de Rutzen (killed in the war) came from a Dutch family long naturalized English, and lived at Slebbich in Pembrokeshire. Sheila de Rutzen is now Lady Dunsany. At the time, they had been returning from Roumania where they had run across military manoeuvres and had their passports confiscated, which sent them scurrying as best they could across Hungary, to shelter at Kohfidisch. Lady Dunsany said: 'When we had stayed once with Gottfried von Bismarck, brother of Otto, I'd met Unity in Berlin, with masses of people – we'd gone through Aberystwyth University because John was a forester. Janos I'd known in Kitzbühel; he was a good host, very welcoming, he spoke faultless English. We'd also met Laczy in Cairo. Everybody knew about Unity but didn't take her seriously. I always felt she was waiting for a sign from Hitler. Janos was second string. He and Unity were very easy with each other, she could walk in and out, she had the run of the house, I felt Marie condoned it. Definitely they were having an affair.

'Hitler sent her little-girl presents, like pocket-knives, her badge and her camera, I saw that – she had a chain from him, but otherwise no jewels. Sometimes we went on walks and she found some little wild flower, she would use the pocket-knife of Hitler's to dig it up; it had a pearl handle and lots of gadgets to it. Hitler sent chocolates to Unity and Diana. Unity was always worrying about her dog. That September she was in tears once or twice. She did talk to Hitler once on the telephone, for hours. She had been to the *Anschluss* and told me how he had taken her on to the balcony of the Imperial Hotel, she was thrilled by that. Through her I replaced my passport in Vienna, she knew the consul. In spring, 1939, we were on our way to Italy and spent a night at Bernstein, I remember her tears then, she was out of contact with Hitler.'

Victor Simaica came to Bernstein on the 20th. Although the weather improved, and the swimming pool, the garden, ping-pong and dressing up in costumes, distracted everybody at Bernstein and Kohfidisch, the international situation worsened, so much so that Janos decided to postpone the holiday in Venice. Chamberlain had been at Godesberg, the British and French ministers were meeting – while at Bernstein the night of the 25th, a Sunday, was celebrated with a choir of forty folk-singers from Mittenwald, with dancing and drinking in the village, Janos seeing in the dawn, home to breakfast in his dinner jacket in the courtyard, with Unity, Baby and Victor in their dressing gowns. Unity spent the day painting, until everybody in the house gathered round the wireless for Hitler's speech at eight o'clock from the Berlin Sportpalast, a howling diatribe against the Czechs.

Sweating it out, Unity, Baby and Victor spent the 27th in Vienna, lunching at the Grand Hotel, calling on Countess Clare Repelaer, known as Fifi, and therefore missing Chamberlain's speech. Next day, the same trio paid a visit to Frau Smital at Oberwart, to mull over her meeting at Nuremberg with the Führer, but that afternoon, over the Kohfidisch wireless, they heard that Mussolini, Daladier and Chamberlain were on their way to Munich. The news thrilled Unity for she perceived that Hitler had his victory, all but the ratification, and the piece of paper. Jimmy Erdödy had returned from Budapest, Count Paul Draskowitch came from Güssing, so that assembled friends and neighbours sat through the morning of the 30th, a dark and rainy Friday, in the big drawing room at Kohfidisch. After lunch Unity had her reward with what she called 'the wonderful news of the Munich Abkommen'. She and Baby and Victor harnessed a pony trap, and then for fun rode in it along the paths of the close, shadowy pines of the Kohfidisch forests.

Respite. Illusion could be spun out for one more twilight year, although to Unity all was radiance and freedom. For a start, she could go to Venice, and on 3 October set off with Janos and Kisebb, Baby and Victor Simaica following behind in another car. Dropping Kisebb at Villach, they had some food and pressed on to the Italian frontier where they caught the broadcast that the German army had crossed into the Sudetenland. The Czechs were offering no resistance to this invasion. Unity was miserable; she was at a frontier all right, but the wrong one; she could have been with the German army, and with the Führer himself, for a repetition of the *Anschluss*, and '*Was! Ihr beide hier!*' Too late. She had to make do with Venice, and a motor boat to the Grand Hotel, dinner in the Taverna Fenice, and a stroll on the Piazza San Marco.

Tourists, they behaved as such for two days, watching glass-making on the far side of the Grand Canal, sightseeing in a gondola, dining on scampi and thrushes. If ever Janos was to have an affair with Unity, no more propitious setting could have been found. On 4 October something happened between them which was described as 'Devils exorcised', which has a sexual ring about it, and suggests fantasies or practices of masturbation, though it might equally be a harmless private joke. Victor Simaica writes to me, 'The trip was great fun. There was a Nazi congress in Venice we stumbled on by chance. Baby and Janos brought forth many amusing remarks. Unity did not seem to hold any political views either way, and her infatuation with Hitler, I am sure, was mental. I remember her once saying to me, "There is a great thrill in desiring the unobtainable." I think her relationship with Janos was more friendly than anything else.'

After lunch on the 6th they were away. They ran out of petrol on the pass before Pontebba, and had to be rescued by Baby and Victor who luckily were behind. In Austria again, Janos took Unity to Osterwitz (a castle surmounted by one of the most spectacular of medieval fortresses), to stay with Prince Khevenhüller, Pimpf to his friends; one of his sisters, Hella, was in a sense a rival to Unity, for she too had been picked up by Hitler and made much of, with a private telephone line installed direct between the Führer and Osterwitz. Janos deposited Unity at Kohfidisch, and from there on the 9th, a Sunday, she drove into Vienna to collect her brother Tom, at the Westbahnhof, for his autumn holiday in the Burgenland.

To enliven the Chekhovian flow of time in the countryside, they smoked a pipe of hashish, introduced to it by Victor. And a quarrel broke out when 'Baby was horrid about the Führer'. Unity rushed off by herself into the woods for a couple of hours and then was still furious enough to shut herself away in her room, lying on the bed reading. ('Could that baby-face of hers really look angry?' wonders Countess Jimmy, of that scene.) On the 14th, Victor left for Stockholm. Two days later Unity accompanied Janos and Count Anty Szapary on a woodcock shoot, and by the 17th she and Tom had moved to Bernstein for two last days.

Driving back with Tom to Vienna on the 19th, Unity had a puncture, and this time Janos caught up with them. They lunched at the Capri Restaurant, where Prince Kari Auersperg joined them before Unity and Tom continued their journey to Munich. But at seven o'clock, near Linz, they crossed the Führer's motorcade in the dark. This was an opportunity Unity could not miss. She turned and followed. The centre of Linz had been blocked by the police, so Unity left Tom in the car, joined the crowd and dogged Hitler to his hotel. Her name and demeanour were enough to get her past the security cordon, and she was taken up to Hitler's room. He was in Linz to pursue plans for the grandiose museum to himself and to German art which he wished to establish there. He was extremely surprised to be gate-crashed by Unity in his room. After a short talk, she left to fetch Tom from the car, and they then waited in the hall downstairs until half past nine when Hitler came down. Unity and Tom dined by themselves across from the hotel, but afterwards they were invited to sit and talk to Hitler and his companion in Linz, Artur Seyss-Inquart, who had prepared the *Anschluss* and until June had been the Reich Commissioner for Austria. It was only at one in the morning that Unity and Tom drove off to find a hotel room. The accosting had been a success on the classic Osteria model.

Unity also profited from the evening's work by culling an immediate invitation to the Obersalzberg. Bormann's notebook records Hitler's journey to Linz on the 19th, and his return to the Berghof next day. Unity and Tom had probably been to Munich in between whiles, for Bormann would normally have recorded their presence as Hitler's guests at meals or overnight. At any rate, he noted on 21 October, 'The Führer drives with Frau Goebbels and the Mitfords to Kehlstein-Haus,' in other words to the tea-house which was perched so high on a crag above his own house that it was later, and splashily, christened The Eagle's Nest. (Obersalzberg, as a description, covers that particular Alpine massif. Hitler's house there, properly speaking, was the Berghof, and confusingly it had another tea-house within walking distance, to which Hitler had gone on the afternoon of Unity's visit of 19 July.) The Kehlstein Haus, almost alone of the whole complex, has survived and may still be reached up seven twisty kilometers of mountain road, which was itself an engineering accomplishment. A tunnel then enters the rock, and an elevator rises up a shaft of over a hundred meters to the interior of the so-called tea-house. Hitler did not care for this ascension, fearing breakdown or sabotage of the essential elevator. That October, however, he was displaying his newly completed tea-house to distinguished visitors, to Prince Philipp of Hesse and Gauleiter Wagner on the 17th, for instance; to the French ambassador, André François-Poncet, on the 18th (an entertaining account of the experience is to be read in his memoirs); then the whole Goebbels family on the 23rd; Generals von Brauchitsch and Keitel on the 24th. The French ambassador may have beaten Unity and Tom to it by three days, but they had beaten the generals, and as far as can be ascertained from the records, no other English people ever saw the Kehlstein Haus in Hitler's lifetime.

'October 25th. Met Unity lunch with her dog . . . November 18th. Unity on radio with Winckler in London.' (She must have done a broadcast for German radio with one of its London correspondents.) These dates in Mary's diary bracket the moment when Unity's routine year-end spell at home began. In fact she had returned in the early part of November, thereby missing the Kristallnacht pogrom of the 10th, in which Streicher's personal anti-semitic dementia became generalized throughout Germany: Europe had experienced nothing comparable since the Middle Ages. The Star of 12 November wrote up what might have been a sequel to the Hyde Park demonstration of April. 'Miss Unity Mitford . . . with her mother, Lady Redesdale, were among the visitors at the conference at Friends' House, in London today, to support the campaign for "Food and Freedom for Spain". They took no part in the discussions. The meeting was addressed by Lord Strabolgi and Madame Tabouis.' On the 17th, the South Kensington Conservatives in their head-quarters in Stratford Road debated the motion 'that whilst National Socialism has been advantageous to Germany it represents a danger to world peace'. Vice-Admiral Usborne proposed the motion. According to the Daily Telegraph, 'he had met Miss Mitford at a recent weekend course at Ashridge [a college of further education near St Albans]. He then suggested that she should act as his opposer. She accepted with alacrity.' The chairman was Lord Sandford. The News Chronicle on the 18th wrote up the debate. 'There were 181 people present. Nine voted for Miss Mitford. Admission was by ticket only, and many who tried to get in were turned away. As she walked with a strong guard to her car after the debate, Miss Mitford, angry at the result, told a News Chronicle reporter: "I have nothing to say about the debate. I spoke for fifteen minutes. I cannot even tell you what I said. I addressed them on the spur of the moment." Miss Mitford's remarks were frequently received with laughter.' It was a far cry from the Hesselberg impromptu with Streicher, and mortifying too that words were so much less effective a lever to publicity among Conservatives than personal display had been among the Hyde Park left-wingers.

In its issue of 25 November, the Kensington News reported the debate ver-batim. Rather unskilfully, Unity conceded right at the start that force was the way for Germany to redress grievances. 'Human nature being what it is, those who do not stick up for their own rights get trampled on. The man with a strong character will be respectfully treated. Likewise the man with a strong body ... Not until Germany was strong enough to enforce justice did the Sudeten Germans regain their rights and freedom.' She went on to the fanciful argument that it was hypocrisy for the British to point the accusing finger at others 'for precisely the same things as they do themselves', for instance, at the present time 'the wholesale bombing of Arab villages'. On her favourite theme that the Nordic races should stick together, she closed, 'I think I can truly say that a war between England and Germany, even if Germany won, would be the greatest tragedy for the Führer ... The Führer and his followers are immensely proud of their wonderful achievements in every field of life. A war would unavoidably put a temporary stop to this programme, if it did not end it altogether. Although the Führer is naturally tremendously proud of the wonderful army he has created, his real interests lie in purely peaceful directions. One of the greatest is architecture ...'

On the 29th she was briefly in the news, in court at Chatham, accompanied by her father, on a charge of exceeding the speed limit. Apparently she had told the pursuing policeman, 'I have just come back from Germany where there is no speed limit, and I am afraid I forgot the limit after four months' absence.' Her licence was endorsed. (Two months later, on 20 January 1939, she was fined ten shillings, with costs of a guinea, for failing to stop at a pedestrian crossing in Sloane Square. The Munich police were altogether more considerate about such things.) Then again on 16 December, a photograph of her, her mother and Captain FitzRandolph of the German Embassy, appeared in the Daily Express, showing the three of them balancing plates of sausages on their knees, 'at the Anglo-German Fellowship's Bloomsbury party last night'. That Hitler, through his adjutant Schaub, would be giving her a Christmas present of an expensive camera to replace the one confiscated from her in Prague, was an item of general news.

Fascinating as it was, morbid, bone-rattling, for the press to dwell upon Unity, the interest was disproportionate to the achievement. This djinn had been summoned out of their bottle, though in fairness it must be said that once she lent herself as a publicists' weapon to the Germans, she could not be ignored in her own country; that would have been to concede her the Nazi game. A democratic press is often in this quandary, spreading the very infections from which it seeks defence, and as a counter it can resort only to ridicule and over-exposure, as was the case here; it can love to hate. Unity-the-monster had permeated the general consciousness as a result, she was the subject of cartoons. ('You can't criticize Unity / with impunity. / If you try to belittle 'er / You have to answer to Hitler' – *News Chronicle* caption to a drawing of them both.) She was frivolous and influential at the same time. Thus in a tatlerizing book, *Europe at Play* (1938) by E. H. Tattersall, a photograph of her, swastika badge prominent, was published with an author's name-dropping aside in the text, about his tea in the Vierjahreszeiten with Hitler, Goebbels, Ribbentrop, Goering and Unity, 'I thought a good bag for one afternoon' – while F. L. Lucas, a man of letters, in his *Journal under the Terror*, 1938, a heartfelt plague-on-both-your-houses outpouring against Nazis and communists alike, gave every snippet of Unity's reported doings as though she were a prime mover of politics. Unity anyhow had no view of herself except through her press-cutting books, those proofs that Nazism really was her life, as she declared it to be. If she was of such consequence that everyone sat up and took notice, how was she to scrub the Pasionaria self?

As a matter of fact, that last winter of peace was the longest continuous span without an outrage since fascism had first overpowered her. She lay low at Swinbrook or in The Garage. Nothing of her is recorded in February, except that on the 19th she was at the Sadler's Wells opera with Nancy and Tom. Not that she was really braking. It was now, for example, that she tried to argue Putzi Hanfstaengl into what would have been a suicidal return to Germany. But her Nazism was in hibernation when compared to the excesses earlier in the year, the rowdiest in her life. Did she, one wonders, have a lull, or in spite of the bragging, an intimation of the ending? Almost everyone else did. The consequences of the Munich Agreement were calamitous, and the suspense of living with certain doom became unbearable. Central Europe, including Russia, had hastened to accommodate Hitler. His military supremacy had been further endorsed when the German army occupied the rump of Czechoslovakia on 15 March; nothing could be done but throw words in the air. Chamberlain, on the 17th, made a resentful speech about resisting Germany though he could not say how. The very next day, the *Daily Mirror* published a half-page article, 'What Miss Mitford would like to see', which must have been written before the final destruction of Czechoslovakia, but chimed in well with it. '*We* don't agree with her,' was the editorial opinion expressed in large type in a top corner of the lay-out, while an insert next to a photograph of Hitler added, 'She wants us to be friends with this man . . . who has just pounced on and ravished an innocent land?'

Precautions against being misunderstood might have been prompted by Unity's text, which in the circumstances was not so inept, though its line was the standard promotion of the German Embassy (where in all likelihood the article had been vetted, if not actually drafted). For the personal tone and challenge of her one and only other excursion into print, namely the *Stürmer* letter, have been ironed out. A more sober Unity was presented than anyone could have expected, though not less Nazi. Hitler, she says, is a dreamer of those dreams capable of fulfilment, 'taking into account his genius for achieving the impossible'. Friendship with England is one of these dreams, and more than that, an expression of Nordic solidarity. 'One of the foundations of Nazi ideology is the racial theory. Germans believe the Nordic race to be the greatest in the world, which indeed it is.' The interests of the two countries therefore coincided humanly and politically. 'The German Army, the British Navy and the two Air Forces combined would police the world and keep "peace in our time".' Slyly she steered racial theory into Nordic waters away from anti-semitism. She also skimped explaining how British interests would be served by a Hitler-controlled Europe, and whether a world under Anglo-German policing was desirable or practical – evasions which might scrape by readers to whom Czechoslovakia really was of no concern, and who prayed above all else to be left alone. The paper stated that nearly twelve hundred readers had written in about the article, of whom eight per cent were in favour of what had been said. Incidentally, Lady Redesdale was to publish an article soon, on 10 June, in the *Daily Sketch*, arguing that National Socialism eliminated class warfare, raised living standards and strengthened religion, unlike its deadly opponent, Bolshevism. Our proposed military pact with Russia, she concluded, would encircle Germany and be divisive. By getting in first with their Russian pact, the Germans were to dynamite the ground on which Lady Redesdale thought she was standing – and Unity too.

Shortly after her article was published, Unity returned to Germany, to her old haunts. As late as 8 May, however, the *Daily Telegraph* was publishing that Unity 'has been away from Germany for the longest period since her acquaintance with leading Nazis. She is reported to have been for a winter holiday in Egypt.' This proved a fine red-herring. The journey could have been dovetailed in only between the beginning of January and the end of March, and we know she was in court at Chatham on 20 January and at Sadler's Wells on 19 February. The Bernstein papers threw only a negative light. Janos had gone there without her in March 1938, which may have somehow got garbled into this report. In his diaries he makes no mention of any second trip to Egypt. When at a loss for anything better, he sometimes jotted 'N v B', for *Nichts von Bedeutung*, Nothing of Importance. He also left blanks, and there are a few in February and March 1939 but not time enough for him to have scrambled from Bernstein to Egypt and back. Could Unity then have gone with Laczy, or Tom, or anyone? Given the time which must be allowed for sailing to Cairo and back, she could hardly have spent even a few days there. The confusion arises in the *Daily Telegraph*, I suspect, because by 8 May she had just come back from Budapest, as will be seen. Nobody confirms what would otherwise have been a rare, a last, bid out of the sprung trap.

A FLAT IN MUNICH

After the *Anschluss*, Gainer's successor in the Munich Consulate was J. E. M. Carvell — with Wolston Weld-Forester as his deputy — and on 27 March 1939, he was sending a despatch (F.O. 371/22989) to Sir George Ogilvie-Forbes, first secretary in the Berlin Embassy, who in turn forwarded it to the Foreign Office. 'Unity Mitford called on me today with the object of informing me that she would be resident in Munich until the autumn of the year. As I thought it likely that she would have visited Herr Hitler while she was in Munich, I engaged her in conversation and learnt that she had taken luncheon with him on the day of his arrival in Munich and also on the following day. In reply to an enquiry on my part as to whether she thought there was a chance of any improvement in Anglo-German relations, Miss Mitford told me that Herr Hitler had said that he was confident that friendship between Germany and Great Britain was still possible, that the German people desired it, and that if he could bring it about he would be deified (*vergöttet*). Miss Mitford then volunteered the statement that Herr Hitler considered Italo-German friendship as unnatural and that he did not expect the Berlin–Rome Axis to last. In the course of conversation Miss Mitford mentioned that Herr Hitler believed that he had been sent by God and that when one heard him say that one believed it too. She also said that Herr Hitler never knew what he was going to do but that when it had all happened he believed that he had known all the time. This was my first meeting with Miss Mitford and although I had heard a great deal about her, I was not prepared to find anyone whose admiration of a man in public life so nearly approached veneration or whose acceptance of a foreign political creed was so blindly fanatical in its fervour.' (To which F. H., later Sir Frank, Roberts minuted, 'Herr Hitler is hardly following the straightest road to his "deification".')

If Hitler had not been informed of Unity's recent article on his behalf, he would have learnt about it at those consecutive lunches. The latest visit to the consulate was to continue maintaining herself as a private circuit between Hitler and the Foreign Office. Carvell, like Gainer before him, was certain to pass on first-hand observations of this kind, but although the repeated anti-Italian slant might have been worth pursuing, Unity was appealing only to emotions: she was taking up her own deification of Hitler where she had left off, a quiet winter notwithstanding.

Something was again amiss between her and Janos, for in the first week of April letters and telegrams were exchanged, until she caught him unawares and uninvited, walking in on him at Bernstein, her dog at her heels, after breakfast on the 7th, which was in fact Good Friday. Jimmy Erdödy and Lady Patricia Russell lunched, and Baby looked in afterwards with Count Imre Zichy, Marie-Eugenie's brother. That week Janos had a series of appointments with the doctor, which perhaps had brought Unity out in such a rush. But Easter weekend was hot and sunny, they sat out in the garden, wrote letters and were entertained by Kisebb. On the Monday Unity set off by herself for another interlude in Budapest. First she stopped at Devecser in the hopes of leaving Boy there, in the care of Countess Tommy Esterhazy, née Countess Wurmbrand, later married to Arpad Plesch. Devecser was an old *Wasserburg* with thick walls, and the estate, together with Papa adjoining it, and also inherited by Count Tommy Esterhazy, comprised eighty thousand hectares. Mrs Plesch said that Unity had been there two or three times. 'She wanted us to take in that dog, it was enormous, a mastiff. She came alone to us, through Janos, he and Marie were great friends of my husband; and Janos was often at Devecser. I thought he was charming and gay, not so good-looking as his brother. We often spent weekends at Bernstein, and at Kohfidisch. We didn't keep that dog at Devecser, I don't know what became of it. The *on dit* was: did she or did she not sleep with Hitler? The fact of gossiping about it gave her a cachet.'

With the wind of Germany filling its sails, Hungary in 1939 was particularly ebullient, grateful for the morsels of Slovakia which had been expediently claimed for their Magyar minorities, and thrown to it as a consequence of the Munich Agreement. Unity was on her own in the Almasy flat, but was whirled into the social round with Marie-Eugenie and Imre Zichy, with Anty and Erzsi Szapary, Count Strachwitz, Count Csekonics, Baby Erdödy in a new flat, Jimmy and Lady Patricia Russell together, lunch with the Malagollas at the Italian Legation, meals at the smartest restaurants like Krist and Ludlab, late-night drinks at the Ritz with the Duke and Duchess of Mecklenburg, a call on Countess Wenckheim, a garden party with Countess Nora Hadik and her sister, a Luise Rainer film, *Dramatic School*, in a cinema in Vaci utca – the whole spiced with the hairdresser, Countess Julia Apponyi's shop, new blouses, even a fur coat made to measure, and of course Boy to be exercised on St Margaret's Island in the Danube. Hubsie Giesen, from Stuttgart, was giving a concert on the 17th, but she was late, coming in for the very end, afterwards dining with him and Baby. That evening was saddened because she had left Boy with Alice Esterhazy, though quite why with her, and in Budapest, remains a mystery. If Janos did not want to have charge of the dog, somebody at Bernstein could have been found. Usually Unity had left Boy at Solln or with Fräulein Becker of the Pension Doering, but these arrangements would no longer do. The summer was to be spent moving into, and arranging, a flat of her own in Munich, and Boy would have been a nuisance. Presumably she had planned to have him back in due course, but as it turned out, this was one preoccupation the less in the final drama, and quite what happened to Boy in the war is now forgotten.

Janos and Marie welcomed her on the 18th. Spring storms and gusts were blowing off the plains below the castle, and for most of the following day Unity closeted herself with Janos before the library fire, or in his study. On the 20th they walked down to the village for her to send a telegram to Hitler. It was his fiftieth birthday. She was missing the celebrations and parties in the Chancellory in Berlin. Since lunching with him on those two consecutive days four weeks earlier in Munich, she had been out of touch, and had become specially Hitler-bereft and weepy, as Lady Dunsany noticed when she passed through Bernstein at this moment. But Unity was out of sight only, not out of favour, and in fact was about to be Hitler's weekend guest. Yet more astonishing as a mark of his approval and affection, he was also about to present her with a flat.

Walking and chatting with Janos whiled away the rest of the week. On the 22nd, the Saturday, they were both woken up by the gamekeeper at three in the morning, to stalk capercailzie in the Bernstein woods, creeping upon these plump, exotic birds deafened by their own song. Having watched the sunrise, they returned home at six, to breakfast, and Unity then slept till lunchtime. She could not know it, but that still and dewy greeting of dawn under the beech and oaks was an adieu to this place of her adoption.

Dropping Kisebb off in the village of Kirchschlag on her way, she spent that night in Vienna, in the Winzinger Hotel, and reached Munich in the middle of Sunday, homing in on the Osteria Bavaria, chancing upon Mary and Das Kind, her husband now, with whom to share a table. And afterwards she drove to Solln, to be greeted there by Erna Hanfstaengl and Pinky Obermayer, and Rudi. With little delay, she set off to chase Hitler in Berlin. Successfully. She was in time to catch with him the display of his birthday presents, as Lucy Butler has already described.

A fortnight later, for the weekend of 6 and 7 May, she was at Berchtesgaden, spending the night in the Berghof itself, seeing Eva Braun plain, as she had not done since the Party Rally of 1936. Hitler's purpose may have been

12 On an inspection with the commandant of an *Arbeitslager*, or work camp. In her arms a puppy, called Fluffy.

13 Unity and her friend Mary at Bayreuth, with Wieland and Wolfgang Wagner (right), grandsons of the composer and future directors of the festival. 'A darling storm' is in the background.

14 *Left to right*, Adrian Stokes the art critic, Deborah, Jessica, Lady Redesdale, Unity. At the Acropolis during one of the many stop-overs of the Hellenic cruise in the early summer of 1936.

15 OPPOSITE ABOVE On the terrace at Haus Wahnfried at Bayreuth, *left to right*, Albert Speer, Frau Hoffmann (the photographer's second wife), Magda Goebbels, Mary, Hitler.

16 OPPOSITE BELOW This photograph from the same tea party at Haus Wahnfried was one of Unity's favourites. Note her respectful manner.

17 At Schloss Fantaisie outside Bayreuth, during the 1937 festival, *left to right*, Count Berchtold, Kukuli von Arent, Princess Carmencita Wrede (whose party this was), Prince Thurn und Taxis, Clementine Mitford (Lady Beit), Count Berghem.

18 Stairs lead up from the inner courtyard at Bernstein to the door on the first floor, past the horoscope which Janos Almasy had painted for himself.

19 Unity with her dog Rebell at Bernstein, at the time of the Munich crisis.

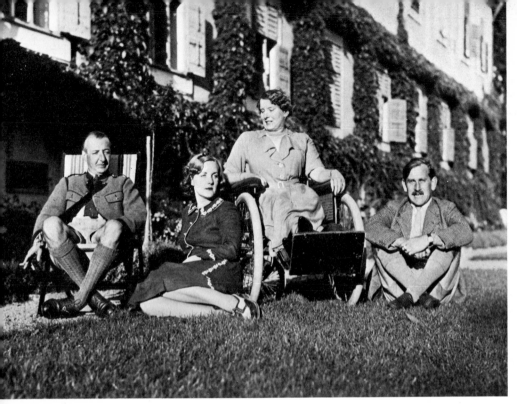

INANITY FARE

You can't criticise Unity
With impunity.
If you try to belittle 'er
You have to answer to Hitler

20 ABOVE In the garden at Bernstein. Unity is between Janos Almasy and his wife Marie in her wheel-chair. Seated to the right, John de Rutzen.

21 LEFT By regularly reporting and commenting on her activities (as in this cartoon from the *News Chronicle*) the press made sure of feeding the fantasies which centred upon her.

22 OPPOSITE ABOVE Lady Redesdale's boat, the *Puffin*, stranded in front of Inchkenneth. Unity's bedroom was on the top floor, with the bow windows.

23 OPPOSITE BELOW On a stretcher at Folkestone quay, 4 January 1940, after the journey home via Switzerland. The wound in the right temple was not visible.

24 Her attendance, seemingly so normal, at Deborah's wedding at
St Bartholomew's, Smithfield, on 19 April 1941, led to more questions in the
House of Commons about interning her.

to remind the ladies of each other, or to show Unity that Eva Braun was well and truly in possession As consolation, Unity would have to make do with the publicizing of her exalted weekend in much of the press – and with preparations for her new flat. On Hitler's orders, his private office, then still under the direction of Hess, had offered her a short-list of four apartments in Munich requisitioned from Jews in the aftermath of the Kristallnacht, and that May she made her choice. She inspected the four apartments.

Some of the Jewish owners, on the eve of their forcible dispossession, were still in their homes, actually looking at her and listening to her in the very rooms which Unity was absorbed in measuring up, imagining colour schemes and decorations and improvements. She was oblivious to the cruelty of the scene. Eyes she had but saw not, as before with the old Angelus couple. Not even victims suffering in front of her could count on simple pity and understanding. And she was the instrument of their victimization. It was cold-blooded, self-seeking, as deliberate as anything the bullies were up to outside. The abstract *Stürmer* hatred culminated here, when she was brought finally to the real meaning of the slogans and swastikas, and did not even notice. This was what Nazism had done for her. Debasement could be carried no further. Anti-semitism at the last meant that Jews had no faces, no children, no anguish, nothing but a suitable flat, and here is the kernel of the horror which was the holocaust.

Janos in his diary for 1939 noted her new address: Agnesstrasse 26, Flat 4, and the telephone number, 372-338. And a deception of monstrous irony was even so being practised upon her, for by 23 May Hitler had alerted the Wehrmacht for the invasion of Poland in September. 'I doubt the possibility of a peaceful settlement with England,' he told the chiefs of the armed services, 'we must prepare ourselves for the conflict.' Had he then arranged for this flat in the expectation that she would live in it as a traitor to her country, or was it a smoke-screen device, or simply a token of personal esteem?

Janos arrived in Munich early on 6 June, and was met by Unity at the station, driven to the Regina Hotel for a bath, and on to breakfast with Erna and Pinky at Solln. While she had her half-hour singing lesson with Raventos, Unity left him at the Franziskaner restaurant, and then they both lunched, back at Solln again, with Erna, Rudi, Arno Rechberg and Eberhard Hanfstaengl. Janos and Unity slipped away to be by themselves, driving down to the river Isar where they sunbathed. In the evening Janos took her to a Constance Bennett film at the Atlantik Palast and to dine at Walterspiel.

What actually was in preparation was the final curtain on Putzi's downfall. Pressed by Erna, Unity was to broach with Hitler the idea of pardoning

Putzi. A new leaf was to be turned over. For this, Janos had come in support. Erna Hanfstaengl explains, 'Hitler wanted Putzi back from London and knew I was the one person who might persuade him. So he had asked me to tea in his flat in the Prinzregentenstrasse' and said how obliged he would be if I could get Putzi back. I thought, that's the last thing I do. Now Randolph Churchill was in my house, and I said to everyone, When war breaks out every German will have to take part whether he is for or against Hitler, we shall have to arm to the last man, and the end will be doubtful. They were impressed. We were at lunch and Randolph shouted across the table to Unity, who was sitting one away from me. You must make sure Erna comes over immediately to talk to Pop. So Unity drove me to the consulate and an hour later I had my visa. When she had to function, she could be quite practical. But I wanted to get out of the scrape of talking Putzi into something. So I put a letter into the mail to Hitler, testing him out, saying that I'd been asked by the Churchill family to go as a guest to Chartwell, and I could not do that unless I had cleared what I could say to Churchill. In the morning I already had an answer, a personal letter written in Hitler's hand, to tell me to act on my own judgement. That settled it, it was much too dangerous to stay with the Churchills on those terms, I could be blamed for anything that went wrong. I could not come out and say what my real anxieties were about Putzi, I thought it better to hide politics with financial matters. I wrote another letter saying that if I went to London I had to be able to assure Putzi that he would have his money paid to him by the party, I wanted a cheque on Hitler's authority, and this letter I gave to Unity, for her to hand to Hitler. I knew that would be the end of the story.'

Erna's visa was issued at the consulate on the afternoon of 7 June, by which time Randolph had come and gone. First thing that morning the masseuse, a Fräulein Ranke, had given Unity a massage. Because it was another hot day, Unity and Janos had driven out of Munich again, on a road famous for its scenery, to Langgries, through Dietramszell, sunbathing once more by the Isar. The dash to the consulate on Erna's behalf ensured that a journey to London was now a possibility, whether to negotiate with Putzi, or in response to Randolph's invitation, though Erna's delaying tactics showed that her heart was never in it.

Unity had to play her part, handing in the latest letter and supplicating for the Hanfstaengls. The 8th started with another singing lesson from Raventos, and then a walk with Janos in the Englischer Garten, pausing to sit on a bench. After lunching at Walterspiel, they endeavoured to pick up Hitler, in the old tracker-style developed to a fine art since Bäumchen's first initiations. They drove out to Schleissheim and lay in wait under the trees of

Hitler's official residence there, then returned to lurk in the Prinzregenten-strasse, where Hitler actually was. Still in pursuit, they caught sight of him later on the terrace of the Haus der Kunst, but they were driving in the car and only a salute from a distance was possible. Rudi and Peter Dornier, the second son of the maker of the Dornier aircraft, joined them for dinner at the Bonbonnière, a Simplicissimus-styled cabaret, performed by Adolf Gendrell.

The chase came to a head only next day, the 9th, which also had begun with a Raventos singing lesson. That Unity could not simply telephone for an appointment is proof of how effectively Hitler's staff kept her at bay. Unity knew her man; she sat lunch out by herself in the Osteria, and Hitler, true to form, walked in at a quarter to two. He invited her to sit beside him in the tiny arbour at the back. When she asked if she could see him alone on a private matter, he answered that she could come to his flat, and at a quarter to three he left. She followed. Alone together, they had tea there, and she handed him Erna's letter. It was, in a way, cussed of Unity to be the bearer of a message which could only seal Putzi's fate as an exile as long as Hitler was in power; but then Erna had every right to ask Unity to stick by her in whatever she thought was for the best. Hitler's reaction was exactly predic-table. He read the first few sentences, he grew extremely angry, ranted against the Hanfstaengls and burnt the letter. To continue living with Erna for even a single day longer, Hitler told Unity, was now impossible for her, he for-bade it outright, and as she now had her own flat she had no excuse for not moving into it at once. Spurred on by that thought, Hitler offered to buy her the furniture for her sitting room. Then, with a return to the list-making habits of old, he asked whom she would be bringing to the Party Rally in September (in which he was being less than candid about his real plans). The hour was over.

It was a quarter to four when she left for the Regina Hotel, and ten minutes later Janos and Rudi turned up from Solln, on tenterhooks to know how the letter had been received. Sitting in the hotel, Unity poured out her story: how he had called the Hanfstaengls unreliable cosmopolitans, money-grabbers, how he had held the letter in the flame of a candle. Then she tried to telephone Pinky Obermayer, but there was no answer. So there was nothing for it but to drive out to Solln, to fetch the copy of the destroyed letter, and also to get hold of Pinky to do the dirty work of breaking the news to Erna. So seriously did Unity take Hitler's wrath against the Hanfs-taengls that she was reluctant to meet Erna. In the end, while Unity was bobbing between Solln and the Regina, Pinky informed Erna what had transpired, and Unity thus contrived to spare herself a full face-to-face account; she did no more than mumble a few sentences to Erna – the years of hospitality shrivelled to nothing on Hitler's say-so.

Janos thought that discretion might be the better part of valour. He gave Unity dinner at the Hofbrauhaus and asked to be driven to the station. Only packing remained. Rudi fetched her car too, and helped clear Unity's clothes and possessions out of Erna's house. Late that night, Unity went to sleep in the Regina Hotel, and if she was conscience-clear and calm in obedience to the Führer in this tale of plain meddling, she at least had a home and a livelihood outside Germany, unlike Erna.

In the morning Raventos gave her another lesson. Loose ends had to be tied up. Josefa, the maid, had not appeared the day before and Unity drove out to say goodbye to her. She was not to see the place, or any of them, again. After lunching with Rudi at Boettners in the Theatinerstrasse (still today the exclusive restaurant it always was), Unity went to the hairdresser, packed her things from the Regina, and left for England.

Rudi Simolin is now Baroness von St Paul. Her father's house, Seeseiten, within an hour of Munich, is now hers. Unity's credential is to have won the friendship of so life-enhancing a person. She was an only child, something of a mad-cap by her own account, independent, still a teenager when she became a pilot at the Hanworth flying school, where her affection for England was shaped. Four years younger than Unity, she was more securely under Erna Hanfstaengl's wing. 'Unity was not much at Erna's in 1938, but a good deal in the spring of 1939,' said Rudi. 'I had a room there and stayed with Erna too. For five days I had been at a school in Munich to learn book-keeping, but I grew so bored I never set foot there again. I went riding instead and spent all my time with Bobo. Erna was not pleased, she said it was too dangerous for me to be so much together with somebody who was such a convinced Nazi and so close to the Nazi party. Of course we had fun – without Bobo I could not have escaped so much. Erna was terribly strict, telling me to behave after my wild time in England. My father knew her and had placed me in her care. Why Bobo and I became such friends was that neither of us wanted anything of the other. We didn't talk politics. I was very impressed by her, she did all the things she wanted to do. Who doesn't want to be as free as that?

'The Obermayers are a very well-known family. They owned the Vierjahreszeiten. Pinky's mother was a Seidl, of the big Seidl bakery in Munich, which owned at least forty shops all over the town, and Pinky used to supervise them. Unity sometimes drove her and I drove her quite often too. We were both fonder of Pinky than of Erna. She had had infantile paralysis when she was a child and had given up, but Erna, who is a great character, had restored her will to live. Pinky was living with her mother and sister in a separate flat in the Sonnenstrasse. After the war, in the fifties, they had bought the old stone house at Uffing, where Erna's mother had lived and where Hitler had been hidden. Erna kept only a little hut for the summer, it was in beautiful country, with nothing, no water, no electricity. In the summer of 1938 Erna was lent a farmhouse on the Untersberg for four weeks by Frau Stöhr, an extraordinary woman, dressed in violet, she kept pugs. We were all there together, with the Redesdales.

'Sometimes we tried to tease Erna. "Horrid little dog" was Titus, her over-bred miniature dachshund, it was always shivering. We painted its nails red, and Erna got so cross she tried to box my ears, but I ducked, so she hurt her hand against a cupboard. Unity loved to shock Rechberg, an elderly bachelor who lived in Kempfenhausen on the Starnbergersee, he'd taken part in the Kapp putsch. His food was marvellous, he gave wonderful parties. Bobo and I used to joke that we must take umbrellas with us when we met him as he spat so much.

'We went walking with Boy, or Rebell, either name would do, her Great Dane, a beauty. When Boy got out of her car, you wondered how he had been able to cram in. He chased sheep and she had left him somewhere in the Hortobagy [the plain of western Hungary], with the Palffys or someone before the war. We had been planning to go riding together in the Hortobagy in the autumn, but the war came. She was so much back and forth from London, bringing her furniture, lamps and curtains. I've still got curtains she brought for me, from a roll of a hundred yards of very nice yellow artificial silk. You can't buy any decent things on the continent, that was her attitude. She had good taste, I thought she dressed nicely.

'Bobo and Janos were very great friends, she spent a lot of time in Bernstein. Hubsie Giesen was a friend of Janos, he was very funny but I never heard such vulgar jokes as his. Janos was fond of Jules Mertz, who lived at Heil-bronn in an eighteenth-century house burnt in the war – he was cultivated, as well as a good shot. Heinrich Bleckmann was another friend of Unity's, he owned a steel factory at Semmering, we both spent a night in his house in Vienna for a dance in 1939, and went afterwards to the Spanish riding school. Erna was with us.

'Raventos lived in the little Pension Fortuna, and Unity once or twice stayed there. He had a very nice wife. She also went to Professor Knappe who was a fine sculptor. He once said to me, If Unity doesn't work and get herself a real interest in life, she is going to commit suicide. She did *Hannibal* several times, and at Erna's I saw the copy given to Hitler.

'I said to her that I would be interested to meet Hitler, so she introduced me to him in the Osteria. I was with my cousin, one of the daughters of Kaulbach, the painter. Hitler suggested at once that we should see round the Kaulbach-Haus where Gauleiter Wagner lived, and we were all escorted round it, that is how I met Wagner for the first time, I could always remind him of that. Wagner anyhow knew about my father. In 1936 the Duke of Windsor, after abdicating, was looking on the continent for a home, and Hitler and Wagner sent a telegram to my father asking if he would sell Seeseiten for the purpose. My father refused. Another telegram stated that a man must do his duty for his country, and Wagner said to me, Your father has given us a lot of trouble.'

'Bobo invited me to the Parteitag and I was dying to go, but my father forbade it. I never had the feeling that Bobo was inhuman. She was really wedded to Hitler and the Nazi party, and if you were attacking them you were attacking her emotional life. Once somebody was trying to pick her brains, and said, All right, Hitler is as wonderful as you say but what about what he's doing to the Jews? Up went her nose. What he's doing to them is wonderful too, she answered. What else could she answer? She was unlikely to say, I quite agree with Hitler in everything but he's wrong about the Jews. Her only hope was to shock people and make them shut up with outrage, and she excelled at that. How much sense and responsibility do you feel at twenty-four? She was a romantic. She would act the heroine, and war would be avoided, like in a simple fairy tale.

'That 9 June interview with Hitler was quite shocking. Hitler had become very livid, very abusive and violent in his language, and Unity was worried about it when she came back to the Regina. *Sie haben auf einem Misthaufen gelebt* – he had shouted words to that effect, You have been living on a dung-heap. He had ordered her not to set foot there again, that was good enough for her.'

It was less a flat than cloud-cuckoo-land which Unity was furnishing that summer, while Hitler and the British and French governments were weighing separately how much they were prepared to concede to a Soviet Russia they all distrusted and feared, in return for a treaty of alliance, and Poland lay like a nut to be cracked. Women with a German husband, like Mary, were deciding whether or not to separate in the contingency of war. Unity must have been virtually the only British subject who with no ties and a free choice was obliviously setting up home in Germany at that moment, although her old acquaintance, William Joyce, and one or two other Nazi hybrids, were to slip into the country once war had become un-avoidable. It was a raid on the London shops, and on Rutland Gate for her things, that she carried out on 10 June. At the same time she arranged transport to Munich of her accumulation of bric-à-brac, furniture and books. She was moving out.

People warned her. Mary, in a chance encounter, spelled out the reasons for being in one's own country in wartime. In his *Daily Mail* obituary of her, Ward Price recounted how he had lunched with her at Rutland Gate in May 1939 (which must be a mistake for June; the whole piece is slipshod) and she had said that she would stay in Munich till November, whether anyone said it was crazy or not. She had even replied to him, 'If there is a war I shall be on the German side.' Urged to think by her friends, she resorted to the escapism of her pistol, as part of the act. Could it be taken any more seriously than the rest of her exhibitionism? Rudbin, for instance, seeing the piled-high car off to Munich, and expressing dismay, had been left in no doubt what Unity would do when the worst came to the worst. The Redesdales did not intervene.

Back and forth, as Rudi said, with car-loads. Unity was certainly in London on 22 June, for that evening Sigismund FitzRandolph of the German Embassy held a farewell party. He had been recalled to Berlin. The signatures on the appropriate page of his guest-book are headed by the Redesdales, with Unity W. (for Walküre) Mitford, Sir Frank and Lady Newnes, Sir Barry Domvile of 'The Link', Sir William Teeling MP, Sir Ralph Glyn MP, Albricht Montgelas, Sir Arnold Wilson – it might have been a list of Ehrengäste at any one of the Nuremberg Rallies. Dr FitzRandolph, it will be recalled, had fetched Unity and Mary at their hotel at the start of the 1936 Rally. He had also met Unity at an Anglo-German Fellowship evening in December 1938. Dr FitzRandolph was running the press department of the German Embassy, and was responsible more to Goebbels's Ministry of Propaganda than to the Foreign Office. Dr FitzRandolph is circumspect to this day, confining himself to saying that he was the only high-ranking official of the embassy who lasted from September 1933 to September 1939. The descendant of a family escaping religious persecution in England in the early seventeenth century, he had an American mother, and speaks a perfect, gentlemanly English. Courteous as he is, he made it plain that it was as dangerous for Germans to see Unity as not to see her. Everybody was watching. What if she unwittingly dropped careless talk in high places?

Herr FitzRandolph said, 'Actually the German Embassy itself would officially always have done its best to keep Unity at a distance, ah yes! because the social attitude in London was to evade her. At the time her views were perhaps harming the German cause more than helping it. She was going much too far – if she'd found a way of saying acceptably what she thought, if she'd only followed the normal lines of arguing on the one hand and on the other, but she didn't, she couldn't. Her views were ruined by being over-stated. Of course she was foolish in many ways but it would not be fair to insinuate that she was a liability. She was a young girl and to turn and rend her was dastardly. The embassy had to be cautious about her. FitzRandolph she called me, You're the only person one can speak frankly to at the embassy, but she added, There are things which can't be discussed. She was afraid that reports might go back to Berlin.

'Did she talk about Hitler? It vexed people that this was her pet subject. She valued her friends on the grounds that they agreed with her about him. She'd boast of the hours spent with Hitler. Her entire ideology was linked with hatred of the Jews, as no doubt Hitler's was. She had it from him. I asked her outright not to speak to me about Jews, she talked such arrant nonsense. She also thought the English didn't understand the danger of the East. I remember her telling me that millions of people had starved to death in the Ukraine and nobody noticed, but the moment people were imprisoned in Germany, they were up in arms about it.

'We discussed the Versailles Treaty. The English don't know the first thing about it, they are like stuffed geese – I can hear her saying the very words, and also, What with all my English friends, if it hadn't been for Versailles they wouldn't have had Hitler to cope with. I never had an intimate talk for two or three hours with her, I'd meet her every year once or twice for a chat. I don't remember her at functions in the embassy. I doubt if Ribbentrop would have invited her. All London was at his Coronation party, but she dis-liked Ribbentrop on many counts. She was violent in her opinions about him. She told me that she had advised Hitler never to send him as ambassador, he would be a complete failure.

'That June I had been recalled to Berlin, my farewell party was in my flat on the 22nd. Unity wrote to me about some items of her furniture, which she wanted shipped across with mine, if possible. I rang up to give instruc-tions about transferring it, some clerk dealt with it, I doubt if it would have been done under diplomatic privilege. She was so grateful to me for helping her and naturally I was delighted to do so, the more so as I was on friendly terms with her family.'

In fact on 20 July Unity arranged with a haulage firm in Munich that some time before the 27th her things should be fetched from Wittelsbachstrasse, where they had been deposited by the official carrier. She was writing to Dr FitzRandolph from the Pension Doering, for her new flat was being painted at that very moment and she hoped to move into it on her return from Bayreuth at the beginning of August. The Tag der Kunst, she observed, had been fun but rather spoilt by rain, though the receptions and theatres were lovely. She also wanted to know how much she owed him, and whether he would prefer to have the sum in marks or pounds. So she had been quick to take advantage of a load going to Germany, but the German Embassy had not necessarily bent the rules, nor shipped her furniture free of charge under cover of Dr FitzRandolph's. For whatever her share of the costs might be, she had at least offered to pay, though in the event she was not required to.

August 8th was her twenty-fifth birthday. She was back from Bayreuth, where she had again edged her way into meals with Hitler at Wahnfried, where, as we know, General Engel had heard her talking of the English anti-aircraft defences. She was now installed in the Agnesstrasse, and as a special treat, Janos had arrived from Bernstein to celebrate with her. This was the last possible blind-folded week in which to chase the will-of-the-wisp of normality. The British Military Mission was bumbling at its own good pace in Moscow, but the Germans were about to increase the stakes there. Unity's birthday was marked by high-decibel screaming in the Nazi press about the supposed persecutions of the *Volksdeutch* minority in Poland, the pretext for mobilization.

Unity had always been lonely, uprooted, the inner emptiness booming with Nazism, the passage of time artificially hectic with what she assumed were Hitler's purposes. Bernstein and Kohfidisch had soothed her through the Munich crisis of the previous year. Had war broken out then, willing people round that wireless in the library would have been at hand to sort out what she ought to do. In the Agnesstrasse, as the cycle of threat and counter-threat sickeningly hastened round again, she was on her own, exposed and caged The flat was on the third and top floor of a house then about ten years old, it was well built and silent, with three rooms and a kitchen. By the time of her birthday, foreign residents of Munich, of Germany indeed, had pulled out, or were in the process of doing so. Abandonment. Exile. True, while Janos was staying there with her, she had company, and the protection of a man, and her *Wohnung*, as she called the flat in would-be identification with what she hoped had become her native city, was the less drear for it. A *putzfrau*, or maid, came every morning. There were last-minute touches, 'pokering about' in her expression for which there was no German equivalent. On the 9th she visited Max, her Brown House contact, and an old steady by now, and then she lunched at the Osteria. Janos was away all day with Hubsie Giesen, and she became worried as she waited, dropping round to the Pension Doering in case a message might be there for her. But at last he did telephone, and asked her to join him and Hubsie for dinner in the Vierjarheszeiten cellar.

Rudi came round to the flat next morning, and the three of them sat about chatting until at half past twelve they were ready to join Hubsie for lunch at the Regina Hotel. Then they did the rounds of the antique shops, for if Hitler had offered her drawing-room furniture, Janos matched him by buying her a dining-room table and a set of chairs to go with it – imitations of the classical English style, Rudi thinks. Hubsie returned home to Stuttgart, but the others dined out at Lombardi, an Italian restaurant, and later occupied the box at the opera which that night Gauleiter Wagner had put at Unity's disposal. *The Merry Widow* was being performed. 'All the singers knew Wagner's box,' Rudi remembers, 'so we received special bows from them.'

Late nights, slow mornings: Janos set the rhythm. He liked expensive shops, such as Küster and Perry opposite the Franziskaner, he insisted on elegance, on externals; inscrutable, in Rudi's word for him. He did not plunge as Unity did, and it was in character for him to spend the morning of the 11th with Erna, mending his fences. Erna was out of bounds for Unity, who went instead to the hairdresser, and then to the Osteria, a reflex move, for Hitler was at Berchtesgaden that day, with Dr Carl Burckhardt, the League of Nations Commissioner for Danzig. Rudi and Janos met up with Unity there, and they drove out to Seeseiten in two cars, Rudi alone, Unity with Janos. On the way, Unity and Janos quarrelled, the supposition being that he was insisting on her leaving Munich, as he was about to do. At Seeseiten only Rudi and Janos bathed in the lake, Unity, in a bad mood, looking on and then leaving sulkily by herself for the Agnesstrasse. The others soon caught up with her, and she scrambled some eggs for their supper. In fact Rudi and Janos were off early in the morning to pay a flying call on Hubsie Giesen at Stuttgart. Unity was left to collect Rudi's tickets for the Salzburg festival from the American Express office, and these she dropped at the Regina for her. Once more she lunched alone at the Osteria – at that moment Hitler was intimidating the Italian foreign minister, Count Ciano, at Berchtesgaden, promising that the fate of Poland would have come to a head by the end of August, no later. Still by herself in the evening, Unity went to the Theater am Karlstor to see *Maskerade*, and a propaganda film *Der Westwall*, boosting German preparations opposite the Maginot line.

From the 13th onwards, she had to square up to the consequences of her actions, to her destiny indeed. That this had its ache is shown by her determination to snatch one more moment with Janos before parting. His train back from Stuttgart arrived at quarter to ten, and the connection to Vienna pulled out at five past ten. For those twenty minutes she was at the station with him. Had he been able to rally her, had she simply dropped everything and accompanied him to Bernstein, her life might have resolved itself other-wise, but commonsense and even the instinct for self-preservation had been inverted long since.

Rudi too was away, with Erna, at the Salzburg festival, where they were to spend the rest of the month with Countess Moy, as paying guests. Nobody and nothing stood between Unity and her own devices.

In his autobiography *Half-Term Report*, William Douglas-Home, the play-wright, has described how a spirit of eleventh-hour missionary goodwill prompted him and a friend, Peter Beresford-Peirse, to drive to Munich, in his Fiat known as 'Mickey Mouse'. Hatred was nowhere in evidence. They reached Munich on 15 August. Peter Beresford-Peirse was already a clergyman. He said, 'One of our dates was to meet Unity in Munich, I'd got to know her at coming-out dances. We stayed in a hotel, I remember waiting there by appointment at two o'clock [this was in the Regina, on the 17th]. She came into the hall, this attractive blonde, clicking her heels and saying Heil Hitler. We were torn between feeling like decadent English, and giggling. She drove up past Hitler's flat several times, saying that she didn't think he was there. Also to the Brown House. In the evening we went to two places, the first was a popular beer-garden, and she watched the cabaret with us, when the local entertainer was cheered to the roof. The trouble with that man, Unity said, is that he is just out of prison, he can't get through his act without making jokes against Goering and Goebbels. The second place was a more sophisti-cated night-club, and I got into an argument with her. She was holding forth about Hitler being the saviour of mankind, the messiah. Hot and strong. As a clergyman I took exception. She ended by warning us that we were most unlikely to get out of Germany as petrol would be requisitioned in the morning. She had been pleasant until then, but gave us the feeling of superiority, that she was sad for William and I, the English pair who didn't see the way things were going. She wasn't behaving like a normal person.'

The Weld-Foresters had been living in the Prinzregentenstrasse, more or less opposite Hitler. As a member of the consulate since the *Anschluss*, Weld-Forester had been with Chamberlain to Berchtesgaden in 1938. He is no longer alive, but his widow, Mrs Weld-Forester, throws light not only on Unity in the ebb of peace, but also on what had been her last evening in the company of other English people. Mrs Weld-Forester said: 'When we first went to the opera in Munich, I'd seen her with Hitler. She hadn't been sitting beside him in the box – the whole house stood up when he appeared. Heil, Heil, they shouted, on and on. I said to my husband, Is this all we're going to get? Then Hitler held his hand up, and had complete silence. My husband whispered, That lovely girl you see behind him is Unity Mitford. We never went out to official parties, but in a restaurant for a meal we'd catch a glimpse of her. You'd see her sitting by herself. I'd say, Wouldn't it be kind to go up to her? but my husband's answer was, No, things are far too risky at the moment. She looked as if she couldn't get out of her chair, it was so awful. We hated to see her in such distress. This was just on the brink of war. But that August she came twice to the consulate, to say to my husband that we were doing the wrong thing and would have to pay for it as a country, there'd be trouble. He told her she had to leave Germany. There was also a girl called Dunne, engaged to a Metternich, and my husband tried to get her home too. Aren't you torn in half? he asked her, and she answered that the only thing she was heart-broken about was her dog Susan.

'Peter Beresford-Peirse and William Douglas-Home threw stones at our window because we hadn't heard them ringing the bell. We had them up, and we went to Platzl's [the popular beer-garden of the earlier account] where the cabaret entertainer mimicked everything including Hitler. It was village life in a way. We had a plate of something, food was already scarce. Unity was at Platzl's, my impression is that she had come separately, and she said to us, You must share some of my chicken, the Führer has just had it sent to me. My husband said, In the circumstances I prefer my sausage.

'The lease on our flat had fallen in, so we could move into a lodging without a fuss. Everything and everybody was sent home. Some of my husband's staff were German Jews, and we had a girl called Oppersdorf, her mother was a Radziwill, we got her out to Zurich as the Germans invaded Poland.

'Unity clung on to the very end. On the first of her August visits to the consulate, my husband had ordered her to leave but she would not. He had said to her, You know you can always come here whenever you want, I can help you. By the 29th I was back in London, and after I'd gone, she went round again to the consulate for her second visit, she must have done so in terror, for then, at the last, there was no getting her out. She was in floods of tears. It was too late to do anything for her. My husband told me, It was terrible to see her. We had a feeling that they'd hold him, the reason being that the French had held their German consuls. On 1 September, sure enough, he knew war was coming. He was walking across the Englischer Garten when he was met by two plainclothes men who asked for his passport. They escorted him to a pension and had him under guard for ten weeks. When he was eventually released, my brother lent us his flat in London, nobody knew, but all the same Lady Redesdale turned up on the very first morning demanding to see him. She wanted to know things my husband didn't know.'

·   ·   ·   ·   ·

August 23rd was literally a red-letter day for Hitler, for it brought the information from Moscow that the pact with Stalin had been signed during the preceding night. His hands had been freed for war. In return he had only to sub-divide a little *lebensraum* in the East with the compliant Russians. England and France, he felt confident, would appreciate their helplessness, their governments would withdraw in self-interest to the side-lines, and the Poles would bite the bullet as the Austrians and the Czechs had done before them. Provided he was right about the English in this respect, the game had concluded in brutal check-mate; the Thousand Year Reich had laid its foundation. During what he took to be a supreme morning, Hitler received Sir Nevile Henderson at Berchtesgaden. Leonard Mosley in his book *On Borrowed Time* gives this account of what happened next. 'Henderson was then dismissed to take lunch in Salzburg. Hitler had a difficult lunch of his own, with Unity Mitford; it was one of the last times he was to see her.' This lunch does not show up in the German records, not even in Bormann's notebook, but that is an insufficient reason for dismissing it, since everyone, Bormann included, was chary on such a thing: the Führer was touchy, the standing of Unity in his private life was uncertain to them, and if really the lunch was difficult then it might well be safest to have no evidence of it. I wrote to Leonard Mosley to inquire what his source for this lunch had been and he answered that Ribbentrop had mentioned it to his aide Erich Kordt, who had referred to it during conversations taped for the book in which it is quoted. Kordt has subsequently died. Ribbentrop himself was on his way back from Moscow and only on the following day, in the Berlin Chancellory, did he and Hitler fall upon each other's necks, as Leonard Mosley expresses it. The chain of hearsay grows. For Unity to have lunched with Hitler at such an hour of crisis – and the British ambassador dismissed as though to the servants' hall – would be phenomenal in itself, but their talk could only have proceeded on fixed sight-lines. Hitler would have happily repeated his conviction that England must acquiesce, and if so, then Unity had nothing to be afraid of, there was no need to panic and leave – she could live the crisis out in peace and quiet in the Agnesstrasse. The Munich crisis of the year before would repeat itself. The Poles would soon surrender, Chamberlain would make speeches. After appeasement would come neutrality, in the penultimate stage of that full Anglo-German cooperation for which Unity had campaigned. Three or four more weeks, and all would be normal again. It might have been bothersome to examine quite why the hated bolsheviks had all of a sudden been transmogrified into peace-loving partners, but Unity would never have questioned the Führer's path to deification. In any case, if the pact with Russia had scared her, as it should have done, she still had time enough in which to clear out. To stay put, as she did, was to misread the situation, and for that she did not need one more lunch at Berchtesgaden. Hitler certainly misled her when he allowed her to select and furnish the Agnesstrasse flat and talked about plans for the coming Party Rally, which he knew would have to be cancelled with the army away in Poland.

Like everyone else, Unity will have realized what was afoot with Poland, and her complete approval was guaranteed in advance. Hitler could give her his cues, but anyone with an understanding of English politics would have realized that 'the worms of Munich' were bound to turn, or be thrown out of office in the general turmoil. Failure to perceive that her contempt for democracy was merely idiosyncratic and unrepresentative was fatal for Unity. Germany's temper she had reckoned on, but not England's.

On the 24th she happened to run into two friends, the Princesses Carmencita and Edda Wrede, identical twins. A statue of their forebear, Field-Marshal Prince Wrede, stands in the Feldherrnhalle. Their mother was Argentinian. The twins – Carmen and Edd, to Unity – were Bright Young Things, social scatterbrains, who loved to be in the political swim, in Berlin especially, for the fun of it. With them, Unity drove that afternoon out to Tutzing, a village on the Starnbergersee, to have tea with Anna Montgelas in her house, Frauenberg. (Possibly through smoking in bed, or upsetting a candle, Anna Montgelas set fire to this wooden chalet not long before the end of the war, and was burnt to death.) Leaving at about half past six, Unity and the twins went on to Schloss Buch on the Ammersee, an estate belonging to Count Hubert Deym.

Count Deym said: 'That night we had a large dinner party, perhaps thirty or forty people. I'd seen Unity twice before with friends, she was an acquaintance. I was always being told about her, so I asked her out to Buch (which is about thirty-five kilometers from Munich). She did very well, she was an intelligent girl. We never spoke politics. As a Czech, I couldn't have risked it. Everyone knew my position. After dinner, Unity begged to be allowed to switch on the radio, she ran to it, there was something very important which she had to listen to, a speech by Halifax. [The foreign secretary that night broadcast on the crisis, reiterating the government's resolve to stand by Poland in accordance with the repeated pledge to do so. With a resolve which he was far from feeling, he warned, 'We mean to fulfil the obligations which we have assumed.'] Unity came back distraught [zerstört].

'Ten days later, after she had shot herself, I was telephoned at Buch by Max Schaumburg-Lippe with a request that I find out which clinic she was in. The accident was top-secret, a Geheime Reichssache. Max was a cousin of

Didi Schaumburg-Lippe, the adjutant of Goebbels', and he was himself in the *Motor Staffel* of the SS, and perhaps getting his information for Goebbels. I had friends in one of the clinics and learnt where Unity was. The Italian consul-general was also in on the story, I remember him telling me that the King of Italy had ordered him to get busy and find out about Unity.'

Princess Carmencita Wrede had spent three months as a volunteer nurse in Spain, and had been in the battered Alcazar of Toledo with Colonel Moscardo. The Wrede house, Schloss Fantaisie, is five short kilometers from Bayreuth, and visitors to the festival used to throng there. In her albums of the period are photographs of English friends, Tom Mitford, Lord Drogheda, Peter Watson who later founded the magazine *Horizon* with Cyril Connolly. In 1934, Putzi Hanfstaengl and Tom and Randolph Churchill lined up to grin at the princess's camera.

She has married Prince zu Solms-Braunsfeld, and she said: 'I was on very friendly terms with Brückner, and in 1935 he told me how everybody was going to this *lokal*, the Osteria Bavaria, and two fine English girls were there. He said, We are hypnotized by them because they are the portrait of Germanism. So at the Bayreuth festival Brückner introduced me to them. He added that Hitler thought they were from a very good English family, and that was enough for him. Unity's *Heil Hitler* was very graceful, she had aplomb and self-confidence, she knew her own worth. She was to be met in Berlin at the Adlon or the Kaiserhof, or in Munich at the Vierjahreszeiten, or at any official reception. Once we had supper in the cellar of the Vierjahreszeiten and Hitler was giving a big speech in the Hofbrau which was being relayed on the radio. We heard how the Führer had finished and the meeting was breaking up and he was leaving for Berlin. Unity said, Quick, quick, come and stand in the street opposite, we can line up as he passes. The huge Mercedes came, with Hitler standing up in it, and Unity shrieked, *Mein Fuhrer!* He stopped for her, he took her two hands in his, and said, Unity what are you doing here? She answered, Tonight I'm going to Berlin. He said, *Melden Sie sich gleich*, let me know as soon as you're there. And she took the night train. It was 1937.

'In Berlin my sister and I lived in the Rauchstrasse, and Unity was there often. We were spare girls. Unity went with each big Nazi, *c'était frère et cochon*, her snobbery was to know everyone. I told her she should drop people like Streicher, but she answered, They help me get what I want. Once she told me about Hitler, I'm never alone with him, or whenever I am, I sit at his feet and then Brückner butts in and stays there – when he wants to be alone with me, he sends his adjutants away but they always come back. I have a feeling that Hitler calculated exactly the correct distance between him and her. Class differences were basic. Unity, Diana, Sigi von Laffert, Hella Khevenhüller, were too fine, really too aristocratic for him. Eva Braun was at his social level. My sister and I knew Eva and her sister, Gretl, well. In 1937 I was with Nevile Henderson – this idiot Henderson, Unity called him – at the Parteitag. Hitler was there, and Eva stood by herself, wearing a little raincoat. Hitler looked round and his gaze fell on her without change of expression. No other woman would have put up with that. Unity could not bear it. She was always badgering me, How is this Eva Braun? what does she have that I don't? how does she do it? She said to me, He never asks me to the Obersalzberg because Eva is always there. She's not in the Reichskanzlei, I replied, so you aren't on the Obersalzberg, fair's fair. There was a proper rivalry between them. Unity was thoroughly jealous. She wasn't jealous of Sigi von Laffert, for instance, because she knew Sigi loved Hansi Wilczek. The Redesdales were at the Parteitag the following year, in 1938, they spoke no German, and Hitler was railing against England. I was sitting slap behind them and Unity. She was giving them a completely false translation of what he was screaming, and she gave me a nudge with the words, Did you see my father clapping? I enjoyed watching how she knew everyone on the platform. She waved at Streicher, and said, He's such a darling – which made a big impression on me.

'What did she talk to Hitler about? His dog and her dog, music, she thought she was musical. Hitler liked to think of her as a distinguished lady. She was his means of acknowledging England, one-sided as that was. Her anti-semitism was extreme. She complained that Stephanie Hohenlohe was Jewish, and how she had told Hitler, Here you are, anti-Jewish yet you have a Jew around you the whole time, this Princess Hohenlohe. Hitler said nothing. She simply hated the Hohenlohe for a rusée, going to tell Lord Rothermere what Hitler was up to. I asked her why she got so upset about it and the answer was short: jealousy again.

'That August of 1939 I had my nursing instructions in my pocket, to go into Templehof in the event of war. The hotel in Munich was full, we camped in the Vierjahreszeiten, we ran into Unity in the street, by sheer luck. She told us, Come along, I have three rooms, so stay for a few days. I told her war was coming. She said she'd been to the consul, and had done her Heil Hitler at him, and he had stood up without saying a word. How is the situation? she asked him, to be told, Very serious, all the English are leaving tomorrow [which means the 29th] and I advise you to go too. I don't contemplate it, she told him. He said, Then you no longer have the protection of Great Britain. I have the much better protection of the Führer, she answered.

The consul said, You are as childish as the man who told me he had to wait because he has tickets for *Tristan*. Oh, she had the last word, who's he? I must get to know him.

'She had a drawing room, a bedroom and a little spare room. The furniture was *Deutsche Werkstätte* style, colourful, with flowers everywhere, a big pile carpet, very chic. She told me that the whole thing was a present from Hitler. Behind her bed two big flags with swastikas crossed over, and their ends folded down on the pillows like drapes. That's too much, I told her – *Doch will ich*, was her answer, that's how I want it. On her bed-side table stood Hitler's photo, with the lips and eyes painted in. I did that, she said, because it looks so nice. In the sitting room she had a writing table, and in one of its drawers a revolver, a little silvered revolver, and she took it out and waved it around, saying, When I'm obliged to quit Germany I will kill myself. We were scared by the way she handled the gun, and my sister told her to put it back in the drawer. We were thunderstruck by the news a week later.

'I slept in the sitting room on a made-up bed, and my sister was in the little spare room. At seven o'clock in the morning the front-door bell rang and Unity sprang to open the door. She was in a very flowing dressing-gown, her hair all over the place. There stood an old SS man with his hands full of eggs and cheese in baskets brought up from the country. She introduced him as Herr Pfeffer, the oldest of the old-time *Kämpfer*. I was furious, lying as I was on a sofa in the sitting room. Unity said to him, Never mind her mood, and she took Pfeffer into her bedroom where I could hear them laughing and joking. I rushed into my clothes and went into the spare room with my sister.'

By the 29th, a Tuesday, the Wrede twins had gone, Unity was alone with her wireless. It became her focus. To listen in to the news became a matter of life and death. She went out for meals, she came back for the news. On the Friday, 1 September, the seven o'clock news announced that Danzig had been incorporated into the Reich. Unity went out shopping, and while she was in her car she listened to the Führer's speech, and found it wonderful. It was as hot and beautiful a day in Munich as it was in London. Unity sunbathed out on her balcony; the *putzfrau* came to clean. The radio replayed Hitler's speech about Danzig. At a quarter to two, Unity lunched at the Osteria Bavaria, one more time, like a shade unable to tear loose from haunts of the past. In the afternoon she changed into a bathing suit, and continued to lie on the balcony in the sunshine. The mail brought letters from Diana and Janos, and she wrote replies to them both. Her course was set. Dressing, she walked to the Vierjahreszeiten cellar for another solitary meal. The German army was thrusting into Poland. The black-out was compulsory. As she walked home, the darkness over Munich was complete. Back in the Agnestrasse, she listened in to the English news.

The British ultimatum to Hitler, to withdraw the German army from Poland, was not delivered until nine o'clock on the morning of Sunday, 3 September, and it expired, unanswered, two hours later. The war had started.

Rudi von St Paul must take up the sequel: 'On the Saturday, Erna and I came back from the Salzburg festival. The soldiers were already mobilized, and were mobilizing further. I went to Seeseiten, I hadn't seen my father for some time, and wanted to be with him. On the Sunday morning Bobo telephoned me, just at eleven o'clock, and said there would now be a war. She said that she heard through the British Consul that war was certain. I was frightened because three or four months beforehand, when the possibility of war had been discussed, she had been trying to persuade Hitler that there could be no war – she had said then that unless she could stop the war, she would have to shoot herself. She had shown me the pistol, not as big as any army pistol, something rather small, we shot a lot with it. I had a much heavier one which I had bought on my permit to have sporting guns. We had shot at targets in the park at Seeseiten. I think she had bought her pistol in Belgium on one of her trips. She came back with it one day, anyhow, and that was her story about it.

'Now I spoke to her for a long time on the telephone. I was terrified for her. I asked her what she was going to do. I would be coming into Munich from Seeseiten on the Monday morning. I urged her not to do anything until then and we would think what should be done for the best. There was no need to shoot herself at all, I told her, I beseeched her to wait until we could meet. We had that plan to go riding in the Hortobagy in the autumn. There must have been friends to go to – the war might be over soon, I said. I had the feeling I couldn't reach her. I tried again but did not get through, the telephone must have been left off.

'On the Monday I got a letter from her enclosing her keys – I can't remember how that letter found its way to me – and in it she had written that she had to kill herself and what I ought to do with her money and possessions. It was her will. Had that letter been left with Gauleiter Wagner? I collected it anyhow. I went to the flat, and it had already been sealed. They had put a seal of paper over the keyhole. And then I went to Wagner in the Kaulbachstrasse – whose house I had visited with my cousin that time a few months before. I went to ask what had happened. It was no news to me. He said that her parents had been told it had happened. They were expecting Diana in at any moment and the parents could enter Germany too, the frontiers had been specially notified that they had permission, he said. I learnt only after the war that this was not true. I do not know if he even believed it himself. He was helpful in any case.'

The name of Julius Schaub has occurred occasionally, as someone who would have been a useful witness. Schaub was an Ancient Pistol in Hitler's household. When he appeared at a denazification tribunal after the war, nothing was found against him and he was released. Thereupon he wrote memoirs of noteworthy events, and stored them in his files, which have not yet been consulted by researchers. Schaub and his wife, Wilma, have both died, but their son, born in 1936, remembered his parents discussing Unity. Rather than repeat what he had heard, he was generous enough to hand me the folder marked 'Unity Mitford' from his father's archive. This consisted of two variant drafts of an essay reconstructing Hitler's relationship with Unity. Writing from memory, Schaub made small slips, but broadly he gave the usual account of the Osteria Bavaria pick-up, he stressed the friendship with Putzi Hanfstaengl; he recorded an evening in the 'Kamaradschaft der Künstler' club in Berlin, when Unity, as the guest of Goebbels and his wife and his sister Maria, was accorded a standing ovation. Prudent people in Hitler's circle, he confirms, naturally saw in Unity a somewhat transparent approach of the English secret service, though Hitler himself believed in the passionate idealism of his young admirer and cut criticism off sharply, with, 'I know very well what I have to say to this young lady.'

Living in Munich, Schaub and his wife came to the fore when Unity shot herself. As will be seen, when she put down the telephone receiver, and left it off, after her conversation with Rudi, her dispositions were complete. Her last letters to Diana and Janos had been posted. Her letter to Rudi, we know, either was in the post for delivery next morning, or was in the envelope prepared for Gauleiter Wagner. If the 'Be merciful to my people' plea to Hitler was really written, as the Goebbels circle believed, it too would have been included in this packet. Then she took her revolver from the writing table where her last two guests had seen it, and towards midday went downstairs, to drive off in her car.

The following extract from Schaub's memorandum is in my translation. 'On the day war broke out . . . Unity drove up to the Ministry of the Interior. "I should like to give you this," she explained in some haste, as she handed over to Gauleiter Wagner a mysteriously heavy envelope. Then she immediately took her leave, and listened only distractedly to the propositions Wagner was making that she should remain calmly in Munich, he would take on himself the responsibility for her safety and see that as a resident she continued unharmed. The Gauleiter was not struck by anything remarkably untoward in her behaviour. He already had more than enough excitements to deal with that day, most likely he took in only that as a young English girl she was indeed worried about remaining. The sealed envelope which she had pushed into his hand did nothing to arouse his curiosity, for he could not imagine that anything important could be contained in it. He busied himself with more important correspondence until finally he opened her small packet. Had the girl lost her reason? A letter of farewell – yes, not just to her beloved Germany, but to life itself. "She could not bear a war between England and Germany, she had to put an end to herself –" Wagner had come to know the girl well enough not to question her consistency. Any doubt about the seriousness of her intentions was quite dispelled when he saw that the envelope also contained what he knew to be treasured souvenirs, her signed portrait of Hitler and her party badge. As an English subject she could not be a member of the party but in order to give her the status of association Hitler had honoured her with the badge which had been worn in the days when the party had been outlawed ... Wagner sprang up and alerted the Sicherheitsdienst. Everything was set in motion to prevent misfortune. But Unity had vanished. She must have driven off very fast in her car. A few hours later the police discovered a young girl on a bench in the Englischer Garten who had shot herself in the temple. Immediately she was brought to the Chirurgische Universitäts-Klinik. At first the casualty could not be identified as she was not carrying any papers, but her clothes and her well-cared-for appearance suggested her background. Only some hours later was she recognized as Unity Mitford. The case seemed quite hopeless. The bullet was lodged dangerously in her head and had affected her movements. She was put in a private room of the clinic and a special sister was on duty day and night. Hitler informed the clinic that he personally would settle the entire costs of her treatment. Her flat was sealed, so that none of her property could be removed.'

One other person in Munich felt personally involved, namely Erna Hanfstaengl, whose predictions of disaster had proved true. She said, 'When she shot herself, I was in Solln. My friend Professor Hönigschmitt [his work as an atomic scientist was original enough to be confiscated by the Americans at the end of the war, whereupon he shot himself] had gone into the Englischer Garten not long after midday, he was a hundred yards in or so, when he heard a small report and saw a figure slump down off a bench. He ran up and recognized Unity. He had met her in my house, he was the man I had consulted to find a mathematics teacher for her. He called for help. The police picked her up, they pushed her at once into a car, they thought she was dead already, and brought her immediately to the *anatomie* [for a post-mortem] and there she showed signs of life, so they rushed her on to the clinic. Professor Hönigschmitt telephoned me. I sat down and thought out the right course of action. Rudi had to go to Wagner, and so she did, the next morning, the Monday. So Unity had already been in their hands all that time. After what had happened in June, I couldn't send a message through to Hitler to make sure she was properly treated. Wagner had to do it. I had to show no personal attachment any more now that my influence with Hitler had weakened, that's why I never visited Unity in the clinic. But Rudi went every day.'

Hitler's Haus der Kunst, at whose inauspicious inauguration in 1937 Unity had been present, stands, a Grecian pastiche, at the corner of the Englischer Garten. Along the street is the low stone parapet of a baroque bridge spanning the stream which twists and writhes into the park, like an English stream, with backwaters and channels, where willows overhang and the bark of mature trees gleams through planted thickets. A gravel path leads from the bridge into the park, and divides into several directions, one of them straight ahead, round one gentle bend and then another, to a bench, still painted green as it should be in a well-appointed place, with behind it a secret trim meadow bordering the stream which widens at that point, its perpetual tumble audible.

There rises the dream-fear, dormant since childhood, of the giant steam-roller which had proceeded inexorably down a road hedged on either side, from which escape was impossible. And who can follow her further?

EXILED HOME

The dead-end which she had reached was cruelly embodied, as well as over-symbolized, by the bullet in the brain. On 3 September, the moment at last was upon her which she had dodged all her life. She had to choose, and to make that choice she had to own up to herself what she had done. There was no longer a Blor, a Miss Boys, a Gainer, a Dame Helen Gwynne-Vaughan, a Hyde Park crowd, the Czechs, before whom to parade in the finery of her naughtiness. Nobody was left to be angry with her, and so she had lost her superiority. Among those she had sought to impress, the other rowdies, Hitler, Streicher, none of them cared enough to cherish her for her own sake, instead of for her exhibition on their behalf. Where to turn? On the one hand, Muv and Farve, the sisters, home, and on the other, Hitler, passion, show-off – the two halves of her life were mutually exclusive, totally irreconcilable, as they always had been, had she paused to think it out, instead of meandering into fantasies about joint armies and navies, and the Nordic races. Her determination not to notice reality had been the cause of general amazement. But what was irritating or amusing to others was destructive to her. For it is the way of the world to indulge young and pretty girls. Unity had received more toleration than was her due. Allowance had always been made for the Mitford humour, on the good old English ground that everything really is a bit of a joke. Everything, that is to say, except the responsibility each person has for himself. The punishment which at last had caught up with her was nothing but hard facts, but so dreadful that they had to be blotted out. She had bunkered herself up in the Agnesstrasse because she had turned control of her life over to Hitler; and rather than face her responsibility for that, she shot herself. Hitler was to do the same, when responsibility for his actions was borne in on him.

The many people who had heard her proclaiming how she would shoot herself if war was declared, had not exactly considered it a figure of speech, for they knew her resolution and fanaticism. Melodrama was in it, nonetheless. She had done no more than make a fool of herself. It would have been easy to emulate Phillip Spranklin and lie low long enough to be satisfied that the war would endure. Hitler would have endorsed whatever she wanted to do. She could have collected herself in Bernstein, and so moved on to

Hungary, which was still neutral, and perhaps home, where the worst even-tuality would have been to share imprisonment under the Emergency Defence Regulations with her sister Diana. She was sincere when she put the pistol to her temple: she had imagined that she had weighed in the balance of politics, that she had had a role, a mission. There was no power behind the throne. Rudi von St Paul found these words, 'She put her life and ambition into avoiding a war between England and Germany, and when she had no success, she killed herself. She could not admit to herself and the public that she had failed to prevent the war. She had been on a pedestal, and therefore was mis-taken into thinking she had influence. She was too loyal to her beliefs.'

'On that Monday,' Rudi continues, 'Wagner told me that she was in the clinic. Erna had been a lifelong friend of Professor Sauerbruch, and Unity knew him well through her, so it was natural to ask that he should look after Unity. I asked Wagner if it was possible, but I don't think this was during my first visit. I was in a school for domestic science about thirty miles outside Munich. Nobody could drive unless on business, and from Wagner I got petrol for this journey, coming in and out every day, to visit Unity. In the hospital, the first thing I heard was that she wasn't able to speak. The first time I saw her, she did not react at all. She was very white and corpse-like. It was a terrific shock.

'I rang Janos, he had no telephone, you had to be connected to the post office at Bernstein, and he had to be fetched down. I think he offered to come to Munich. I said, There's no point, she's unconscious. It took about a week before she recognized me. After some time she started talking, but she could be muddled over a sentence – for instance, she said, Please give me the table over there on the fruit. Every day I cabled or telephoned Janos, hoping that he and Unity's parents might get in touch with each other, if he was in Hungary. I was in constant touch with Erna as well. Unity never spoke about whether she was upset or regretted what she had done. She skated over it. That was a terrible fall I had, she would say, That's why I'm ill. I am con-vinced that she knew what she had done, but I was told by Professor Magnus that one should not discuss this. He was very off-hand. I had suggested to him that Professor Sauerbruch should come, but he didn't like that one bit and gave a nasty answer. Unity made another attempt at suicide, trying to swallow her swastika brooch, one of the Ordensschwester told me that.'

Bormann's notebook has this entry for 8 November 1939. 'The Führer visits among others Miss Mitford in the clinic; evening speech in the Burgerbräu-keller from 20.10 hours to 21.07 hours; thence 21.31 hours departure. In

Nuremberg the news reaches us in the train that eight minutes after our departure the Munich Burgerbräukeller was destroyed by a dynamite explosion: 8 dead, 60 wounded.' On leaving Unity, in fact, Hitler had been to one of the annual appointments he never missed, in the cellar where his 1923 putsch had been launched. Georg Elser, a former communist, had been manipulated by the Gestapo into placing this bomb for complex and devious motives of discrediting opposition to Hitler, while at the same time fabricating his image of invulnerability and deification. This was Hitler's only visit to Unity in hospital, and the last occasion on which they were to see each other.

Schaub's memorandum best describes this visit, as well as her second suicide attempt: '. . . when Hitler entered her sick-room he was accompanied by the doctor in charge, Professor Magnus, and his adjutant Schaub, and he was deeply shaken by the fearful alteration to the beautiful, lively girl. Unity lay thoroughly apathetic and lamed in the bed, and took notice neither of the visitors whom she barely recognized, nor of the flowers they had brought. Hitler remained only a few minutes. He had further talk outside with Professor Magnus over the prospects of recovery and the possibility of extracting the bullet, which Professor Magnus had declined to undertake after the event as her life would have been endangered.

'When Unity was in better shape, Frau Wilma Schaub watched over her during regular visits to the clinic. Hitler was responsible for this, in the hopes that some suitable person could help Unity find her way back to the land of the living. At first, she appeared completely beyond reach, and stared straight ahead. Her condition made such regular progress that she could make conversation to Frau Schaub and started to show an interest in everyday things at least. Gauleiter Wagner decided that this was an appropriate moment to return the packet she had handed over in farewell. Frau Schaub, who brought it back, was certainly surprised that the invalid should have almost snatched the envelope from her hand and clutched it against herself as though to hide it, but judged this to be from Unity's embarrassment at being reminded of what she had done. For a brief moment only, she was alone in her room. Frau Schaub had let herself out, and told the sister on the floor how she had handed over some souvenirs. Frau Schaub was no sooner home than the sister rang up in a fluster because the party badge had vanished. Unity had shown her the photograph of Hitler in the packet, and had had nothing to say to a question about the badge. When searches were fruitless, the suspicion grew that in her determination to kill herself Unity had swallowed it. Professor Magnus did indeed get it out of her stomach with a probe. All efforts were in vain, the girl did not want to recover from the collapse of her values. Nor did Unity wish to discuss the incident when Frau Schaub went on visiting her afterwards, so the subject was dropped.'

The clinic on the Nussbaumstrasse was part of the university medical faculty, and its excellence justified its reputation. Professor Magnus, its director, was internationally known, and he was also aware of the accusation which might be trumped-up if Unity were to die under operation. She was in safe hands. At the end of the war, the clinic was evacuated, its medical records destroyed, and Professor Magnus has long been dead. Erna Hanfstaengl had put me in touch with Dr Felix Frey, who had joined the staff of the clinic halfway through the war, and he had mentioned the name of Dr Helmut Reiser. Better than that, Frau Hess introduced me to him. Dr Reiser invited me to dine with him privately in the hospital which he now runs, and he sprang a surprise on me: the other guest was *Das Kind*, once Mary's husband, but divorced after his return, long after the war, from penal servitude in Russia. He is again a practising doctor. We spoke of Unity, of the whole period and the spell which Hitler had nefariously cast upon it. Unity, he thought, had been bored and dismissive with his family, and with him, though he had been a handsome, blond young German in a black uniform. Erich, he recollects, had been motionless and silent, an outline of a man, most probably with a watching brief. 'Unity must have noticed how I never wanted to meet Hitler, and that put her off.'

Dr Reiser had been hardly older than Unity when he had to look after her. 'I was *Dozent für Chirurgie* [lecturer in surgery] in the university clinic, and private assistant to Professor Magnus. I was there in the early evening when she was brought into our clinic in an ambulance, and next morning I realized that I still had no idea who she was. I knew only that she had been delivered to the clinic after an attempted suicide. She was in the care of the first *Oberarzt* [senior physician] of Professor Magnus, Professor Jaeger, brother of the Archbishop of Paderborn. He was a neuro-surgeon, and took over her case, with Magnus as supervisor.

'When I examined her on the morning of 4 September, she was unconscious. She was not so gravely wounded. A few days later she came to herself, and then we took an X-ray of her skull. This showed that the bullet was in the back of the skull, having come through the right temple, but not penetrating through. Her face was severely swollen by the wound. She was taken into the operating theatre for minor attention, but not to extract the bullet, which could not have been done. She never uttered a single word. We thought that she had suffered a motor aphasia, we assumed some disturbance in the centre of the brain.

'Unity had a large room in the front, giving on to the Nussbaumstrasse She was looked after by an *Ordenschwester*, a sister of mercy, and their head matron was Sister Tetwina. Only sisters from this order came to wash Unity, and change her. She had to be fed. She could look around, but perhaps was not there in spirit. With Professor Magnus, I went in to her twice a day. One could not discover what she wanted, or did not want. Not the least clue. We did not have the impression that she did not wish to speak, but that she could not. There was no question of Unity getting up or moving, she had spells of vertigo, as is the case with head wounds.

'Professor Sauerbruch may have been telephoned, but he never came to the clinic, he had the Charité Hospital in Berlin. Frau Schaub came to visit her, certainly. And Hitler came just that once. Professor Magnus received him at the clinic, and accompanied him into Unity's room. We had warned Hitler that she was not speaking. He accepted that. He went in and stayed about a quarter of an hour, and when he came out he asked those of us waiting out-side in attendance whatever had we meant by telling him that she wasn't speaking. She had found her tongue with him all right. Of course we asked what she had said, and he answered, She would like to go back to England. And then Hitler said he would set things in motion so that somehow she would be able to travel home.

'After that, the clinic was informed by the Bavarian Innenministerium that contact had been made through Switzerland, and Unity was to be taken there, and English doctors would then fetch her. A special carriage from the railways was to be prepared, and a sister of mercy and a doctor were to accompany her. The sister selected was the one who had been with her, and I was the doctor. Because of diplomatic procedures the whole affair had been dragged out into December, and I wanted to be home for Christmas. Shortly before-hand, we had the necessary permits for money and exit visas. I had been granted a thousand marks. Time passed, and one day a Hungarian count rang up out of the blue, and said that he knew the Redesdales very well and wanted to come too. He had spoken to the Innenministerium and had been given permission to travel with us. Professor Magnus had no objection, so the count came too, which was very nice for me. Hungarians were neutral at the time, and I had no idea how the English doctors might react to me.

'We left from the Hauptbahnhof in Munich. Unity did not get up, because of her vertigo, which would also have prevented her from convalescing with Frau Schaub, or anything like that. She had never left the clinic until then. We had this large railway carriage to ourselves, with a bed in it specially arranged for transporting the wounded. The sister sat beside her. The count and I went to the dining-car on the train, for he liked his food. I had the money from the Ministry of the Interior to pay expenses for myself and the count at a hotel. We came to Berne. An ambulance was waiting, Unity was transferred into it and went on to the clinic of Professor Matti. I then had to wait until the English doctor came. But he didn't arrive, and as I had personally handed over to Professor Matti all the medical documents, my mission was over. The count stayed as well, and in my presence he telephoned Lord Redesdale in England, to learn that the English doctor had problems over his visas.

'Next day I visited Unity and Professor Matti asked, What's all this about her not speaking? She has been singing Hitler's praises. In the clinic in Munich, flowers had been sent from Hitler, from several Gauleiters, Ribbentrop, Goebbels. It would have been impossible for her to have taken roses from Hitler back to England. I waited until 24 December. I never saw the mother. I left. The count visited me on his way back through Munich and told me that at least a week more had passed, and he had spent all the money, and had to ask for more at the embassy in Berne. We went to the Innenministerium together, and were told that it would be all right.'

Since those few days in the middle of August, Janos had not stirred from Bernstein. Could he have imagined, one wonders, in those twenty minutes when Unity had waved him off between trains, how before the close of the year they were to be together in a far more agonizing send-off at the same station? September 3rd, in Janos's diary, was an N v B day, Nothing of Importance. On 4 September he lunched at Kohfidisch with Marie-Eugenie Zichy and Baby Erdödy, and noted, 'Informed about Unity. Telephone Munich hospital.' Next day, still at Kohfidisch, 'Telephone Rudi'. And on the 6th he discussed the situation with the consul (Hungarian, presumably) in Graz. For a week he was active, running between the consulate and the local party officials for permissions and petrol, to the garage for servicing his car, and then he relapsed, on Rudi's instructions. He was biding his time. From December 9th to the 15th he was in Budapest, then in Vienna, reaching Munich as late as the 19th. His first visit to Unity was on the following day. Then he noted, 21st, Thursday. Imminent departure Unity [plötzliche Abreise Unity] ... 22nd, Friday. 6.30 Vienna. Hospital in the evening with Tima Auersperg, Hannah Mikes ... 23rd, Saturday. Off early [früh ab] with the doctor. Evening in Berne. Unity in Salem hospital [he had scribbled the name of Professor Matti at the bottom of the page] ... 24th, Sunday. Early to Matti's clinic. Doctor leaves at midday. Midnight mass ... 25th, Monday.

Midday Wettstein [a private reference]. Unity in the evening at Matti's.
Telephone Redesdale.'

The apparent discrepancy concerning Dr Reiser's memory of telephoning
to Lord Redesdale can mean only that Janos did not record all his calls to
London. There may have been a last-minute delay to account for the 'plötzliche
Abreise' of the 21st, which more properly translates as 'sudden departure'. But
the entry '6.30 Vienna' cannot be linked to this journey, as it might confusingly seem to be. The train went straight through to Berne, and in any case
Lady Redesdale, interviewed by the Daily Express in Paris on their way back,
settled any doubts about these dates and directions: 'On December 23rd when
the Nazi doctors said she was fit to be moved, the Nazi authorities put her in
a special hospital train, which entered Switzerland through Bregenz, and
finally arrived in Berne.'

Janos hung on by himself until the 29th, when, he wrote down, 'Lady
Redesdale and her daughter arrive', the daughter being Debo. So by the 30th,
without further hitch, he was grateful to be back in Munich. New Year's Day
he spent with Rudi at Seeseiten, that night taking the Auerspergs to the theatre
in Munich – and so to Bernstein on 4 January 1940, while Unity was crossing
to England.

That Christmas Himmler was away in Italy, and his absence, according to
Erna Hanfstaengl, was a stroke of luck. Only Himmler might have argued in
favour of holding Unity as a hostage, or exchanging her for someone in
English hands, or at the worst, out of spite, obstructing her release. But the
request to go home to England would not be thwarted against Hitler's direct
orders to expedite the matter, and a delay of six weeks does not seem unduly
protracted in the circumstances. But what was the meaning of that silence
maintained before Professor Magnus and Dr Reiser? Has Dr Reiser lengthened
in his mind the period when she was speechless? Was she prepared to talk to
Rudi, but not to the doctors? It looks as if she was reserving for Hitler the
one statement she had to make, afraid otherwise of being dragged through
the war in Germany in her condition. If there was method in it, there was no
recanting. To the first stranger she met, Professor Matti, she started upon the
old song.

Rudi could have accompanied the train to Berne, but was too frightened to
do so. She had brought Unity some clothes in the clinic, and in the middle
of November she had packed up ˌhe Agnesstrasse, helped by an old family
maid of hers. 'I cleared up,' Rudi says, 'and then nothing happened for a bit.
All her personal things went with her, but nothing Nazi. Some of that I kept
at Seeseiten, including quite a lot of her books with her name on the fly-leaf,

and a swastika. At the end of the war, the Americans occupied the house, found them within the hour, and took the whole lot away. All the photos which she had taken were lost, including many of her and Hitler which he had given her. Her furniture was stored until 1949 when Lady Redesdale removed it. I could not remember where it had been stored; there were thirty-four separate firms in Munich, and only the fifth name on the list was correct. Lady Redesdale very kindly made me a present of Bobo's writing desk, which had been brought from England. She asked me to keep it in memory of Bobo. It's Edwardian, with five drawers on either side, in mahogany with different inlays. I have been using it ever since. Hitler paid for all the moving and storing of the furniture until 1945. After that, Lady Redesdale paid.

'Janos had the rest of her things. I told him I didn't feel happy about keeping the diaries – in our house we were all aware that Germany would lose the war – my father said that if Hitler ruled Europe people like us would anyhow have no place in it. So Janos took the diaries.'

Hannah Mikes, as we know, had temporary custody of the diaries, but Janos recovered them. For a few years it did not seem as if the war would catch up with Bernstein, horoscopes or not, and Janos lived undisturbed. Laczy, true to his form, was away in the Western Desert with Rommel; and afterwards he had a secret assignment in Constantinople as liaison between King Farouk and the Germans. Had he been on the winning side, his exploits would have made him a schoolboy-hero. As the tide turned, and the Russians smashed across Central Europe, retreats and alibis had to be secured. Janos made a bonfire of the Hungarian boyar's costume which he had loved dressing in, and also burnt the unique copy of Mein Kampf which Hitler had given to Unity, with observations in the margins which he had thought particularly suitable for her. This loss he apparently regretted afterwards.

To Janos's niece, Baroness Stoerck, fell the lot of one last service. She said, 'Laczy was at Tobruk. You know how he infiltrated a German spy into Cairo behind the British lines, a film was made about him, starring Peter van Eyck. After the debacle he left Egypt in 1943 and was on his mission in Turkey before he returned to his flat in Budapest. A company of SS men were billeted on my parents at Mezőkeresztes and he got them to go away. After September 1944, I lived in his flat in Budapest too. Laczy had a German car with an Egyptian numberplate, and in April or May 1944 he smuggled a child, a nephew of Artur Rubinstein's, into the Salesianer convent. The child was given false papers with the identity of Antal Arkus, and they hid him on the floor of the car. The roadblocks waved them through to the station, and on the train safely to the convent. That was a big risk for Laczy. The Russians arrested him in Budapest, and he gave my mother's name as a witness in his defence, so they arrested her too, on 24 April 1945, the very day after we had arrived in Bernstein. In the end Laczy was tried by a so-called People's Court but he was acquitted with the help of a well-known orientalist, Dr Gyula Germanus, a member of parliament, and a Jew who had become a Moslem. Laczy's book about Rommel was used in his defence at the trial, it showed him to be nothing but a brave officer.

'Now Janos had Unity's diaries for two or three years, and then was anxious to be rid of them, so he handed them over to our possession. In those diaries there was a regular time-table, what she was doing, whom she met, Goebbels was there, Hitler was wonderful, she was thrilled, that kind of thing. Horrible platitudes. I read them and could hardly believe it was possible. To have been there, and to have taken in so little! So Laczy hid the diaries in Horthy Miklos út. The servant there we called Uncle Pek, and he asked me to carry away the diaries, he didn't want the Russians to find them. I put them into a rucksack, and went from Budapest by train to Szombathely, then on to Kösag, and walked to Bernstein. The journey should have taken four hours but actually took thirteen. People living in the frontier zone could get permission for local crossings. I had twenty-three kilometers to do on foot, and the diaries were heavy, five or six booklets bound in black linen-cloth, some other albums and press-cuttings and pictures of Hitler. Janos was half-crying with fear when he saw them but they were hidden in Bernstein, until a few years later a Dutch priest, Father Koster, took them to Lady Redesdale.'

Finally the Bundesarchiv contains a little clutch of bills. On 1 November 1939, the Staatssekretär of the Bavarian Ministry of the Interior wrote to the Adjutantur des Führers in the Wilhelmstrasse, acknowledging receipt of 1,039 reichsmarks and 29 pfennig, and requesting payment of a further 255 marks, 9 pfennig, to be paid into an account number 4415 in the Bavarian Gemeinde-bank for Unity – the sum made up from 161 marks, 14 pfennig, for hospital treatment between 11 and 20 October, 90 marks to Dr Albert Kohler for two X-rays, and 3 marks and 95 pfennig to the Theatiner Shoe Shop.

On 8 January, just after Unity's departure, Professor Magnus sent in his bill for over three thousand marks, and settlement of this dragged on in Hitler's office until April. However account 4415 was credited in February with 250 marks from the sale of some cupboards specially built by Unity in the Agnesstrasse. The flat, so the Obersturmführer in the Ministry then de-clared to Hitler's office, was available for further re-letting. The expenses had been high. Hitler paid. It was the least he could do.

A SHORT NOTE OF GOODBYE

'A number of British subjects still remain in Germany,' runs a Foreign Office memorandum of 5 September 1939 (see F.O. 369, Vols. 2534, 2535, 2536 for this information). 'We are receiving appeals from their relatives for assistance in getting them out. We require to find out as quickly as possible what is happening to them and whether the Germans are likely to let them go in the near future . . . Above all, we wish to make sure that our nationals will get out before we allow all the Germans to go from here and so lose our bargaining weapon.' After the outbreak of war, British interests in Germany were represented by the American Embassy, and on 11 September Counsellor Herschel V. Johnson was reporting back that the process of rounding up British subjects had started the previous afternoon, though the Germans were willing to let them depart on principles of reciprocity. Lists began to be drawn up, though the very first of them contained only forty-seven adults, with some children as well: for the most part they were governesses or nannies, and a few people in hospital, such as a Mrs Wickert who had had the misfortune to be operated for appendicitis at Bad Kreuznach on 22 August. Charles Watkinson was in a hard-luck category of his own, pleading guilty at his trial in Dresden on 20 November to accepting five hundred marks as payment for taking out of the country some of the belongings of a Jewish refugee, and receiving a prison sentence.

Unity was on the first list. Her address was unknown, and the space for 'Last heard of' was left blank. The Foreign Office filed notes of a telephone call on 5 September from Lord Redesdale. 'He has begged her to come home but without success so far. He hopes she will now repent and asks that she should be put on any list of British subjects requiring assistance to be submitted to the American Embassy in Berlin.' Arrangements were made that as soon as Weld-Forester returned home, he would telephone Lord Redesdale.

Throughout October the lists of British subjects in Germany were emended and expanded, but it was not until 6 November that the Redesdales' persistent requests for information from official sources were rewarded. Ted Achilles of the American Embassy in London was asked to cable Berlin, and on the 9th F. M. Shepherd of the Foreign Office was writing to Lady Redesdale at Old Mill Cottage with the results of this initiative. 'I had a telephone message from the United States Embassy just after you left for the country this morning saying that your daughter was in the surgical hospital at Munich and was well on the road to recovery. According to the information received by the embassy, your daughter had attempted to do away with herself on 3 September. She had not communicated with the United States consul-general at Munich, otherwise no doubt we should have had earlier news.' To which Lady Redesdale answered next day that it was a great relief to know Unity was getting on well. Can it be a coincidence that this official news should have been delayed at the German end until the very day after Hitler had seen Unity, and learnt for himself what she wanted to do?

The Redesdales had already been prepared for the shock. The ominous silence from Munich had been broken in the second week of October by a letter from Janos, guarded, to be sure, skirting the truth, with the information merely that Unity was ill in Munich and might require an operation. Although the letter had been posted from Budapest, Janos was conscious of the long arm of the Gestapo, especially in a *Geheime Reichssache* like this. A second letter from him, two weeks later, suggested that an operation would perhaps not be necessary after all.

On top of their anxiety, the Redesdales had to endure press comment and speculation, which in the absence of facts, was abusive. *Good Riddance* – to 'Unity'!, an article in the *Daily Mirror* of 1 October, for instance, presumed that Unity would be living happily in Germany for the duration of the war, which was damaging at the very moment when treason was in the air with Lord Haw-Haw's broadcasts, whose impact alarmed the government. Internal evidence revealed him at that stage only as someone at ease in the language and tone of the British fascists. But Joyce's Hitlerization began where Unity's ended, and such parallels as exist in their lives – their attendance at the Nuremberg Rally of 1933, their preference for German expressions when English would have done, their anti-semitism – cannot be ridden too hard.

As always, rumours flowered around Unity and her fate. The censorship in the German press was cast-iron, and nothing appeared there until the following July, when a bulletin purporting to originate in Stockholm was published, alerting Germans to Unity's supposed death in an English prison – this was a last little gift to her from Goebbels's Ministry of Propaganda. On 5 November, however, Prince Nicholas Orloff gave an interview to the *Sunday Dispatch* representative in Belgrade, and then the news that Unity had shot herself was out, if not yet believed, or believable.

A White Russian émigré, Prince Orloff had been the English-speaking announcer of the Berlin radio station, but had fled after the outbreak of war. His information about Unity had come from 'somebody in close touch with Hitler's personal staff' and also from a lady who had been a close friend of hers whom he had met in the train travelling from Munich to Vienna. These two unnamed people had indeed grasped the outline of what had happened, though the details were distorted, and the prince wrongly asserted that Unity was dead.

Sensation-mongers were soon embellishing what was tendentious enough in itself. Unity was supposed to have had a row with Hitler, banging doors on him, her consequent depression culminating in an overdose of veronal. Alternatively, she and Hitler had had 'stormy scenes', and she had been murdered. 'Whether Hitler knew of her execution, or even gave the order for it, may be a secret for ever ... She was sitting in the bedroom of her Munich hotel flat recovering from an illness when Gestapo officers entered her room and a shot was heard ... She simply disappeared – and it is believed she was buried under a false name.' To Madame Tabouis, ineffable old French war-horse and public menace among roving correspondents between the wars, goes the credit of inventing the hardy fiction that Unity was shot down on her usual walk in the Englischer Garten. Madame Tabouis was imaginative enough to provide a killer, twenty-nine-year-old Gruppen-führer August Scharenbach, who 'fired twice from a considerable distance, thus failing to kill her'. So fluent a writer might have reflected that a Gruppen-führer bungling lamentably what purported to be orders from Himmler might have been advised to turn his gun at close range on himself. The legend that Unity had been shot by the Germans was further boosted when Uncle Jack Mitford docked at New York on the *Lancastria* in February and told reporters that Unity's bullet wounds were not self-inflicted, and his niece's memory was a blank about the incident.

In the doldrums of the Phoney War, Unity's homecoming was a nine days' wonder. From Berne, her mother had hired, said the papers, 'the special first-class railway carriage Number 1002 and guard's van' at a cost of about £1,600. The ordinary cross-channel ferry from Calais had landed her at Folkestone in the late afternoon of Tuesday, 3 January. From the newspapers again: 'Unity was held one hour and a quarter for Customs and immigration inspections. She sat up in bed in her state cabin while half a dozen customs men went through her twenty pieces of luggage. Immediately the ship was tied up, Sir Arthur Jelf, Chief of the Field Security Police, and also the chief immigration officer of the port, both went on board. They went into the state cabins B and C occupied by Unity, her mother and her sister Deborah.

They questioned Unity, looked at her passport, and asked to see her documents ... When the search was completed Unity climbed out of bed, and with a rug wrapped round her, walked two steps out of the cabin and was helped on to the stretcher lying in the corridor. She was told that her landing card and food ration card had been given to her mother.'

Sir Arthur Jelf, it seems, had either lost all sense of proportion, or more probably, was over-reacting to a flap in Whitehall. Folkestone harbour had been blocked off at the gates. Nobody and nothing was allowed in, not even rail traffic. Armed guards patrolled every entrance, as well as the railway tracks. Sentries had been posted on the highways, even outside the harbour perimeter, the police force had been trebled and plain-clothes men drafted in. The station and quayside had been searched.

Lord Redesdale had been allowed to drive in with the ambulance which he had hired from the Walton Private Ambulance Service. 'When he saw his daughter being carried down the gangway he ran to the stretcher. Then he kissed her twice.' A few miles outside Folkestone, however, the ambulance broke a spring, and had to return to the town, where the whole party were obliged to spend the night in a hotel. The massed reporters were now able to have virtually unrestricted access, and the grapevine whisper spread, rather implausibly, that the broken spring was a Fleet Street ruse which had cost good money.

Next morning, the papers were able to splash the story for all it was worth, with photographs of Unity, on the stretcher or on her father's arm, a ghoulish sight. Here was retribution. 'I am not ashamed of Unity,' the Daily Mail rubbed salt into the wounds by using this quote from Lord Redesdale in its heading. 'I have been offered £5,000 for her story. I would not take £25,000. I would not like to make money that way,' the Evening Standard had him saying. Editorials trundled ahead. 'Nobody can pretend that the same facilities would have been given to an unknown Miss Unity Brown,' Vernon Bartlett wrote in the News Chronicle, in a column entitled 'Has the Press Gone Mad?' 'All this fuss is made either because she is a friend of Hitler's or because she is the daughter of a rich peer.' 'Censorship by Bayonets' was the title of the article in the Daily Express, by Hilde Marchant, who argued, 'She has come back. She has a right to – but we are fighting for those rights. The right for Unity Mitford to go bellowing in Hyde Park or marching down Piccadilly without being lynched. But don't waste our soldiers' time or poke bayonets at a Press who still want facts.'

Of course the public which in its mercy might have been disposed to think that Unity had paid the price for folly, was outraged by the bewilderingly extravagant precautions surrounding her landing, as though she were being accorded privileged treatment or protection by that turn-out of armed soldiers at the harbour. Underlying resentment had been whipped into odium. Questions were asked in Parliament. Oliver Stanley (a friend and distant relation of the Redesdales) had just succeeded Hore-Belisha as secretary for war, and he tried to shuffle out of his responsibility for this mismanaged affair on the grounds that Folkestone harbour was a prohibited area. Herbert Morrison then asked about the steps taken to facilitate Unity's return, and Neville Chamberlain, still prime minister for a few months longer, in reply described how her name had been on the list of British subjects whom the American Embassy in Berlin had been asked to help.

Newsreel companies, Pathé for instance, had released films of the Folkestone arrival in a similar slightly uplifting spirit of malice. But a three-minute spoof film from Paramount was an indignity better suited to the German Ministry of Propaganda, which did indeed pick it up and screen it, eventually, to instruct their audiences to what levels the British had sunk. This montage had shots of sailors scanning the horizons, destroyers laying smoke-screens, squadrons of aircraft, ironically heralding Unity's entry. The commentary, in doggerel couplets, was rounded off with crude musical blurps – the whole accompanied by a second clip about Hore-Belisha's dismissal from the government. A well-known literary agent, Raymond Savage, wrote a letter to *The Times* protesting that these two newsreel items, contentiously run together, were an abuse sufficient to justify censorship. In the House of Lords, the motion that censorship, or supervision at least, was a wartime necessity was thereupon moved by Lord Denman, who was actually flying a kite: his interest was that he had married Aunt Daphne, one of Lord Redesdale's sisters, and like Uncle Jack, was wrong-headedly establishing solidarity. Lord Dufferin and Ava, under-secretary for the colonies, replying for the government, did not wish to erode liberty through further controls but he agreed that 'as an example of sadistic brutality the Unity Mitford film would be hard to beat'.

Meanwhile the *Daily Mail* had invited its readers to list their wartime grouches, and this straw-poll threw up good-sense results: Women in Uniform was the chief complaint, followed by the black-out, BBC programmes, horse-power car tax, torch-flashers, and the Ministry of Information, in that order. On this scale Unity Mitford was in fourteenth place, below patriotic songs, but above the Civil Service, the evacuation of businesses, and sympathy for German prisoners. On 26 January the *Daily Mirror* was writing that, 'the Mitford girl who has openly been consorting with the King's enemies (surely a treasonable offence?) goes scot free. Why? God and the House of Lords only know.' Here was apparently a hideous plot to import National Socialism, 'to exploit the working classes and keep them where they belong – in the gutter'. As late as May, the *Daily Express* was still close behind, mentioning Unity's 'active interest in Christian Science . . . several of the Nazis' leading chums here were strong Christian Scientists . . . she still takes a mainly pro-Nazi view of events but her manner has lost its former violence, is quiet and vague.' For the duration of the war, the hounds of the yellow-press, like Hannen Swaffer and William Connor, yelped intermittently on this trail.

A second ambulance, its springs in order, drove Unity away from Folkestone after breakfast on the 4th, to the cottage at High Wycombe. Three policemen there kept away a knot of villagers as she was carried in on a stretcher. On the 22nd she was driven, still by ambulance, to the Radcliffe Infirmary in Oxford, to be attended by Professor (later Sir) Hugh Cairns, one of the foremost neuro-surgeons of his day. Just a week later the Radcliffe announced that, 'Her general health is good and the wound from which she suffered in Germany in September and for which she was skilfully treated in Germany, has healed in a normal and satisfactory manner. After consultation it has been decided that no operation is advisable or desirable.' Professor Cairns had concurred with Professor Magnus.

The sister on Unity's ward was Dorothy Day, who said, 'I was in Nuffield Ward I, which was four-bedded, with six private patient rooms, in one of which Unity was. She was very friendly with the nurses. She was up and about, dressed, or in her dressing gown. Apparently an uncomplicated English girl. Her parents used to drift in and out, every day they came. There were political overtones, but ours not to reason why, I wasn't to mention her being there to my colleagues. They were doing X-rays and confirming what the Germans had found. She had got a weakness in the right hand, and her limp. She was not there long.'

Until Saturday, 5 February, in fact, when she returned to High Wycombe. That same day, incidentally, Mosley, who had been stranded as high and dry in his illusions as the communists in theirs by the Russo-German pact, but still had some anti-war speeches in him, defended Unity at a meeting in the Manchester Free Trade Hall, as 'my very young sister-in-law upon whom attacks are made, many of them in the hope of doing me some damage'.

Lord Redesdale proposed removing Unity to the island of Inchkenneth, off Mull, which he had bought two years beforehand. Out of sight, out of mind, as he rightly thought. The Western Isles, however, were declared 'protected under the defence regulations', and the news on 20 February that Unity might be in retreat there caused another ruction. A Labour MP, for Maryhill, Glasgow, asked in Parliament whether permission had been given for Unity to reside on Inchkenneth. Once bitten, twice shy: Oliver Stanley now swung in the other direction, and Unity was forbidden to travel to Inchkenneth. The prohibition was a very small bone easily thrown to public opinion. The decision had been influenced by the conduct of Mosley and the fascists, who were viewed as a dangerous fifth column, and whose days at large were therefore numbered. Unity, in her condition, was no risk to national security, but she was tarred black with the same brush.

Lord Redesdale was goaded by the latest pinprick into issuing a statement on 10 March. 'My only crime, if it be a crime, so far as I know, is that I was one of many thousands in this country who thought that our best interests would be served by a friendly understanding with Germany. In this, though now proved to be wrong, I was, at any rate, in good company.' As for Unity's exclusion from Inchkenneth. 'It is a decision arrived at by those responsible for the safety of our country after due consideration and it would be highly improper for me to question it. What I do resent, however, is the undoubted undercurrent of suspicion and resentment created by publicity to which, however inaccurate its statements may be, there is no right of reply ... One other matter which I find very wounding is that I am constantly described as a "Fascist". I am not, never have been, and am not likely to become a Fascist.'

Humble pie tastes like this. Another large helping of it had to be eaten at the end of June when Lady Mosley was detained in the round-up of English fascists under defence regulations. France had fallen, and while Hitler was mobilizing for Operation Sea-Lion, as the invasion of England was code-named, the government could not indulge in the luxury of finding out whether or not Mosley and his followers would prove to be patriotic. Lord and Lady Redesdale were now gradually to drift apart; he in old age to become a lonely, broken man; she still sheltering in her maternal feelings for Unity a complete, obtuse misunderstanding of Nazism.

Swinbrook had been taken by Sir Charles Hambro for the shooting, until in 1935 Mr and Mrs Duncan Mackinnon rented the house, furnished, for a year, after which they bought it, with the estate. Lady Redesdale kept a toe-hold, however, in what was confusingly called Mill Cottage, in pretty Cotswold stone, attached to the Swan Inn on the edge of the village, by the stream flowing alone from Asthall. The purchase of Inchkenneth had followed the sale of Swinbrook as though in the foreknowledge that the family would be withdrawing from the centre of the stage to an outer rim. Banned from the island, Unity was cared for at Mill Cottage (in October 1942 a stray German bomber dropped its load close enough to shatter the windows), or at High Wycombe, or in The Garage.

Mabel, and her husband Mr Woolven, were invited to live at High Wycombe to look after her. She said, 'I can see his lordship now, when we had the news she'd shot herself. He went down to meet her off the boat, they tried to mob the ambulance. Lord Redesdale said, I shall never be able to hold up my head again. I told him, I should hold it up higher, it would have been terrible if she'd shot herself dead, now she'll have time to repent. Mabel, he held on to me, you've been a friend to us. Unity would go funny but fierce. We had to quarrel. She would say, What time are you going to have your lunch, I think I'll have mine, but I'm going out – and then she'd say, I've changed my mind, we'll have our lunch together. She'd go off with her stockings all down, and come back saying, I've not got enough change, Mabe, I gave five shillings to the taxi for a tip. Whatever did you do that for? I'd say, I'm not going to help you if you're going giving away your money. All kinds of trouble. Once she was in the bathroom for a long time, in the water right up to her neck, her eyes staring out. What a fright I got. Now, no games with me, I said and pulled her out. She was not herself, oh no.'

There was much rallying round. Nanny Blor came over from Staines. Rudbin came. 'Once she was convalescent, I saw her in the Easter of 1940,' she said. 'Bobo had got much more huge. She used to wear Tom's shoes, her feet had got so much bigger. She hadn't taken any pains to remain in trim. She used to sing a lot, a very small but true voice. Muv played the piano for her.' Later Unity was often to spend weekends or longer periods at Brayfield. Miss Hussey was to find her able to hold discussions 'about all sorts of things. Once we went to a Methodist congregation for evening service.'

Mary Ormsby-Gore saw her regularly. 'I went to High Wycombe in the time between Unity's return and her entry to the Radcliffe. She always had a fetish about gloves, and in order to comfort her Muv had bought for her expensive fur gloves, more like gauntlets. When she went to see Diana in Holloway, she was wearing these gloves and put them up on the grill, and Diana said, Oh Dorly, grouse? Unity thought she had gone through suffering for the cause, and then came this remark. She adored Tom, and thought it all right about him being killed in Burma, not Germany. She wore his Sam Browne belt under her clothes like a hair shirt. She used to go down to Whitechapel to scrub floors, so she must have felt guilt about it, someone must have arranged that for her. She'd say, Why didn't you stop me? and I answered, We tried to. On the other hand we saw those awful films of camps after the war, and she said, 'That's all propaganda, there was a typhoid epidemic and it's the way of getting rid of the bodies.'

Her cousin Timothy Bailey said, 'After she shot herself she was all sideways, those peals of laughter were slightly maniacal. Hooper had come to help, with Mrs Hoops. I remember those sessions at High Wycombe. Bobo'd make an effort, I'd take her on a drive. She showed no sense of repentance.' But her atheism was replaced by an interest, indeed an obsession, in religion for its own sake. Margaret Durman said, 'After her illness, Unity was taken with the parish church. The Rev. Float helped her. She used to give a hand with local parish work. One day she came into my mother's house and said she'd like to see Margot. She's not due for leave, my mother said, but Unity came several days to sit and stare at a photo of me. When I came home, I went to Unity but she didn't recognize me after all. My uniform could have upset her, and given her a mental block.'

The Rev. Wilfred Float was vicar of All Saint's Church from 1925 to 1950, and therefore has known the Mitfords since first they lived in Old Mill Cottage. In spite of his ninety years, he is as sprightly as ever, his blue eyes clear. 'As a schoolgirl Unity had charm, and that aristocratic manner, as I call it. She wanted to be somebody. She told me how the elder children were not playing with her, and asked what she should do about it. You wait, I answered, You may be able to lord it over them one day. Even then I noticed her attitude. She was at home from St Margaret's, and present at some function for a good purpose, and Coningsby Disraeli was there putting in for a raffle. He was Disraeli's nephew, an MP and churchwarden for Hughenden. I was opposite Unity at tea and saw from her behaviour that she had some objection to Jews. She asked Coningsby how he spelled his name. Where she acquired this dislike of Jews I don't know. She could be rude, and this rudeness was due to dissatisfaction with her position. That led her to turn against England and the English. She very bitterly attacked me over our national disloyalty to the Duke of Windsor. It was our duty, she said, to support the King of England whatever he did. The new Queen she found a common shopgirl.

'Just before the war I was having tea with Lady Redesdale and Unity, and we had an argument over Hitler. You tell her, Lady Redesdale encouraged me, She ought to learn how people think, and how they'll think of her. Unity was running down everything English. She told me that if only I went to Germany and talked to Hitler I would understand. He was their saviour who could do no wrong, and that's how the King of England ought to be. I told her, Even if you scrub their floors to them you are still Unity Mitford, you don't realize what you owe to England and to your family. I am certain that whatever Hitler had asked her to do, she would have done, which showed that her morals had gone. Her ideas were those of a slave-mind. If she'd been Miss Snooks Hitler would not have bothered with her. The Redesdales were scared of communism, they thought Hitler was for the Right, a great man. Unity also disliked the working class for being so powerful.

'After the suicide attempt, I first saw her in church when she came to communion and foolishly I didn't recognize her. When I called round some time later, I recognized the tremendous change in her. Her peculiarities at that time were due to brain damage and people ought to have recognized it. She was peeved with the Church of England because its members were not ready to receive her. She took a violent emotional feeling for the Congregationalist minister Mr Spooner, who was a married man, she used to persecute him, lying in wait for him – I never discussed it with Spooner, he was very nice, and terribly worried about it. The chapel was at the other end of The Rye, on East Street. It wasn't religious mania she had, no. My wife had a concert, Unity sat up towards the front, she seemed to enjoy it. It used to be said that High Wycombe wasn't bombed because Unity was there. The last time I saw her was when two girls were curious about her, so I asked her to tea with them. She said, I've got to go up to Scotland but I feel some fatal accident might happen. That presentiment was strange.'

The Rev. E. Sidney Spooner and his wife (whom Unity also pestered) have both died, but their eldest son, Dr A. G. Spooner, writes from Australia: 'She used to sit near the back of the church on the right-hand side, facing the minister and leave immediately the service was finished, so it was three or four weeks before my father knew who she was. He was naturally interested that someone like her should attend, and after due interval, she came home to tea on two or three occasions. On these and a few later meetings she poured out her troubles to him, as he made a sympathetic audience . . . She did afterwards on a few occasions try to contact him in the street . . . In retrospect I feel that Unity was in no way different from any other depressed female who leans on, psychologically speaking, ministers of religion or their doctor . . .'

On 19 April 1941, she was at St Bartholomew's, Smithfield, for the wedding of Debo. 'As she drove off with a woman companion she shielded her face with a small blue pochette decorated with U.M. in gilt letters.' The press and the photographers were quick off the mark. If she was well enough to be out and about in the world, she was well enough to be interned, and the suggestion was raised in Parliament, to be rebuffed now by Herbert Morrison, whose views as Home Secretary had broadened. 'My information as to the condition of this person's health and the circumstances in which she is living does not indicate that there is at present any ground which makes it necessary in the interests of national security to exercise control over her.'

A couple of years later, Lady Dashwood spent a day learning from Lady Redesdale how to rear goats, when Debo appeared after a lengthy bus-ride feeling ill as she was expecting. Unity exclaimed that she would love to have a baby. Before the war Lady Dashwood had invited Nancy to lunch at her house, West Wycombe, and Unity had been brought along, only to turn up afterwards at the Wycombe Town Hall at a meeting of the Conservative Association, which she scandalized by interrupting with the Nazi salute, the gesture being all the more tiresome because Lady Dashwood was an officer of the association. She said, 'In the war Unity wasn't allowed into High Wycombe because of the American air force bases. That day she said to me, Will you help, I do want to go and see my favourite friend, Lady Astor – she and the Other One are the two stars in my life – if you were to drive me to Cliveden it would be all right.'

Nancy, living near the Regent's Park Canal and working in Heywood Hill's bookshop in Curzon Street, made the effort to fit Unity into her social life. Her companion in the bookshop as from January 1943 was Mrs Friese-Greene, now Mrs Handasyde Buchanan. She said: 'I came back from lunch one day. Nancy was out, and this stranger came up and said, Do you think it is wicked to commit suicide? I don't think I've ever thought about it, I said, let's have a chat. Then Nancy came back, but Unity had taken to me. All she wanted from life was a husband, which of course by then was out of the question. When I get married, I should like to have ten children, she would say. Harvey Nichols was within walking distance, we'd lunch there and were always looking through the *Matrimonial Times* for a husband for her. We'd shriek with laughter about it. I never asked about Hitler, but once she told me how he had said that she had beautiful legs. I was only trying to keep her amused. She'd ring up or pop into the shop two or three times a week at that stage, she'd be sent to spend the afternoon in the Curzon cinema. Now Miss, Nancy would tell her, you're being a perfect nuisance, go away. It was like having a child to go out with. They kept her very short of money. I went to stay at High Wycombe and we had a long walk together when she spoke of becoming a Catholic, because the nursing sisters had been so good to her in Munich. In the evening there we played racing demon, and Lady Redesdale whispered to me, I always let her win, she might mind if she lost. Bobo would have been a religious girl – she'd found it in Nazism instead.'

Derek Hill remembers how Nancy rang him up with instructions to look after an old friend by inviting Unity out to lunch, which he did. She told him how she had just joined the Congregationalists, in a ceremony which involved shaking everyone by the hand. 'She said, It's wonderful to have two hundred people shaking one's hand because now nobody does that to me.' Osbert Lancaster was similarly roped in, when at a party Nancy placed him next to Unity, 'this Mitford giantess, unmistakable, aggressive', he says. 'On the other side was Pierre Roy, with the Free French, some sort of ADC to General de Gaulle. His opening remark to her was, I expect you speak far better French than I do English. She answered, Thank the Lord, not a word of the beastly language. She went on about her hatred of the French. No holds barred. Extraordinarily mad. I was trying to keep off the subject of the war, when she said how much she loathed the blitz. I said, It sends shivers down my spine to hear the siren. It's so odd for me because I want to die, was her come-back.'

Charles Ritchie, the Canadian diplomat, in his entertaining diaries, The Siren Years, recorded an evening of the kind at Nancy's on 27 November 1942. 'I had a long conversation with Unity Mitford. She started the conversation by saying, "I have just hit my left breast against a lamp-post as I was bicycling here." She said, "I tried to commit suicide when I was in Germany but now I am a Christian Scientist – not that I believe a word of it, but they saved my life so I feel I owe it to them to be one." "I hate the Czechs," she said suddenly in a loud emphatic voice, "but that is natural – they tried to arrest me and I had not done anything. I did not even have the Führer's picture in my suitcase as they said I had." She had just recently returned to England where her role as Hitler's English friend does not make her popular. I must say I liked her better than anyone else at the party. She has something hoydenish and rustic about her.' In conversation with me, Charles Ritchie added that the incident with the suitcase seemed to be obsessing her.

Lady Harrod said, 'After the shooting we saw a lot of her. She was terribly lonely. Poor old Bobo, Nancy said to us, do be nice to her, she runs up to everybody like a huge big dog wagging her tail, and nobody is nice to her. Bobo worked in a British Restaurant where you got cheap meals in High Wycombe. Because it was so cold she had a fur coat with wide sleeves and kept it on. Nancy said, If you were hungry all you'd have to do is wring out Bobo's sleeves and you would have a plateful of soup. I can see her so well in my drawing room at 91 St Aldate's. She used to come into Oxford by bus, for regular check-ups at the Radcliffe most likely. All I remember of her conversation is her saying that she was going to have six sons, the eldest to be called Adolf, and all the rest John. We talked trivialities, I don't think I dared embark on Hitler. I used to go to the Swinbrook cottage. We all went to her funeral. Nancy came over from Paris and arrived on the early train at Oxford in a scarlet mackintosh. With her was Mark Ogilvie-Grant, with a cross of rosemary from his garden at Kew – that was put on the grave. They all had lunch with us. Lord Redesdale came back in my car from Swinbrook, but not to the lunch. Lady Redesdale talked so much about it, how Bobo had always been planning her funeral, and would have liked the hymns and everything.'

Though in tolerable shape outwardly for those last years of her life – sometimes heavier, sometimes thinner – Unity required constant nursing. She was incontinent. She also suffered from loss of balance, she continued to limp, and had had to relearn certain muscular activities, such as writing. Lady Redesdale never wavered. It made little difference where they both were; from the physical point of view, High Wycombe was much like the Swinbrook cottage. In the latter place, next door in the Swan Inn lived old Mrs Bunce, who had a goitre and wore a black dress; she was the mother of Mrs Timms, whose husband had been the farm bailiff, and had bought the Swan Inn from Lord Redesdale. Unity used to bicycle about the village, singing aloud. She was ignored. The Peacheys, staunchest of Swinbrook families, used to invite her to tea, and once she told Tom Peachey, the churchwarden, that soon she would be dead and wished to be buried as near as possible to the church, in order to hear the hymn-singing. Her favourite hymn, they say, was 'Praise, my soul, the King of Heaven'.

In Burford there was a Miss Bowerman who ran an antique shop, and had married an Austrian refugee; and the Misses Jones, one a suffragette, the other an author of biographies, were friends in Asthall village. Miss Nan Lovett-Campbell had run a canteen in Burford for soldiers, together with Lady Piercy, the wife of a Labour MP. She said, 'Unity came and helped there for a bit, but our elders and betters put a stop to that. She took a fancy to my sister and me. People said, You can't have her in the house, but it was wartime pettiness and I'd answer, If I'd got off with someone so powerful I'd have been flattered too. She talked about Hitler to show she was not a traitor. To Lady Piercy she said she had adored her Führer. Miss East on Witney Street was a hairdresser, and Unity was her customerr. She said Unity had told her about shooting herself.' Similarly when she had lunched at Lodge Park with Mr and Mrs Christopher Harris, she had said that she could not sit with her back to Germany. Mrs Harris said, 'It was an undertaking having her to lunch. My brother-in-law, Robert Harris, the actor, was there, and she rang him up later on, they had clicked. She used to go into Oxford for singing lessons [at Taphouse's, the music shop] and I was once coming out on the bus with her. Her mother met her at the Swinbrook turn. The whole way she was very talkative about how marvellous Hitler was. Everybody in the bus knew what she was talking about, and nobody batted an eyelid.'

Family embarrassments were lightened when the Mosleys were released from detention in November 1943, and Unity received permission to live on Inchkenneth, as from 29 July 1944. Until the end of her life, she was to spend at least six months of the year there. It was a long haul by night sleeper, to Oban in those days, and then by steamer, the *Lochinvar*, across to Mull, landing at Salen or Craignure. A winding road crosses the fifteen miles or so of Mull, to the scattering of houses which is Gribun. Opposite lies Inchkenneth, a short mile off-shore, at the mouth of Loch-na-keal. Dr Johnson and Boswell on their Highland Tour had been much taken with the island, but the Maclean house in which they had slept no longer exists. Instead, something of a home-counties mansion scours the horizon, on three floors, bow-fronted, white in that stern and elemental landscape. The main work here had been done by Sir Harold Boulton, composer of popular songs, from whom Lord Redesdale had bought the island.

The house, as it looks towards the peak of Creag Mhor on Mull, seems anchored below it, yet the strand between Inchkenneth and Mull is a very real divide, to be crossed as winds and tides dictate. Lady Redesdale kept an ancient Morris in a shed at Gribun; she had a boat and a boatman; and a contraption signalled from shore to shore. The island, a cliff-girt plateau, is gentler than its rugged setting, its grass emerald green, its hundred and sixty odd acres ideal for the sheep and cattle and Shetland ponies which Lady Redesdale reared along with the goat and her hens. She farmed, she made her own butter and cheese, and her own bread, she gardened, and there was nothing to shake the equilibrium of the Good Body.

Inchkenneth is timeless, numinous, a Valhalla where the affairs of man do not disturb. Across a field to one side of the house, the crumbly walls of the unroofed church in which Unity improvised her services – and the shade of Hitler was conjured – bear witness to other exiles and hermits. It was as though Unity had been marooned, would slip away of her own accord into folk-memory. The house is bleaker now, sold, though immovable pieces like the Aga cooker and the grand piano and Unity's four-poster remain behind like fossils. In the bookshelves upstairs is the 1926 inventory for insurance of Rutland Gate, totalling £27,984. 7s. 6d. And other books too. Detritus. Borkenau, Louis Golding's *The Jewish Problem*, *The Ludwigs of Bavaria* by Henry 'Chips' Channon, *What Hitler Wants* by E. O. Lorimer, *Britain's Jewish Problem* by M. G. Murchin, a Nazi tract in which passages have been scored – there flutters out a page of anti-semitic jottings. In several of these expended books, the references to Unity have been underlined, for instance in Frederick Oechnser's *This is the Enemy*. 'No!' and 'Traitor!' and 'This, as published here is a total misrepresentation of the passage referred to in *Mein Kampf* and must be consciously so. Is the author himself one of the Great Masters of Lies?' are all disfigurations of the pages of Vincent Sheean's *Not Peace but a Sword*. Here is another apparition from the past – Ward Price, whose *Year of Reckoning* has Hitler saying, 'What do they think I want a corridor for? To run up and down it?' with the pencilled clarification, 'To Tom and Unity.' (At that meeting at the Kehlstein-Haus?) This house, they say, is haunted. A chill prickles the spine at the revelation of mother and daughter closeted here in isolation, their state of mind locked up tight, as though nothing had changed and Europe was not ruined, and the seepage of so many sad days was to be suspended by these poor gibberings and scratchings in books. And this is how my quest had begun.

People here have a proper reserve, a proper respect. Unity could not be judged in the context of Hitler; she was harmless to them, and even the fairy-tale of lights winking on Inchkenneth to attract German ships cannot have been much by way of a diversion in the evenings. Lady Redesdale had local friends like Lady Congleton on nearby Ulva, or the five Misses Turner of Salen – the one surviving sister remembers her first meeting with Unity, on the boat crossing from Oban. 'A small boy, the son of a neighbour, was also travelling and the two of them hit it off, pretending to shoot at each other like cops and robbers. I have a revolver and I used to play with it, she said to him, and for a moment I was frightened by the thought that she might go too far. Unity said to me, I haven't been well, I'm going to stay with my mother, I don't get enough good food, my mother says. You will at Inchkenneth, I answered, and went on, Is she a good cook? Oh no, Unity said. Lady Redesdale was completely innocent, a nice woman, with not the least idea of what it was all about. The death of Tom knocked her sideways. She deserved better.'

Dr Macdonald would come across from Mull for Unity's health. His widow, Dr Flora Macdonald, now retired from practice herself, said that he had been called in at the start of her last illness. But Inchkenneth depended upon reliable men to help, and this meant, for a good part of the time, the Macfadyeans. Archie Baldy (as he is known) and John Macfadyean were brothers, and relations of the Mrs Macfadyean who had the small post office in her shop at Gribun.

Mrs John Macfadyean said: 'Unity came up with her father that time to buy the island, just the two of them, in the spring of 1938. They fell in love with it and decided right then and there. She was a lovely girl. When she came back a few years later you could see she wasn't the same girl, in her gait she was different altogether. Yet her faculties were there. Until 1944 we lived in the bungalow, when our children were of school age we had to come over here [to Mull]. The Campbells came after us, she's on Coll now, her husband's dead. The cook came with Lady Redesdale from High Wycombe. That man of mine thought the world of Lady Redesdale's boat, the Puffin, and said she could sail anywhere in the world. Unity would come across and visit us. She loved to go fishing, my husband would take her out. She came to see the children, she saw my eldest daughter in a cradle and asked if she could nurse her. She gave the pram-cover she'd made, pink, all crocheted, and this little rabbit [she produces a woolly toy] was stuffed by her – my girl's over thirty now. She would sit here and enjoy her tea, she got into Salen too with the car, going to concerts. She was a great one for walking round the island in all sorts of weather. They entertained quite a lot, at Easter specially, for the local people, Lady Redesdale had a piper brought across. Unhappy? Yes, you would see it in her eyes. I often think she'd known what she'd done. We could never talk about it. Her past was no concern of ours.'

The MacGillivrays replaced the Campbells as a couple on the island, but they had little time to know Unity. Mrs MacGillivray said: 'When we went there, in March 1948, the whole place was in a shambles, workmen were in. The launch had been smashed in the bad weather, and we had to carry our household possessions over in the dinghy. Unity used to be up to all kinds of silly things at the end and Lady Redesdale was often coming to me to say how naughty she'd been. Once she made a cake, mixing in four or five dozen eggs but no flour. Unity and her mother were out in the boat a lot, the two of them, Unity rowing. How else did they spend the day? Reading, sewing, embroidery. Lady Redesdale loved painting woodwork. Photos and albums of Unity's were lying in the drawing room and Lady Redesdale would think we'd known Unity before and would tell stories of her in the past. Afterwards she used to think Unity was around the house. Lady Redesdale wouldn't come with us to Iona on one occasion because she was sure Unity was outside the house, waiting for her. There were noises, too, which she declared was Unity. I remember her saying of Unity, How sad it all was.'

Mr MacGillivray added, 'I once took Unity to a little dance, a ceilidh, in the schoolhouse at Gribun. Johnny Russell was playing the accordion and I was dancing with Unity when she said to me, I think Scots people are frightfully lucky to wear the kilt. She was reasonably well at least, she was a good sport.

For that dance Unity got across with the boatman they had at the time, he would not cross in the dark so she sat in the garage shed till dawn.'

The West Highland Cottage Hospital at Oban was built in 1895, the year of St Margaret's too, as a prosperous villa standing on a hill above the town. Recently it has been enlarged and extended to provide thirty-three beds Unity was admitted there on 28 May 1948, already too ill for anything to be done for her. The hospital secretary was Miss Macleod, who is now rising eighty. She said, 'They had to charter a special boat for Lady Redesdale and Unity. She had a brain complaint, there was only one brain unit in Scotland, at Killearn in Stirlingshire. They brought her up the hill by ambulance. She was treated as an ordinary ill patient, people went about their duties. She was beyond speaking when they brought her in. I know she was in the operating theatre. Lady Redesdale was to stay in the Station Hotel [which has been re-named The Caledonian]. The wards have changed a lot, I'm not sure which one she was in, maybe one of the two private rooms, I never saw her in bed. The late Mr Crawford was the surgeon in charge, an Irishman, he had come here in December 1946. He was in touch with the brain specialist, it was arranged to transfer her, Mr Crawford was giving her emergency treatment. However, during the last lot of treatment he was giving, he saw her condition was worse, deteriorating too quickly, and he decided not to let her be moved. The ambulance for Killearn was at the door. The chief matron, Miss Gordon, was with her. A few hours later, she died.'

At 9.50 p.m. according to the death certificate, dated the same day, which lists as cause of death 'Purulent Meningitis, Cerebral Abscess, Old Gun-shot Wound.'

Professor Sir Hugh Cairns to E. J. Crawford, 5 June 1948:

Lord Redesdale tells me that you looked after Miss Mitford in her final illness and he says that I may write to you about it. I looked after her when she came back from Germany with a bullet in her left occipital lobe and a missile track showing bone fragments, coming from the right frontal region. Subsequently we had further X-rays which showed that the bone fragments had not moved at all. At one stage I wondered whether she had had a fracture of her frontal or ethmodial sinuses, but we had some X-rays and didn't feel that there was any evidence of this ... looking at these X-rays now, I suspect that there was a fracture to the roof of the right ethmoid, in which case that would probably provide the explanation for the meningitis.

E. J. Crawford to Professor Cairns, 7 June 1948:

... My own connection with the case started on May 27th 1948 when I was called over to Lady Redesdale's house on the island of Inchkenneth – a difficult journey by motor boat to Mull – across the island by car and ferry to Inchkenneth. Dr Reginald Macdonald, the practitioner in charge of the case, told me that he had been in attendance for four days, the illness having started as a 'chill', accompanied by intense headache and vomiting. Sulphathiazole had been prescribed in the usual doses, with apparent benefit for two days, vomiting ceasing after three days' treatment, though fever – around 101°F – continued. The pulse had not been significantly slow until the morning of the 27th, when it was stated to be between 60 and 70, and the question of a cerebral abscess was considered, with also the possibility of meningitis. Dr Macdonald told me that a scar in the right temporal region had been tense since he first saw the case and had been bulging for the past 24 hours. I saw Miss Mitford at 6.30 p.m. . . . Her pulse was full, not unduly slow – 80 – but possibly slowish in view of her temperature at that time (102). From Lady Redesdale I learned of the history of a gunshot wound and hemiplegia consequent on this. The patient herself could help very little, disliking disturbance . . .

The general picture suggested meningitis and with this in mind I did lumbar puncture and puncture of the bulge . . . I advised Lady Redesdale that the patient was suffering from purulent meningitis, probably connected in some way with the original injury, and recommended immediate removal to the mainland where the services of a brain surgeon might be obtained. She agreed. Miss Mitford was removed with surprising comfort considering the difficulties of the journey, by motor boat, ambulance, motor boat and second ambulance, to this hospital, arriving in fairly good shape, at midnight, when penicillin treatment was initiated.

In the morning it was arranged for the patient to be taken to Killearn Hospital Cranial Surgery Centre [Mr Robertson] and the ambulance was actually waiting when there was a sudden change for the worse – the most obvious sign being rapid and extensive dilation of the pupils. This was followed by an epileptiform seizure which I witnessed, this in turn being followed by Cheyne-Stokes respiration and death about 10 pm. A post-mortem was thought of . . . I hesitated to mention it. Also, I was at the time in no doubt as to the cause of death – i.e. purulent meningitis. As to the presence or otherwise of cerebral abscess I was much less confident, but in view of all the tragic circumstances I decided against asking for one. As the case was one of death from violence, I reported the facts to the Procurator-Fiscal who advised me, after private inquiry (as can be done in Scotland) to certify . . .

Professor Sir Hugh Cairns to E. J. Crawford, 14 June 1948:

I have compared these X-rays with our X-rays taken some years ago and the position of the bone fragments in the right frontal region have not altered at all; nor has the position of the missile in the left occipital lobe altered. I think, therefore, it is reasonably certain that there was no brain abscess. The course of the case has been very similar to others which we have seen and I think it means that there was a fracture of the roof of the ethmoidal air cells at the time of the wound and that ever since she has had a connection between the subdural part of the cranial cavity and the ethmoidal air cells; and that only now she developed this pneumonococcal meningitis ... Lady Redesdale is coming to see me today and I shall certainly make a point of giving Lord Redesdale your message that Miss Mitford died peacefully.

Mrs Helmut Schroder was returning from Islay when she heard a voice calling her on the platform at Glasgow Station. It was Lady Redesdale. 'You're looking terribly ill, I told her. She said, Don't you know what's happened? – we've got Unity with us. They were bringing her down from Oban that night. I knew the stationmaster and I said to him that Lord and Lady Redesdale had to be given sleepers. The coffin could go into the guard's van. The train's full, he said, but in the end he did get them sleepers from Kilmarnock.'

The funeral was at Swinbrook church on 1 June. Sir Oswald and Lady Mosley were among those present. Somehow during these events Lady Redesdale had found time to write a letter to the *Daily Mail*, which was to be published on the 2nd, to take issue with some of the statements in the long obituary, already referred to, by Ward Price, 'The Secret Life of Unity Mitford'. Lady Redesdale made some assertions of her own, as when she declared that Hitler had visited Unity several times in hospital, and had offered to give her German nationality, but she had this to say in the context, 'It is not true that she wrote to Hitler on the outbreak of war and received no reply, nor that he refused to see her. The reason why she tried to kill herself is very simple, and was not a personal one. The idea of war between the two countries she loved was intolerable to her. On the day that England declared war against Germany she went out to the English garden in Munich and shot herself. She communicated with no one, but left a short note of goodbye for us. She never renounced her nation or her family, and was never cast off by anyone.'

EPILOGUE

A sad life, then, a wasted life, but even Lady Redesdale insisted in the newspapers that Unity should not be thought of as tragic. There had been extravaganza enough in it to amuse and arouse, to make her seem lovable to those prepared to place politics and her political carry-on in baulk. To Jessica, at the close of *Hons and Rebels*, the unsolvable riddle in the events leading to Unity's attempted suicide was how someone so human had turned her back on humanity for an alliance with the Nazis. 'How could Boud, a person of enormous natural taste, an artist and poet from childhood, have embraced their crude philistinism?' Such gaiety, to come to nothing. 'She was always a terrific hater – so were all of us, except possibly Tom – but I had always thought she hated intelligently, and admired her ability to reduce the more unpleasant of the grown-up relations to a state of nervous discomfort with one of her smouldering looks of loathing. But when she wrote gaily off to *Der Stürmer*, "I want everybody to know I am a Jew-hater", I felt she had forgotten the whole point of hating, and had once and for all put herself on the side of the hateful. It is perhaps futile to try to interpret the actions of another – one may be so completely wrong; but it always seemed to me that this last really conscious act of her life, the attempt at self-destruction, was a sort of recognition of the extraordinary contradictions in which she found herself, that the declaration of war merely served as the occasion for her action, which would in any case have been inevitable sooner or later. I mourned my Boud of Boudledidge days, my huge, bright adversary.'

While Nazism flourished, Unity had thrown herself into it as completely as she knew how. She had thoroughly enjoyed it. She was confident in her election by the winning side; this had put her in touch with the times, with manifest destiny, justifying the importance of who she was, and the superiority of what she did. To acquaintances or strangers, she liked to stress that she was 'the notorious Unity Mitford', and something of her effect was lost if she failed to shock, if the bourgeoisie was not as *épaté* as it ought to have been. She had frozen herself in what might have been the attitudes of a joke, a laugh against the rest of the world. At the back of it, no doubt, was a desire to escape the stultifications of her upbringing and find fulfilment of her own, but this was more natural activity than idealism. The Redesdales had never really led from strength; where their children were concerned, they followed suit.

Not that idealism was absent. She had sincerely wished for a peace between England and Germany, and the ordering of the world between them; which was the outlook of the BUF. Its translation into practical politics was unrealistic. For if Hitler was to be encouraged to expand into central and eastern Europe, then war was certain. If, in its course, Germany were victorious, England would have had to accommodate to what must have become far and away the most fearsome continental power, a Thousand-Year Reich well and truly founded. Subordination through alliance would have been the logical end of previous appeasements, of the understandable desire to find in Hitler's aims justice enough to make conflict unnecessary. But if Germany were to be driven back in the war of expansion, Europe would belong to Soviet Russia. A fundamental fascist, Unity believed that Hitler was not only entitled to be released from the Versailles boundaries, but was manning the defences against communism. Plenty of conservative-minded people in England had similar trains of thought, but steadied themselves with the realization that whoever won a Slav-Teuton struggle to the death would be far too ugly a customer to live with, a certain strangler of English independence once and for all. Peace was to be had up to 1939 and beyond, but its price was acquiescence in Hitler's aims, wherever they might lead. For a few more years, countries like Hungary and Roumania were spared the reckoning which came with such a deal.

A drastic miscalculation of fascists everywhere, especially those outside Germany and Italy, was to put their trust in Hitler's star. It was a matter of faith for the ordinary BUF member, for Unity, that Hitler and his state incarnated the future. For many reasons, psychological, personal, political, it served to believe that he was always in the right, and must therefore be rightness itself. Did not every year bring its proofs? The gleaming columns of healthy men, rising employment and prosperity, the Olympic Games, blood and soil ever on the increase? To Unity, it was incredible that people resisted the obvious. She was convinced that sceptics had only to visit Germany and see for themselves, in order to be converted to National Socialism on the spot: Hitler had done his statesman's duty to his nation, and none but assorted 'poors', communists or Jews, could be honest in holding otherwise. The means whereby he had done it did not enter into consideration, nor did his final purposes. Nazism, as Goebbels once defined it correctly, depended upon instinct, not knowledge. Deep in the bones was where the cause was felt. Argument, for which Unity had neither the inclination nor the gifts, was second-best to example, and that accounted for her defiance and the publicizing of herself. A scrap, or what Mosley in his context called 'the good old British fist', was to be grasped quicker by the unconverted than any amount of preaching. Which was why Unity stuck out as a curiosity, a one-man band, rather than a successful propagandist.

A romantic, in any case, does not pause for the pros and cons of the situation. Unity was a Lady Hester Stanhope of Nazism, impelled to seek abroad the adventure, the identification, she had not found at home. The more dramatically coloured and outlandish the new values, the more thorough-going their adoption. Like many emotional freebooters, she came to project every unrest in herself on to one person, Hitler, her Führer, father-figure, hero and true love, holder of keys to all doors. To have spent so much time simply trailing after him has its adolescent despair. She was eccentric in the clock-work of her devotion, but then a more ordinary character would not have held Hitler's imagination in its turn. It will always remain a historical freak that Hitler, whose destruction also brought down the old order of England, should have had an English girlfriend brought up at the heart of that old order.

Her enterprise stranded her on what have been called the wilder shores of love. She might instead have been an agitator, if she had continued in BUF. campaigning, but that was like joining the family business, with none of the reflected heat and light of the Loved One. Her Mitford talent for dressing up a part was able to fulfil itself in Germany: she could act while being per-fectly serious; the darling Führer in his sweet mackintosh was smiling over the heads of his army, and 'we roared'. At the time, she looked, and indeed was, sensational, perverting herself and her genuine impulses, but now she can be seen as an early path-finder for the many children of the rich and secure classes who are her kindred spirits in opposition to the custom of their society. Those who have since screamed for foreign causes and alien tyrants, or faute de mieux, pop stars, are so many Unity Mitfords: so are the writers, politickers, dons, who undermine everything which has allowed them to become what they are, in praising totalitarian systems of whatever kind. Pre-dating them, Unity used her position of fortune to destroy it, and thus herself. She was distinguished in that she came within striking range of the illusion that the world-historical moment had elected her for the fresh departure – at least getting her hands on Hitler, so to speak, when the great majority with her frame of mind must make do with slogans and party meetings and emblems in the lapel. But to find refuge in other people's con-ventions has itself become conventional since Unity – let alone long-lost Lady Hester Stanhope – tried it.

The death-wish is there. From the very beginning, in that Sleeping Beauty childhood which sought awakening, Unity had been injuring herself, placing herself in punishment's way, contriving to be disgraced and rejected. The pattern of self-destruction grew fixed. The one inner hope which was in combat with her fascism had been to marry and have plenty of children, and this was all she had to cherish, with increasing pathos, after the suicide attempt. She had only herself to blame for having always pushed this kind of normality impossibly out of reach. She had left herself only with wants in life which were not for the having. Her very virtues of courage and forth-rightness drove her deeper into opposition for its own scandalizing sake; such contempt could, would be bound to, turn back on her. In the end she was more out on a limb than she could have imagined, having closed behind her all retreats – and half-loved easeful death alone remained.

SELECT BIBLIOGRAPHY

Books referred to and briefly quoted:

Acton, Harold, *Memoir of Nancy Mitford*, Hamish Hamilton, 1975
Aigner, Dietrich, *Das Ringen um England*, Munich, 1969
Boothby, Robert, *I Fight to Live*, Heinemann, 1947
Bruce-Lockhart, Sir Robert, *Diaries* edited by Kenneth Young, Macmillan, 1973
Carrington, Dora, *Letters and Extracts from her diaries*, chosen by David Garnett, Cape, 1970
Cowles, Virginia, *Looking for Trouble*, Hamish Hamilton, 1941
Cross, Colin, *The Fascists in Britain*, Barrie & Rockliff, 1961
Delmer, Sefton, *Trail Sinister*, Secker & Warburg, 1960
Dietrich, Otto, *The Hitler I Knew*, Methuen, 1957
Ebermayer, Erich and Roos, Hans, *Die Gefährtin des Teufels*, Hamburg, 1952
Engel, Gerhard, *Heeresadjutant bei Hitler 1938–1943*, Stuttgart, 1974
Fromm, Bella Steuerman, *Blood and Banquets*, Geoffrey Bles, 1943
Golding, Louis, *The Jewish Problem*, Penguin, Harmondsworth, 1939
Graham, Sheilah/Gerald Frank, *Beloved Infidel*, Cassell, 1959
Guinness, Bryan, *Singing out of Tune*, Putnam, 1933
Gun, Nerin E., *Eva Braun: Hitler's Mistress*, Frewin, 1969
Hanfstaengl, Ernst, *The Missing Years*, Eyre & Spottiswoode, 1957
Heiber, Helmut, *Goebbels*, Robert Hale, 1972
Heygate, John, *These Germans*, Hutchinson, 1940
Hoffmann, Heinrich (transl. Lieut-Col. R. H. Steven), *Hitler was my Friend*, Burke, 1955
Home, William Douglas-, *Half-Term Report: An Autobiography*, Longmans, Green, 1954
Lehmann, Rosamond, *The Swan in the Evening*, Collins, 1967
Mitford, Jessica, *Hons and Rebels*, Gollancz, 1960
Mitford, Nancy, *The Water Beetle*, Hamish Hamilton, 1962
— *Wigs on the Green*, Thornton Butterworth, 1935
Mosley, Leonard, *On Borrowed Time*, Weidenfeld & Nicolson, 1969
Mosley, Oswald, *My Life*, Nelson, 1970
Nicolson, Harold, *Diaries and Letters*, 3 Vols, Collins, 1970

'Oscaria', In Memory of Dorothy Ierne Wilde, privately printed, 1952

Oven, Wilfred von, Mit Goebbels bis zum Ende, Buenos Aires, 1949

Pope, Ernest Russell, Munich Playground, G. P. Putnam, New York, 1941

Powell, Violet, Five out of Six, Heinemann, 1960

Price, G. Ward, I Know these Dictators, Harrap, 1937

— Year of Reckoning, Cassell, 1939

Ravensdale, Irene, In Many Rhythms, Weidenfeld & Nicolson, 1953

Reck-Malleczewen, Friedrich Percyval, Tagebuch eines Verzweifelten, Stuttgart, 1947

Trevor-Roper, H. R. (Intr.) Hitler's Table Talk 1941–44, Weidenfeld & Nicolson, 1953

Wagner, Friedelind, The Royal Family of Bayreuth, Eyre & Spottiswoode, 1948

Wiedemann, Fritz, Der Mann der Feldherr Werden Wollte, Velbert, 1964

Williamson, Henry, Goodbye West Country, Putnam, 1937

We are also grateful to Her Majesty's Stationery Office for giving us permission to quote extracts from Foreign Office Papers at the Public Record Office and Documents on British Foreign Policy 1919–1939.

INDEX